AmV.

Writing for Television and Radio

WRITING FOR TELEVISION and RADIO

By ROBERT L. HILLIARD

SECOND EDITION

COMMUNICATION ARTS BOOKS

Hastings House, Publishers   •   New York 22

To Mary Ellen

Library of Congress Catalog Card Number: 62-13983

Published simultaneously in Canada
by S. J. Reginald Saunders & Co., Ltd., Publishers,
Don Mills, Ontario

Printed in the United States of America

CONTENTS

PREFACE

It is gratifying to know that this work has been of sufficient value in meeting the needs of students, teachers, practitioners and the public that a second edition is necessary. Because the first edition was published only five years ago, it did not seem fair to those students and teachers in the nearly 100 colleges and universities which have adopted this book as a text and where it is being used and reused in continuing semesters, to create an extensively revised work so soon. This, then, is an *updated,* rather than a revised edition, with primarily a substitution where necessary of information and material that reflects the pertinent changes in television and radio writing since 1962. The original material has been retained wherever possible. The basic content and organization remain unchanged.

The mass media of television and radio are closely related in the development and practice of writing techniques. Indeed, it is usual for television and radio writing to be combined in one course in most colleges and universities. For a number of years good texts and resource books have been available on television writing alone and on radio writing alone. In addition, there are several fine works oriented primarily toward dramatic writing.

From the practical point of view, however, relatively few opportunities exist today for the serious television or radio playwright. The jobs available for television and radio writers are most frequently found among the program types which exist on local as well as network levels, including news, sports, talks programs of various kinds, panel-games-audience participation shows, women's and children's programs, music and variety shows, special features and, sometimes, documentaries. Extremely important is the writing of announcements and commercials. Those who wish to write for the mass media, the playwright included, can benefit from a knowledge of the non-dramatic areas.

Over a number of years of teaching television and radio writing, I was unable to find a text devoted predominantly to the above "bread-and-butter" aspects of the two media. Consequently, I developed my own teaching materials which, after several years of testing and revision, now make up this book. My purpose is not to slight the play, which I believe to be the highest form of writing (about one-fifth of this book is devoted to dramatic writing). My primary aim, however, is to make available to all who are concerned with broadcast writing that which was heretofore unavailable: a book devoted principally to the non-dramatic forms of both television and radio. By concentrating on the practical elements needed to prepare one for a writing job, and on the areas of writing that comprise most of current broadcast fare, I hope that this book may serve as a single, comprehensive work for all who wish to learn some of the basic principles and techniques of the craft, and as a useful reference source for professional writers.

From my experiences in teaching television and radio writing, I have found that the student needs and learns most effectively from an understanding of both the aesthetic and the technical bases of specific areas of broadcast writing, and from careful study and analysis of sample scripts before attempting to develop scripts of his own. Therefore, each chapter is organized around principles and motivations before going on to examine specific techniques. Where necessary for clarification of pertinent points, script excerpts and other illustrative material are analyzed. The sample scripts in this book have, for the most part, been previously produced commercially or professionally. The questions and exercises for application and review at the ends of chapters are designed to supplement the within-the-chapter analyses.

In order to know what he can or cannot do in any given script, the writer should understand the potentials and limitations of television and radio, including time, space, audience, subject matter, and the audio and video effects possible with cameras, sound and music, visual devices, control room techniques, and other mechanical and electronic forms. The first two chapters of this book are consequently devoted to an examination of these basic elements, prior to consideration of specific program types and their writing problems and approaches.

Because radio preceded television and because many of radio's procedures and techniques were adapted by television, material pertaining to radio writing frequently is treated before that on television in this book. I have, however, attempted to note the similarities and differences between the two art forms throughout.

The terms "continuity" and "script" often are used interchangeably. Script may refer to the written material which indicates the verbal and nonverbal action that is to go into a program. Continuity may refer to exactly the same thing. Sometimes the term script denotes only the dramatic story, comedy routine, musical number or other element comprising the main body of the program, while continuity may then refer to all the other material outside the main program content. Further, continuity may designate just the outline of the program material to be used for a specific broadcast or for an entire broadcasting day. As used in this book, the terms "continuity" and "script" encompass all three definitions, and include all material presented "on the air." When a specific definition is meant, however, it will be so indicated.

Continuity must move and develop with each passing minute, even second, of a broadcast. It must hold the attention of the viewer or listener at all times. It must build in a rising rhythmic pattern so that the audience does not want to—cannot—switch the dial. "Transition" continuity—between program segments or between entire programs—should be strong enough to hold the audience not only through an entire program and into the next, but for a complete broadcast day. The latter goal is of particular significance to the program manager-writer of the small station, who frequently is responsible for both the continuity of individual programs and for the planning of the daily broadcast schedule.

The most direct approach in presenting continuity is through the verbal delivery of a performer—an announcer, master of ceremonies, moderator, narrator, actor, speaker, studio guest, or anyone else who delivers words prepared by the writer. In addition to this verbal form of continuity, which may be called dialogue, there are sound effects and music—and silence—on both television and radio, and also live action, film, tape, slides and other mechanical devices and electronic effects on television. Familiarity with all forms of continuity in all program types is essential for the writer who aspires to competence in his craft in television and radio.

The mass media are potentially the most powerful forces for communicating ideas and impressions to the minds and emotions of the peoples of the world. Perhaps the lack of clear, honest and effective communications among all people is most responsible for the continuing crises of civilization. The most important element in the mass communication process is the script. The writer who has something to say and knows how to put his ideas into the proper and most effective form can have great influence and, if he wishes, make a contribution of infinite value.

In the Preface to the first edition, written in Chapel Hill, North Carolina in July, 1962, I expressed my appreciation to the many persons and organizations that cooperated in providing illustrative materials used in this work, with special thanks to Albert Book, Martin Carmichael and George Brenholz. I will add here my thanks to those others who have helped in obtaining new materials, and to Russell F. Neale, editor of Communication Arts Books, for his faith in this book and his efforts in making its availability known to all those who might find value from it. I am grateful to the people whose interest in television and radio writing have made this second edition possible.

Washington, D.C.
May, 1967

1

THE MASS MEDIA

THE TELEVISION and radio writer aims at an audience that at one and the same time is very small and very large, that has much in common and almost nothing in common, that is a tightly knit group and a disunified mass.

Millions of people may be listening to or seeing the material developed by the writer. Yet, any one group within this vast audience is apt to be a small one — usually a family group, at home, in everyday surroundings. The distractions of everyday life are constantly at hand, continuously operative, and likely to pull the individual viewer or listener away from the program. Unlike the theatre or movie audience, the television and radio audience is not "captive." It has not paid a fee and, if it doesn't like what it sees or hears, it is under no compunction to stay. The theatre and film audience is, to varying degrees, selective; moreover, with the availablity of newspaper reviews, it generally knows something about the play or film it is going to see. The television audience is less selective, and frequently will tune in a program from force of habit or because it has nothing else to do at the time. The writer for television and radio, therefore, must capture the imaginations and interests of this undiscriminating audience as soon as possible. Each word, each picture must be purposeful, must gain attention and hold interest. Ideally, there should be no irrelevancies in the writing, no extraneous moments.

Psychologists tell us that the smaller the group and the further apart the individual members of the audience, the better chance there is to appeal to the intellect. The physical groupings of the television and radio audience offer this opportunity to a greater extent than has been utilized thus far. On the other hand, because it is an audience that can remove itself quickly and easily with only the flick of a finger, emotional empathy must also be established. The use of universal emotional impressions is important because the audience largely is unknown to the writer and no immediate responses to determine the audience's reaction can be felt or measured.

Theatre audiences and, to some degree, film audiences — or at least those within any given movie house — may have common interests or backgrounds: a common geographical location, the same relative economic or social status within the residential area of the city where the movie house is located, or similar educational backgrounds or cultural interests which prompted their attendance. The television and radio audience, as a whole, watching or listening to any one given performance, is likely to have more diverse opinions, emotional prejudices, educational, social and political backgrounds, and personal creeds than the theatre or movie audience. The audience of the mass media is as varied as is the population of the United States.

To make any single piece of material effective, the writer often is told that he must find a common denominator that will reach and hold as many as possible of the groups and individuals watching the 70 million television sets and listening to the 245 million radios in use in this country (in 1966). The Federal Communications Commission hearings in 1961-1962 and its 1965 proposals for diversity in program control suggested that business rather than artistic considerations (through the network, the advertising agency and the sponsor) controlled television and radio programming. The sponsor's primary aim, it seems, is to present material that will not offend anyone. The sponsor and the producer thus far in the history of our mass media have searched for and often found the broadest common denominator, which frequently turns out to be the lowest. Innumerable rating organizations substantiate the advertising agency approach by measuring the percentages or numbers of people who allegedly watch any given program. Presuming that the ratings do have some validity — and many observers believe that the exceedingly small sample purportedly representing the entire American populace, as well as uncontrolled factors in interviewing techniques, nullify the claims of the rating systems — they do not measure accurately (although some of the ratings attempt to do so in part) the audience's reaction, its potential buying power, or the effectiveness of either the program or the commercial message.

Because of the acceptance of the lowest common denominator and the reliance upon a *quantitative* measurement, the cultural contributions of our mass media have become, for the most part, comparatively low in quality and repetitive in nature. The outstanding casualty of this trend has been serious drama. In March, 1965, after a study of competition and responsibility in network television broadcasting, the FCC stated: "By and large, episodes of television series are produced on the basis of 'formulas' — approved in advance by the network corporation and often its mass advertisers — which 'set' the characters, 'freeze' theme and action and limit subject matter to 'tested' commercial patterns."

RADIO AND THE MASS AUDIENCE

Radio is not limited by what can be presented visually. The writer can develop a mind picture which is bounded only by the extent of the audience's imagination. Sound effects, music, dialogue — even silence — are combined and integrated to provide the most effective presentation. However, the setting, physical characters, characterization, plot and all of the other elements of the dramatic or non-dramatic show must be conveyed through sound alone. This absence of sight may be a handicap as well as an advantage.

Radio permits the writer complete freedom of time and place. There is no limitation on the setting or on movement in time or in space. The writer can create unlimited forms of physical action and can bypass in the twinkling of a musical bridge minutes or centuries of time. Orson Welles' radio adaptation of H. G. Wells' *War of the Worlds* is famous for its many provocative productions throughout the world. Television once attempted a similar adaptation. It was unsuccessful. Limiting the action to what one can present visually restricts the imaginative potentials of word and sound.

In radio the audience is not selective. It does not pick out what it wants to, but hears only what the writer wants it to. In this way the writer controls the direction of the attention of the radio audience. Of course, different listeners may imagine the same sound stimulus in different ways because each person's psychological and experiential background is different. In the creation of a mind picture in the imagination, the audience does "see." The radio writer can create this mind picture more effectively than can the writer in any other medium. The audience "sees" places, characters and events just as the writer wants it to. The audience sometimes even experiences the emotions the writer wants it to. The subjectivity of the medium permits the writer to place the audience right alongside of or at any given distance from the character or participant in the radio show, providing the writer makes it quite clear exactly where that place is. Voice distances and relationships of the performers to the microphone determine the "view" the audience has of the characters and of the setting. For example, if the audience is listening to two characters in conversation and the writer has the first character "fade off" from the microphone, the audience, in its imagination, stays with the second character and sees the first character moving away.

Although a scene must be set in dialogue and sound rather than established through sight as in the other performing media, such orientation and exposition must not be done too obviously. Radio often uses a narrator or announcer to set the mood, establish character relationships, give information about the program participants, describe the scene, summarize previous action and even comment on the attitude the audience might be expected to have toward the program, the participants or the characters in the play. This background material may be given through dialogue, music, sound effects or, sometimes, even through silence.

TELEVISION AND THE MASS AUDIENCE

Television makes use of the same subjective potentials as does radio, but is more specific in directing the attention and feeling of the audience. Television utilizes many of the techniques of the theatre and of the films, and the audience is directed through sight as well as through hearing. With its use of mechanical and electronic devices, television has more flexibility than the theatre but, because of the limitation of sight as previously pointed out, not so much flexibility as has radio. Nevertheless, television can combine the sound and the audience-orientation of radio, the live continuous performance of theatre and the electronic techniques of the film. It is capable of fusing the best of all previous communications media.

On the other hand, television also has specific limitations. Although it can break the always flexible unities of time and place, it is greatly restricted in production by *physical* time and space. Time-wise, the writer cannot develop a script as fully as he might desire. The actual program length, after commercial and credit time has been subtracted, is approximately 12 minutes for the 15-minute program, 24 minutes for the half-hour program, 51 minutes for the hour program, and 75 minutes for the hour-and-one-half program. This limitation is a particular hindrance in the writing of a dramatic program. Space-wise, the writer is hampered by the limitation of the camera view, the limitation of settings for live television and live-type taped television (the term "live-type taped television," as used here, refers to the taped program which uses the continuous action, non-edited procedure of the live show; it is done as if it were a live show) and the comparatively small viewing area of the television receiver. The writer must orient his work toward small groups on the screen at any one time, make extended use of the close-up shot and, excluding filmed television, limit physical sets and outdoor nature effects. These limitations have prompted the intimate, subjective approach in dramatic writing, and the result, in television's mid-1950's "golden age," was the probing, slice-of-life play.

Television does have a reasonable freedom of movement, however. The camera serves, in a sense, as a moving proscenium arch. The writer may use detail sets, projections, electronic inserts, film clips and multiple sets to achieve a broadening or a variety of place.

Television combines both subjectivity and objectivity in relation to the audience, fusing two areas that are usually thought of as being mutually exclusive. Through use of the camera and electronic devices, the writer and director frequently may give the audience's attentions and emotions a subjective orientation by directing them to specific stimuli. The close-up, the split screen and similar devices are especially useful. The television audience cannot choose, as does the theatre audience, from the totality of presentation upon a stage. The television audience can be directed to a specific stimulus which most effectively achieves the purpose of the specific moment in the script. Attention can be directed to subtle reaction as well as to obvious action. At the same time, the television audience can be given an objective orientation in that the personality of the performer as a person can be brought more openly and directly to the viewer than can be done in the large auditorium of the theatre or movie-house. Although the purpose of most drama is to create illusion, the television narrator, master of ceremonies, announcer, actor or other performer can achieve excellent non-illusionary relationships with the audience.

The basic exposition of a television program should be presented through the action, logically and quickly. In radio it is more difficult to reach the audience through the action, and a narrator or announcer frequently is necessary.

Television may use a narrator or announcer, of course, but preferably as voice-over or in filmed or taped inserts. Visual devices such as title cards, pantomime and other art work are effective, too. It must be remembered that radio is aural while television is essentially visual, and where a visual element in TV can achieve the desired effect, it should take precedence over sound — in many instances, dialogue even may be superfluous. There is the story told about the famous Broadway playwright, noted for his scintillating dialogue, who was asked to write a film script shortly after sound movies became practical and popular. He wrote a 30-page first act treatment in which a husband and wife, on vacation, went up to their hotel room. Through 30 minutes of witty and sparkling conversation it was revealed that the wife was becoming increasingly disturbed over her husband's attention to other women. An experienced movie director went over the script and thought it presented a good situation. He changed one thing. He substituted for the entire 30 pages of dialogue visual directions in which the husband and wife enter the hotel, register and walk to the elevator perfunctorily, the husband looks appraisingly at the female elevator operator, and a look of great displeasure comes over the wife's face as the elevator doors close. Sound should be considered secondary in television production; the essential ingredient is visual action. This principle applies to most non-dramatic forms, as well as to the play.

SUBJECT MATTER

Not only is the writer faced with a problem in the quality level of his material, but he faces concrete manifestations of this problem in the selection of specific subject matter. Television and radio writing is affected greatly by censorship. In commercial television and radio the control over the final script to be presented seems to rest primarily in the hands of the advertising agencies representing the sponsor. In some cases, the person in charge of the television and/or radio division of the agency or of the individual account is an advertising executive, a businessman with little or no knowledge of the artistic needs or potentials of the media. It has been alleged that three hostile postcards from a vacant lot will influence a sponsor or advertising agency to do almost anything. The sponsor, however, isn't the only potential censor. The originating station — or the continuity acceptance departments of the networks — may reject material it deems unsuitable. The industry itself has set up codes concerning permissible subject matter. The Communications Act of 1934 authorizes license suspension for "communications containing profane or obscene words, language, or meaning. . . ."

Censorship falls into two major categories: material that is "censorable" and material that is "controversial."

Censorable Material

Censorable material, as discussed here, is that which generally is considered not in good taste for the home television audience, although this same material might be perfectly acceptable in the legitimate theatre. Profanity, the sanctity of marriage and the home, suicide, unduly provocative sex and other similar items are theoretically governed by censorship codes or, as sometimes called, standards of good conduct.

The general approach taken seems to be, as Eric Heath has observed, that ". . . grandma [representing the audience] may be a little old-fashioned and may object to forms of entertainment in which the children will be extremely interested. For this reason censorship [has] . . . an even stronger hand than in motion pictures."[1]

The most publicized codes of good standards are those of the National Association of Broadcasters, an organization to which virtually all of the major television and radio stations, including the networks, belong and subscribe. (The writer would do well to obtain, for reference and study, *The Television Code* and *The Radio Code* from The National Association of Broadcasters, 1771 N Street, N.W., Washington, D.C. 20036.)

On paper the codes seem almost idyllic. The orientation of television and radio programming in terms of the recommendations in these codes would, for the most part, raise the artistic and cultural levels of programming and of the public. Unfortunately, there is no really effective enforcement of the codes. The decision to follow code procedures, or whether a given segment of material falls under a category of the codes, is usually up to the individual director, producer or agency representative. Networks and larger stations do have "censors" or "reviewers" who attempt to check material for obvious breaches of the code or for material which, even if it might fulfill some of the cultural or public service provisions of the code, conflicts with the desires of the sponsor or of the policy of the station itself. It is in this latter area that the greatest danger lies. Many of the items censored are not necessarily in bad taste. When they are not, then any censorship constitutes not the censorship of *censorable* material, but the censorship of *controversial* material.

Erik Barnouw, discussing censorship in the movies in his *Mass Communication,* indicates an approach which just as readily may be applied to television and radio. Mr. Barnouw writes: "Banning evil example . . . does not ban it from life. It may not strengthen our power to cope with it. It may have the opposite effect. Code rules multiply, but they do not produce morality. They do not stop vulgarity. Trying to banish forbidden impulses, censors may only change the disguises in which they appear. They ban passionate love-making, and excessive violence takes its place."[2]

Controversial Material

Censorship of controversial material is of concern to the writer. Controversial material refers to subject matter which in the broadest sense might disturb any viewer. Such material might relate to any area of public thinking, including certain aspects of political, social, economic, religious and psychological problems. "When a story editor says, 'We can't use anything controversial,' and says it with a tone of conscious virtue, then there is danger," observes Erik Barnouw.[2]

There is a great danger today to freedom of expression and the democratic exchange of ideas in American television and radio because many of the media executives fear controversy. On the grounds of service to the sponsor and on the basis of high ratings for non-controversial but mediocre entertainment, anything controversial has been avoided in too many cases. Many sponsors will reject material as controversial if they feel it will in any way alienate any potential customer anywhere in America. It can be said that if a sponsor permits his product to be identified with a controversial issue that may offend even small groups of citizens, there may be damage to the company's prestige. It can also be said, on the other hand, that anyone using the public airwaves has a responsibility not only to a private company, but to the public as a whole. Censorship of controversial material is particularly prevalent in dramatic programs. Writer Reginald Rose, who has had some plays censored because they contained alleged controversial material, believes that such controversial productions help more than harm advertisers — people are made more aware of the program and of the product, as opposed to their barely noting the sponsorship of innocuous shows.[3]

In the early 1960's the Federal Communications Commission heard many sponsors testify concerning their control over the content of television programs. With few exceptions, almost all of the leading industries in this country went on record as stating that their television programs must be oriented toward their sales policies and must reflect their corporate images. Jack Gould summed up the attitude of the television sponsor: "As a business man governed by concern for his customers and stockholders, the advertiser wants to avoid displeasing any substantial segment of the public, wants to establish a pleasant environment for his product, wants to make sure the private life of a performer is not embarrassing to his company, and wants to skirt any possibility of being accused of taking one side in a situation where there are two sides."[4] For example, the nation's biggest television advertiser, Procter and Gamble, administers a strong editorial policy in relation to its shows. It does not believe its policy constitutes program control, however, but believes that what it is "exercising is a wholesome influence on our programs." The company believes that its editorial policy should apply to news documentaries as well as to dramas. "The moral tone of Procter and Gamble sponsored broadcasts should reflect the moral code of the bulk of the American people," one of its representatives told the Commission, adding that the interpretation of what constituted "moral tone" rested with him and with the company.[5]

While most advertisers, such as Du Pont ("We're careful not to present programs which might antagonize a large number of people") and Chrysler ("Generally speaking, I would avoid controversy") agree with a policy of sponsor control, some do not. Standard Oil of New Jersey, which sponsored "The Play of the Week" and "The Age of Kings" series, had no voice in the subject matter, production or casting of the programs. The Bell & Howell

Corporation told the F.C.C. that despite threats of boycott as a result of its sponsorship of controversial programs on the "Closeup" series, it would not abandon either the "conviction and faith that most Americans are fair-minded people who realize they must know more if our society is to survive," or "the principle that has served this country so well — the idea that the press should be free of advertising influence."[6] Many of the witnesses at the F.C.C. hearings agreed that "in no other sphere of American life does the advertising community exercise power over content that lies outside of advertising per se."[7]

Whatever the arguments for or against the merits of censorship of controversial material, it is a special characteristic of the television and radio media that the writer must recognize. Let us look at some of the kinds of materials that have been censored. A talk by a clergyman on interdenominational friction was cancelled by a network. A play about homesteading in the southwest was cancelled because the sponsor didn't want anything presented which touched on the government giving economic help to farmers. The writer of a play about discrimination against a Negro family, based on headline newspaper stories, was forced to change the protagonist from a Negro to an ex-convict because of sponsor and network censorship. Two of the mass media's most prominent writers, Rod Serling and Reginald Rose, wrote a pilot film script for the Ford Foundation's Fund for the Republic series titled "The Challenge." The series was to deal with controversial topics of the day and the pilot film presented both sides of the issue of loyalty oaths, asking the audience to make any necessary decisions. The film was not given air time.

An ironic example of the kind of censorship the writer may expect was the cancellation of a play about a network censoring a commentator, even after the script had been put into production and publicity about it had been released. It may be significant that the network which cancelled this play had not long before censured one of its top commentators.

Some instances of censorship of alleged controversial material are based neither on the sponsor's vested interest nor on feared public reaction, but on the direct prejudice of the sponsor. One program, the true story of a Jewish owner of a large concern who gave away his entire fortune to fight cancer, was stopped by the sponsor because the play allegedly would give Jewish owners of department stores an unfair advantage over other department stores owners.

If such censorship seems incredible, the writer should be aware of even more petty instances which border on the ridiculous. One script, dealing with the Korean war, had an enlisted man who was referred to as having attended a certain Ivy League university. The advertising agency ordered this changed because certain agency executives felt that a person from this university should be an officer!

A frequent form of censorship is that which eliminates any material which might put the sponsor's product, even by implication, in an unfavorable light or which might, even obliquely, suggest a competing product. For example, in a program dealing with the German atrocities of the 1930's and 1940's, the sponsoring gas company eliminated any reference to the "gas chambers." In another instance, one of the country's leading popular singers was prohibited from presenting a certain love song on a program because she had just announced plans to get a divorce. On another occasion, the name of President Lincoln was deleted from a program because it is also the name of an automobile produced by a competitor of the sponsor. A leading cigarette manufacturer and distributor has told the Federal Communications Commission that in its programs tobacco products were not to be used in a derogatory or harmful way, that "no reference or gesture of . . . dissatisfaction . . . be made in connection with them . . . cigarettes should not be ground out violently in an ash tray or stamped out under foot . . . no cigarette should be used as a prop to depict an undesirable character."[8]

A leading television and radio writer has stated that censorship covers a far wider range than that specified in the NAB production codes and by individual stations and networks. Each sponsor, this writer has said, has his own special list of unacceptable subjects or ideas, stemming either from what he is selling or from his own personal prejudices. For example, on one program series sponsored by an auto manufacturer no one ever had an auto accident, nor was one ever referred to by any character. A cigarette manufacturer whose advertising proclaimed that their filters were favored by the medical profession made certain that no doctor ever appeared in any story done on the program series sponsored by the company. Even a flattering portrayal of a doctor might be construed as unfavorable by some doctor in the audience, whose good will the sponsor wished to retain or acquire. According to this writer, one can find similar examples for every sponsored show on the air, and these are problems that any writer must face if he would write for that show.

Although the most dramatic examples of censorship, as noted in this chapter, occur in plays, censorship applies just as strongly to other forms of television and radio writing.

In French television, until the political crises of the past few years, the major censorable items were "bad words" and non-dramatic, purposely provocative sex. When material of a censorable or controversial nature is presented on French television, material which generally is deemed acceptable to a mature and intelligent audience but which may not be entirely acceptable to the audience at home, an announcement before the program asks the audience to watch the program with indulgence and to put the children to bed. On the British Broadcasting Corporation programs there is virtually no dialogue code. Although good taste is a general guide for writers, in a dramatic show, for example, a character can make any reference that is necessary to the play.

Sydney W. Head, a leading teacher and writer in the communications field, has written that ". . . television, as a medium appears to be highly responsive to the conventional conservative values," and that a danger to society from television is that it, television, will not likely lend its support to the unorthodox, but that "it will add tremendously to cultural inertia."[9]

Former Federal Communications Commission Chairman Newton N. Minow characterized television programming as a "vast wasteland," and former Chairman E. William Henry called it an "electronic Appalachia." The immediate prospects for the serious creative writer are not too bright.

Theoretically, the writer can help to fulfill the responsibility of the mass media to serve the best interests of the public as a whole, can raise and energize the cultural and educational standards of the people and thus strengthen the country. Realistically, the most well-intentioned writer is still under the control of the network and advertiser whose first loyalties seem to be directed toward their own interests and not necessarily toward those of the public. Occasionally, these interests coincide. The writer who wishes to keep a job in the mass media must orient his work toward the first consideration — the employer.[10] It is hoped that conscience will not permit him to sacrifice the second entirely.

NOTES TO CHAPTER 1

[1] Eric Heath, *Writing for Television* (Los Angeles: Research Publishing Company, 1950), p. 18.

[2] Erik Barnouw, *Mass Communication* (New York: Holt, Rinehart and Winston, Inc., 1956), pp. 148; 267-268.

[3] Reginald Rose, *Six Television Plays* (New York: Simon and Schuster, 1956), pp. 249-251.

[4] *The New York Times,* October 8, 1961.

[5] *New York Herald Tribune,* September 28, 1961.

[6] *The New York Times,* September 28, 1961, and *New York Herald Tribune,* September 28, 1961.

[7] *The New York Times,* October 8, 1961.

[8] *The New York Times,* September 29, 1961.

[9] Sydney W. Head, "Content Analysis of Television Drama Programs," *Quarterly of Film, Radio and Television,* IX (Winter, 1954), pp. 192-193.

[10] For a tragi-comedy account of the writer's problems, the reader is referred to the book by Merle Miller and Evan Rhodes, *Only You, Dick Daring* (New York: William Sloane Associates, 1964).

2

BASIC ELEMENTS
OF PRODUCTION

MANY PROFESSIONAL WRITERS from other media — especially the novelist and the journalist — state in the same breath that they are trying to write for television or radio and that they haven't bothered to learn anything about the media. This is roughly equivalent to the painter who doesn't know how to choose a canvas or mix paints. He could be a successful painter, but probably will not be.

It is necessary to know the elements of television and radio that affect writing technique. The writer must learn what the camera can and cannot do, what sound or visual effects are possible in the control room, what terminology is used in furnishing directions, descriptions, and transitions, and what other technical and production aspects of the media are essential for effective writing.

RADIO

THE PRIMARY TECHNICAL and production potentials the radio writer should be aware of and should be able to indicate in the script, when necessary, pertain to microphone use, sound effects, and music. He should understand how the studio and control room can or cannot implement the purposes of his script.

The Microphone

The basic element of radio broadcasting is the microphone. The number of microphones used in a show usually is limited. There may be one or two for the announcer and the cast. Another may be used if there are any live sound effects. A live orchestra may require still another. Not all microphones are the same. The audio engineer selects certain types of microphones in terms of their sensitivity and uses for specific effects. The writer has only one important responsibility in this area: he must indicate the relationship of the performer to the microphone. It is this physical relationship which determines the orientation of the listener. For example, the audience may be with a character riding in a car. The car approaches the edge of a cliff. The writer must decide whether to put the sound of the character's scream and the noise of the car as it hurtles down the side of the cliff "on mike," thus keeping the audience with the car, or to fade these sounds into the distance, orienting the audience to a vantage point at the top of the cliff, watching the character and car going downward.

There are five basic microphone positions. The writer should indicate every position except "on mike," which is taken for granted when no position is designated next to the line of dialogue. Where the performer has been in another position and suddenly speaks from an "on mike" position, then "on mike" should be written in.

On mike.   The performer speaks from a position right at the microphone. The listener is oriented to the imaginary setting in the same physical spot as the performer.

Off mike.   The performer is some distance away from the microphone. This conveys to the audience the impression that the sound or voice is at a proportionate distance away from the physical orientation point of the listener, which is usually at the center of the scene. The writer may vary this listener orientation and, by removing the performer's voice but through the dialogue indicating that the performer has remained in the same physical place, it is the listener and not the performer who has been removed from the central point of action.

Fading on.   The performer slowly moves toward the microphone. In the mind's eye of the listener, the performer is approaching the physical center of the action.

Fading off.   The performer moves away from the microphone while speaking. He thus moves away from the central orientation point.

Behind obstructions.   The performer sounds as if there were a barrier between him and the focal point of the audience's orientation. The writer would indicate that the performer were behind a door, outside a window, or perhaps under the bandstand.

The writer may indicate the need for special microphones. One is the filter mike, which creates the impression that the voice or sound is coming over a telephone. The voice at the focal point of the audience's orientation, even though speaking over the telephone, too, would be on mike. Another is the echo chamber, which creates various degrees of an echo sound, ranging from an indication that a person is locked in a closet to the impression of a voice in a boundless cavern.

Note the use of the five basic positions in the following sample material*:

---

* The radio or television script is usually typed with double-spacing between speeches, sound effects, music directions and (for television) video directions. However, in the interests of a more compact typographic arrangement, single spacing has been used within most scripts in this book.

COMMENTARY	AUDIO
1. There is no mention of position. The character is assumed to be on mike.	GEORGE: I'm bushed, Myra. Another day like the one today, and I'll just . . . (THE DOORBELL RINGS) MYRA: Stay where you are, George, I'll answer the door. GEORGE: Thanks, hon. (DOORBELL RINGS AGAIN)
2. The orientation of the audience stays with George as Myra leaves the focal point of the action.	MYRA: (RECEDING FOOTSTEPS. FADING) I'm coming ... I'm coming. I wonder who it could be at this hour.
3. George must give the impression of projecting across the room to Myra who is now at the front door.	GEORGE: (CALLING) See who it is before you open the door.
4. Myra's physical position is now clear to the audience through the distance of her voice. Then as soon as we hear her ON MIKE, the audience's physical position arbitrarily is oriented to that of Myra at the front door.	MYRA: (OFF) All right, George. (ON MIKE) Who is it?
5. This is an example of the "behind an obstruction" position.	MESSENGER: (BEHIND DOOR) Telegram for Mr. George Groo.
6. The physical orientation of the audience stays with Myra. George is now OFF MIKE.	MYRA: Just a minute. (CALLING) George, telegram for you. GEORGE: (OFF) Sign for me, will you Myra? MYRA: Yes. (SOUND OF DOOR OPENING) I'll sign for it. (SOUND OF PAPER BEING HANDED OVER AND THE SCRATCH OF PENCIL ON PAPER) MESSENGER: Thank you, Ma'am. (SOUND OF DOOR BEING CLOSED) MYRA: (SOUND OF TELEGRAM BEING OPENED) I'll open it and . . . (SILENCE FOR A MOMENT) GEORGE: (OFF) Well, Myra, what is it? (STILL SILENCE)
7. Note the complete shift of audience orientation. After Myra goes to the door the audience stays with her, hears George from the other end of the room, finally knows that George, who is coming on or fading on, is approaching the spot where the audience and Myra are. Finally, George is at that spot. Note the use of the term ON MIKE at the end, when the character comes to that position from another position.	GEORGE: (FADING ON) Myra, in heaven's name, what happened? What does the telegram say? (ON MIKE) Myra, let me see that telegram!

23

The Studio

The physical limitations of a radio studio sometimes may affect the writer's purposes, so, if possible, the size of the studio should be checked to see if it is large enough. In addition, though most professional studios are satisfactorily equipped acoustically, some smaller stations are not, and the writer should attempt to determine whether he will be able to achieve the sensitivity of sound he may have planned for his script.

The Control Room

The control room is the focal point of operation in which all of the sound, music, effects and broadcast silence are coordinated — carefully mixed by the engineer at the control board, and sent out to the listener. The control room usually contains the turntables on which transcriptions and recordings can be incorporated with the live action in the studio. The control room also contains recording and taping equipment which permit the capture of the program either for rebroadcast or for initial public broadcast at a later time.

The control board regulates the volume of output of all microphones, turntables and tapes, and can fade or blend the sound of any one or combination of these elements.

Sound Effects

There are two major categories of sound effects: those that are recorded, and those that are made manually or live. Virtually any sound effect desired may be found on records. Examples range from various types of airplane motors to the crying of a baby. For split-second incorporation of sound into the live action of the program, however, manual or live effects are more effective. Manual effects would include such sounds as the opening and closing of a door (coming from a miniature door located near the microphone of the sound effects man) or the rattling of cellophane to simulate the sound of fire. Under this category fall natural effects — those emanating from their natural sources, such as the sound of walking feet in which the microphone might be held near the feet of a sound effects man marking time. In some instances — Norman Corwin's radio plays are prime examples — entirely new combinations of sounds may be necessary, including an amalgamation of recorded, manual and natural effects.

Inexperienced writers occasionally have a tendency to overdo the use of sound. Sound effects should be used only when necessary, and then only in relation to the psychological principles which determine the orientation of the listener. Reflect on your own orientation to sound when listening to the radio. For example, a high pitch or high volume or rising pitch usually suggests a climax or some disturbing element, while a low pitch or low volume or descending pitch usually suggests something soothing and calm. However, combinations of these sounds and the relationship of the specific sound to the specific situation can alter these generalizations. For instance, a low pitch in the proper place can indicate something foreboding rather than calm; or the combination of a low pitch and a high volume, as in thunder and an explosion, can create anything but a soothing effect.

Sound can be used for many purposes and effects, as follows:

Establish the locale or setting. For example, the sound of marching feet, the clanging of metal doors and the blowing of a whistle will suggest the locale or setting of a prison. The soft sounds of violin music, the occasional clatter of dishes and silverware, the clinking of glasses and the whispered sounds of talking would suggest not only a restaurant, but perhaps an old world Hungarian, Russian or Gypsy restaurant.

Direct the audience attention and emotion by emphasis on a particular sound. The sudden banging of a gavel in a courtroom scene will immediately direct the mind's-eye view of the audience toward the judge's bench. In a sequence in which the audience is aware that a person alone at home is an intended murder victim, the sound of steps on a walk and the sound of knocking on a door, or the more subtle sound of the turning of a doorknob, will direct the audience attention toward the front door and orient the audience's emotions toward the suspenseful terror of inevitable and perhaps immediate violence.

Establish time. The clock striking the hour or the crowing of the cock are obvious, oft-used but nevertheless effective devices. The echo of footsteps along a pavement, with no other sounds heard, would indicate a quiet street very late at night or very early in the morning. If an element referred to in the program, such as an airplane or the rumbling of a subway train, has been established as indicating a certain time, then the moment the sound effect signifying that element is used, the audience will know the time.

Establish mood. Anyone who has heard a dramatization of a Sherlock Holmes story is familiar with the mood created by the echo of a baying hound followed by the muffled strokes of a clock striking twelve. The sounds of laughter, loud music and much tinkling of glasses would establish a much different mood for a party than would subdued whispers and the soft music of a string quartet. Sound may be used effectively as counterpoint in setting off an individual character's mood. The attitudes and emotions of a character who is worried, sullen, morose and fretful may be heightened by placing him in the midst of sounds indicating a wild, gay party.

Signify entrances and exits. The sound of footsteps fading off and the opening and closing of a door, or the reverse, the opening and closing of a door and the sound of footsteps coming on, are unmistakable in indicating an exit or entrance. Transportation sounds and human and non-human sounds may be used to signify a character's coming to or leaving a place. The departure of a soldier from an enemy-held jungle island after a secret reconnaissance mission could be indicated by the sound of boat paddles, the whine of bullets and the chatter of jungle birds and animals. If the bullet, bird and animal sounds remain at a steady level and the paddling of the boat fades off, the audience remains on the island and sees the soldier leave. The audience may leave with the soldier if the paddling remains at an on-mike level and the island sounds fade off.

Serve as a transition between program segments or between changes of time or place in a dramatic program.   For example, if the transition is to cover a change of place, the sound used may be the means of transportation. The young man is about to leave home to travel to the big city to make his fortune. Tender farewells are said. The farewells cross-fade into the sounds of a train, with appropriate whistles. The train sounds cross-fade into the sounds of the hustle and bustle of the big city. These sounds in turn cross-fade into the live sequence in which the young man makes arrangements for the renting of a room from the big-city landlady. The change of place has been achieved with sound providing an effective transition.

If the transition is to cover a lapse of time, the sound may be that of a timing device, such as a clock striking three, the tick of the clock fading out, fading in again, and the clock then striking six.

The sound indicating the transition may not relate necessarily to the specific cause of the transition. It may be of a general nature, such as a montage of war sounds to cover a change of place or lapse of time when the action relates to a war. Sometimes a montage, or blending of a number of sounds, can be particularly effective when no single sound fits the specific situation.

In a non-dramatic program, sounds relating to the content of the next segment may be used for transition. In some situations the sounds may have a relationship to the program as a whole rather than to a specific circumstance, such as the use of a ticker or telegraph key sound as a transition device for a news program. On comedy shows sounds completely irrelevant to the material may be used for transitional purposes, serving at the same time, because of their irrelevance, as comedy material.

Create unrealistic effects.   Note Norman Corwin's description in "The Plot to Overthrow Christmas"[1] of the audience's journey to Hades, "To the regions where legions of the damnéd go."

> (CLANG ON CHINESE GONG. TWO THUNDER PEALS. OSCILLA-
> TOR IN AT HIGH PITCH BEFORE THUNDER IS ENTIRELY OUT.
> BRING PITCH DOWN GRADUALLY AND FADE IN ECHO CHAMBER
> WHILE HEAVY STATIC FADES IN, THEN OUT TO LEAVE NOTH-
> ING BUT OSCILLATOR AT A LOW OMINOUS PITCH; THEN RAISE
> OSCILLATOR PITCH SLOWLY. HOLD FOR A FEW SECONDS.)

Combinations of sound and music may be used to create almost any unrealistic effect demanded, from the simplest to the most complicated.

Sound also may be used to achieve not only one, but a combination of the various purposes already noted. For example, who could ever forget, once having heard it, the sound sequence accompanying Jack Benny's periodic visit to his private vault? The sounds used establish setting, orient the audience's emotions and direct its attention, establish mood, signify entrances and exits, serve as transitions between places and indicate lapses of time, and create unrealistic effects.

SOUND:	FOOTSTEPS . . . DOOR OPENS . . . FOOTSTEPS GOING DOWN . . . TAKING ON HOLLOW SOUND . . . HEAVY IRON DOOR HANDLE TURNING . . . CHAINS CLANKING . . . DOOR CREAKS OPEN . . . SIX MORE HOLLOW FOOTSTEPS . . . SECOND CLANKING OF CHAINS . . . HANDLE TURNS . . . HEAVY IRON DOOR OPENS CREAKING . . . TWO MORE FOOTSTEPS (DIALOGUE BETWEEN THE GUARD AND JACK) . . . LIGHT TURNING SOUND OF VAULT COMBINATION . . . LIGHT TURNING SOUND . . . LIGHT TURNING SOUND . . . LIGHT TURNING SOUND . . . HANDLE TURNS . . . USUAL ALARMS WITH BELLS, AUTO HORNS, WHISTLES, THINGS FALLING . . . ENDING WITH B.O. FOG-HORN . . .

Courtesy of J & M Productions, Inc.

The writer must keep in mind that many sounds, no matter how well or accurately done, sometimes are not immediately identifiable to the audience, and often may be confused with similar sounds. It may be necessary for the writer to identify the sound through the dialogue. For example, since the rattling of paper may sound like fire, and the opening and closing of a desk drawer may sound like the opening and closing of almost anything else, note the need for identifying dialogue in the following sequence and the attempt to make the designation of the sound logical and a natural part of the dialogue.

DICK:	(RUFFLING THE PAGES OF A MANUSCRIPT) Just about the worst piece of junk I've ever done in my life.
ANNE:	Well, even if you don't like it, I think it can become a best seller.
DICK:	(RUFFLING PAGES AGAIN) Three hundred and forty-two pages of pure unadulterated mediocrity. Listen to them. They even sound off-key. (SOUND OF A DESK DRAWER OPENING). There. That's where it belongs. (SOUND OF MANUSCRIPT BEING THROWN INTO THE DRAWER.)
ANNE:	Don't lock it up in your desk. I think it's good.
DICK:	Nope! That drawer is the place where all bad, dead manuscripts belong. (SOUND OF DESK DRAWER CLOSING) Amen!

Music

Music is an important part of all radio programming. The writer should understand its several uses, including the following:

As the content for a musical program. Live music, in the form of an orchestra or a musical performer, has virtually disappeared from radio. Recorded or transcribed music is the primary content of radio today, as exemplified in the popular disc jockey type of program.

As the theme for a dramatic or non-dramatic program. Who could have failed to identify even the first few bars of "Love in Bloom" with the Jack Benny show or "A Hard Day's Night" with The Beatles? Music may be used not only as a theme for a program as a whole, but for a specific event or a particular character. The action or character is immediately identifiable when the theme music is heard. This may be true in the dramatic program or with the personality on the non-dramatic program. Every time "Love In Bloom" is heard we know Jack Benny is about to make his appearance. Theme music is used in dramatic shows, too. It is similar here to its use as a bridge, described next, except that it is not applied during the action but only for the opening, closing and sometimes during the commercial breaks. Note the use of music as a theme in the following excerpts from the beginning and end of one program of a dramatic series entitled "The Delaware Story."

ANNOUNCER:	WDEL presents "The Delaware Story."
MUSIC:	THEME IN, UP, AND UNDER.
NARRATOR:	When we think of lawless robber barons and land pirates, our thoughts turn to the early wild and unsettled west. Yet, in the late seventeenth century . . . if it had not been for the interference of the King of England, the State of Delaware, through the unscrupulous efforts of one man, might have become annexed to Maryland and never become a separate state at all.
MUSIC:	THEME UP AND OUT.
ANNOUNCER:	COMMERCIAL
	And now, back to today's "Delaware Story," "The Man Who Almost Stole A State."
MUSIC:	THEME IN, UP AND OUT.
NARRATOR:	In 1681 Charles II of England granted to William Penn a charter . . .
	The narrator introduces the live dramatic action. Following the dramatic sequences, the narrator again resumes, completing the story.
NARRATOR:	. . . but Talbot did not succeed in stealing a state, and he remains, fortunately, a not too successful chapter in "The Delaware Story."
MUSIC:	THEME IN, UP AND OUT.

After the final commercial and program credits, the theme is again brought in, up and out to close the show.

For the bridging of divisions in the non-dramatic program, or for a change of time or place in the dramatic program. The musical bridge is the most commonly used device for transitions. Music lasting only a few notes or a few bars or, in some cases, of longer duration may be used to indicate the break between segments of the non-dramatic presentation. For example, in the variety show the writer would indicate a music bridge following the completion of an act, before the master of ceremonies introduced the next act. Sometimes the bridge may also serve as a short musical introduction or finale. The musical bridge also may be used to demark the commercial insert from the rest of the program.

In the dramatic program the musical bridge frequently is used to indicate a change of place or a lapse of time. Care must be taken that the bridge is representative of the mood and content of the play at that particular moment. The musical bridge usually is only a few seconds long.

Note the use of the bridge separating dramatic sequences and narration in the following condensed excerpt, again from one of "The Delaware Story" series.

LORD BALTIMORE:	Go to Philadelphia and speak with William Penn. Ask him to withdraw. If he does not, then we can consider other methods.
MUSIC:	BRIDGE.
TALBOT:	(FADING IN) . . . and if you choose to remain, we are left with only one recourse. I need not amplify, my dear Mr. Penn, need I?
PENN:	You have had my answer, Talbot. If you think you can frighten me from land legally deeded to me, then your presumptuousness is exceeded only by your stupidity.
MUSIC:	SNEAK IN SHORT BRIDGE.
NARRATOR:	Talbot returned to Maryland and immediately began his campaign to regain the land he believed rightfully belonged to Lord Baltimore . . .

SOUND:	CROWD OF MEN'S VOICES, ANGRY, UNDER.
TALBOT:	We must fight for the right. I've called you together because we shall and must fight like vigilantes. Our first line of defense will be Beacon Hill. The firing of three shots means danger . . . the blowing of horns will mean we assemble to ride. Are you with me?
ALL:	(SHOUTING) Aye! Aye!
MUSIC:	SNEAK IN SHORT BRIDGE.
NARRATOR:	And ride they did. Talbot now assumed dictatorial powers . . .

As a sound effect. For example, brass and percussion instruments often may be very effective in conveying the sound of a storm or in heightening the feeling of a storm presented through sound effects alone. Some effects cannot be presented potently except through music. How better could one convey on radio the sound of a person falling from the top of a tall building than through music moving in a spiral rhythm from a high to a low pitch and ending in a crash?

For background or mood. Music can heighten the content and mood of a sequence, especially in a dramatic presentation. Background music is an extremely important part of film making, and is used effectively in non-musical stage plays. The music must serve as a subtle aid, however, and must not be obvious or, in some instances, even evident. The listener who is aware of a lovely piece of background music during a dramatic moment has been distracted from the primary purpose of the production. The music should have its effect without the audience consciously realizing it. Background and mood music should not be overdone or used excessively in the manner of the piano player accompanying a silent film. Well known compositions should be avoided, to prevent the audience from being distracted from the dialogue by too great a familiarity with the music.

Sound and Music Techniques and Terms

Several important terms are used by the writer to designate the techniques used in manipulating sound and music. These techniques are applied at the control board.

Segue (pronounced *Seg-way*). The smooth movement from one sound into the next. This is particularly applicable to the transitions between musical numbers, in which one number is faded out and the next is faded in. Technically, it is used in the dramatic program as well as in the musical show, but in the dramatic program the overlapping of sounds makes the technique a cross-fade, rather than a segue.

An example in the musical program:

ANNOUNCER:	Our program continues with excerpts from famous musical compositions dealing with the Romeo and Juliet theme. First we hear from Tchaikowsky's "Romeo and Juliet" overture, followed by Prokofieff's "Romeo and Juliet" ballet, and finally Gounod's opera, "Romeo et Juliette."
MUSIC:	TCHAIKOWSKY'S "ROMEO AND JULIET," SEGUE TO PROKOFIEFF'S "ROMEO AND JULIET." SEGUE TO GOUNOD'S "ROMEO ET JULIETTE"
ANNOUNCER:	You have heard . . .

An example in the dramatic program:

ANNOUNCER: And now, to today's mystery drama.
MUSIC: THEME IN AND UP, HOLD FOR FIVE SECONDS AND OUT,
            SEGUE INTO
SOUND: TINKLING OF GLASSES, VOICES IN BACKGROUND IN ANGRY
            CONVERSATION, JUKEBOX PLAYING.

Cross-fade.   The dissolving from one sound into another. The term cross-fade sometimes is used interchangeably with the term segue. The cross-fade is, however, the crossing of sounds as one fades in and the other fades out, while the segue is simply the immediate following of one sound by another. In the following example

MUSIC: THEME IN AND UP, HOLD FOR FIVE SECONDS, CROSS-FADE
            INTO THE RINGING OF A TELEPHONE.

the telephone ringing becomes blended for a second or two with the theme before the theme is entirely out and then only the telephone ringing remains.
An example in a dramatic program:

CLARA: I don't know where Harry is, but if he's with some blonde in some
            bar . . .
MUSIC: STAB IN BRIDGE, HOLD FOR THREE SECONDS, CROSS-FADE
            INTO SOUND OF PIANO IN A BAR PLAYING A BLUES NUMBER.

Blending.   Two or more different sounds combined and going out over the air at the same time. These may include combinations of dialogue and music, dialogue and sound effects, sound effects and music or a combination of all three. The earlier example of the combination of tinkling glasses, angry voices in the background, and the playing of a jukebox is illustrative of blending dialogue, sound effects and music. The blending of sounds may be used effectively to create unrealistic effects.
Cutting or Switching.   The sudden cutting off of one sound and the immediate intrusion of another. It is a jarring break and sometimes is used for special effect purposes. It may simply designate the switching sharply from one microphone to another microphone or sound source. It also may be used for remotes:

ANNOUNCER: We now switch you to Times Square where Tom Rogers is ready
            with his "Probing Microphone."
CUT TO REMOTE, ROGERS AT TIMES SQUARE
ROGERS: Good afternoon. For our first interview, we have a gentleman over
            here . . .

Fade In and Fade Out.   Bringing up the volume or turning it down. This is a relatively simple operation. It frequently is used to fade the music under dialogue, as well as to bring it into the program and out of the program. The writer indicates that the music should be "faded in," "up," "under," or "out."

The following excerpt from the Five Star Matinee dramatic production, "A Girl of His Own," illustrates the above uses of theme and introductory music. Note the qualifying descriptions of how the music should be used, such as "fast and full."

ANNCR: NBC Radio brings you two full hours of drama in the afternoon. Next . . . "FIVE STAR MATINEE"

(MUSIC: THEME: "SEQUOIA" IN FAST AND FULL . . . ON CUE, FADE UNDER)

MERRITT: But Orville's supposed to be writing a book!   He can't fall in love at a time like this!

MARK: It's happened before, Mr. Merritt.

MERRITT: Now, see here, Hampton. You know Orville -- he can only write when he's feeling miserable -- if he starts feeling happy, it'll ruin him as a novelist. No, this girl has got to go!

(MUSIC: "B" THEME OF "SEQUOIA" UP TO FULL, THEN FADE FOR:)

ANNCR: "FIVE STAR MATINEE" . . . A complete story, brought to you live each weekday afternoon. This is your host, Fred Collins, and in just a moment, you'll hear Russell Beggs' romantic comedy titled - "A GIRL OF HIS OWN."

(MUSIC: THEME OUT HERE)

ANNCR: But first, hear this:

                    (FIRST COMMERCIAL POSITION)

(MUSIC: TEN SECOND INTRO . . . DOWN UNDER)

ANNCR: Now, Five Star Matinee . . . and our story - "GIRL OF HIS OWN"!

(MUSIC: UP AND DOWN)

MARK: When I walked into Mr. Merritt's office . . . .

                              Courtesy of Galahad Productions, Inc.

The following example illustrates the use of the fade in and fade out on the disc jockey show.

MUSIC: THEME, "Sunny Side of the Street," IN, UP, AND UNDER.

ANNCR: Good evening, ladies and gentlemen, boys and girls, guys and gals.   Welcome to the Rollicking Rollo Rock and Roll Repertory.

MUSIC: THEM UP, HOLD FOR FIVE SECONDS, THEN UNDER AND OUT.

ANNCR: This is Rollicking Rollo Rollins bringing you another half hour of popular melodies from the top forty. Our first selection, in response to a request from all the cool chicks and shook-up gents at P.S. 943, is a number that's been sweeping the nation.

MUSIC: SNEAK IN AND HOLD UNDER, "Jail House Juke Box.'

ANNCR: If you listen real close you can hear it playing in the background. That's right, you guessed it. It's the "Jail House Juke Box."

MUSIC: UP FAST, HOLD TO FINISH, AND OUT.

TELEVISION

Many programs, particularly the popular situation comedy-adventure-western and similar type play series being produced in the mid-1960's, follow the Hollywood (or filmed) rather than the New York (or live-on-tape) approach. The writer, therefore, will find the terms and techniques of film writing used more in the preparation of many scripts than the terms representing purely television technique. (See the section on the filmed play in Chapter 9.) But the medium is still television, and a primary, basic grounding in television skills — many of which are similar to film skills — will not only provide the most practical preparation, but will permit the writer to move more easily and ultimately more effectively, when necessary, into film-for-television writing.

Although the writer for television does not have to know the various coordinate elements of theatrical production as does the writer of the stage play, it would add to his competence to know how to use and integrate settings, lights, costumes, make-up and the visual movement of actors into his script, dramatic or non-dramatic. The television writer, like the radio writer, has at his disposal all of the elements of sound. In addition, the television writer must achieve an understanding of the special mechanical and electronic devices of the television medium. There are five major areas pertaining to television production that the writer should be aware of: the studio, the cameras, the control room, special video effects, and sound.

The TV Studio

In the ETV station (about one out of six stations on the air is non-commercial) and in some local and regional commercial stations, the writer has an opportunity to write the live-type program. In such instances he must be aware of his studio limitations, especially the need to avoid too many sets or large sets in any one production. Exterior sets and large nature effects frequently are not possible.

The Camera

The writer should consider the camera as a moving and adjustable proscenium through which the attention of the audience is directed just as the writer and director wish. There are three major areas of audience attention that may be changed via the camera: the distance between the audience and the subject, which includes the amount of the subject the audience sees; the position of the audience in relation to the subject; and the angle at which the viewer sees the subject. Various uses of the camera, including camera movement, lens openings and types of shots, may be made to effect all of these approaches in varying degrees.

Camera movement may change the position, angle, distance and amount of subject matter seen. There are five specific movements the writer must be aware of and be prepared to designate, when necessary, in the script.

Dolly in and dolly out. The camera is on a dolly stand which permits smooth forward or backward movement. This movement to or away from the subject permits a change of orientation to the subject while keeping the camera on the air and retaining a continuity of action.

Tilt up and tilt down. This consists of pointing the camera up or down, thus changing the view from the same position to a higher or lower part of subject area. The tilt also is called panning up and panning down.

Pan right and pan left. The camera moves right or left on its axis. This movement may be used to follow a character or some particular action or to direct the audience attention to a particular subject.

Follow right and follow left. This is also called the "travel" shot or the "truck" shot. It is used when the camera is set at a right angle to the subject and either moves with it, following alongside it or, as in the case of a stationary subject such as an advertising display, follows down the line of the display. The audience's eyes, through the camera lens pointed sharply to the right or left, pick up the subjects in the display. This shot is not used so frequently as are the previous ones.

Boom shot. The camera boom is a familiar part of Hollywood film making. Equipment, usually attached to the moving dolly, enables the camera to "boom" from its basic position in or out, up or down, at various angles to the subject. The boom is becoming more and more part of standard television production practices.

Note the use of the basic camera movements in the following hypothetical script situation. Ordinarily, the writer would not include so many camera directions as indicated here, but would leave their determination to the director. The writer should study the following to become aware of the various camera and shot possibilities. The left hand column, as shown here, would almost entirely be written in on the mimeographed script by the director.

VIDEO	AUDIO
	DETECTIVE BYRON
ESTABLISHING SHOT.	(AT DESK, IN FRONT OF HIM, ON CHAIRS IN A ROW, ARE SEVERAL YOUNG MEN IN DUNGAREES, LEATHER JACKETS AND MOTORCYCLE CAPS.) All right. So a store was robbed. So all of you were seen in the store at the time of the robbery. So there was no one else in the store except the clerk. So none of you know anything about the robbery.
DOLLY IN FOR CLOSE-UP OF BYRON.	(GETTING ANGRY.) You may be young punks but you're still punks, and you can stand trial whether you're seventeen or seventy. And if you're not going to cooperate now, I'll see that you get the stiffest sentence possible.
DOLLY OUT FOR LONG SHOT OF ENTIRE GROUP. CUT TO CU. PAN RIGHT ACROSS BOYS' FACES, FROM ONE TO THE OTHER, AS BYRON TALKS.	Now, I'm going to ask you again, each one of you. And this is your last chance. If you talk, only the guilty one will be charged with larceny. The others will have only a petty theft charge on them, and I'll see they get a suspended sentence. Otherwise, I'll send you all up for five to ten.

FOLLOW SHOT ALONG LINE OF
CHAIRS IN FRONT OF BOYS, GETTING
FACIAL REACTIONS OF EACH ONE
AS THEY RESPOND.

(OFF CAMERA) Joey?

JOEY

(STARES STRAIGHT AHEAD, NOT
ANSWERING.)

BYRON

(OFF CAMERA) Al?

AL

I got nothin' to say.

BYRON

(OFF CAMERA) Bill?

BILL

Me, too. I don't know nothin'.

BYRON

(OFF CAMERA) O.K., Johnny. It's up to
you.

JOHNNY

TILT DOWN TO JOHNNY'S BOOT AS HE
REACHES FOR HANDLE OF KNIFE.
TILT UP WITH HAND AS IT MOVES AWAY
FROM THE BOOT, INTO AN INSIDE
POCKET OF HIS JACKET. CUT TO ME-
DIUM SHOT ON BOOM CAMERA OF
JOHNNY WITHDRAWING HAND FROM
POCKET. BOOM INTO CLOSE-UP OF
OBJECT IN JOHNNY'S HAND.
(ORDINARILY, A BOOM SHOT WOULD
NOT BE USED HERE. A ZOOM LENS
WOULD BE EASIER TO USE AND AT
LEAST AS EFFECTIVE.)

(THERE IS NO ANSWER. THEN JOHNNY
SLOWLY SHAKES HIS HEAD. UNPER-
CEPTIBLY, BYRON NOT NOTICING, HE
REACHES DOWN TO HIS MOTORCYCLE
BOOT FOR THE HANDLE OF A KNIFE.
SUDDENLY THE HAND STOPS AND MOVES
UP TO THE INSIDE POCKET OF HIS
JACKET. JOHNNY TAKES AN OBJECT
FROM HIS POCKET, SLOWLY OPENS
HIS HAND.)

Lens Openings

The image orthicon camera and the less expensive vidicon camera, which
is used primarily for closed-circuit educational purposes, usually are equipped
with four lenses, each of which creates a different distance between the viewer
and the subject. Lenses are divided into two categories of use: studio work and
field work. Studio lenses have a shorter focal length than do field lenses, offer
a greater depth of field and require comparatively little adjustment for close-
up scenes. Lenses most often used for studio work with the image orthicon
camera are the 2-inch 50-millimeter lens, the 4-inch 90-millimeter lens, the 6-
inch 135-millimeter lens, and either the 8½-inch lens or the zoom lens. There
are several types of zoom lenses; the most commonly used has a range of
from 60-millimeters to 240-millimeters. In recent years the use of the 3-inch
75-millimeter lens has been growing, and the wide angle 1½-inch 35-milli-

meter lens especially has found favor in large studios where distance or height shots are possible. Field lenses have special long focal lengths and sometimes are called telephoto lenses. Although the 8½-inch lens is used sometimes for field work, it is essentially a studio lens. Standard field lenses include those of 13-inch, 15-inch, 17-inch and 25-inch dimensions. These lenses, picking up objects at a longer distance in direct proportion to their lengths, are excellent for sports events and for taking close-ups where the action is 50 feet or more away.

Although the writer does not need to indicate the lens used for any of the shots in his show — this remains the prerogative of the director — he should be aware of the lens potentials. For example, if the writer expects that a certain scene in his script would call most effectively for a two-shot, it might help him plan his action if he knows that he can get the same two-shot at 6 feet distance with the 50-millimeter lens and at 29 feet distance with the 8½-inch lens. The 135-millimeter lens is usually used for the close-up, the 90-millimeter for the medium shot, the 50-millimeter for the long, wide angle shot, and the 8½-inch lens for a close-up at a relatively long distance. The zoom lens is effective for quick continuous movement from a long to a close shot and vice versa.

Types of Shots

The writer should be familiar with the types of shots used in television and their designations. Ordinarily, the writer does not indicate the kinds of shots, but leaves their determination up to the director. In many instances, however, he will find that he needs to capture a specific subject for the logical continuity of his script and for the proper psychological effect upon his audience. When the shot might not be obvious to the director the writer has the prerogative of inserting it into the script. There are various shot designations, ranging from the close-up to the medium shot to the long shot. The writer may indicate the kind of shot and specific subject to be encompassed by that shot. Let us examine some of the most commonly used shots.

Close-up. This may be designated by the letters CU. The writer states in the script: "CU Harry," or "CU Harry's fingers as he twists the dials of the safe," or "CU Harry's feet on the pedals of the piano." The close-up of the immediate person of a human subject will usually consist of just the face and may include some of the upper part of his body, with emphasis on the face, unless specifically designated otherwise. The letters XCU or ECU stand for extreme close-up and designate the face alone. The term shoulder shot indicates an area encompassing the shoulders to the top of the head. Other designations are bust shot, waist shot, hip shot and knee shot.

Medium Shot. This may be designated by the letters MS. The camera picks up a good part of the individual or group subject, the subject usually filling the screen, but usually not in its entirety, and without too much of the physical environment shown.

Long Shot. The writer may state this as LS. The long shot is used primarily for establishing shots in which the entire setting, or as much of it as necessary to orient the audience properly, is shown. From the long shot, the camera may move to the medium shot and then to the close-up, creating a dramatic movement from an over-all view to the impact of the essence or selective aspect of the situation. Conversely, the camera may move from the intriguing suspense of a close-up to the clarifying broadness of the long shot.

Full Shot. This is stated as FS. The subject is put on the screen in its entirety. For example, "FS Harry" means that the audience sees Harry from head to toe. "FS family at dinner table" means that the family seated around the dinner table is seen completely.

There are, of course, various gradations within each shot. Just as the tight two-shot (T2-S, close-up of two people) is a variation of the close-up, there are medium close-ups, medium long shots, and similar minor changes of distance and amount of subject seen.

The writer should be aware of any necessity to change lenses, focus the lenses or dolly the camera for a new shot. Depending on the number of cameras used in the show, the writer should leave enough time between shots for the cameraman to properly perform these functions.

Note the use of different types of shots in the following hypothetical script example. The video directions are necessary at the beginning of this script because the writer is dealing solely with pictures. Subsequent video directions may be left out by the writer, except, as at the end, where necessary to convey the meaning and action. Examine the script beginning on page 299 for an example of how few video directions the author has to provide.

Control Room Techniques

The technicians in the control room have various electronic techniques for modifying the picture and moving from one picture to another — thus giving television its ability to direct the attention and control the view of the audience, and its means of bypassing the unities of time and place effectively. The writer should be familiar with the terminology and function of all of the control room techniques so that he can know what the potentials of his medium are and so that he can indicate, if necessary, special picture modification or change of time and/or place.

The Fade. The fade-in consists of bringing in the picture from a black screen. The fade-out is the taking out of a picture until a black level is reached. The fade is used primarily to indicate a passage of time, and in this function serves much like the curtain or blackout on the legitimate stage. Depending on the sequence of action, a fast fade-in or fade-out or slow fade-out or fade-in may be indicated. The fade-in is used at the beginning of a sequence, the fade-out at the end. The fade sometimes also is used to indicate a change of place. The writer always indicates the fade-in or fade-out in the script.

VIDEO	AUDIO

FADE IN ON LONG SHOT OF OUTSIDE OF BAR. ESTABLISH STREET FRONT AND OUTSIDE OF BAR. DOLLY IN TO MEDIUM SHOT, THEN TO CLOSE-UP OF SIGN ON THE WINDOW: "HARRY SMITH, PROP." CUT TO INSIDE OF BAR, CLOSE-UP OF MAN'S HAND DRAWING A GLASS OF BEER FROM THE TAP. FOLLOW MAN'S HAND WITH GLASS TO TOP OF BAR WHERE HE PUTS DOWN GLASS.
DOLLY OUT SLOWLY TO MEDIUM SHOT OF HARRY, SERVING THE BEER, AND MAC, SITTING AT BAR.
CONTINUE DOLLYING OUT TO LONG SHOT, ESTABLISHING ENTIRE INSIDE OF BAR, SEVERAL PEOPLE ON STOOLS, AND SMALL TABLE AT RIGHT OF BAR WITH THREE MEN SEATED, PLAYING CARDS.

JOE

(AT TABLE) Harry. Bring us another deck. This one's getting too dirty for honest card players.

HARRY

Okay. (HE REACHES UNDER THE BAR, GETS A DECK OF CARDS, GOES TO THE TABLE.)

JOE

TIGHT 2-S HARRY AND JOE

(TAKING THE CARDS, WHISPERS TO HARRY.) Who's the guy at the bar? He looks familiar.

HARRY

Name of Mac. From Jersey someplace.

CUT TO CU JOE

JOE

Keep him there. Looks like somebody we got business with. (LOOKS AROUND TABLE) Right, boys? (THE MEN AT THE TABLE NOD KNOWINGLY TO HARRY.)

CUT TO FS TABLE

HARRY

Okay if I go back to the bar?

JOE

Go ahead.

HARRY

PAN WITH HARRY TO BAR. DOLLY IN TO BAR, MS HARRY AND MAC AS HARRY POURS HIM ANOTHER DRINK. MCU HARRY AS HE WRITES. CUT TO CU OF WORDS ON PIECE OF PAPER.

(WALKS BACK TO BAR, POURS DRINK FOR MAC. SCRIBBLES SOMETHING ON PIECE OF PAPER, PUTS IT ON BAR IN FRONT OF MAC.)

37

The Dissolve.   The dissolve is similar to the cross-fade of radio. While one picture is being reduced to black level, the other picture is being brought in from black level, one picture smoothly dissolving into the next. The dissolve is used primarily to indicate a change of place, but is used sometimes to indicate a change of time. There are various modifications of the dissolve. An important one is the matched dissolve, in which two similar or identical subjects are placed one over the other and the fading out of one and the fading in of the other shows a metamorphosis taking place. The dissolving from a newly lit candle into a candle burned down would be a use of the matched dissolve. The dissolve may vary in time, and may be designated as a fast dissolve — almost a split-second movement — or as a slow dissolve — anywhere up to five seconds. The writer always indicates the use of the dissolve in the script.

The Cut.   The cut is the technique most commonly used. It consists simply of switching instantaneously from one picture to another. Care must be taken to avoid too much cutting, and to make certain that the cutting is consistent with the mood, rhythm, pace and psychological approach of the program as a whole. The writer ordinarily is not concerned with the planning or designation of cuts, but leaves it up to the director.

The Superimposition.   The "super," as it is sometimes called, means the placing of one image over another, thus creating a fantasy kind of picture. This sometimes is used in the stream-of-consciousness technique when the thing being recalled to memory is pictured on the screen. The superimposition may be used for non-dramatic effects very effectively, such as the superimposition of titles over a picture or the superimposition of commercial names or products over the picture. To obtain necessary contrast in the superimposition, when the two pictures are placed on the screen together one picture must be of a higher light intensity than the other. The writer usually indicates the use of the superimposition.

The Wipe.   This is accomplished by one picture literally wiping another picture off the screen in the manner of a window shade being pulled down over a window. The wipe may be from any direction: horizontal, vertical, or diagonal. The wipe may also blossom out a picture from the center of a black level or, in reverse, envelop the picture by encompassing it from all its sides. The wipe can be used to designate a change of place or time.

The Split Screen.   In the split screen the picture on the air is actually divided, with the shots from two or more cameras occupying adjoining places on the screen. A common use is for phone conversations, showing the persons speaking on separate halves of the screen. The screen may be split in many parts and in many shapes, as is sometimes done when news correspondents report from different parts of the nation. One segment of the screen of virtually any size may be split off from the rest, as often is done in sports broadcasts; for example, one corner of the screen may show the runner taking a lead off first base while the rest of the screen encompasses the main action of the ball game.

Film and Slides.   The use of the film clip (a short length of 16-millimeter moving picture film) and slides is important in live or taped television production. The film clip often is used to provide background shots necessary to the production, which cannot be achieved in the limited settings of the studio. The film clip can provide exterior scenes and nature effects for the live show. The slide frequently is used in documentary, news and sports programs. The split-second electronic adjustments make it possible to integrate the film or slides with live action.

"Cover" material. The film clip sometimes is used as cover material which continues the sequence of live action while permitting the character or characters involved to change costume, alter make-up or get to another set in the live show. Voice-over pre-recorded material is another electronic "cover" device. The writer must be certain to allow the actor sufficient time between sequences for any necessary costume or make-up changes or movement to a new set. When such time cannot possibly be permitted in the script, the writer may "cover" the performer by various means, including concentration on some action or on a close-up of another performer, giving the impression that a particular character is present but is involved in the action off-screen. The writer may cut to other characters in another set or substitute a similarly dressed performer, showing only the back of the head or an incomplete image of that performer, creating the impression that the original character is still there.

Note the use of different control room techniques for modifying the picture and moving from one picture to another in the following hypothetical script example:

COMMENTARY	VIDEO	AUDIO
		FEARLESS
1. The fade-in is used for the beginning of the sequence.	FADE IN ON SHERIFF'S OFFICE. SHERIFF FEARLESS AND DEPUTY FEARFUL ARE SEATED AT THE DESK IN THE CENTER OF THE ROOM.	I wonder what Black Bart is up to. He's been in town since yesterday. I've got to figure out his plan if I'm to prevent bloodshed.
		FEARFUL
		I've got faith in you, Fearless. I heard that he's been with Miss Susie in her room.
		FEARLESS
		Good. We can trust her. She'll find out for us.
		FEARFUL
		But I'm worried about her safety.
		FEARLESS
		Yup. I wonder how she is making out. That Black Bart is a mean one.

COMMENTARY	VIDEO	AUDIO

2. The dissolve is used here for a change of place without passage of time. This scene takes place simultaneously, or immediately following the one in the sheriff's office.

DISSOLVE TO MISS SUSIE'S HOTEL ROOM. BART IS SEATED IN AN EASY CHAIR. SUSIE IS IN A STRAIGHT CHAIR AT THE OTHER END OF THE ROOM.

BART

I ain't really a killer, Miss Susie. It's only my reputation that's hurting me. Only because of one youthful indiscretion.

SUSIE

What was that, Mr. Bart?

3. The superimposition is used here for a memory recall device.

SUPERIMPOSE, OVER CU BART, FACE OF MAN HE KILLED AS HE DESCRIBES SCENE.

BART

I can remember as well as yesterday. I was only a kid then. I thought he drew a gun on me. Maybe he did and maybe he didn't. But I shot him. And I'll remember his face as sure as I'll live--always.

SUSIE

I guess you aren't really all bad, Mr. Bart.

BART

You've convinced me, Susie. I've never had a fine woman speak to me so nice before. I'm going to turn over a new leaf.

4. The cut would be used without indication from the writer throughout this script. Here, the cut specifically indicates a different view of the character in the same continuous time sequence.

PAN WITH BART TO THE HALL DOOR. CUT TO HALL AS HE ENTERS IT.

(WALKS INTO THE HALL. AN EARLY MODEL TELEPHONE IS ON THE WALL.) I'm going to call the Sheriff. Operator, get me the Sheriff's office.

FEARLESS

Sheriff's office.

5. The wipe here moves from left to right or right to left. It designates a change of place. The use of the split screen indicates the putting of two different places before the audience at the same time.

HORIZONTAL WIPE INTO SPLIT SCREEN. BART IN ONE HALF, SHERIFF PICKING UP TELEPHONE IN OTHER HALF.

BART

Sheriff. This is Black Bart. I'm going to give myself up and confess all my crimes. I've turned over a new leaf.

FEARLESS

You expect me to believe that, Bart?

40

  BART

                                                No, I don't. But all I'm
                                                asking is a chance to prove
                                                it.

                                                        FEARLESS

                                                How do you propose to
                                                do that?

                        WIPE OFF SHERIFF OF-   BART
                        FICE SCENE. CU BART'S
                        FACE AS HE MAKES HIS   I'm coming over to your
                        DECISION.   office. And I'm not going
                                                to be wearing my guns.

6. The fade here indicates   FADE OUT. FADE IN ON   SUSIE
the passage of time. If this   MISS SUSIE SEATED ON
next scene were in the Sher-   HER BED.   That's all there was to it,
iff's office, the fade would   Fearless. The more I
have indicated a passage of   talked to him, the more I
time and change of place.   could see that underneath
                                                       it all he had a good heart.
7. The sustained opening on   (SHE WALKS TO THE
Susie is necessary, for live   SMALL TABLE AT THE
television, to provide time   FOOT OF THE BED, TAKES
for Bart to get off the set   A GLASS AND BOTTLE,
and for Fearless to get on.   THEN WALKS OVER TO
The 15 or 20 seconds at the   THE EASY CHAIR. WE
opening of this scene, in   SEE SHERIFF FEARLESS
which we do not yet see   IN THE EASY CHAIR.)
Fearless, though Susie's
dialogue indicates he is
there, should be sufficient   Here, Fearless, have a
"cover" time.   Sarsaparilla. You deserve
                                                one after what you've done
                                                today.

                                                        FEARLESS

                                                No, Susie. It was you who
                                                really did the work. And
                                                you deserve the drink.
                                                (AFTER A MOMENT.)
                                                You know, there's only one
                                                thing I'm sorry for.

                                                        SUSIE

                                                What's that?

                                                        FEARLESS

                                                That Bart turned out to be
                                                good, deep down inside,
                                                and gave himself up.

                                                        SUSIE

                                                Why?

                                41

COMMENTARY	VIDEO	AUDIO

FEARLESS

Well, there's this new gun
I received this morning
from the East that I
haven't yet had a chance
to use!

8. Fade is used to signify the end of a sequence, and, note the next scene, a passage of time and change of place.	THEME MUSIC IN AND UP STRONG. SLOW FADE OUT.	
9. Since this is a live show, the film clip is necessary for the exterior scene, not reproduceable in a studio. Such film clip inserts could be used at any time during the play itself. For example, there might have been a short chase on horses between Fearless and Bart, the stationary scenes played live, with the pre-filmed chase sequences integrated in the live action.	FADE IN FILM CLIP FEARLESS AND SUSIE ON THEIR HORSES ON THE TRAIL WAVING GOODBYE TO BART, WHO RIDES OFF INTO THE DISTANCE.	
10. "Super" refers to superimposition. "Telop" refers to the opaque projection transmission into a camera and to a monitor, titles, credits and other written, drawn, printed and similar material. The superimposition is used here for credits.	SUPER TELOP WITH CREDITS OVER THE SCENE AS FEARLESS AND SUSIE CONTINUE TO WAVE.	

Special Video Effects

Titles. Although the writer is not responsible for the kind of titling done, he should be aware of the various types of titling devices at his disposal — such as title cards, title drum, book titles, slides, superimpositions and others.

Nature Effects. Though it is difficult to achieve realistic nature effects in some studios, it is possible to obtain some through special effects. These include snow, rain, smoke and flame.

Miniatures. In lieu of film or live exteriors, a miniature of a setting that cannot be duplicated in full in the studio may serve very well for establishing shots. For example, a miniature of a castle may be used for an opening shot. The camera dollies toward the front gate of the miniature. Then a cut is made to the live set which may consist of the courtyard or an interior room.

Detail sets. Detail sets serve to augment the close-ups of television. Where the camera might find it difficult to pick up the precise movements of the fingers turning the dial of the safe on the regular set, another camera may cut to a detail set of the safe and capture another actor's fingers in every precise action. Detail sets are used frequently in instructional TV.

Puppets, Marionettes, and Animation. These devices may be integrated with live action and are particularly effective in commercial presentations.

Rear, Front and Overhead Projection. Scenes or effects may be electronically projected from the front or the rear onto the background. Use of overhead projectors for special effects in titling and in graphic presentations has been an important development of the mid-1960's, especially in ETV.

Remotes. One or more cameras may be set up at a place remote from the studio and send back material for incorporation into the program. An entire program may be done "remote," increasingly so on video tape.

Although the writer should be aware of the possible uses of special effects, he need not be concerned with their implementation.

Sound

Basically, sound is used in television in the same way as in radio, as analyzed earlier in this chapter. There are, however, some obvious modifications. Sound in television does not convey movement and does not physically orient the audience as it does in radio. The microphone in television usually is not stationary, but is on a boom and a dolly to follow the moving performers. The dialogue and sound on the set emanate from and must be coordinated with the visual action. Off-screen sound effects may be used, but they clearly must appear to be coming from off-screen unless they represent an action taking place on-camera. Sound may be pre-recorded or, as in filmed productions, added after the action has been shot. Television may use narration, as radio does. In television the voice-over may be a narrator, an announcer or the pre-recorded thoughts of the character. Television uses music as program content, as background and as theme. If a performer in television purportedly plays an instrument, the impression must be given that the person involved is really playing the instrument. Other uses of sound and music in radio may be adapted to television, so long as the writer remembers that in television the sound or music does not replace visual action, but complements or heightens it.

NOTES TO CHAPTER 2

[1] Norman Corwin, *Thirteen by Corwin* (New York: Holt, Rinehart and Winston, Inc., 1942), p. 90.

REFERENCE BOOKS ON RADIO AND TELEVISION PRODUCTION
This chapter is necessarily only a brief summary of the basic production elements in radio and television. The writer is advised to consult books such as the following for detailed, illustrated explanations of production techniques.

Charles W. Curran, *Screen Writing and Production Techniques* (New York: Hastings House, 1958). A non-technical handbook on the techniques of both television and motion picture production.

Gerald Millerson, *The Technique of Television Production* (New York: Hastings House, 1961). Detailed analyses of every aspect of production with illustrations throughout to provide "visual explanations." The treatment of the aesthetics of camera movements and shots will be of particular interest to writers.

Alec Nisbett, *The Technique of the Sound Studio* (New York: Hastings House, 1962). Descriptions of equipment potentials and techniques for recording sound.

Robert Oringel, *Audio Control Handbook: For Radio and TV Broadcasting* (New York: Hastings House, Revised Edition, 1963). Microphones, sound effects and music techniques.

The following titles may also be helpful: Peter Jones, *The Technique of the Television Cameraman* (New York: Hastings House, 1965); Harry Wayne McMahan, *Television Production: The Creative Techniques and Language of TV Today* (New York: Hastings House, 1957); Edward Stasheff and Rudy Bretz, *The Television Program: Its Direction and Production* (New York: Hill and Wang, 1962); Herbert Zettl, *Television Production Handbook* (San Francisco: Wadsworth, 1961).

FOR APPLICATION AND REVIEW

RADIO

1. Write a short sequence in which you use all five microphone positions.
2. Write one or more short sequences in which you use sound effects to: establish locale or setting; direct the audience attention by emphasis on a particular sound; establish time; establish mood; signify entrances or exits; create transitions between program segments; create unrealistic effects. More than one of the above uses may be indicated in a single sequence.
3. Write one or more short sequences in which you use music: as a bridge; as a sound effect; to establish background or mood.
4. Write a short script in which you use the following techniques: segue; cross-fade; blending; cutting or switching; fade in or fade out.

TELEVISION

1. Write a short sequence in which you use the following camera movements: the dolly in and dolly out; the tilt; the pan; the follow shot.
2. Write a short sequence in which you, the writer, must indicate the following shots: CU, M2S, LS, FS.
3. Write one or more short sequences in which you, the writer, must designate the following effects: fade in and fade out; dissolve; superimposition; wipe; split-screen; film insert.
4. Watch several television programs and analyze the use of the dolly, the tilt, the pan, the close-up, the long shot, the fade, the dissolve, the superimposition, the wipe and the split-screen. Can you determine the writer's contributions in relation to the use of these techniques as opposed to the director's work?

3

ANNOUNCEMENTS
AND COMMERCIALS

MANY COPYWRITERS use a word count scale to determine the number of words that will go into a given time segment of a radio announcement or commercial, but, at best, such word counts are approximate. The length of individual words, the complexity of the ideas, the need for emphasis through pause and variation in rate, and the personality of the performer delivering the announcement are some of the factors which may affect the number of words that may be spoken effectively in a given length of time. Some generalizations may be made, however. The 10-second ID will contain about 25 words; the 20-second announcement, about 45 words; the 30-second announcement, about 65 words; the 45-second announcement, about 100 words; the one-minute announcement, about 125 words; the minute and one-half announcement, about 190 words; and the two-minute announcement, about 250 words. These word counts cannot be applied to television, except in the instance of a continuous spoken announcement, because the visual action in television may be expected to take up a portion of the time without dialogue or verbal narration.

ANNOUNCEMENTS

Spot announcements may be commercial or non-commercial materials. Programs do not end at the "minute" mark. Actual time lengths taken by networks and stations vary for, as it is called, the station break. The 1965 NAB Codes specify up to 130 seconds per break, not exceeding 16 minutes and 20 seconds total commercial time per hour for television; and no specified station break limits, with a maximum of 18 minutes of commercial time for a single hour on radio. Spot announcements may be, therefore, of varying lengths. The station break announcement may be a station identification; a public service announcement concerning almost any civic matter, such as keeping the streets clean; a news flash; a service announcement, such as a weather report attached to a commercial message; a station "cross-plug" for one of its upcoming programs; or, of great importance to a profit-minded industry, a straight commercial message. Spot announcements of the same type, excepting the station identification, sometimes are inserted into a break in a given program, no matter at what time that break occurs. Let us look first at the non-commercial spot announcement.

The ID

The purpose of the station break is for the station identification, or ID. The ID is usually 10 seconds long. If accompanied by a commercial announcement, it may be a brief 2 seconds long, followed by an 8-second commercial. The ID consists of the call letters of the station, the city in which the station is located and, sometimes, the operating frequency of the station. Occasionally, the station will attempt to find an identifying phrase to go with the ID.

A simple, direct ID would be: "You are listening to NBC, six-sixty, WNBC, New York."

A special identification for radio would be: "America's number one fine music station, WQXR and WQXR-FM, New York."

CBS-TV has used the following audio-video slogan as a special identification:

VIDEO	AUDIO
SLIDE: Channel 2's "Eye"	Keep your eye on Channel 2. CBS, New York

Some radio stations use singing commercials for ID's as promotion material. A frequently used break is the video picture of the identifying seal of the NAB, with the voice-over announcing that "This seal of good practice identifies this station as a subscriber to the code of the National Association of Broadcasters," followed by the name of the station, its channel and city.

In writing an ID, the writer must remember that he is creating a public relations trademark for the station, and must find something that is identifying and distinctive at the same time.

Public Service Announcements

Announcements in the "public service" ordinarily are given as part of the ID, and may be of any length. The local station usually receives such announcements in a form already prepared by the writer for the distributing organization. The American Foundation for the Blind, for example, has issued a radio and television kit containing various forms of announcements. One of their 10-second public service announcements reads:

> There is a book without pages. For the latest information about the Talking Book for the blind contact the Library of Congress or the American Foundation for the Blind, 15 West 16 St., New York City.

The American Heritage Foundation's non-partisan "Register, Inform Yourself, and Vote" program issued public service announcements of 10 seconds, 20 seconds, 30 seconds and 60 seconds in length. The following examples illustrate the form the public service announcement should take.

● *Analyze each of the following announcements. Determine the kind of writing approach in each and the kind of material added with each subsequent time extension.*

<u>10-SECOND ANNOUNCEMENT</u>

ANNOUNCER

You can't vote if you're not registered. Protect your right to vote. Register now at

_____, _____, _____.
        (place)   (dates)   (hours)

<u>20-SECOND ANNOUNCEMENT</u>

ANNOUNCER

The right to vote is a great right. It helps you run your government. But you can't vote unless you're registered. Register now so you can vote on Election Day. Register now at

_____, _____, _____.
        (place)   (dates)   (hours)
Register now.

<u>30-SECOND ANNOUNCEMENT</u>

ANNOUNCER

It's not much bigger than a phone booth. But it's the place where your town gets its schools built and its streets paved. What is it? It's your precinct voting booth. And you'll be locked out of this year's important elections on _____ -- if your
                                    (date)
name's not in the book . . . the voter's registration book. So get your name in the book.
Go to _____, _____, _____.
          (place)   (dates)   (hours)
Register before the deadline _____. Register now.
                                (date)

<u>60-SECOND ANNOUNCEMENT</u>

ANNOUNCER

It's not much bigger than a telephone booth. And it's open only a couple of days a year. But it's the place where your schools are built, roads are paved, streets are lighted. What is it? It's the voting booth in your precinct. And you'll want to be there on Election Day, along with your friends and neighbors, helping to make the decisions that make your town a better place to live in. But--is your name in the book? Because if it isn't--if you haven't registered--you'll never see the inside of that voting booth. So be sure you aren't left out. Registration closes _____. Go now to _____,
                                    (date)   (place)
_____ and get your name in the book. And then, on Election Day, we'll see you
  (hours)
at the polls.   <u>Courtesy of American Heritage Foundation</u>

The Public Service Announcement may include the station identification. Note the following incorporation of the ID into the message:

This is _____, your election station. If you've been listening to the important campaign issues on _____, you'll want to <u>vote</u> on Election Day. Register today so you <u>can</u>.

Public Service Announcements — Special Groups

Service groups and organizations devoted to activity related to public welfare, such as Public Health Departments, educational associations, societies aiding the handicapped and fund raising institutions, among others, have devoted more and more time in recent years to special television and radio workshops for their regular personnel and volunteer assistants. The foregoing public service announcements on voting, presented by such an organization, are general spots and illustrate form only. In view of the increasing interest in and use of the mass media by these groups, it is important to mention type. Special service announcements are written also for special program types and in terms of special occasions. Such spot announcements are written for disc jockey, news, women's, sports and other programs. They may be prepared for delivery with a weather bulletin or with a time signal. They can relate to a given national or local holiday. The following examples will illustrate how the "organization" writer goes beyond the general spot announcement.

WASHINGTON'S BIRTHDAY SPOT (20 SECONDS, RADIO)

This is station ____ reminding you that a holiday like Washington's Birthday brings a sort of break into the routine of daily living. This applies also to America's estimated 355,000 blind people--or had you thought of them as a group apart? They certainly aren't. For information about blindness contact your nearest agency for the blind or the American Foundation for the Blind, 15 West 16th Street, New York City.

TIME SIGNAL (20 SECONDS, RADIO)

ANNOUNCER

It's _____ . . . and right now an emotionally disturbed child in _____
     (time)   (town or area)
needs your help and understanding. This is National Child Guidance Week. Observe it . . . and attend the special program on emotionally disturbed children in _____
                                                      (town or area)
presented by the _____ PTA, on _____ at
                                                            (date)
_____ .
        (place)

DISC JOCKEY PROGRAM (30 SECONDS, RADIO)

(AFTER MILLION-RECORD SELLER)

DISC JOCKEY

_____ . . . a record that sold a million copies.
       (title and artist)
Easy listening, too. But here's a figure that's not easy to listen to: Over 1,000,000 American children are seriously emotionally ill. During National Child Guidance Week, the _____ PTA, in cooperation with the American Child Guidance Foundation, is holding a special meeting to acquaint you with the problems faced by children in _____ . It's to your benefit to attend. Be there . . .
       (town or area)
_____ . . . learn what you can do to help.
     (date and address)

WOMEN'S PROGRAM (30 SECONDS, RADIO)

WOMAN

Women are traditionally the moving spirits behind community efforts concerning children. And now comes a problem so close to us, as women, that I can't stress its importance enough. I'm speaking about the many emotionally disturbed children in _____ .
(town or area)

Your help is needed . . . and you can start by attending the ___ _____ PTA meetings during Child Guidance Week on _____ at _____ .
                                       (date)   (place)

Attend this meeting . . . learn about the nature and extent of emotional illness affecting our children. And learn how you can help.

LOCAL WEATHER FORECAST (20 SECONDS, RADIO)

ANNOUNCER

That's the weather forecast for _____ , but the outlook for children with emotional illness is always gloomy. This is National Child Guidance Week, and
                                  (town or area)

you can help by learning the facts about the problem in _____ .
                                        (town or area)

Attend the _____ PTA meeting on _____ at
                                                (date)

_____ .
      (place)

● *The preceding announcements on child guidance specify the time, date, place and sponsor of a meeting. What if there is no meeting scheduled? Reread the previous announcement written for the disc jockey show and then read the following announcement, written for the same show, but without the information on a specific meeting. Note how the specifics are transferred smoothly into generalities — and vice versa.*

DISC JOCKEY PROGRAM (30 seconds, radio)

(AFTER MILLION-RECORD SELLER)

DISC JOCKEY

_____ . . . a record that sold a million copies.
(Title and Artist)

Easy listening, too. But here's a figure that's not easy to: Over 1,000,000 American children are seriously emotionally ill. During National Child Guidance Week, many PTA groups, in cooperation with the American Child Guidance Foundation, are holding special meetings concerning these problems faced by children. Find out when your meeting will be . . . and attend . . . Learn what you can do to help.

Prepared for American Child Guidance Foundation, Inc. by its agents, Batten, Barton, Durstine & Osborn, Inc.

COMMERCIALS

In early radio and television there were few commercials, and what there were were usually gratis. In television, for example, the stations, needing material, were happy to present films dealing with "electronics for progress," or showing "how rubber is made" — films which, incidentally, carried the clearly indicated brand name of the rubber company or of the electrical appliance manufacturer. The television viewer and radio listener today, frequently accustomed to seeing and hearing what seems to be more commercial than program content on some stations, would not be surprised to learn that the total expenditures by advertisers on television in 1964 amounted to $2,289,000,000, and on radio for the period to $832,900,000.[1] Of these totals, advertisers on television spent $1,132,000,000 on network commercials, $779,800,000 on spot announcements and $377,200,000 on local station commercials. Advertising on radio amounted to $58,600,000 spent on network commercials, $242,500,000 on spot announcements and $531,800,000 for commercials on local stations. The importance of the local radio station for the advertiser — and for the commercial writer — is evident.

Almost all of the writing of commercials is done in advertising agencies. However, local commercials most often are prepared locally, frequently by someone connected with the station.

Techniques of Writing Commercials

Emotional Appeals. The appeal of the commercial is an emotional one. By emotional we do not mean the evoking of laughter or tears. Emotional appeal means, here, the appeal to the non-intellectual, non-logical aspects of the prospective customer's personality. It is an appeal to the audience's basic needs or wants. For example, one of the basic wants in our society is prestige. Look at the next commercial you see for an automobile. Does it appeal to logical, intellectual needs? Does it recommend that you buy the car because it is shorter than the other makes, thus enabling the driver to find a parking space more easily? Does it emphasize lower horsepower as one of the car's major advantages, enabling the owner to save on gasoline consumption and at the same time still achieve the maximum miles-per-hour permissible on our highways without risking a speeding ticket? Sometimes, in a buyer's market, yes. But most of the time the appeal is to prestige, to our emotional needs, not to logic. The commercial stresses the longer length of the car, longer than that of the competing make. The commercial emphasizes greater horsepower for umpteen miles-per-hour speeds, faster than the other make. Have the longest, fastest car in the neighborhood!

The development of commercials for the compact car is a good case in point. "Big car room" became an important ingredient in selling small cars. The compact must be bigger than the competing compact. One couldn't own a small car; one had to own a king-sized small car! And how many automobile commercials show the driver climbing into the car to be seated next to a pretty girl looking as much as possible like Brigitte Bardot! The emotional implication is, of course, that men who drive this make of automobile have sitting with them women who look like movie stars. This is the prestige factor again. Or, so goes the implication, if the prospective customer does not have such women immediately available, the very presence of the automobile in his driveway will draw them. This would be an appeal to power, in this instance the power to draw women — a strong emotional appeal.

There are a number of basic emotional appeals that have been particularly successful and upon which the writer of commercials may draw as the motivating factor within any individual commercial. The appeal to self-preservation is perhaps the strongest of all. Drug commercials, among others, make good use of this appeal. Another strong appeal is love of family. Note the next commercial presented by an insurance company. Other widely used emotional appeals include patriotism, good taste, reputation, religion, loyalty to a group and conformity to public opinion.

The following commercial illustrates, primarily, the effective use of the appeal to prestige. The implications are that if one does not serve Libby's foods, one does not have *good taste,* is not a *smart* shopper and, by further implication, would not have the prestige of sophistication and intelligence of those who do serve Libby's. The use of well-written emotional appeals in this commercial in no way suggests that these implications may not be valid.

● *As you read the commercial see if you can find an additional emotional appeal and a sample of what we shall call logical appeal.*

VIDEO	AUDIO
1. MCU ANNOUNCER BESIDE LIBBY'S DISPLAY.	ANNOUNCER:
	LIBBY'S presents a word quiz. What is the meaning of the word "epicure?" Well, according to our dictionary the word means a person who shows good taste in selection of food. And that's a perfect description of the homemaker who makes a habit of serving . . .
2. INDICATES DISPLAY.	LIBBY'S famous foods. Yes, everyone in every family goes for
3. INDICATES EACH PRODUCT IN SYNC (IF POSSIBLE CUT TO CU LIBBY'S PEACHES . . . THEN PAN IN SYNC.)	LIBBY'S Peaches . . . Fruit Cocktail . . . LIBBY'S Pineapple—chunks, Crushed or Sliced . . . Pineapple Juice . . . LIBBY'S Peas . . . Beets . . . Corn—Whole Kernel or Cream Styled . . . LIBBY'S Tomato Juice . . . Corned Beef Hash . . . and LIBBY'S Beef Stew. AND right now, smart shoppers are stocking up on LIBBY'S famous
4. HOLDS UP LIBBY'S COUPONS (IF POSSIBLE CUT TO CU LIBBY'S COUPONS)	foods . . . because there's still time to cash in those LIBBY'S dollar-saving coupons you received. You can save a whole
5. MOVE IN FOR CU LIBBY'S DISPLAY	dollar on this week's food bill. So stock up now on LIBBY'S famous foods . . . and cash in your LIBBY'S coupons and save! Always make LIBBY'S a "regular" on your shopping list!

Courtesy of Libby's Famous Foods

You may have noted the appeal to love of family in the statement that "everyone in every family goes for. . . ." The logical appeal was the emphasis, at the end of the commercial, on the saving of money through the use of Libby coupons. Logical appeals are those which strike the intellect, the logical, analytical thinking processes. An example of a logical appeal would be that which, with accurate information, emphasized that the electronic structure of the television set being advertised has certain elements that make it longer lasting or which provide a clearer picture than other makes. This kind of logical appeal may be contrasted with the emotional appeal which ignores the organic functioning of the television set but emphasizes the shape, color or styling of the cabinet, items which have nothing to do with the logical purpose for using a television set.

Commercials frequently use logical appeals in combination with emotional appeals. Commercials often only *seem* to use logical appeals; closer examination reveals that the appeals are really emotional in content. Emotional appeals are far more effective in commercial advertising than are logical appeals.

Audience Analysis.   Before choosing and applying the specific emotional or logical appeal, the writer must know, as fully as possible, the nature of the audience to which he's directing his message. In the mass media of television and radio it often is impossible to determine many specifics about the audience. The audience is a disunified mass of many attitudes and interests, economic, social, political and religious levels, spread out over a broad geographical area. In some instances, however, the writer may be able to do some analysis. For example, examine the following commercial, presented on "Omnibus."

> ● Determine the kinds of audiences to which this commercial would appeal. Can you discover any emotional appeals? Any logical appeals? After you have studied the commercial and answered the above questions, read the brief analysis following it, then study the commercial again. Can you find any further elements of audience analysis? Can you find any further emotional or logical appeals?

VIDEO	AUDIO
1. OPEN ON HIGH ANGLE SHOT LOOKING ACROSS SAN FERNANDO VALLEY. IN THE DISTANCE ARE TOWERING MOUNTAINS. THE TIME IS LATE AFTERNOON OR EARLY EVENING. PAN SLOWLY ACROSS THE MOUNTAIN PEAKS. THEN . . .	MUSIC: WE HEAR A SOFT MELODY ON A GUITAR. IF IT CAN BE CLEARED, USE "SAN FERNANDO VALLEY," AND BRING UP VOCAL AT THE PHRASE: "And make the San Fernando Valley My Home."
2. . . . TILT DOWN SLOWLY TO SHOW SEVERAL HOMES ON VALLEY MEADOW ROAD.	ANNOUNCER: (VOICE OVER, OVER MUSIC) In the San Fernando Valley, in Southern California, it's often said . . .
3. CUT TO CLOSER SHOT OF THE DOUGHTY HOME, SHOWING HOUSE, YARD AND SWIMMING POOL.	. . . that no one ever willingly moves away. Such a tradition is easy to understand . . .

4. CUT TO SHOT OF THE DOUGHTY HOME, SEEN ACROSS THEIR SWIMMING POOL. PAN DOWN TO CLOSE SHOT OF THE NEAR EDGE OF THE POOL.

. . . when you visit the home of Stan and Laura Doughty, and their two sons . . .

5. THE TWO BOYS PUSH THEIR HEADS QUICKLY UP OVER THE EDGE OF THE POOL, AS THO' THEY HAD BEEN HIDING TO SURPRISE A VISITOR. THEY ARE DRIPPING WET.

. . . John and Bobby. The Doughtys live on Valley Meadow Road, Encino . . .

6. CUT TO THE DRIVEWAY, AS STAN DRIVES IN HIS JAGUAR. THE TWO BOYS ENTER TO GREET HIM AS HE GETS OUT. THEY ARE STILL DRIPPING WET AND HE TRIES SIMULTANEOUSLY TO GREET THEM AND TO KEEP THEM FROM GETTING WET.

. . . just 30 minutes, in Stan Doughty's sports car, from his business in downtown Los Angeles. Here they find Valley living is outdoor living . . .

7. DISSOLVE TO LAURA DOUGHTY ARRANGING SCOTKINS ON DINNER TABLE ON THE LANAI. PAN AWAY FROM HER AND AROUND THE LANAI, PICKING UP PHONOGRAPH, TEA WAGON, CHAISE LOUNGES, ETC. IN TURN.

. . . and much of their time is spent on their terrace—known in Southern California by its Hawaiian name: Lanai.

8. DISSOLVE TO THE KITCHEN AS LAURA ENTERS. READY TO PREPARE DINNER.

Valley living is easy living, too—a life . . .

9. SERIES OF QUICK CUTS SHOWING CU WOMAN'S HANDS TEARING OFF STRIP OF CUT RITE, CUTTING VEGETABLES ON SCOTTOWELS, DRYING HANDS ON SCOTTOWELS, GRATING CHEESE ON CUT RITE, TAKING SCOTTIE FROM BOX.

. . . made even easier with those wonderful paper products by Scott . . . products that make work more pleasant . . . and leave more time for family fun.

10. DISSOLVE TO STAN AT BARBECUE, COOKING SOMETHING FOR DINNER. HE LOOKS UP, CALLS OFF CAMERA.

Stan's a master of the barbecue and that's one of the few things that can . . .

11. CUT TO SWIMMING POOL AS THE TWO BOYS HEAR HIS CALL AND SPLASH WETLY OUT, RUN TOWARD CAMERA.

. . . tempt John and Bobby away from their favorite playground.

12. CUT BACK TO THE LANAI, WHERE LAURA HOLDS TWO LARGE TOWELS, WAITING FOR THE BOYS. JOHN ENTERS, SNEEZES, AND GRABS FOR A SCOTTIE.

Evenings in the valley are cool, and sometimes there's an irresistible urge to . . . SNEEZE! . . .

13. CUT TO CU SCOTTIES BOX AS HIS HAND TAKES OUT ANOTHER.

. . . But new Scotties stand up to a man-sized blow . . .

14. CUT TO LAURA HELPING BOBBY WHO WEARS BIG TOWEL. SHE WIPES HIS FACE WITH A SCOTTIE. PAN WITH HER HAND AS IT RETURNS TO BOX FOR ANOTHER SCOTTIE.

. . . even though they're soft and gentle as a mother's touch. New Scotties are sturdy, even when wet . . .

15. DISSOLVE TO ANOTHER SCOTTIES BOX AND PULL BACK TO REVEAL IT IS ON VIEWER'S RIGHT OF AN UNMARKED TISSUE BOX.

. . . because Scotties have wet strength.

VIDEO	AUDIO
16. CUT BACK AS WOMAN'S HANDS HOLD FIRST A TISSUE FROM UNMARKED BOX, THEN A SCOTTIE, UNDER A WATER TAP. FIRST TISSUE SHREDS, SCOTTIE HOLDS.	When you hold an ordinary tissue under running water, you can see how quickly it tears and shreds. But a wet-strength Scottie holds . . . and holds . . . and holds. No wonder . . .
17. DISSOLVE TO BOX OF SCOTTIES ON A SIDE-TABLE. TILT UP TO DOUGHTYS AT DINNER.	. . . new Scotties are right at home in the modern lives of families like Stan and Laura, John and Bobby Doughty. Here . . .
18. DISSOLVE TO KITCHEN CUPBOARD OR SHELF ON WHICH SCOTTIES, SCOTKINS, SCOTTOWELS AND CUT RITE ARE SEEN.	. . . and in homes all over the United States, paper products by Scott are part of the American scene.

Courtesy of Scott Paper Company

"Omnibus" was a prestige and cultural program, and appealed to an intelligence and educational level above that of the average television viewer. There is a direct correlation between income and educational level. It would seem that a fair portion of the audience might very well own their own homes, or live in a community of the relatively high economic level of the family pictured in the commercial. Direct empathy, or identification, then, may be made. But the emotional appeal of all viewers is not overlooked. The family pictured is on a comparatively high economic and social prestige level. If this family uses the product involved, certainly any family can feel a measure of prestige and pride in using the same product. The logical appeal, indicated in the reference to the tested strength of the product, is not overlooked either.

There are several elements of analysis the commercial writer should apply to the potential audience to the greatest degree possible. These are: age, sex, size, economic level, political orientation, primary interests, occupation, fixed attitudes or beliefs, educational level, knowledge of the product and geographical concentration.

The writer should try to include appeals to all the major groups he expects to reach. However, he must be careful not to spread his message too thin.

Familiarization with Product. Before the writer can apply his audience analysis or choose the emotional appeals to be used, he must become familiar with the product being advertised. This does not imply that the male writer needs to use a girdle before preparing an ad for it, or that a female writer must test the efficiency of a certain shaving cream. The writer should, however, obtain as much information as he can about the product from those closely connected with it. A good source of information is the sales department of the company. From the information obtained about the product, the writer can then, by coordinating his audience analysis and emotional and logical appeals, develop a unique or novel way of presenting the product most effectively to the audience.

54

Organization of the Commercial. Inasmuch as the commercial's primary purpose is to persuade, the writer should be aware of the five basic steps in persuasive technique. First, the commercial should get the attention of the audience. This may be accomplished by many means, including humor, a startling statement or picture, a rhetorical question, vivid description, a novel situation or suspenseful conflict. Sound, specifically the use of pings, chords and other effects, effectively attracts attention, too.

Second, after attention is obtained, the audience's interest must be held. Following up the initial element with effective examples, testimonials, anecdotes, statistics and other devices, visual or aural, should retain the audience's interest.

Third, the commercial should create an impression that a problem of some sort exists, related vaguely to the function of the product advertised. After such an impression has been made, then, fourth, the commercial should plant the idea in the audience's mind that the problem can be solved by use of the particular product. It is at this point that the product itself may first be introduced. Finally, the commercial must finish with a strong emotional and/or logical appeal, one which achieves the fifth step in persuasion — getting action. This final step prompts the audience to go out and buy the product.

The following commercial illustrates the five steps in persuasion. For purposes of explanation, the Roman numerals I through V, designating these steps, have been placed next to appropriate sections of the video and audio columns. (This is not done, of course, by the writer or director; the Arabic numbers 1 through 6 on the original commercial script refer to the video sequences for production purposes.)

Attention is achieved through a combination of humor, a novel situation and a startling statement — when Bud Collyer indicates that he is going to play the part of a housewife and has an apron tied onto him. The visual picture continues the interest of the audience, as does the statement which describes the meal. The impression that a problem exists (the picture and statement also contribute to the holding of the audience's interest) is made clear by the appearance of the dirty, sprouting potatoes and Collyer's discovery that the entire bag is sprouting, making preparation of the dinner impossible. The question "So, *now* what do we do?" leads into the step in which it is disclosed that the problem can be solved by the use of the sponsor's product. The film clip demonstrating the use of the product, with Collyer's voice-over explanation, confirms the value of the product. The final step in persuasion is made with the display of the package and the appeals in Collyer's concluding statement.

● *Could any of these steps in commercial writing have been made more effective within the same one-minute time limit?*

VIDEO	AUDIO
COLLYER STILL WITH CONTESTANTS. AS HE CROSSES OVER TO TABLE SET UP FOR FIP COMMERCIAL.	COLLYER (ON CAMERA)
	And now—let's have a little real-life I Sunday dinner drama. I'm playing the part of the housewife.

- -

VIDEO	AUDIO
I 1. COLLYER AT TABLE. MADELINE II OR BETTY TIES PRACTICAL, COVER-UP APRON ON HIM.	COLLYER: We're having roast beef II and brown gravy for dinner. And at <u>our</u> house . . . that means <u>mashed potatoes</u>! So . . .
III TABLE HAS TWO SACKS ON IT. ONE CONTAINS SPROUTING POTATOES (DIRTY). THE OTHER (WITH BOTTOM CUT OUT) CONTAINS BOX OF FIP.	
2. REACHES IN BAG AND PULLS OUT SPROUTING POTATO. POTATO IS DIRTY SO THAT DUST OR DIRT CAN BE BRUSHED OFF WHEN COLLYER HANDLES SPUD. THEN ANOTHER.	What's this??? A potato tree! Oh, III no! The whole bag's sprouting! So, <u>now</u> what do we do?
IV 3. TAKES OFF APRON. BETTY OR MADELINE PUTS CUTE, HALF-APRON ON HIM.	We <u>change aprons</u> and be a <u>smart</u> IV housewife who . . .
4. YANKS OFF SACK TO REVEAL BOX OF FIP.	uses New French's Instant Mashed Potato! Because French's are made from perfect, selected <u>Idaho</u> potatoes. No waste! No storage problem! Just delicious mashed potatoes <u>every</u> <u>time</u>. Watch!
5. FILM CLIP - 20-SEC. #20070-"DEMO-FINISHED FIP." DEMONSTRATION SHOWING MILK BEING POURED INTO BOILING WATER. FIP POURED FROM FOIL ENVELOPE INTO LIQUID WHILE FORK STIRS. MASHED POTATOES FORM BEFORE YOUR EYES. DISH OF MASHED POTATOES. HAND COMES IN AND PLACES PAT OF BUTTER.	COLLYER (VOICE OVER): All you do is add milk to boiling water— stir in French's Instant Mashed Potato . . . and whip 'em up! Like <u>that</u>—you have fluffy, Sunday-dinner mashed potatoes. In <u>seconds</u>, they're creamy-smooth and <u>ready</u> to serve. Enough for 8 hungry people.
V 6. COLLYER WITH BOX. POINTS TO POTATO ON BOX.	Let your family just <u>taste</u> New V French's Instant Mashed Potato and you'll never peel another potato for Sunday dinner!
	<u>Courtesy of the R. T. French Company</u>

● *See if you can find the steps of persuasion in the following commercial. How do the approaches, within each of the steps, differ from those of the previous commercial? Note the different script form.*

1. MAYEHOFF TIGHT CLOSEUP.

MAYEHOFF

I want to have a word with you cars out there. Do you feel sluggish, overheated, steamed up?

2. MAYEHOFF, TIGHT ECU, LOOKING LIKE DOCTOR GIVING DIAGNOSIS.

Ah ha! Your trouble is rust . . . rust in your cooling system!

3. CUT TO HOOD OF CAR POPPING OPEN AS MAYEHOFF SAYS "OPEN WIDE."

Now then . . . open wide! Ah! That's fine.

4. MAYEHOFF PUTS ON WHITE GLOVE AND THRUSTS FINGER INTO RADIATOR.

This won't hurt a bit! Look at this! Um hm!

5. CLOSEUP OF MAYEHOFF LOOKING AT FINGER OF DIRTY GLOVE.

Rust in your cooling system. You could overheat . . . stall . . . embarrass your owner this summer!

6. MAYEHOFF HOLDING UP CAN OF NO. "7" ANTI-RUST, TALKING TO CAMERA.

Now car-owners (PATRONIZING) don't let this happen to you. Keep rust out of your cooling system this summer with Du Pont liquid anti-rust.

7. MAYEHOFF PULLS DOWN CHART WHICH SHOWS SIMPLE DIAGRAM OF CAR ENGINE.

Without Du Pont anti-rust, your engine can get rusty . . .

7A. CUT IN CLOSE ON DIAGRAM WHICH ANIMATES TO SHOW RUST BUILDING UP AND WATER UNABLE TO CIRCULATE.

. . . like this . . . the water can't circulate properly.

8. MCU MAYEHOFF, AS HE PULLS DOWN ANOTHER CHART, SHOWING CLEAN ENGINE.

It's so easy to prevent rust from forming.

8A. CLOSE ON DIAGRAM WHICH ANIMATES TO SHOW ANTI-RUST BEING POURED IN.

Just pour in a can of Du Pont Anti-Rust. It keeps your cooling system clean . . . keeps the water circulating. Your engine stays healthy . . . you avoid costly repairs.

9. CUT TO MCU MAYEHOFF IN FRONT OF CHART. PAN WITH HIM AS HE CROSSES TO DISPLAY RACK.

Remember, it's not enough to start with a clean cooling system . . . you gotta keep it clean.

10. CUT TO MAYEHOFF CLOSE, HOLDING NO. "7" ANTI-RUST, IN DISPLAY RACK AREA.

Don't let your car overheat this summer. Keep cool . . . keep goin' with Du Pont Anti-Rust — one of the Du Pont No. "7" line of automotive products that take good care of your car.

11. ECU MAYEHOFF WITH CAN OF DU PONT ANTI-RUST.

Hm . . . mm . . . mm . . . don't take chances. Get Du Pont Anti-Rust now.

12. ZOOM IN FOR ECU NO. "7" ANTI-RUST.

Wherever auto supplies are sold.

1961 TV commercial script reprinted with permission of E.I. du Pont de Nemours Co., Wilmington, Delaware.

Writing styles. The writer constantly must be aware of the necessity for keeping the commercial in good taste. Although there have been commercials from time to time which have been repugnant to individuals or groups, the sponsor tries not to alienate a single potential customer. The style should be direct and simple. If the commercial is to seem sincere, the performer presenting it must have material of a conversational, informal nature that permits him to present it so that the audience really believes what it hears or sees. This does not mean that the writer uses ultra-colloquial or slang words. The vocabulary should be dignified, though not obtuse; it must be attention-getting, but not trite. Usually, the writer will avoid slang and colloquialisms entirely unless these forms have specific purposes in specific places in the commercial.

The writer should be certain that the writing is grammatically correct. Action verbs are extremely effective, as are concrete, specific words and ideas. If an important point is to be emphasized, the writer must be certain to repeat that point in the commercial, although in different words or in different forms. One exception would be the presentation of a slogan or trade mark which the sponsor wishes the audience to remember; in this case word for word repetition is important.

The writer should avoid, if possible, the use of superlatives, false claims, phony testimonials and other elements of obvious exaggeration which might antagonize a large part of the audience, even if particularly effective in deceiving another part. Network commercials are sometimes more honest than those on independent stations. Frequently, the commercial on the small station is not only presented, but written by the disc jockey or announcer who may have sold the show or the air time in the first place. Extravagant claims sometimes are made in order to keep the account. In the 1960's three commercial types grew in importance: the realistic, human interest approach, emphasizing people and families; the so-called sophisticated commercial in which wit, humor and satire replaced some of the more obvious and direct techniques; and the obvious exaggeration, the "camp" commercial with a comment on life that sometimes resembled pop art. The following is an example of the "family" type:

1. CAMERA OPENS ON LOW ANGLE REAR VIEW OF SMALL BOY (5 OR UNDER) IN COWBOY SUIT. HE DROPS HIS GUNS AND RAISES HIS HANDS TO THE SKY.

    STOCK (MUSIC: ESTABLISH WESTERN THEME) DOWN AND UNDER.

                                         CUT TO:

2. REVERSE ANGLE, MCU, REVEALING WORRIED YOUNG COWBOY.

              HUGH (V.O.)

Meet Fearless Dan . . . the unlucky cowboy.

3. PULL BACK TO REVEAL COWGIRL (3 OR UNDER) ON ROCKING HORSE BESIDE DAN. SHE'S RAISING HER HANDS, BUT SHE HAS FORGOTTEN TO DROP GUNS.

And here's his sidekick . . . Bad New Sal . . . These critters have just been caught by the law . . .

4. BOTH KIDS MAKE WRY, CRIMINAL FACES.

   . . . for playing in the basement.

CUT TO:

5. MCU YOUNG MOTHER, WITH MARSHAL'S STAR PINNED ON HER APRON. SHE LEANS ON HER BROOM, LOOKING DOWN AT COWHANDS WHO ARE O.S.

The law says she aims to run 'em out of that basement everytime, because that dusty cement floor down there ain't fit to play on.

CUT TO:

   (MUSIC OUT)

6. REACTION SHOT: HIGH ANGLE: DEJECTED BOY AND GIRL LOOKING UP IN MOTHER'S DIRECTION.

Well, if you were a grownup, would you want . . . cowhands trackin' up dust from the basement all over your clean house? (BEAT) Rough, but that's how matters stood . . . until . . .

DS TO:

7. MS, DAD ON HIS KNEES, FACING CAMERA. DAN AND SAL STAND BESIDE HIM. WE SEE SEVERAL CARTONS OF EXCELON ON FLOOR, ALONG WITH A PAIR OF SCISSORS AND A BRUSH. DAD HOLDS AN OPEN CARTON TO CAMERA. KIDS APPROVE.

Dad came to the rescue! One night he brought home a new vinyl tile floor for their pesky old basement.

CUT TO:

8. ECU, DAD'S HANDS POINT TO LETTERING ON CARTON: "ARMSTRONG EXCELON." HE HOLDS UP SCISSORS AND BRUSH IN SYNC.

It was Excelon Tile, by Armstrong. The kind you install yourself with a pair of household scissors and a brush.

CUT TO:

9. ECU REACTION SHOT, BOY AND GIRL STARING AT EACH OTHER IN DISBELIEF.

HUGH (SOTTO, VOICE OVER)

What? Dad — install it himself? But he can't even fix a screen door.

SLOW DS TO:

10. MS DAD LAYING TILES.

HUGH (V.O.)

But were those kids ever surprised when the loveable old varmint really did install it himself.

DS TO:

11. MEDIUM TWO-SHOT: SMILING BOY WATCHING DAD FINISH CUTTING AN ODD-SHAPED TILE WITH A PAIR OF SCISSORS.

Dad used those scissors to cut the tile . . . wherever he needed an odd shape to fit an odd place.

59

12. MEDIUM TWO-SHOT: SMILING GIRL WATCHING DAD BRUSH ON CEMENT.

He used that brush to brush on the Armstrong Cement that holds the tiles in place.

DS TO:

13. WIDE SHOT: DAD PUTTING FINISHING TOUCHES ON LARGE DESIGN AREA.

HUGH (V.O.)

And the easy way Dad put that custom design down amazed the whole family.

DS TO:

14. WIDE SHOT OF COMPLETED BASEMENT PLAYROOM: WHITE PAINT WALLS, POSTERS ON WALLS, TWO SLING CHAIRS, AND A TRESTLE PICNIC TABLE AND TWO BENCHES; TWO KIDS IN SAME OUTFITS AS SCENE 1 & 3 SEATED ON FLOOR PLAYING.

Here's how their basement looked when Dad had finished up a couple of nights later. (ENTER PARENTS) They had a brand-new basement playroom.

14A. CU KIDS ON FLOOR. GIRL REACTS TO MOTHER.

— a place for the whole family to play and relax. And look, Mom — no dust.

14B. WIDE SHOT MOTHER AND FATHER WITH CHILDREN.

All it took was a coat of paint for the walls, some inexpensive curtains, and Armstrong Excelon Tile for the floor.

CUT TO:

15. MCU HUGH AT DEALER COUNTER. HE HOLDS TILE. ON CUE, HE FLIPS TILE, REVEALING $60.

HUGH (ON CAMERA)

Why not turn your basement into a family playroom this very weekend? You can install 200 square feet of Excelon vinyl tile in your basement playroom for under $60 if you do it yourself.

16. HUGH PUTS DOWN TILE. HE PICKS UP SCISSORS AND BRUSH, IN SYNC. AS HE BRUSHES ACROSS SCREEN, LETTERING IS REVEALED: "EXCELON TILE, BY ARMSTRONG."

Remember — all you need to install new vinyl tile floors is a pair of scissors . . . a brush . . . and Excelon Tile, by Armstrong.

Courtesy of Armstrong Cork Company.

Among the most effective and artistic commercials in the sophisticated humor and camp categories have been those produced by Stan Freberg. The following example won the 1966 American Television Commercials Festival award for the best 20-second spot.

VIDEO	AUDIO
OPEN ON MAN WITH FRANKS IN HIS BREAST POCKET LINED UP LIKE CIGARS. HE EXTRACTS ONE AND PUTS IT IN HIS MOUTH.	
	MAN
HE TAKES IT OUT AND HOLDS IT LIKE CIGAR.	Trying to cut down on smoking? Switch to ESSKAY Quality Frank! All meat, no fillers. Hickory smoked, too! Delicious, barbecued.
HE PUTS IT BACK IN HIS MOUTH AND LIGHTS LIGHTER UNDER THE END OF THE WEENY, AS THOUGH HE WERE BARBECUING IT.	MAN (CONTNG.) I'm down to a pack a day.
HE STARTS TO EAT IT.	
CUT TO PACKAGE OF ESSKAY WEENIES, AND FADE	

Courtesy of Freberg, Ltd.

In some instances the TV commercial audio portion is adaptable to radio use. Such was the case for another Freberg production, "E Pluribus Mellon," which received the 1966 International Broadcasting Award and the 1966 American Television Commercials Festival award as best animated 60-second commercial. The following is the TV track re-recorded as a radio spot.

1ST MAN:	HEY YOU THERE WITH THE CREDIT CARDS CASCADING OUT OF YOUR WALLET LIKE A PLASTIC WATERFALL...
GUY:	WHO ME?
2ND MAN:	NOW THAT YOU'VE A MELLON BANK CREDIT CARD, HAS IT OCCURRED TO YOU, YOU MAY NOT NEED THOSE OTHER CARDS AT ALL...
GUY:	NOT AT ALL?
1ST MAN:	NOT AT ALL...
2ND MAN:	NOT AT ALL...
BOTH:	LET'S SAY SELDOM, IF EVER!
1ST MAN:	DON'T YOU REALIZE THAT... TREE SURGERY YOU MAY HAVE DESIRED,
2ND MAN:	GOLD PLATED TUBAS CAN BE ACQUIRED,
BOTH:	ALL ON YOUR MELLON BANK CREDIT CARD
1ST MAN:	MELLON BANK!
2ND MAN:	CREDIT CARD! TRIPS TO THE DENTIST,
1ST MAN:	OR THE BAHAMAS,
2ND MAN:	SPORTING EQUIPMENT
1ST MAN:	SHORTIE PAJAMAS,
BOTH:	ALL ON YOUR MELLON BANK CREDIT CARD.
1ST MAN:	(CAUSE YOU CAN CHARGE) MORE THINGS, MORE PLACES

2ND MAN:	SNOW SHOVELS OR...
1ST MAN:	CRYSTAL VASES!
ORCH:	DING!
2ND MAN:	BICYCLES OR A STUFFED ALLIGATOR,
1ST MAN:	WIGS MADE TO ORDER,
2ND MAN:	SOONER OR LATER
FULL CHORUS:	YOU WILL NO DOUBT DISREGARD,
	ANY OTHER BUT YOUR MELLON BANK,
	CREDIT CAAAAAARD! (UP TO BIG FINISH. ORCH. CUTS OFF.)
GUY:	You mean, now that I have my Mellon Bank Credit Card, I might as well throw most of these other cards away?
1ST MAN:	Why not? Who wants a fat wallet?
ORCH:	TAG.

Courtesy of Freberg, Ltd.

The following Freberg 60-second radio spot, "Stretching the Imagination," has won many honors, including the 1966 International Broadcasting Awards as best radio musical spot, best radio humor and the IBA Sweepstakes Award. The content of this commercial is particularly appropriate here.

MAN:	Radio? Why should I advertise on radio? There's nothing to look at ... no pictures.
GUY:	Listen, you can do things on radio you couldn't possibly do on TV.
MAN:	That'll be the day.
GUY:	Ah huh. All right watch this. (AHEM) O.K. people, now when I give you the cue, I want the seven-hundred foot mountain of whipped cream to roll into Lake Michigan which has been drained and filled with hot chocolate. Then the Royal Canadian Air Force will fly overhead towing the ten-ton maraschino cherry which will be dropped into the whipped cream, to the cheering of twenty-five thousand extras. All right...cue the mountain...
SOUND:	GROANING AND CREAKING OF MOUNTAIN INTO BIG SPLASH!
GUY:	Cue the air force!
SOUND:	DRONE OF MANY PLANES
GUY:	Cue the maraschino cherry...
SOUND:	WHISTLE OF BOMB INTO BLOOP! OF CHERRY HITTING WHIPPED CREAM.
GUY:	Okay, twenty-five thousand cheering extras...
SOUND:	ROAR OF MIGHTY CROWD. SOUND BUILDS UP AND CUTS OFF SHARP!
GUY:	Now...you wanta try that on television?
MAN:	Well....
GUY:	You see...radio is a very special medium, because it stretches the imagination.
MAN:	Doesn't television stretch the imagination?
GUY:	Up to 21 inches, yes.

Courtesy of Freberg, Ltd.

Further evidence that the writer's art is not overlooked in commercial script writing are the yearly awards of the Advertising Writers Association of New York. That group's 1965 Gold Key for the best written radio commercial went to the following humor-oriented script.

1. EFX: MUSIC
2. EFX: DEPARTMENT STORE SOUNDS
3. 1st Lady: Do you have something called Shant Daromees?

     MUSIC UP

1st Man: (embarrassed) Miss, I don't know whether I'm saying this right, but do you have that new perfume Chandaroms?

     MUSIC UP

2nd Man: (Laughingly) May I have a bottle of Shandodrames, please?

     MUSIC UP

2nd Lady: May I have a bottle of Shandoromeez please?

     MUSIC UNDER

ANNCR: Because Chant d'Aromes is new French perfume, it seems no two people pronounce it the same way. But it really doesn't matter. When she wears Chant d'Aromes it speaks for itself. Chant d'Aromes, a new, young fragrance from Guerlain, creators of the classic Shalimar . . . and that in itself says a lot.

> Harry J. Gittes, Associate Creative Director,
> Gilbert Advertising Agency, Inc., and Tony
> Schwartz, New Sounds, Inc.

● *Restudy the scripts above with respect to their use of the five steps of persuasive technique. Can you discover any emotional appeals? Compare the effectiveness of these commercials with the approaches of the Elgin commercials beginning on page 69.*

The 1965 Gold Key for the best written television commercial, awarded by the Advertising Writers Association of New York, was for the script illustrated (and written) in the story board on pages 64 and 65. Sometimes the story board will contain only the visual illustrations, with a separate script containing the written out video descriptions and audio portions. In this case all the material was incorporated in the story board captions.

The Television Story Board

The basic commercial continuity is the same for both radio and television. However, it must be remembered that while the radio commercial must convey everything through sound, the television commercial is essentially visual. The television announcement should be able to hold the viewer with

Video: DS TO MATCHING TELESCOPIC VIEW OF WHISPERJET TAKING OFF AT CAMERA.

Audio: VOICE: To fly. To rush at the wind and, having caught it, to climb as high as the wind itself.

Video: BIRD SOARS.

Audio: MUSIC.

Video: END MONTAGE WITH BIRD FLYING TOWARD CAMERA IN HIS TAKE-OFF

Audio: MUSIC.

Video: DS TO VIEWS OF A WHISPERJET SOARING. . .ABOVE THE CLOUDS. . .

Audio: VOICE: To soar.

Video: BIRDS TAKE FLIGHT

Audio: MUSIC.

Video: AN EAGLE HOVERING ALONG ABOVE A PLAIN. A SEA BIRD BATTLING THE WIND.

Audio: MUSIC

Video: OPEN ON MONTAGE OF BIRDS TAKING OFF.

Audio: MUSIC: EASTERN THEME BEGINS WHEN WE FIRST SEE THE WHISPERJET.

Video: DS TO BIRDS SOARING IN FLIGHT.

Audio: MUSIC UP

Video: DS TO VARIOUS VIEWS OF WHISPERJETS LANDING GRACEFULLY

Audio: To come home.

Video: DS TO BIRDS CIRCLING FOR LANDINGS. . . THEN SHOW BIRDS LANDING

Audio: MUSIC.

Video: EASTERN LOGO

Audio: MUSIC: UP AND OUT.

Video: SHOW IT FROM ABOVE. . .WITH THE MINISCULE EARTH BELOW.

Audio: To look down upon a world made trifling, and look out to the freedom of a horizon without bounds.

Video: SHOT OF WHISPERJET LANDING

Audio: For the people of Eastern Air Lines, the miracle, the exaltation, the serenity of flight are a ceaseless wonder. Come share it with us.

Video: . . .INTO THE SUN

Audio: To hover serenely beyond reality.

EASTERN

Video: BIRD LANDS IN NEST

Audio: To return to the world again.

Written by Jim Nickel, Young & Rubicam; Courtesy of Eastern Air Lines.

the picture. It seems that many writers, directors and producers lack confidence in the visual effectiveness of their own creations. Listen to the sound on your television set the next time there is a commercial break in the program. Chances are you will be able to hear the sound all the way to your refrigerator, or even, depending on your acuity and tastes, all the way to your wine cellar. The visual continuity in the commercial should be such that the technician in the control room does not have to turn up the sound for every advertising message. Well-written commercials don't need to rely solely on a high volume of sound. The video, in other words, should not be treated merely as an adjunct to the audio. In fact, commercial producers (and sponsors) like to see as fully as possible the visual contents for a prospective commercial in its early stages. For this purpose a "story board" is used. The story board usually is a series of rough drawings showing the sequence of picture action, optical effects, settings and camera angles, and it contains captions indicating the dialogue, sound and music to be heard. A good example is the Eastern Air Lines "Birds" story board on pages 64-65. There are frequently many refinements from the story board that sells the commercial to the advertiser to the finished film or tape that sells the product to the viewer. Most agencies prepare story boards. Some, Freberg, Ltd. in particular, do not. Mr. Freberg strongly feels that a visual commitment at too early a date, leading an advertiser to expect a finished product close to the story board, limits the flexibility for artistic creation on the part of those producing the commercial. He uses a "rough" story board as a "road map" for his staff as production develops.

Types of Commercials

The Codes of the National Association of Broadcasters suggest time limits for commercials, which vary according to prime time and non-prime time. Some stations are fairly conscientious in following the NAB code recommendations. Some are not. There are almost as many commercial lengths as there are time periods in the day. During the station break, as indicated, and within sponsored programs the commercial time may be divided in many ways. Let us examine some of the major time lengths.

ID's and Service Announcements. As indicated earlier, the station identification is a 10-second announcement. Attached to the station identification there may be a commercial announcement. The following is an example of the 10-second radio ID.

The following are the television counterparts of the radio ID, an 8-second commercial with slides and a 10-second commercial on tape or film.

There's a new kind of personal car at your Ford Dealer's. It's the Falcon Futura . . . compact cousin of the Thunderbird. See the Futura today at your Ford Dealer's.

Courtesy of J. Walter Thompson Company for Ford Division, Ford Motor Company.

VIDEO	AUDIO
1. SLIDE: CARTOON OF SICK CAR (SLIDE #751)	ANNOUNCER: (OVER) Stop wasting your money trying to keep your old car alive!
2. SLIDE: BEE AND LEGEND: "FORD DEALER'S SWAPPING BEE." (SLIDE #1242)	Visit your Ford Dealer's Swapping Bee, and <u>swap</u> it for the car that outsaves 'em all . . . the new Ford!

Courtesy of J. Walter Thompson Company for Ford Division, Ford Motor Company.

VIDEO	AUDIO
1. OPEN ON STODGY COUPLE IN THEIR ORNATE BEACON STREET PARLOR. THEY HARDLY MOVE AS THEY SIT STIFFLY AND SIP TEA.	MUSIC: HARPSICHORD UP BRIEFLY, THEN CONTINUE UNDER. ANNOUNCER (OVER) Proper Bostonians . . .
2. BUTLER'S HANDS APPEAR, CARRYING TRAY WITH BOSTON CREAM PIE ON IT. THEY START TO SMILE.	. . . drop all formality . . .
3. THEY GET UP, EACH WITH DISH IN HIS HAND, AND BREAK INTO FAST CHA CHA.	MUSIC: SEGUE INTO CHA CHA RHYTHM, UP
4. CUT TO PIE AND PKG. SUPER "NEW" IN SYNC.	When it comes to new and improved Betty Crocker Boston Cream Pie!

Courtesy of General Mills, Inc.

The foregoing IDs were agency-produced. Note how the following commercial, written for the local station, includes the actual identification.

VIDEO	AUDIO
SLIDE: C-2010	TV TROUBLE? CALL A SPECIALIST! CALL CORN'S TV! WRAL-TELEVISION, CHANNEL FIVE, RALEIGH-DURHAM!

The service announcement ordinarily accompanies or follows the ID, and usually is 5 to 10 seconds long, consisting of a commercial message accompanying public service information, such as a time signal or a weather report. The following is an example of the service announcement on radio.

It's _____ PM, B-U-L-O-V-A , Bulova Watch Time. See the Bulova Miss America — 17 jewels — expansion band. Only $35.75.

Courtesy of Bulova Watch Company.

Chain Breaks. The chain is another name for the network. The time available between the network station identification and the local station identification is sold to advertisers either on a network or local basis. This is an especially good source of revenue for local stations. Television advertisers on the chain break usually fill the time with 20-second commercial films. Radio advertisers use an announcement of about 50 to 60 words in length.

30- and 60-Second Announcements. As noted at the beginning of this chapter, programs do not end at the 30-minute or 60-minute mark. Time is allowed for the ID and one or more commercials. In some instances, a sponsored program following another sponsored program will start late to permit more time for the ID and announcements. Sometimes the network affiliate will fade out a program early or fade in a program late to permit more time for commercials in the time break. 20-second, 30-second and full-minute commercials, recorded, live, or on film, are most often the lengths used for both television and radio.

Participating Announcements. When a show is unable or unwilling to get just a single sponsor, it may get a number of participating advertisers. The various advertisers jointly share the cost of the entire program, and the length and frequency of their commercials vary in proportion to the share of the program cost they have contributed. Disc jockey shows on radio, with their frequent and constant commercial announcements, and films on television, with their interminable interruptions for commercials, are examples of the participating announcement program. Large budget shows and television "spectaculars" frequently have participating advertisers.

Program Announcements. When a single sponsor has purchased the entire show, either as a one-shot arrangement or a series, all the commercials on that program will come from that sponsor. The commercials are called program announcements. The sponsor may space his commercials into short announcements, or may lump the commercial time for one long commercial.

The program announcements for the longer programs, those which are half-hour, hour, or 90-minute shows, will follow a fairly standard transitional form, each one building upon the previous one, but nevertheless containing enough variety so that the audience does not become bored through repetition. The average show usually has three program announcements: at the beginning, in the middle and at the end. Occasionally there are four commercials, divided into short opening and closing "billboards," and two insertions within the program itself.

● On the following pages are commercials from a Perry Como show, illustrating the use of the opening and closing billboard and two program insertions. 1) Analyze the emotional and logical appeals, 2) analyze the five steps in the persuasive process, 3) determine the audience analysis used.

ELGIN BILLBOARD FOR CHRISTMAS - OPENING BILLBOARD

VIDEO	AUDIO
1. LARGE "ELGIN" LOGO IN STARRY SKY. BELOW IT, THE WORLD HORIZON.	ANNCR (VOICE OVER): Elgin . . . the most beautiful watches since time began . . .
2. SAME SCENE. BUT REPLACE THE WORD "ELGIN" WITH CU OF LORD ELGIN VISTA #7512.	. . . with exclusive new "Horizon styling." Remember, whatever they're like there's an . . .
3. SAME SCENE. BUT REPLACE CU OF LORD ELGIN VISTA WITH CU OF AN OPEN LORD ELGIN BOX. IN IT, ONLY THE WORD "ELGIN" IS SEEN, AND THE LORD ELGIN VISTA WATCH.	. . . Elgin they'll like for Christmas!

1 MINUTE FILM
ELGIN #1 (HORIZONTAL STYLING)

VIDEO	AUDIO
1. LS OF HORIZON OF A WINTRY WORLD GLOBE, WITH A DARK STARRY SKY ABOVE. IN THIS SKY, DISSOLVE IN THE LARGE LOGO WORD "ELGIN."	MUSIC: APPROPRIATE SCORING THROUGHOUT WITH A BRIGHT, SIMPLE MELODY AND SOUND EFFECTS AS NEEDED; ANNCR: (WITH WARMTH AND QUIET ASSURANCE): This Christmas give the most . . .
2. SAME SCENE. BUT DISSOLVE OUT WORD "ELGIN" AND DISSOLVE IN A CU OF THE LORD ELGIN VISTA (#7512)	beautiful watch since time began . . . a twenty-three jewel Lord or Lady Elgin — the only watch with "horizon styling."
3. SAME SCENE. BUT DISSOLVE OUT THE WATCH, AND DISSOLVE IN THE VISTA'S HORIZON CRYSTAL. IT IS IN THE SKY, AND LIES PARALLEL TO THE HORIZON OF THE GLOBE BELOW.	Elgin's horizon styling features a large picture-window crystal . . .
4. SAME SCENE. BUT FROM BEHIND THE WORLD HORIZON, THE WATCH CASE MOVES UP IN A HORIZONTAL PLANE TO MEET THE CRYSTAL. THEY JOIN, BECOMING ONE WATCH.	. . . that not only extends to the edge of the watch, but actually wraps around it to form a trimmer, thinner profile ---
5. SAME SCENE. BUT DISSOLVE OUT THE HORIZONTAL WATCH, AND DISSOLVE IN THE LORD ELGIN VISTA WITH ITS EDGE PRESENTED TO US VERTICALLY.	--- reveals up to thirty-three percent . . .
6. SAME SCENE. BUT WATCH TURNS FULL-FACE TO US.	more of the dial. No other watch but Elgin offers "horizon styling."
7. DISSOLVE OUT THE LORD ELGIN VISTA. TILT UP TO SKY TO LOSE THE HORIZON LINE OF THE GLOBE.	For her . . . . MUSIC: GLISSANDO AS WE TILT UP TO SKY.

VIDEO	AUDIO

8. SAME SKY SCENE. DISSOLVE IN THE LADY ELGIN VALERA (#7231). TITLE "LADY ELGIN."

. . . Elgin's high styling gives the ultimate in beauty.

9. STAR-SHAPED IRIS TO FAST SERIES OF FULL-SCREEN CUs, ALTERNATING BETWEEN PEOPLE AND THE WATCHES:
(LORD ELGIN MARLIN #9902. PLUS THE WORDS "LORD ELGIN. SELF-WINDING. WATERPROOF."
NOTE: AT BOTTOM OF FRAME WE MUST CARRY THE LEGEND "WHEN CROWN, CRYSTAL AND CASE ARE INTACT." THIS LETTERING CAN BE VERY SMALL.)

Ideally, the gift should . . .

9a. ACTIVE MAN.

fit the person.

9b. LADY ELGIN DEVOTION #7158. PLUS THE WORDS "LADY ELGIN. DIAMOND SET."

And each Elgin watch has been . . .

9c. SENTIMENTAL GIRL.

personality-styled . . .

9d. LORD ELGIN DUNBAR #7614. PLUS WORDS "LORD ELGIN. SHOCK RESISTANT."

to fit a particular type.

9e. CASUAL MAN.

Whatever they're like . . .

9f. LADY ELGIN CONSTANCE #7328. PLUS WORDS "LADY ELGIN. 23 JEWELS."

. . . there's an Elgin they'll like for Christmas.

10. STAR-IRIS BACK TO STARRY SKY TO SEE AN OPEN ELGIN GIFT BOX. IN IT THE WORD "ELGIN." BELOW IT THE WORDS, "FROM $33.75."

From thirty-three seventy-five . . . at Elgin jewelers everywhere.

11. SAME SCENE. BUT DISSOLVE OUT THE GIFT BOX AND TITLE, AS WE TILT BACK DOWN TO THE WORLD HORIZON.

This Christmas, give the . . .

12. SAME SCENE. REPEAT SCENE #5 AS WE DISSOLVE IN THE LORD ELGIN VISTA STANDING WITH ITS EDGE IN A VERTICAL PLANE TO US.

most beautiful watch . . .

13. SAME SCENE. BUT THE WATCH TURNS FULL-FACE TO US.

since time began . . .

14. SAME SCENE. BUT DISSOLVE OUT THE WATCH, AND DISSOLVE IN THE LOGO "ELGIN" IN THE STARRY SKY, AS IN SCENE #1.

. . . a horizon-styled Elgin!!

ONE MINUTE FILM

ELGIN #2 - ARCHIE GARDNER AS SANTA

NOTE: IN WATCH SHOTS, HAVE WATCHES
MOVING SLIGHTLY.

VIDEO	AUDIO
1. CU ARCHIE, WEARING SANTA CLAUS HAT, WHISKERS PULLED DOWN. HE IS TALKING ON THE PHONE.	ARCHIE: Duffy, you call later.
2. ARCHIE HANGS UP PHONE.	Thanks, Duffy.
3. CUT TO MLS TO SHOW ARCHIE ON THRONE ON DAIS ATOP STAIRS; HE ADJUSTS WHISKERS, PAYS AT-TENTION TO GORGEOUS GALS LINED UP ON STAIRS, TRYING TO GET HIS ATTENTION. LARGE LOGO "ELGIN" IN B.G.	
4. CUT TO MCU AS FIRST GAL CUD-DLES UP TO ARCHIE.	GAL #1: Santa, I want a new Elgin Watch Personality-Styled just for me.
5. GAL CUDDLES EVEN CLOSER, PLAYS WITH ARCHIE'S WHISKERS. HE EN-JOYS IT, BUT STILL TRIES TO RE-MEMBER HE'S SANTA.	ARCHIE: Yeah, yeah . . . . well,
(HE REACHES INTO BAG, PULLS OUT LADY ELGIN.)	for you . . .
6. CUT TO CU OF LADY ELGIN (7158) BEING SLIPPED THRU A WEDDING RING, SUPER: "23 JEWEL" "LADY ELGIN" AND "DIAMOND SET."	ARCHIE (VOICE OVER): . . . this here diamond-set Lady Elgin. So petite, it passes the wedding ring test.
7. CUT TO ARCHIE AND GALS. SEC-OND GAL SLINKS UP TO ARCHIE.	GAL #2: My boyfriend wants Elgin's ex-clusive new "Horizon styling."
8. GAL WRAPS HER ARMS AROUND ARCHIE, HE BEAMS.	He just l-o-v-e-s that wrap-around crystal.
9. ARCHIE BEATS HER OFF.	ARCHIE: For him . . .
(ARCHIE REACHES INTO PACK, HOLDS UP ELGIN.)	
10. CUT TO CU LORD ELGIN VISTA. SUPER: "LORD ELGIN" AND "EX-CLUSIVE HORIZON STYLING."	ARCHIE (VOICE OVER): . . . Okay, for him here's an extreme-ingly handsome Lord Elgin. Big, picture-window crystal.
11. CUT TO ARCHIE AND GALS. GAL IN BATHING SUIT CUDDLING UP TO ARCHIE.	GAL #3: My boyfriend wants a water-proof Elgin.
12. ARCHIE REACHES INTO SACK, PULLS UP A LORD ELGIN.	ARCHIE: Waterproof --- Okay here we are . . .

71

VIDEO	AUDIO
13. CUT TO CU LORD ELGIN MARLIN (9902) SUPERS: "SELF-WINDING WATERPROOF "WHEN CROWN, CRYSTAL AND CASE ARE INTACT."	ARCHIE (VOICE OVER): . . . this here Lord Elgin . . . waterproof, shock-resistant and self-winding.
14. GAL TAKES WATCH, POISES ON BACK OF PLATFORM, DIVES OFF. SUPER THE WORD: "SPLASH"	GAL #3: I'll take it! SPLASH
15. ARCHIE OBSERVES THIS, SHRUGS HIS SHOULDERS PHILOSOPHICALLY	ARCHIE: Well . . .
16. ARCHIE INDICATES ALL THE GALS, SPEAKING DIRECTLY TO CAMERA. HE HOLDS UP OPEN ELGIN GIFT BOX WITH WORD "ELGIN" IN IT, AND THE LADY ELGIN VALERA.	. . . whatever they're like . . .
17. CUT TO CU OPEN GIFT BOX AND LADY ELGIN VALERA SUPER ON WORDS: "FROM $33.75."	. . . there's an Elgin they'll like for Christmas.
18. GALS REACT WITH DELIGHT, SWARM ALL OVER ARCHIE, KISSING AND HUGGING HIM. PHONE RINGS. HE PICKS IT UP.	PHONE RINGS: Hello. Duffy? Okay. With 23 jewels.
19. CUT TO ARCHIE'S FACE AS HE COVERS PHONE. WHISKERS AWRY, LIPSTICK ALL OVER HIM, CAP KNOCKED TO ONE SIDE, AS MORE GALS ARE TRYING TO GRAB AT HIM. HE WINKS AT CAMERA.	ARCHIE (TO US): Folks, see 'em at Elgin jewelers everywhere.

ELGIN BILLBOARD FOR CHRISTMAS - CLOSING BILLBOARD

VIDEO	AUDIO
1. LARGE "ELGIN" LOGO IN STARRY SKY. BELOW IT, THE WORLD HORIZON.	ANNCR (VOICE OVER): Elgin . . . the most beautiful watches since time began . . .
2. SAME SCENE. BUT REPLACE THE WORD "ELGIN" WITH CU OF LORD ELGIN VISTA #7512.	. . . with exclusive new "Horizon styling." Remember, whatever they're like there's an . . .
3. SAME SCENE. BUT REPLACE CU OF LORD ELGIN VISTA WITH CU OF AN OPEN LORD ELGIN BOX. IN IT, ONLY THE WORD "ELGIN" IS SEEN, AND THE LORD ELGIN VISTA WATCH.	. . . Elgin they'll like for Christmas!

Courtesy Elgin National Watch Company

Cowcatcher and Hitchhiker.   Prior to the actual start of a scheduled program, but after the station break and in the time segment of the program, a commercial announcement may be inserted. This is the "cowcatcher." When such an announcement is inserted following a program, but prior to the station break, it is called a "hitchhiker." These usually are short announcements, but they may vary from 5 seconds to more than a minute. The cowcatcher and hitchhiker usually advertise other products of the sponsor of the program.

Co-op announcements.   These are the commercials of several sponsors who have purchased a particular network show. They differ from participating announcements in that the co-op sponsors are in different cities, and instead of their announcements being consecutively on the same show, they are given simultaneously. The network leaves fixed commercial time in the program for the local station to fill in with the message from the co-op sponsor in that locality.

Commercial Formats

There are six major format types for commercials: straight sell, educational, testimonial, humorous, musical, and dramatization. Any single commercial may consist of a combination of two or more of these techniques.

Straight Sell.   This should be a clear, simple statement about the product. Be careful about involving the announcer or station too closely with the product. Do not say "our product" or "my store." Only if a personality is presenting the commercial, the combination of testimonial and straight sell techniques may permit such personal involvement.

The following 20-second and one-minute films illustrate two different straight sell forms for the same product.

VIDEO	AUDIO
1. CLOSEUP OF TUBE OF STRIPE BEING SQUEEZED OUT ON BRUSH.	ANNOUNCER: (OFF SCREEN) New! Stripe toothpaste! The pink stripe tells you it's Stripe, the only toothpaste.
2. SUPER TITLE: "HEXACHLORO-PHENE" AND ZOOM IT UP FROM THE TOOTHPASTE TO UPPER FRAME.	with Hexachlorophene!
3. DISSOLVE TO GERMS TITLED "BAD BREATH" AND "DECAY GERMS IN YOUR MOUTH" AND X OUT WITH STRIPE TOOTH PASTE TUBE STILL SHOWING.	That's why Stripe kills bad breath and decay germs . . .
4. STRIPE SQUEEZED OUT IN "X" OVER TUBE LABELED ORDINARY "TOOTH-PASTE." "X" OUT TUBE AND LET-TERING.	Better than any leading toothpaste . . .

VIDEO	AUDIO
5. STRIPE SQUEEZED OUT IN "X" OVER BOTTLE LABELED "MOUTH-WASH."	or mouthwash . . .
6. STRIPE SQUEEZED OUT IN "X" OVER ORDINARY TOOTHPASTE AND MOUTHWASH.	or <u>both</u>!
7. DISSOLVE TO BOY & GIRL KISSING.	For a breath that's
8. DOLLY IN WITH HEART OF STRIPE TOOTHPASTE AROUND MOUTH (AS IN PRINT AD)	close-up clean, get
9. POP ON CARTON UNDERNEATH HEART. TITLE: LEVER BROTHERS COMPANY.	Stripe with Hexachlorophene.
ANNCR WALKING FROM OFF LEFT TO CENTER SCREEN. MCU STANDING BE-HIND DESK CHAIR.	<u>SHIPLEY</u> (TO CAMERA) I want to talk to you about toothpaste and your family's teeth. Now to start with tooth decay is caused by germs - just as an in-fection is caused by germs.
HE PICKS UP PACKAGE	So the thing to do is to kill those germs be-fore they can attack the teeth . . . and Stripe contains the most effective killer of decay germs ever put in a toothpaste. Let me repeat that - it's important: Stripe contains the most effective killer of decay germs ever put in a toothpaste.
ANNCR MOVES AROUND DESK, PACKAGE IN HAND. SITS DOWN ON DESK.	What's more Stripe's germ-fighting action stays in the mouth for hours. That makes it especially helpful to children, what with all the candy and soft drinks they go thru.
CUT TO CU OF STRIPE BEING SQUEEZED ON BRUSH.	Decay germs, of course, thrive on sweets. But here's another thing . . . Children brush longer and more often, as dentists recom-mend, because Stripe looks good and tastes good too.
CUT BACK TO ANNCR, WHO GETS UP FROM DESK AND MOVES INTO ECU, HOLDING PACKAGE UNDER FACE.	So, mother, here's the easy way to get your family to fight tooth decay germs by brushing more often every day - give them Stripe toothpaste.

Courtesy of Lever Brothers Company

The straight sell may hit hard, but not over the head and not so hard that it may antagonize the potential customer. The straight sell is straightfor-ward, and although the statement about the product is basically simple and clear, the writing technique usually stresses a "gimmick," usually emphasizes something special about the product, real or implied, that makes it different or extra or better than the competing product. A slogan frequently character-izes this special attribute. The following is a good example of the straight sell with a gimmick.

ANNOUNCER: Ever hear a tiger with a European accent?
SFX: TIGER GROWL
ANNOUNCER: Here's one—the new Overhead Cam Sprint by Pontiac—like no car you've ever seen or driven before! It comes with a revolutionary new overhead cam six engine... with its camshaft mounted up over the valves like the European road machines have them ...to develop more rpm's...and a brisk 207 horsepower that acts like its coming out of a V-8. There's a four-barrel carburetor under the hood of the Sprint, too...along with a special low-restriction exhaust out back...a special suspension under you that hangs on like a tiger...a quick-action Hurst floorshifter inside...and a set of tiger stripes around you. You can order the Sprint package on any 1966 Pontiac Tempest, and Tempest Custom except station wagons...and on the LeMans. Come in soon and tie into this European-inspired tiger ...Sprint by Pontiac. It's at your Pontiac dealers now...
SFX: TIGER GROWL
ANNOUNCER: ...tiger country!

John Lapp, Group Creative Supervisor, MacManus, John & Adams.

Educational. The educational commercial usually uses logical appeals and gives rational reasons, not emotional ones, why the product should be purchased. The educational commercial may sometimes reflect institutional rather than product advertising. Institutional advertising attempts to gain good will for the individual organization or industry rather than sell anything specific. There are various kinds of educational commercials, from those which may simply present a single logical appeal in a 10- or 20-second spot to the following three-minute example, almost all of which is presented here. This commercial uses a semi-documentary approach to combine institutional and product advertising.

"PURE FOOD AND DRUG ACT"

1. FADE IN - CLOSE UP ANIMATED TITLE
Stars moving in dark sky behind words -

> Du Pont
> Cavalcade
> Theater

ANNOUNCER O.S.

We will return to Cavalcade Theater right after
after tonight's story of Du Pont Chemistry.

. . . FADE OUT

2. FADE IN - CLOSE UP GIRL
Wearing light colored coat -

GIRL

And I'd like a loaf of bread, please.

. . . VERTICAL WIPE TO

CLOSE UP MAN
Wearing hat - speaks

MAN

A box of aspirin, please.

. . . VERTICAL WIPE TO

CLOSE UP WOMAN IN CHECKERED DRESS
Holds lipstick in hand - extends it forward -

75

2. (CONTINUED)

                              WOMAN

              I'll take this lipstick.

    . . . DISSOLVES INTO

    MED CLOSE SHOT INT. OFFICE
    Commentator, John Kennedy, stands by
    display of drugs & foods -

                              KENNEDY

              These little scenes illustrate a very important
              point. Today you buy foods, drugs or cosmetics -
              and you never worry as to whether they're safe
              to use. You trust the manufacturers. You buy
              with confidence.

    . . . DISSOLVES INTO

    MED CLOSE SHOT EXT. OLD GATE
    Sign over gate reads

    E. I. DU PONT DE NEMOURS & COMPANY
    1802 EXPERIMENTAL STATION 1903

                              KENNEDY O.S.

              But about fifty years ago the story was a lot
              different.

    . . . DISSOLVES INTO

    MED SHOT CORNER IN DU PONT LABORATORY
    AROUND 1906
    Chemists working - man moves forward & picks
    up bottle of liquid - looks intently at it -

                              KENNEDY O.S.

              Science had really started to advance. Big steps
              were made —

    . . . DISSOLVES INTO

    MED CLOSE SHOT INT. OFFICE
    Kennedy standing by display of drugs & foods -
    camera dollies as he moves to desk - points
    to plaque on desk -

                              KENNEDY

              but with them came potential dangers. You see,
              no effective controls existed to enforce safety
              standards to protect the public health. So -
              in Nineteen Six, the Food and Drug Act was
              passed. This year marks its —

3. LARGE CLOSE UP PLAQUE ON DESK
   Kennedy's hand at side points to plaque -
   Lettering on plaque reads

   FOOD, DRUG & COSMETIC LAWS
     50th Anniversary
       1906 - 1956

                              76

A HALF CENTURY OF
PROGRESS

INDUSTRY
CONSUMERS   A HEALTHY
GOVERNMENT   NATION IS A
IN CO-OPERATION   STRONG NATION

KENNEDY O.S.

Fiftieth Anniversary which is being celebrated
under the — sponsorship of the Association of
Food and Drug Officials of the United States.

4. CLOSE SHOT OF DESK
Kennedy sits on desk · holds up a book
of regulations - puts it down on desk -

KENNEDY

Today all reputable manufacturers abide by the
codes and regulations of federal and state
governments.

. . . DISSOLVES INTO

MED SHOT INT. DU PONT'S HASKELL LABORATORY
Camera pulls back to longer shot - chemists working
around long lab table b.g. - woman busy at a micro-
scope in f.g.

KENNEDY O.S.

- Companies like Du Pont have established research and testing programs to make sure you
get top quality products that are safe to use.
This is Du Pont's Haskell Laboratory, expecially
set up —

5. CLOSE HIGH SHOT OVER LAB TABLE
Chemist working with equipment -

KENNEDY O.S.

— to do work of this sort. Here are some ex-
* * *

8. CLOSE UP LOAF OF BREAD
As Kennedy, partly in scene, lifts it -

KENNEDY O.S.

— year it's used in over five billion loaves of
bread.

. . . DISSOLVES INTO

CLOSE UP WOMAN TECHNICIAN
Applies nylon patches to girls' legs - girls
in line to b.g., exit past camera -

KENNEDY O.S.

- And when nylon was new, Du Pont's Haskell
Laboratory supervised many tests. Eight thousand volunteers wore test stockings or patches
of nylon to determine the possibility of any
irritation.

. . . DISSOLVES INTO

CLOSE SHOT INT. LABORATORY
Analytical chemist (woman) working with equipment - camera pulls back as she moves forward -

KENNEDY O.S.

- In the laboratory insecticides and other agricultural chemicals are studied to make certain that
harmful residues do not remain on food crops. This
special testing equipment was designed and built
by Du Pont to measure the presence of the residue —
in parts per million.

. . . DISSOLVES INTO

MED CLOSE SHOT IN OFFICE
Kennedy standing back of desk by window - holds
can of food - puts it on desk - Word come on
over scene -

"CYLAN"

KENNEDY

- Today, in special dietary foods, there's another
product of chemical research - a non-caloric
sweetener called "Cylan" calcium cyclamate,
and you can be sure it's safe to use because
scientists of industry worked closely with scientists of the Food & Drug Administration in extensive research and testing programs.

9. CLOSE UP KENNEDY
Turns to side - camera pans away from him &
moves up close to Du Pont Oval on wall -
Slogan under oval -

Better things for better living
. . . through Chemistry

KENNEDY

- In many other ways, Du Pont takes every possible step to fulfill its obligation to the public.
That is why you can have complete con- (O.S.)
fidence in products that bear the Du Pont oval
trademark - your assurance of safe, high-quality
products - of - Better Things for Better Living —
through Chemistry.

ANNOUNCER O.S.

- And now, back to Cavalcade Theater.

. . . FADE OUT

1956 TV commercial script, reprinted with permission of E. I. du Pont de Nemours & Co.,
Wilmington, Delaware.

The Testimonial. The testimonial commercial is very effective when properly used. When the testimonial is given by a celebrity — whose social and economic status is likely to be quite a bit higher than that of the average viewer — the emotional appeals of prestige, power and good taste are primary. What simpler way to reach the status of the celebrity, if only in one respect, than by using the same product he or she uses? The writer must make certain that the script fits the personality of the person giving the endorsement.

The traditional celebrity testimonial has been replaced, in part, by the testimonial from the ordinary housewife, worker and other man- or woman-in-the-street with whom the viewer at home can more easily identify. By virtue of such identification, the viewer may more easily accept the existence of a common problem set in a physical area of common experience, and may more readily accept the solution adopted by the subject of the commercial — using the sponsor's product. The following is an example of this approach.

VIDEO	AUDIO
BOB BARKER ON SET.	BARKER: Is there anybody here who could stand some help on washday? Well, listen to Mrs. Eugenia Schaefer, of Milwaukee, Wisconsin . . .

FILM

1. (OPEN ON)
   MEDIUM SHOT OF MRS. SCHAEFER IN LAUNDRY AREA OF HOME. CLEAN WHITE LAUNDRY AND WRAPPED PACKAGE ON TABLE BESIDE HER. SHE HAS HAND ON PACKAGE.

   ANNOUNCER #1 (VO): See that package under Mrs. Schaefer's hand? It contains a washday product she's been testing for three weeks, following regular directions, but she does not know the product's name . . .

2. (CUT TO)
   CLOSE SHOT OF MRS. SCHAEFER. SUPER THROUGHOUT SCENE: "MRS. EUGENIA SCHAEFER."

   MRS. SCHAEFER (OC): It was just wonderful. Everything was so much whiter and brighter than it had been before.

3. (CUT TO)
   MEDIUM SHOT OF MRS. SCHAEFER

   Mostly, I would think, in the white clothes. For instance, in a slip I can get comparisons. I have left some of the things out and have compared what has been washed with this product, and they are many, many

4. (CUT TO)
   CLOSE SHOT OF WHITE LAUNDRY ON TABLE. MRS. SCHAEFER'S HAND PARTLY RAISES ARTICLES ON TOP.

   (VO): shades whiter and brighter.

   ANNOUNCER #2 (VO): Are you a little bit

5. (CUT TO)
   MEDIUM SHOT OF MRS. SCHAEFER.

   curious about what is in that box?

   MRS. SCHAEFER (OC): Yes, I am.

   ANNOUNCER #2 (VO): Why don't you open it and find out?

   MRS. SCHAEFER (OC): Now?

VIDEO	AUDIO
6. (CUT TO) CLOSE SHOT OF WRAPPED PACKAGE AS MRS. SCHAEFER TEARS SIDE OFF.	ANNOUNCER #2 (VO): Please. MRS. SCHAEFER (VO): All right. Thank you. Oh, it's <u>Cheer</u>!
7. (CUT TO) MEDIUM SHOT OF MRS. SCHAEFER WITH UNWRAPPED CHEER PACKAGE.	(OC): The new Blue <u>Cheer</u>! Well, this is wonderful. It really is wonderful. ANNOUNCER #1 (VO): <u>You'll say the same</u> when you see the <u>deeper</u>, <u>fresher</u> white you get with Cheer.
8. (CUT TO) CLOSE SHOT OF UNWRAPPED CHEER PACKAGE.	Cheer, with exclusive <u>Blue-Magic Whitener</u>. Try it <u>soon</u>! <u>Courtesy of The Procter & Gamble Company.</u>

Another widely used form of the testimonial has the star or stars of a dramatic program — sometimes remaining in, sometimes stepping out of character following a given episode — present a commercial for the product. Sometimes the statement may be given by the star alone, in the manner of the traditional testimonial approach. At other times dramatization is incorporated, as in the following sequence between Dick Van Dyke and Mary Tyler Moore of the "Dick Van Dyke Show."

DISH DOING SCENE IN THE PETRIE KITCHEN. LAURA IS FINISHING UP THE WASHING. ROB IS DRYING. SHE TURNS AND WATCHES HIM. 2 SHOT	ROB What're you lookin' at?
HE PUTS DOWN THE DRIED DISH	LAURA I was waiting for you to notice.
AND LOOKS AT HER	ROB Notice. Aha! Your eyes are a different color tonight.
ROB PICKS UP THE PLATE HE'S JUST DRIED. LOOKS AT IT (IN IT), THEN AS THOUGH HE'S JUST BEEN GIVEN AN ELABORATE PRESENT	LAURA No, Rob, didn't you notice the new dishes?
	ROB Aw, honey, you shouldn't have!
	LAURA (CONFUSED) Huh?
STILL STARING AT PLATE. CUT TO ANGLE SHOT SO WE SEE HIS REFLECTION IN PLATE	ROB Getting my picture put on all the plates!

VIDEO	AUDIO

HE ADMIRES HIMSELF. CUT TO 2 SHOT. PICKING ONE
UP, HER REFLECTION IS REVEALED.

                                            LAURA

Rob, these are perfectly
plain plates.

CUT TO CU REFLECTION IN PLATE

                                            ROB

Oh, I see you got some with
your picture, too.

                                            LAURA

Oh, silly, I didn't do that.
The Joy did! Joy gets dishes
so clean I can see myself.

PICKING UP POT

                                            ROB

Pots too?

CUT TO 2 SHOT

                                            LAURA

Pots too—JOY gets them so
shiny you can see yourself.

ADMIRING HIMSELF IN THE PLATE

                                            ROB

Can't get over the likeness.
Joy did that, huh?

                                            LAURA

Uh huh.

                                            ROB

Boy, think what it could do if
we sent it to art school.

DISS TO BOTTLE CU

Humor. Humor is extremely effective and may be presented in a number of ways, including live action, film, music and animation. The commercials on pages 61-63 and 80-83, of different physical types, all illustrate the use of humor.

ANNOUNCER: Here are the 4 Lads and Mitch Miller!

> Super Shell gives you extra power
> Cause it's loaded with toluene.
> Super Shell gives you extra mileage
> Try this great new gasoline!
>
> Drive up to the Shell white pump and
> Get the gas that's making news
> Fill your tank with Super Shell
> Most powerful gas any car can use
> Get more power with new Super Shell,
> It's the gasoline to choose.
>
> Get more power with Super Shell
> Get more mileage, come see what we mean
> Drive to your dealer and fill the tank
> Try this great new gasoline.

ANNOUNCER: Super Shell with TCP is the most powerful gasoline any car can use. See your Shell Dealer.

Courtesy of Shell Oil Company.

Dramatizations. The dramatized commercial may be a 20-, 30-, or 60-second announcement such as that of the "doctor" advising the patient to use a certain patent medicine. If the commercial is a program announcement it may be longer and may be able to utilize more than stereotyped characters. The dramatized program announcement is especially effective when it can be incorporated into the action of the show itself. In a play, particularly if it is a situation comedy, the characters of the story can be put into a dramatic sequence which seems to be an extention of the plot line and in which they can extol the virtues of the sponsor's product. In the variety program the same approach may be employed, except that actual personalities rather than fictional characters are used. The dramatized commercial offers good opportunity for the presentation of a problem which can be solved by the utilization of the product. Note how this is done in the following illustration.

ONE-MINUTE COMM'L - 20-SEC. FILM: 40-SEC. LIVE

VIDEO	AUDIO
1. MCU JACK PAAR	JACK: Right now, you're probably asking yourself: "What do people drink?"

FILM (20-SECONDS)

2. ROLL FILM #138 - 20-seconds "PICKLE PACKER"	SOUND ON FILM

3. DISSOLVE TO MCU OF DODY GOODMAN.	JACK (VOICE OVER): Here's an alert looking woman. What is your occupation and your favorite drink?
4. PULL BACK TO MS OF DODY BEHIND A COUNTER OR TABLE. IN FRONT OF HER ARE A STACK OF CLAMS AND SOME SMALL BOXES. SHE PACKS CLAMS INTO THE BOXES. HIDDEN BELOW TABLE TOP IS AN OPENED BOTTLE OF SEVEN-UP WHICH SHE WILL REVEAL ON CUE.	DODY: I pack clams. All day I'm packing clams. I get exhausted after packing clams all day, and I'm ready for a quick, refreshing lift. That's when I wrap my clammy hands around a chilled bottle of Seven-Up. (DRINKS)
5. CUT TO MCU JACK WITH OPENED BOTTLE OF SEVEN-UP.	JACK: (POLITELY) Ladies and gentlemen. May I suggest that you wrap your pickle packing, clammy hands around a chilled bottle of Seven-Up. For a quick, refreshing lift — Nothing does it like Seven-Up. (DRINKS)

Courtesy of Seven-Up Bottling Company.

● *Write a TV commercial for a soft drink, using the dramatization approach. Present a problem and show how the product solves that problem. Orient the commercial around a human, realistic, sympathetic family with whom the audience can or would wish to identify.*

Physical Types of Commercials

In radio the commercial may be live or recorded. In television, however, there are a number of approaches combining various potentials of the live and filmed presentation. You may have already noted differences in type in the examples presented earlier.

● *As you examine the following commercials in relation to physical type, format and length, try to analyze them in terms of the previously discussed elements of good commercial writing.*

Live, with realistic action, the talent in view and being heard.

60 SECONDS

VIDEO	AUDIO
1. OPEN ON CU CULLEN	CULLEN: One of the troublesome symptoms of the Asian flu is the sore, aching muscles that accompany it.
2. CUT TO ECU PILE OF TUBES OF DEEP HEAT RUB. (NOT IN VIEW: HE PICKS UP TUBE OF DEEP HEAT RUB, TAKES OFF CAP AND SQUEEZES ABOUT AN INCH OUT ONTO HIS WRIST)	Well, here's a suggestion to help you through the aches of the flu — new Metholatum Deep Heat Rub.

3. CUT BACK TO MS CULLEN MASSAG-
ING THE RUB INTO HIS WRIST.

Massage it into those agonized muscles
whenever and wherever you ache.

4. DOLLY IN TO CU HIS WRIST.

You'll notice that Mentholatum Deep Heat
Rub soaks right into your skin. Its major
active ingredients stimulate the blood into
soothing action.

5. DOLLY BACK TO MS CULLEN.

Soon . . . a warm, pleasing glow is felt
right where you hurt. Deep Heat Rub makes
your sore muscles feel good again.

6. CUT TO SIDE VIEW CULLEN. HE
TURNS AND LOOKS INTO CAMERA.
(DOES NOT DEMONSTRATE AUDIO)

— Something else: because new Mentholatum Deep Heat Rub is greaseless and
stainless, you can massage with it in the
morning and still wear your finest clothing.

7. HE SMELLS TUBE, SMILES.

It's got a pleasing smell, too.

8. CUT TO ECU GLAMOR SHOT OF
PRODUCT.

Buy a large economy size tube of new Mentholatum Deep Heat Rub today. Deep Heat
Rub's available in both the United States
and Canada!

Courtesy of Mentholatum Company.

Live, with voice-over narration. This may include pantomime, slides,
photos, cards or other artwork.

20 SECONDS

VIDEO

AUDIO

ANNOUNCER:

1. OPEN ON SLIDE #922
(EVERYBODY TALKING)

Good news travels fast!

2. CUT TO SLIDE #923
(ABOUT SUPER SHELL)

Super Shell is the most powerful gasoline
any car can use!

3. CUT TO SLIDE #925
(FULL OCTANE EVERY)

It has the full octane you need for any
driving situation . . . And TCP additive in
Super Shell neutralizes harmful engine deposits . . . insures high octane.

4. CUT TO SLIDE #246
(SHELL BANJO SIGN)

See your Shell Dealer for Super Shell with
TCP.

Courtesy of Shell Oil Company.

LIVE: ONE MINUTE

VIDEO	AUDIO

1. OPEN ON CU OF RECORD ALBUM (SKETCHES BY SKITCH) IN WOMAN'S HANDS. AS SHE LEANS BACK INTO HUSBAND'S ARMS WE REVEAL IN STYLIZED SECTION OF ULTRA-MODERN LIVING ROOM. EVERY-THING FREE FORM. YOUNG COUPLE SITTING ON FLOOR LISTENING TO MUSIC ON SYLVANIA HI FI (MODEL #4801).

MUSIC IN SOFTLY . . . FROM ALBUM "SKETCHES BY SKITCH."

SAME MUSIC SWEEPS UP DRAMATICALLY, THEN HOLD UNDER.

ANNOUNCER:

2. SUPER CU SKITCH HENDERSON OVER ENTIRE SCENE LEADING ORCHES-TRA.

It's like hearing favorite recording stars like Skitch Henderson in person — with music from his new album — "Sketches by Skitch." You hear music as you've never heard it before on . . . Sylvania High-Fidelity!

MUSIC: UP . . . THEN UNDER

3. DOLLY INTO CU CONSOLE (MODEL #4801). TAKE OUT SUPER OF SKITCH.

The newest, the finest in high-fidelity! Magnificent custom consoles . . . a complete home music center such as this with . . .

4. CUT TO ECU RECORD CHANGER AND DIAMOND STYLUS IN CONSOLE. HAND IN POINTS THEM OUT.

MUSICAL PUNCTUATION

. . . 4-speed automatic record changer . . . and diamond stylus!

5. PAN TO ECU RADIO ON CONSOLE. HAND POINTS IT OUT.

MUSICAL PUNCTUATION

. . . rich toned AM-FM radio!

6. PAN TO ECU TAPE RECORDER. HAND LIFTS UP MIKE.

MUSICAL PUNCTUATION

. . . and special built-in two-speed tape recorder!

7. DISSOLVE TO CU HI-FI CONSOLE (MODEL 4702) . . . THE ROOM DIVI-DER SET. DOLLY AROUND TO SHOW ITS FASHION FINISH ON ALL SIDES.

MUSIC: UP . . . THEN UNDER

For something fresh in high-fidelity styl-ing . . . this smart Sylvania phonograph radio console! Fashioned finished on all sides . . . it makes an attractive room divider.

8. DISSOLVE TO CU HI-FI PORTABLE (MODEL 4501) HAND LIFTS IT UP TO SHOW PORTABILITY. PORTABLE RESTS ON STAND.

MUSIC: UP . . . THEN UNDER

Sylvania goes portable, too . . . with light-weight high-fidelity radio-phonographs . . .

9. PAN TO MATCHING PORTABLE TAPE RECORDER.

. . . and portable tape recorders!

10. PULL BACK TO REVEAL COMPLETE HIGH-FIDELITY AND TAPE RE-CORDER LINE

MUSIC: SWEEPS UP . . . DRAMATICALLY

Hear your favorite symphonies, popular songs and recording artists . . .

11. "SYLVANIA" LOGO ZOOMS UP FULL SCREEN.

. . . on Sylvania High-Fidelity . . . the finest in high-fidelity sound!

MUSIC: UP STRONG AND OUT

Courtesy of Sylvania Electric Products, Inc.

Film, with realistic action.

FILM: ONE MINUTE

VIDEO	AUDIO
1. OPEN ON MS SUZANNE STORRS WALKING TO SMALL TABLE IN SECTION OF MODERN LIVING ROOM. ON TABLE ARE ONE CARTON EACH OF COOL-LIGHT AND BUG-LITE. SUZANNE IS DRESSED IN A PRETTY SUMMER COTTON. ESTABLISH THEN DOLLY IN.	SUZANNE: (SMILING) We're all ready for summer at our home . . .
2. SUZANNE PICKS UP CARTONS, ONE IN EACH HAND.	with these wonderful new Sylvania light-bulbs . . .
3. CUT TO ECU COOL-LIGHT CARTON IN SUZANNE'S HAND.	beautiful aqua-tinted Cool-Light for indoors . . .
4. PAN TO BUG-LITE CARTON IN SUZANNE'S OTHER HAND.	and soft yellow-tinted Bug-lite for outdoors.
5. CUT BACK TO MS SUZANNE. SHE REPLACES CARTONS ON TABLE. PAN WITH HER TO LAMP TABLE BY CHAIR. SHE GESTURES AS SHE WALKS.	Indoors, this marvelous new Cool-Light makes everything seem fresher . . . cooler!
6. SUZANNE SWITCHES ON TABLE LAMP, GESTURES TO ROOM	Look what it does for my living room. The soft aqua tint brings out all the cool colors . . . makes the whole room look fresh . . . airy . . . so much cooler!
7. DISSOLVE TO MS. SUZANNE ENTERS THROUGH DOOR TO MODERN, ATTRACTIVE PATIO, WHICH IS LIGHTED BY MOONLIGHT AND HOUSE LIGHTS. SUZANNE SWITCHES ON PATIO LIGHTS.	Out here . . . Sylvania's new Bug-lite keeps our patio practically bug-free! The yellow-tinted light of Bug-lite doesn't attract insects like ordinary light. We can enjoy all the light we need out here - without attracting all the bugs in the neighborhood!
8. DISSOLVE TO MCU SYLVANIA DISPLAY: COOL-LITE AND BUG-LITE BINS.	Look for these Sylvania serve-yourself displays in your favorite store . . . along with all the wonderful other Sylvania household lightbulbs . . .
9. DOLLY IN FOR ECU COOL-LITE BIN.	Cool-lite for indoors . . .
10. PAN TO BUG-LITE BIN.	Bug-lite for outdoors . . .
11. DISSOLVE TO ECU OF TWO 4-PACKS (COOL LIGHT & BUG LIGHT)	They'll make your whole summer seem cooler . . . and happier!

Courtesy of Sylvania Electric Products, Inc.

Silent film, voice-over.

● **As you examine the following commercial, study its use of emotional appeals.**

VIDEO	AUDIO
1. Open on MLS of couple getting out of row boat onto island. As couple walk over rocks on island, camera dollies back to ELS of couple and island. Camera then pans slowly to bay of water, screen left.	1. SALEM THEME UP, THEN UNDER ANNOUNCER: If you had your choice ... where would you spend today? On an island in a wind-freshened bay? Well, let me tell you about a cigarette whose taste is as refreshing as that breeze
2. Salem pack zooms up from b.g. to screen left. Titles: MENTHOL FRESH, RICH TOBACCO TASTE, and MODERN FILTER, TOO come on screen next to pack in sync with audio.	2. across the bay ... Salem Menthol fresh Rich tobacco taste Modern filter, too
3. Dissolve to MCU two-shot of couple. Girl in f.g. taking puff from cigarette. Man in b.g. lights cigarette, then takes puff.	3. That's Salem, the cigarette that brought something new to smoking ... the cigarette that refreshes your taste. When you smoke a Salem, you enjoy good rich
4. Cut to MCU of girl. Bay in b. g.	4. tobacco taste, but with a surprise softness ... a refreshing
5. Cut to MLS of couple seated on rocks. Man takes girl's hand to help her up from rock. As couple walk across screen, and out of frame, Salem pack zooms up from sky b.g. Title: NEW IDEA IN SMOKING comes on below pack in sync with audio.	5. quality that brings new ease and comfort to smoking. Through Salem's pure-white filter flows the freshest taste in cigarettes. Smoke refreshed. Try Salem ... a new idea in smoking.

Courtesy of R. J. Reynolds Tobacco Company.

Animation.   The following is an excerpted script segment from an animated public service film on smoking entitled "Breaking the Habit," which was nominated for an Academy Award in 1965. It has been shown since as a 60-second TV spot. The animation consists of two blob-type characters in limbo, in conversation, one with a cigarette.

FIRST BLOB (MUMBLES): Well, that's ... ah ... certainly a modest ...
SECOND BLOB (THE SMOKER): That's all I had today!!
FIRST: Well, you ... you look a lot better, I must say.
SECOND: I feel a lot better, too. I really do. Yesterday I was a nervous wreck and ...
        ah ... today it's all different!!
FIRST: Yea ... you better ... ah ... take another one.
SECOND: Oh, have you got another one???
FIRST: Yeah.
SECOND: All right. Here. Gimme a match!
FIRST: Yeah ... yeah ... just wait till you finish this one though, first.
SECOND: Well, why not??
FIRST: When you get the last puff ... ah ... if you can.
SECOND (MUMBLES): Doesn't mean a thing.
FIRST: Things are expensive.
SECOND: I can ... look ... (MATCH STRIKES)

FIRST: Oh, yeah ...
SECOND: There are two cigarettes at once ... and I'm chewing, too ... and, ah ... yet the
         thing is not a habit because I can just take and put 'em out as quick as I want...
FIRST: Well, is this ... ah ...
SECOND: And I've been smoking for ...
FIRST: Ah ...
SECOND: Ten years ... and I should make a point of that!!
(SUPER WORDS ON FILM: WHO ARE YOU KIDDING?)
(WORD KIDDING LAP DISSOLVES INTO WORD KILLING, SO AS TO READ:
WHO ARE YOU KILLING?)

> Produced for the American Cancer Society by Henry Jacobs
> and John Korty, San Francisco.

Other Formats. In addition to other uses of film with non-realistic action, there are puppets, live or on film, electronic and mechanical effects as the
major components of the commercial, and combinations of two or more techniques, as you may have noted in the use of live action plus film in some of
the commercials presented earlier. The following commercial is a good example of the frequently used insertion of film with live action.

LIVE AND FILM CLIP, 2 MINUTES

VIDEO	AUDIO
1. OPEN ON ED AND JULIA IN COMMERCIAL AREA. BESIDE THEM ON STAND IS STAR-FLEX OUTFIT.	SULLIVAN: With Christmas so close, I'll bet you feel the way Julia and I do: time is really racing along. Isn't that right, Julia? MEADE: Sure is, Ed. SULLIVAN: But tonight, Julia Meade is going to show you how to slow it down — in fact, how to stop time completely.
2. DOLLY IN TOWARD OUTFIT.	MEADE: It's easy Ed. Just give someone a Kodak camera outfit . . .
3. CUT TO CU OUTFIT AS HER HAND PUTS "OPEN ME FIRST" TAG ON TOP OF IT.	. . . with this tag that says: "Open Me First." And then watch what will happen on Christmas morning.
4. DISSOLVE TO FILM CLIP #14. CAMERA IN WOMAN'S HANDS, SEE FROM REAR. IT IS AIMED AT CHILD OPENING PRESENT IN LIGHT FROM CHRISTMAS TREE. FILM: WOMAN'S HAND PUSHES BUTTON AND TAKES PICTURE OF CHILD WITH TEDDY BEAR	MEADE: (LVO) Some lucky family will really stop old father time because their pictures will save all the happiness of Christmas for keeps . . . . . . save those "look what I got" smiles . . .

FILM: FAST DISSOLVE TO ECU SNAPSHOT SHE TOOK.	. . . that light up the house like a hundred Christmas candles . . .
FILM: DISSOLVE TO MCU. BOY HUGS TEDDY BEAR.	. . . save those hugs that could almost break a teddy bear in two . . .
FILM: DISSOLVE TO SNAPSHOT SHE TOOK.	There! Look at that!
5. WIPE TO JULIA BESIDE OUTFIT.	Yes, a Kodak camera outfit saves it all even while the other presents are being unwrapped. You can take pictures indoors or out, first thing Christmas morning.
6. CUT TO CU AS JULIA'S HAND POINTS TO ITEMS IN SYNC.	. . . because it's complete with camera . . . flashholder . . . bulbs . . . batteries . . . and film. Now this outfit . . .
7. CUT BACK TO JULIA BESIDE OUTFIT AS SHE LIFTS OUT CAMERA AND LOOKS IN VIEW-FINDER. SHE POINTS TO VIEW-FINDER ON CUE, "RIGHT IN THERE"	. . . is ideal for Mother, because this Starflex camera lets her see her picture big and clear before she shoots . . . right in there. What's more, she can take three kinds of pictures: black-and-white snapshots, color snapshots, and even color slides.
8. CUT TO CU AS SHE REPLACES CAMERA IN OR NEAR OUTFIT. SUPER $16.50.	The Starflex outfit costs only 16.50 . . . and there are many other camera outfits . . .
9. DISSOLVE TO DISPLAY. JULIA WALKS IN.	. . . ranging in price from 9.95 up. So you go see your Kodak dealer. You don't have to wander around looking for gift ideas because . . .
10. SHE TURNS AND FACES CAMERA	. . . almost everyone will want a modern Kodak camera . . . the gift that says: "Open Me First."
11. CUT TO AUDIENCE & SUPER SYMBOL.	APPLAUSE.

Courtesy of Television Department, Eastman Kodak Company.

NOTES TO CHAPTER 3

[1] *Television Factbook,* Number 36 (1966 Edition), p. 55-a.

REFERENCE BOOKS ON TELEVISION COMMERCIALS

The writing of effective commercials (which must *sell* a product, service or idea) is a technique requiring considerable "know-how" and much practice. This chapter has covered the fundamentals, but the writer is advised to consult books such as the following for more information on this subject.

A. William Bluem, John F. Cox and Gene McPherson, *Television in the Public Interest: Planning, Production, Performance* (New York: Hastings House, 1961). Includes an extensive section on public service scriptwriting techniques with numerous sample scripts of announcements, together with production methods for local stations.

Harry Wayne McMahan, *The Television Commercial: How to Create and Produce Effective TV Advertising* (New York: Hastings House, Revised Edition, 1957). A standard work on the subject. Includes cartoon, stop motion, photo animation and other techniques as well as the singing jingle, station break spots, sound effects and how to evaluate the finished TV commercial script.

Charles Anthony Wainwright, *The Television Copywriter* (New York: Hastings House, 1966). Comprehensive examination of all aspects of the process of writing TV commercials — from the idea to the finished production. Practical experiences of agency and network writers and producers.

FOR APPLICATION AND REVIEW

1. Review this chapter to clarify the several steps a writer should take in preparing the commercial announcement. Choose a product, a program and a station. Then develop the commercial, step by step, according to the following points: audience analysis; determination of emotional and logical appeals; familiarization with the product and outlining of the commercial according to the five steps of persuasion: attention, interest, impression of a problem, solving of the problem, getting action. If you have understood the analyses as you went through the chapter and carefully studied the sample scripts, writing the basic commercial announcement should be that much easier.

2. Write a television and a radio ID for your local station. Write a 30-second public service announcement for your local station.

3. Analyze the specific emotional appeals used in several television commercials. Write television and radio commercials in terms of the analysis of the audience of your locality, using the following emotional appeals (one or more of which may be used in each commercial): prestige, power, good taste, self-preservation.

4. Study television and radio commercials until you are certain you can identify each of the following approaches: straight sell; educational; testimonial; humorous; musical; dramatization. Write short television and radio commercials which illustrate each of the above.

5. Write a commercial for each of the following television physical types: live, realistic action, talent in view; live, voice-over narration; film, realistic action; silent film, voice-over; a combination of live action and film.

4

NEWS AND SPORTS

NEWS

ANY HAPPENING that is real that may have an interest for people is news. The television and radio reporter has a limitless field. Anything from a cat up a tree to the outbreak of a war may be worthy of transmission to the mass media audience. The gathering of news, however, is not our primary concern here. The writing of news broadcasts is.

Sources of News

Two major agencies, the Associated Press and United Press International, which serve as news sources for the newspapers, also service television and radio stations. The same information given to newspapers is made available for broadcasting. For broadcast purposes, however, the style of writing of the news should be changed so that the stories become shorter and more pointed, oriented toward the needs of television and radio transmission. In television, in addition, the news stories are not used alone, but are coordinated with visual elements such as films, slides, photographs and wirephotos. A number of organizations provide special news material, particularly pictorial matter, for television. Special newsreel and photo companies operate in almost every city containing a major television station. The larger networks have their own news gathering and reporting organizations. The Columbia Broadcasting System, for example, operates a most effective newsfilm division which supplies material to various stations throughout the country.

All television and radio stations of any consequence, even small local stations, subscribe to at least one wire service. The independent station also may use more immediate sources for local news, such as telephoned reports from city agencies or even private citizens, special information from the local newspapers, word of mouth communications, and sometimes special reporters of their own. The local news story must be written from scratch and, for television, written to fit in with the available visual material.

In the large network station, the news usually is prepared by writers in a special news department. Most small stations do not have separate news departments, so news broadcasts are prepared by available personnel. The continuity department, if there is one, will prepare the special local reports. Generally, the job will fall to the program director or to the individual announcer. The news received through teletype, as well as from other sources, is edited in the large station by the producer or director of the news program or by the individual commentator. The commentator on the small station does this job. The announcer has to make certain that the news reports he reads fit his personality, vocabulary and, often, station policy. More important, he must make certain that the amount of news he has prepared fits the time limit of his show and that the organization of the material adheres to the format of his program. A writer preparing news for a particular program and for a particular announcer will edit it so that it conforms to the above requirements as the specific case demands.

In some instances the writer may do little more than prepare the transitional continuity for a particular program, leaving out the news content itself. It is then up to the individual commentator to edit the news to fit his own announcing abilities, his personality, and his program approach. In many cases the writer prepares only the opening and closing for a program, the broadcaster or his special writer filling in the news portions with wire service reports and material of his own design. An example of this kind of approach was the Edward R. Murrow news show. Here is the prepared format for one of his 15-minute news broadcasts.

EDWARD R. MURROW - FORMAT

BRYAN: The FORD ROAD SHOW presents EDWARD R. MURROW with the news . . . This is George Bryan speaking for Ford, <u>whose new Interceptor V-8 engine brings you gas-saving Precision Fuel Induction.</u>

          (One minute commercial) — Now, Edward R. Murrow.

MURROW: (11 minutes of news) . . . . . I'll be back in a moment with the word for today. Now, a word from George Bryan.

BRYAN: (1-minute 30-second commercial) Now here is Mr. Murrow with his word for the day.

MURROW: Word for the day.

BRYAN: The FORD ROAD SHOW has presented Edward R. Murrow with the news. This is George Bryan speaking for Ford, <u>whose new Interceptor V-8 engine brings you gas-saving Precision Fuel Induction.</u> Listen through the week for the other FORD ROAD SHOWS with Bing Crosby, Rosemary Clooney, Arthur Godfrey, and the morning World News Roundup.

CBS Radio Broadcast.

Styles of Writing

The writer of the news broadcast should remember that, first of all, he is a reporter and has as his primary duty the conveying of the news. The traditional "5 W's" of news reporting must apply. In the condensed space of a few sentences, comparable to the lead paragraph of the newspaper story, the television or radio report must contain information as to What, Where, When, Who, and, if possible, Why. In addition, the television and radio news writer must include as many of the details as possible within the limited time devoted to the story. The key word is *condensation.*

The writer must be aware of the organization of the broadcast so that he can provide the proper transitions, which should be clear and smooth between each story. The writer should indicate to the audience the different divisions of the broadcast. For example, note the introduction: "Now here is Mr. Murrow with his word for the day," in the format on page 92. Similar divisions might be: "And now the local news," or "Now, the feature story for the day," or "Now, the editor's notebook."

The writer must be aware of the content approach, whether it is straight news, analysis or personal opinion, so that he will not confuse editorializing with news. It is wise not to try to fool the audience, at least not too often, although some of our most popular commentators have been doing so for years. Distortion of stories or the presentation of only one side of the picture can change a news story into an opinion comment. Incomplete statements and the excessive use of color words can do the same thing. It is wise to avoid unnecessary sensationalism, unless the purpose of the particular broadcast or the policy of the station leaves the writer no choice. Remember that the newscaster is coming into the home as a guest, and is generally accepted as a personal visitor. His approach should be informal, friendly and — hopefully — honest. The NAB Codes provide some criteria for the treatment of news.

Inasmuch as the announcer tries to establish an informal and friendly relationship with the audience, it is wise not to use antagonizing or shocking stories, at least not in the very beginning of the broadcast. Consider the time of the day the broadcast is being presented — whether the audience is at the dinner table, seated comfortably in the living room, or rushing madly to get to work on time. The writer should think of the news as dramatic action. The story with an obvious conflict (the war, the gang fight, the divorce case, the baseball pennant race) is a good one. Because action is important, write the stories with verbs. The immediacy of television and radio, as opposed to the relatively greater time lapse between the occurrence and reporting of the incident in journalism, permits the use of the present tense in stories about events which happened within a few hours preceding the newscast. The television and radio writer should be cautioned about the use of questions as opposed to direct statements as the opening element of a story. Although the rhetorical question is an excellent attention-getting device in speech making, the nature of objective broadcasting makes its use in radio and television dubious. Rather than beginning with a question such as: "What will happen to the Mars space capsule . . .?," it is more dramatic to say: "The question in all the capitals of the world tonight is: What will happen to the Mars space capsule?" Negative approaches to the news should be avoided. It is better to give whatever details are available without comment than to say: "This is an incomplete story, but . . ."

The writer should begin the news story with precise, clear information. The opening sentence should be, if possible, a summary of the story as a whole. Be wary of including too many details. Remember that the audience hears the news only once and, unlike the newspaper reader, cannot go back to clarify any points in the story. The audience must grasp the entire story the first time it hears it. The writing, therefore, must be simple and understandable and, without talking down to the audience, colloquial in form. This does not imply the use of slang or illiterate expressions, but suggests informality and understandability. Repetition must be avoided, and abstract expressions and words with double meanings should not be used. The information should be accurate and there should be no possibility of a misunderstanding of any news item. Make certain that the terminology used is correct. For example, don't refer to a figure in a story as a "car thief" if the person has not been convicted and is, in actuality, an "alleged car thief."

The writer must help the announcer to convey numbers accurately and to pronounce words correctly. The writer should not put long numbers in figures, but should write them out in words. It is sometimes helpful to place the numerical figures in parentheses. The writer should avoid using long, difficult words or tongue-twisters. After foreign words and difficult names the writer should place in parentheses a simplified sound spelling of the word. Note the following newswire excerpts and pronunciation guide.

HERE IS THE LATEST NEWS FROM THE ASSOCIATED PRESS:

SOUTH VIETNAMESE PREMIER KY AND THE LEADER OF REBELLIOUS GOVERNMENT TROOPS, LIEUTENANT-GENERAL NGUYEN CHANH THI (NWEN CAHN TEE), MET SECRETLY TODAY AT THE U-S MARINE BASE AT CHU LAI (CHOO LY). RESULTS OF THE MEETING WERE NOT REVEALED BUT THERE WAS SPECULATION THAT THE PREMIER IS MOVING TOWARD A SHOWDOWN WITH HIS BUDDHIST AND MILITARY OPPONENTS IN HUE (HWAY).

IN HUE (HWAY), WHERE STUDENT MOBS SET FIRE TO THE U-S INFORMATION SERVICE BUILDING YESTERDAY, THE U-S HAS EVACUATED MANY AMERICAN AND OTHER CIVILIANS TO SAIGON. AMERICAN CONSULATE EMPLOYEES STILL IN HUE HAVE MOVED FROM THEIR HOMES TO THE U-S MILITARY ASSISTANCE COMMAND COMPOUND, WELL PROTECTED BY U-S SOLDIERS.

AN OFFICIAL OF THE MALAYSIAN FOREIGN OFFICE SAYS THE VISIT BY AN INDONESIAN MILITARY DELEGATION TO MALAYSIA PROMISES AN END TO THE THREE-YEAR-OLD UNDECLARED WAR BETWEEN THE TWO COUNTRIES. THE INDONESIANS ARRIVED IN KUALA LUMPUR (KWAH'-LAH LOOM'-POOR) TODAY TO COMPLETE PREPARATIONS FOR PEACE TALKS SCHEDULED TO START IN BANGKOK, THAILAND, NEXT MONDAY.

RELIABLE SOURCES IN SANTO DOMINGO SAY NEGOTIATIONS ARE UNDER WAY FOR THE WITHDRAWAL OF WILLIAM BONNELLY FROM NEXT WEEK'S DOMINICAN PRESIDENTIAL ELECTION SO THAT HIS FOLLOWERS CAN SUPPORT DR. JOAQUIN BALAGUER (WAH-KEEN BAH-LAH-GHEHR'). AN ANNOUNCEMENT ON THE RESULT OF TALKS BETWEEN THE PARTIES CONCERNED IS EXPECTED WITHIN THE NEXT TWO DAYS. THE NEGOTIATIONS STARTED THREE DAYS AGO. SUPPORTERS OF JUAN BOSCH (WAHN BOHSH) ARE CONFIDENT HE CAN DEFEAT BALAGUER, EVEN IF BALAGUER GET THE SUPPORT OF BONNELLY'S FOLLOWERS.

PARTS OF WESTERN TEXAS SUFFERED HEAVY FLOOD AND FIRE DAMAGE TODAY
IN THE WAKE OF CLOUDBURSTS AND VIOLENT THUNDERSTORMS. WATER WAS SIX
FEET DEEP IN THE STREETS OF ANDREWS, WHERE ALMOST THREE INCHES OF RAIN
FELL IN HALF AN HOUR. ANOTHER THREE INCHES FELL IN MIDLAND, TURNING
STREETS INTO SMALL RIVERS. FIRES STARTED BY LIGHTNING DESTROYED A COT-
TON WAREHOUSE AT PYOTE (PY-OHT') AND DAMAGED AT LEAST TWO HOUSES IN
MIDLAND.

-PRONUNCIATION GUIDE-
  BRIGADIER-GENERAL PHAM XUAN NHUAN, COMMANDER OF VIETNAMESE FIRST
DIVISION — FAHM ZWAHN NWASHN
  GUYANA, NEW NAME OF FORMER BRITISH COLONY OF GUIANA AFTER DECLAR-
ATION OF INDEPENDENCE — GHEE-AH'-NAH.
  MILTON OBOTE, UGANDA OFFICIAL IS CENTER OF POLITICAL TURMOIL — OH-
BOH'-TAY.
  TUY HOA, SCENE OF BUDDHIST DEMONSTRATIONS IN VIET NAM — TWEE HWAH.
  GROTON, CONNECTICUT, SCENE OF SEA TRIALS OF NUCLEAR SUBMARINE
"FLASHER" — GRAHT'-UN

United Press Broadcast Wire.

Types of Broadcasts

There are several types of television and radio news broadcasts. The
most common is the straight news presentation, which may be seen or heard
in 5-, 10- or 15-minute segments, presenting the news without editorial comment. There are also commentator-personalities who present news analyses
and/or personal opinions on the news. In recent years news analysis in depth,
stressing feature stories and dramatic aspects of the news, has become more
common. Networks and stations frequently have "specials" which probe the
news. Many of these programs utilize serious research and present their findings in documentary or semi-documentary form. Edward R. Murrow and Fred
W. Friendly were among the pioneers in this field with the "Hear It Now" and
"See It Now" series. Other news program types include the press conference,
the panel and the interview. We will not discuss these types here, but will
examine them in the chapter dealing with "talks" programs.

In addition to the general news program types, there may be programs
devoted to specific topics, such as the international scene, the financial reports,
garden news, women's news, educational or campus news and so forth. The
approaches within these categories may vary, of course, such as stressing the
public service aspect or the human interest elements.

Most news programs originate in the studio, live. Some, particularly the
feature story and documentary types, are often recorded or filmed. There are
also multiple news pickups from various studios, involving reporters closer to
the scenes of the events. The networks frequently present news roundups,
either from various parts of the country or, in radio, from various parts of the
world. There are also frequent — though, perhaps, not frequent enough —
on-the-spot news broadcasts which show or narrate the event actually taking
place. This latter news program type suggests one of the most important contributions television can make; it deserves fuller exploitation.

Organization of the News Program

There are specific kinds of news programs, as indicated above, including those emphasizing a special topic or a special approach. In the straight news program the writer should look for a clear and logical organization, no matter what the topic or approach. One such organization is for the placement of stories to follow a topical order; that is, the grouping of similar stories into sections, although the order of the sections themselves may be an arbitrary one. A geographical grouping and order is another organizational form. For example, the news coverage may move from North America to Europe to Asia to South America to Africa to the rest of the world. Another frequently used grouping organizes the material into international, national and local news categories. The order of presentation often moves, within these categories, from the largest (international) to the smallest (local). Probably the most common approach is to place the most important story first in order to get and hold the audience's attention, much as does the lead story in the newspaper.

The organization is determined, in part, by the audience being reached. In the mid-morning newscast, for example, stories should be chosen and placed so as to appeal primarily to women, the bulk of the listening group at that time. In the evening the organization should be one that will reach most effectively the male listener or viewer who has just returned from work. The time of day is also important in relation to what the audience already knows of the news. In the early morning newscast it is desirable to review the previous day's important late stories. In the late evening broadcasts the current day's news should be reviewed and the audience should be prepared for the next day's possible happenings.

The physical format of the news show may vary. It may begin with an announcer giving the headlines, then a commercial, and then the commentator coming in with the details. It may start with the commentator himself beginning directly with the news. It may be a roundup of different reporters in different geographical areas. A simple, direct, and frequently used format is that of the Murrow show on page 92.

● In the following pages, purposely presented in haphazard order, are the contents of a 9 a.m. CBS Radio Network news broadcast.

1) How would you rearrange this material to develop a news broadcast oriented around a clear, effective organization? Organize the newscast along geographical lines; organize it according to international, national and local news; organize it along topical lines, grouping similar types of stories; organize it according to the importance of the stories. After the major stories are organized, where would you place the "fills"? The "briefs"?

2) After you have practiced organizing the material, analyze the writing itself to determine whether: the five W's are clearly included; the principle of conflict is utilized; clarity, simplicity and the direct statement are evident; informality is present.

3) What kind of news broadcast is this? Straight news? Commentary? Documentary? Rewrite this news broadcast into at least one form other than its present orientation.

CBS NEWS — TEN MINUTE HOURLY RADIO
00:00 SFX UP & UNDER FOR:
                This is CBS News . . . .
(HEADLINE SUMMARY)

VIETNAM: U-S jets strike closer-than-ever to Hanoi; Buddhist leader pushes for an end
to anti-government demonstrations...
CAPITOL HILL: Secretary Rusk goes before the Senate Foreign Relations committee,
again....
THE NATO CRISIS: French and West German foreign-ministers talk it over in Bonn....

        These and other top stories of this hour on CBS Radio News.
00:29   (one second pause)
00:30   This is Mike Wallace in New York

VIET

        American Air Force jets have come closer than ever before to the North Vietnamese
capital of Hanoi . . . coming in at low altitude, to attack Russian-built missile-sites and a
radar complex, just outside the city.
        A U.S. spokesman in Saigon said the missile-sites were 15 and 17 miles south of Hanoi,
. . . and that they apparently were completely knocked out. Only one missile was fired at the
incoming planes . . . and it missed. All the U.S. planes returned safely.
        Reaction from Hanoi was swift and predictable: the North Vietnamese New Agency said
an urgent protest had been sent to the International Control Commission.
        In South Viet Nam, the country's most-militant Buddhist leader — 45-year old Thich
Tri Quang — barnstormed through rebellious cities in the northern provinces today . . .
calling for an end to anti-government demonstrations. But he warned that the Buddhists will
not ease their pressure for new elections, which the Saigon government has promised within the next 3 to 5 months.

GOLDWATER

        Back in this country, former Senator Barry Goldwater – (in copyright interview in U-S
News and World Report) – says today that the war in Viet Nam is going badly, because –
in his words – we are still not trying to win.

LONDON

        Published reports in Johannesburg said today that more than enough oil is now being
transported across the South African border into Rhodesia to maintain the breakaway
colony's needs. Meanwhile, in London, Prime Minister Harold Wilson met today with senior
British Cabinet members, to discuss future moves in the government's drive to dry up
Rhodesian oil-supplies.

POLAND

        Poland's Communist chief and the head of that nation's Roman Catholic Church were
only a mile apart yesterday . . . but, philosophically, they were widely separated, as each
spoke out on church-state policy. Communist party leader Wladyslaw Gomulka denounced
the Catholic primate, Stefan Cardinal Wysznski as "an irresponsible shepherd." Cardinal
Wysznski, in a more conciliatory tone, said the Catholics want to cooperate with the nation,
because it needs God.
        The cardinal has invited Pope Paul and other church leaders to attend ceremonies on
May 3rd — commemorating one thousand years of Christianity in Poland . . . but the government, so far as is known, has not issued any visas.

COAL

        The nation's largest soft-coal strike in 15 years enters its 2nd week today, with thou-
sands of miners off the job, in half-a-dozen states. Contract talks between the striking union and the coal-operators are reported still deadlocked. Coal stockpiles at the nation's
steel-mills continue to dwindle, and production cutbacks are forecast if the walkout lasts
much longer.

FOREIGN RELATIONS

In Washington, the Congress resumes its work — following an Easter recess — and, once again, top attention is paid to Viet Nam. On tap today, another session of the Senate Foreign Relations Committee . . . with Secretary-of-State Dean Rusk the star witness. Day-after tomorrow, Defense-Secretary Robert McNamara is scheduled to go before the committee.

Meanwhile, some congressmen — particularly on the Republican side — say that holiday pulse-taking among voters in their districts pointed up a growing concern among Americans with the war in Viet Nam.

President Johnson, by the way, is still at his Texas ranch . . . although he's scheduled to return to Washington this week, possibly tonight.

NATO

The foreign-ministers of France and West Germany began talks today in Bonn on the future of European defense; the first such meeting since French President DeGaulle decided to pull his country out of the NATO alliance. They're trying to work out an agreement on the status of French troops in West Germany — some 72-thousand of them — after the withdrawal. DeGaulle has indicated the French forces will go home, rather than be subjected to any new allied controls . . . and the West Germans are seeking assurances from Paris that the French troops, in the event of war, will be available for a common-defense effort.

"A" — :30 fill

Two Johns Hopkins University scientists say that new studies indicate there are large regions on the planet Venus where man would find the temperature comfortable . . . and where life as we know it "is likely to exist." Dr. William Flummer and Dr. John Strong — writing in the current issue of the Astrophysical Journal — further say that Venus appears to be the only planet in the solar-system which could readily support life.
But not near Venus' equator, where the temperature reaches 580 degrees.

"B" — :30 fill

An 11-year research project, published today in Boston, has come up with some new conclusions about human sexual response. The study, dealing with the reactions of 382 women and 312 men between the ages of 18 and 89, is said to be the most wide ranging treatment of the subject since the publication of the Kinsey report nearly a generation ago.

BRIEFS

Union electricians, at dawn today, set up picket-lines at all 5 entrances to Cape Kennedy's space-complex . . . in a wage dispute with a California aerospace firm. It was not immediately clear whether the Cape's 3-thousand man construction work-force would honor the picket-lines.

In an East German courtroom today three men were sentenced to prison-terms ranging from 12 years to life . . . for spying for the West. Two of the defendants — a West Berlin butcher and a Dresden schoolteacher — admitted they'd spied for the C-I-A in East Germany. The third man — an East Berliner — confessed to working for the West German Secret Service for 12 years.

FEATURE

A leading British psychiatrist arrives in the United States today, with word that we are "the most worried people in the world."
Dr. Joshua Bierer, editor in chief of the International Journal of Social Psychiatry, says that prosperity . . . and women . . . are the root of our trouble.
Prosperity confuses us, he says.
But women, they're worse. They rule American society, according to the doctor. He says American men, having worked themselves to death, leave rich widows . . . so the United States has become a matriarchy, which he finds unhealthy.
Concludes Dr. Bierer: "The whole American society is in danger."
He'll be here for three weeks, to help straighten us out.

Mike Wallace, CBS News, New York.

Script written by John Armstrong, CBS Radio News.

98

Another organizational approach frequently used is the concentration on one major news story, with the orientation of all other news around that story. This kind of news-in-depth approach sometimes requires the incorporation of film (for television) or tape recordings (for radio). For example, Edward R. Murrow began one news broadcast with: *

"This is the news:

The Federal Reserve Board today cut the margin requirement on stock purchases from 70 to 50 percent."

(Mr. Murrow went on to give the details of the story, indicating the stand of the federal government. Then he stated:)

"President Eisenhower told his first news conference in two and a half months that he has no intention of asking Congress for any direct economic controls.

"The first question put to President Eisenhower . . . was . . . Here is Mr. Eisenhower's reply."

(The taped reply, plus questions from a reporter and further answers were inserted at this point in the news broadcast. Murrow introduced similar taped excerpts of the President's news conference. For example, Murrow stated:)

"Later, in the news conference, a reporter asked Mr. Eisenhower to expand on what he said in his State of the Union message about unification of the armed forces."

(The taped reply of the President followed.)

The news broadcast developed into an exploration, in terms of the President's taped replies to reporter's questions, of other important news of the day, including foreign affairs, national defense, and Eisenhower's physical health. Following the presentation of the taped excerpts of the news conference, Murrow narrated the other news.

Content Approaches

Some news broadcasts deal exclusively with the straight news, giving it without comment or coloration. Other broadcasts interpret the news, through objective analysis, or color it through purely subjective personal opinion. Some broadcasts combine two or more elements, unifying the actual news story with an interpretation or prognostication of its implications.

The following example of the personal analysis approach was selected from an Edward P. Morgan radio news broadcast (February 15, 1966), not only as an example of approach, but because of its special pertinence for the student, practitioner and critic of the mass media.

A crisis in the broadcasting industry, in which the public has an enormous stake, broke into the open today. The resignation of Fred W. Friendly as president of CBS News was not a whimsical decision. It was not caused by a mere clash of personalities. The issue was far more basic. It involved the responsibility of radio and television of keeping the public informed on matters of major concern. The incident which triggered Friendly's withdrawal was an order of his newly-established superior, John A. Schneider, cancelling live television coverage last Wednesday of the Senate Foreign Relations Committee hearings on U. S. policy in Vietnam.

---

* CBS Radio Broadcast

Friendly deplored this "business decision" over "news judgment" and in his letter of resignation to Board Chairman William Paley and CBS President Frank Stanton he wrote that it "makes a mockery of the Paley-Stanton . . . crusade of many years that demands broadest access to Congressional debate . . .

"We cannot, in our public utterances," he went on, "demand such access and then, in one of the crucial debates of our time, abdicate that responsibility."

Friendly added that while he watched the Senate hearings on NBC Thursday morning, CBS was showing "a fifth rerun of 'Lucy', then followed by an eighth rerun of 'The Real McCoys'."

If bitterness is detectable in that passage it is undoubtedly genuine and comes from one of the most respected newsmen in broadcasting. Friendly is every inch in the Edward R. Murrow tradition and won his spurs in TV as producer of Murrow's crusading series of documentaries, "See It Now," and went on to produce the excellent "CBS Reports." He became president of CBS News two years ago.

It now behooves all networks and all stations, radio and TV, to examine, critically, their news and public affairs policies. As for ABC, it has plans for early modest and later major growth in these areas but some critics seem to find its intentions wanting of performance. Yesterday New York Timesman Jack Gould wrote that "journalists in TV note with apprehension that the American Broadcasting Company appears to have virtually withdrawn from competition in special public-service programming."

It is pointless, for the moment, to make comparisons. The stark fact is that the broadcasting industry as a whole consistently moves along the minimal instead of the maximal lines of its responsibilities in news and public affairs. The explanation is simple: money. With the rarest of fleeting exceptions, special news broadcasts, documentaries, panel shows and studio discussions cost more money than they bring in, if any. Undoubtedly the new CBS major-domo, John Schneider, saved the network a lot of revenue last week by continuing regular programming—soap operas, reruns and other fun and games—instead of tuning in on the testimony before the Foreign Relations Committee of one of the country's top experts on Communists and Communism, George F. Kennan. Undoubtedly too, countless housewives and others watching would have switched the hearings off.

That is not the point. The point is that broadcasting has far more of a responsibility to the public than pandering to the widest common denominator of its tastes for profit. It is no defense to argue that special programs of information are a burden on the budget. Broadcasting is a rich and thriving industry and it can afford to absorb a lot more losses than it has ever thought of in fulfilling its trust as a public service. It is no defense, either, to argue that "nobody looks or listens" to such programs as a Congressional hearing. There is always an audience and because it is small does not mean that it is not important. The opposite may often be the case.

Regard the following spectacle: the United States is deeply involved in a bloody conflict in Vietnam which could precipitate or—possibly—avert World War III. More and more men, money and machines are being committed to the battle. The issues are confusing, the objectives blurred. Senator Fulbright's committee hearings provide the first sustained, sober, public review of the U.S. position in this crisis. Is it frivolous to think that these proceedings, however inconclusive they may be, are not of less value to the population than "Queen For a Day"?

Some of the broadcast coverage of the war in Vietnam has been magnificent. Some of the attempts on radio and television to clarify the issues have been courageous and illuminating. But the performance—in the printed media as well, for that matter—has not been good enough. Nor has it been good enough on other major stories. The news is capsulized, synthesized, sensationalized and approached like a gladiatorial event, including "body counts" on the battlefield. Is this the way to employ the most marvelous instruments yet invented to convey news and ventilate issues?

Fred Friendly called his resignation as president of CBS News a "matter of conscience." One wonders anxiously whether his courageous act of protest will impel the decisionmakers of broadcasting to check and see what they did with theirs. Radio and television displayed what electronic journalism can be on the weekend of November 22, 1963. These talents are adaptable to other events besides the assassination of a president.

Edward P. Morgan, ABC Washington Correspondent

The following broadcast by Edward P. Morgan illustrates the combination of news and opinion analysis. The first part of the broadcast is oriented first around a dramatic lead item, and then around the crucial United States concern which serves as a focal point for much of the rest of the news. The last part of the broadcast is devoted to Mr. Morgan's analysis of a news situation, with no attempt made to disguise the analysis as straight news, something occasionally done by broadcasters.

Good evening. Here is the shape of the news.

A heart attack has taken the life of Indian Prime Minister Shastri just hours after he signed a limited agreement with Pakistani President Ayub Khan that might bring some slight measure of stability to troubled Asia.
Shastri, who was 61 years old, had a history of heart disease, suffered a serious attack in 1959, again in 1964 shortly after succeeding the late Jawaharlal Nehru as premier. He died in Tashkent, Russia, where he and Ayub had been meeting — at Soviet invitation — to discuss differences. The agreement they signed calls for withdrawal of troops from disputed border areas in Kashmir, restoration of full diplomatic relations. By helping to work out the agreement, the Russians scored a major diplomatic victory over Communist China, which had backed Pakistan in the fighting over Kashmir.
President Johnson and U. N. Secretary General U Thant both hailed the agreement as worthwhile, despite the Russian role. Their statements came before Shastri's death. Shastri was to visit the White House in February. The President mourned his loss. Indian Home Minister Nanda has been sworn in to head a caretaker government.

The White House says it is a "safe deduction" that the U.S. has been in direct contact with North Vietnam in efforts to end the war in Vietnam. A Yale professor just back from Hanoi charged yesterday there had been no such contact. The White House also disclosed today that Ambassador-at-Large Harriman's next stop will be Saigon. He is now in Australia.

The second session of the 89th Congress was gaveled to order today. Members faced a touchy "guns or butter" debate at the start, elections at the finish. Both the Senate and the House took up only routine matters, recessed until Wednesday, when both chambers will meet separately, then convene jointly to hear President Johnson deliver his State of the Union Address. It is expected to deal largely with Vietnam, probably will sound the legislative tone for months to come.
The Republicans, outnumbered 2 to 1 in both houses, have served notice they will fight for reductions in domestic Great Society spending so that war costs can be met without a large budget deficit. Other important legislation is expected to relate to labor, legislative reapportionment, discrimination on juries, consumer protection. Reportedly, the Administration will ask this year for about 60 billion dollars for the military, almost half the anticipated record budget of some 115 billion dollars. But the White House hopes the booming economy will bring in enough added tax money to provide for reasonable continuation of Great Society programs, without a tax increase.
The "guns or butter" debate is expected to go far beyond a simple dialogue over money. So far, polls indicate a safe majority of Americans back the Administration's handling of the War. But the stuttering peace offensive could spell trouble at home, as well as overseas. Typical of the Vietnam debate beginning on Capitol Hill, Republican Senator John Sherman Cooper of Kentucky proposed today that the U.S. offer a five-year ceasefire, to be followed by a vote in North and South Vietnam on whether to reunite under a common government. But Democratic Congressman Mendel Rivers of South Carolina urged an immediate resumption of U. S. air strikes against North Vietnam "to help Ho Chi Minh make up his mind."

The lull has now lasted 16 days but still the Communists offer nothing but scorn and belligerence. In South Vietnam, the bitter ground fighting continues, while U.S. fighter-bombers — apparently operating from bases in Thailand — are smashing night and day against hundreds of North Vietnamese filtering through Laos into South Vietnam. In one of three large ground operations today, U. S. troops moved to within a few yards of the Cambodian border in search of guerrillas. American officials claim Cambodia is a refuge for some Red troops, have warned they may be pursued. But Cambodian officials deny the charge and newsmen have found little evidence of Communist troop activity within Cambodia. Today, Great Britain rebuked the Soviet Union for criticizing U. S. policies regarding Laos and Cambodia.

The most controversial domestic legislation the second session of the 89th Congress is likely to face will be a renewed effort to repeal the section of the Taft-Hartley Act that permits states to enact so-called "right-to-work" laws. Another serious controversy could develop over a proposal to water down the Supreme Court's "one man-one vote" ruling. A strong effort also will be made to push through a higher minimum wage and a revision of unemployment compensation regulations. Democratic Congressman William F. Ryan of New York announced just today he will seek repeal of a controversial section of the Medicare Act that requires some applicants to disclaim any Communist affiliations.

Before going to Capitol Hill today, a number of legislators — along with President Johnson — attended a special congressional prayer service at National Presbyterian Church. The Senate swore in a new member, Democrat Harry Byrd Jr. of Virginia, to succeed his father, who has retired. The House took in two new members, California Democrat Thomas Rees and Ohio Republican Clarence J. Brown, Jr., who was elected to fill the unexpired term of his late father. Byrd was given a seat on the powerful Senate Armed Services Committee, an unusual assignment for a freshman legislator.

The Georgia legislature opened its 1966 session today and immediately bogged down in a dispute over whether to seat a newly-elected Negro state representative who has denounced U.S. policy in Vietnam. A committee that includes two of the legislature's nine other Negro members was appointed to study the case of Julian Bond. Civil rights leaders threatened to demonstrate if Bond is not eventually seated.

At Hattiesburg, Mississippi, one person was fatally burned and two others were injured when a grocery store and home belonging to a civil rights worker was burned. Police blame nightriders.

The police commissioner of Baltimore announced today he will retire. Yesterday, a special committee reported there is much organized crime and "flagrant" vice in the city. The report also said some public officials may have been "reached" by unlawful elements.

Still no end in sight to the 10-day-old New York City transit strike. Today's traffic crush was the tightest yet. Reportedly, the economic squeeze is growing worse, is beginning to spread to other parts of the nation dependent on New York products and services.

A labor demonstration in the tense Dominican city of Santo Domingo got out of hand briefly today. One person was fatally shot when troops moved in to return order.

The African State of Burundi has ordered the ouster of the U.S. ambassador and two American embassy members for alleged contact with "conspirators." Apparently, the charges relate to an abortive coup attempted last October.
That's the shape of the news. In just a moment I'll have a comment.

Thanks to the astuteness and candor of a Senate team headed by Majority Leader Mike Mansfield of Montana, the government and the country have been brought still closer to the issue which will dominate almost every action of the second session of the 89th Congress — namely, the war in Vietnam.

Even on opening day, of course, there were predictable diversions. The Republicans wasted no time in hitting out at big government and Democratic spending. House Minority Leader Ford of Michigan called for an examination of the size of the executive branch and Congressman Cunningham, Republican from Nebraska, warned Congress will have to "prune down" the Great Society spending programs ". .so hastily enacted last year."

At a dulcet and dainty little ceremony on the Senate side, the senior Senator from Maine, Margaret Chase Smith, looking far younger and fresher than her own 68 years, presented to Senate Minority Leader Dirksen of Illinois, who has just turned 70 himself, a floral bouquet in the shimmering shape of the fountain of youth as a tribute to his leadership of the loyal opposition. A marigold man by gardening choice, Dirksen also wore in his lapel a red rose as big as a tail-light, to complement the traditional floral adornment of Senator Smith.

But nobody on Capitol Hill kidded himself that there would be any surplus of hearts and flowers at this election year session. And the harshness of circumstance was underlined by a report, released yesterday, to the Senate Foreign Relations Committee by Mansfield and four other senators on their 35-day round-the-world pursuit of a solution to the Vietnam crisis. With Mansfield went Democrats Muskie of Maine, Inouye of Hawaii, Republicans Boggs of Delaware and Aiken of Vermont. Their grim conclusion: continued fighting in Vietnam may lead to a general war in Asia while there is also little hope now of a satisfactory settlement by negotiation. President Johnson, who endorsed the trip, is said to have remarked a little ruefully that they didn't need to girdle the globe to discover that; he was aware of the difficulties before the senators set out. What he wanted was some sound suggestions leading to a solution.

The traveling senators have performed a service, however, in pointing up anew the monstrous and enveloping dilemma of the war. They noted that despite some sympathy for the U.S. policy and position, no other country was giving or was likely to give more than the merest token of military support in South Vietnam except South Korea — confronted herself, paradoxically, with a tenuous truce at home. They noted that "none of the nations in the area desires the domination of either China or the United States," though, if given a choice, these countries would not welcome withdrawal of American influence from Southeast Asia entirely. They found "no reason to believe that the Soviet Union is anxious to play a significant role (now) to assist in bringing an end to hostilities in Vietnam."

The senators' report seemed tempted at times to speak almost in terms of the "futility" of the American military assignment. It noted, to be sure, that without strengthening of U.S. support last summer South Vietnamese resistance might well have collapsed. But given the escalation, the Viet Cong escalated in response and furthermore appears capable of increasing its strength by even more substantial numbers in a short time. Meanwhile the "same over-all control of the country remains about as it was at the beginning of 1965: some 60 per cent of the population under some sort of government control, 40 per cent directly or indirectly dominated by the Viet Cong, who also control or threaten large geographical areas of the country except the strongholds of the cities."

Thus there is "no assurance as to what ultimate increase in American military commitment will be required before the conflict is terminated" because instead of a defined military objective the situation is "open-ended. . . . All of mainland Southeast Asia, at least, cannot be ruled out as a potential battlefield." The senators noted the war "has already expanded significantly into Laos and is beginning to lap over the Cambodian border while pressures increase in the northeast of Thailand. ...

"...The situation, as it now appears," the report concluded darkly, "offers only the very slim prospect of a just settlement by negotiations or the alternative prospect of a continuance of the conflict in the direction of a general war on the Asian mainland."

Under similar if less spread-eagled circumstances in World War I, Marshal Foch sent his famous telegram to his superior, Marshal Joffre, noting his predicament and observing: "situation excellent; I attack." But far more than a battle is now at stake. The important thing for the country to grasp at this juncture is how terribly painful are the alternatives left to the president. And the important thing for the White House to remember is that the durability of public support depends largely on the understanding of the ramifications of those alternatives. If we're going somewhere we need to know where, why and the probable cost of the journey.

This is Edward P. Morgan saying goodnight from Washington.

Edward P. Morgan, ABC Washington Correspondent.

Special TV Techniques

The types, styles, organization and approaches are essentially the same for the television and for the radio news broadcast.

The radio program can incorporate live interviews, taped interviews and reports, live remotes consisting of interviews or reports, and live or taped sounds of the event.

In television the physical setting as well as the news content is important. The reporter should have an interesting visual personality. The content must be presented so that there is physical action. For example, the nightly weather report of Tex Antoine on WABC-TV, New York, employs Mr. Antoine's artistic abilities to create movement through drawings and to indicate the next day's weather by putting the appropriate outer clothing on a "dummy" used as part of the program format.

Television news should stress the visual and may use photographs, video-tape, film, slides, inanimate objects or live guests. Television commentary frequently is used to caption silent film of the news event. When insufficient time or great distance has made it impossible to show film of the event, a blown-up photo of the scene or of the persons involved may be used as background.

The following excerpts from the rundown sheet and the script of a Huntley-Brinkley television news broadcast illustrate the use of the live personality, film, video-tape, static visuals (such as slides and maps), and the live switch or remote. Note the organizational approach incorporating various geographical vantage- and viewpoints. The symbols on the rundown sheet refer to descriptions of materials and to audio and video means of presenting those materials, such as SOF for sound-on-film, VTR for video tape recorder, VIZ for visual, SL for slide, FM for film.

The rundown sheet is important for the director and for the technicians, and lists not only materials and means, but the exact timing of each segment. On the final script, in preparation for the program, the director designates the specific places where the visual is to be placed, where to "roll film" and where other audio and video techniques begin and end. The numbers at the far left of the rundown sheet correspond to the numbered pages of the final script. Examine particularly how VIZ, VTR pretape, film, live switch and PAD are used in the rundown sheet and script.

> ● *1) Analyze the following script according to the principles of good newswriting, including the use of the five W's, and the principles of conflict, clarity and informality.*
>
> *2) What is the organizational approach of this news broadcast? Is it the most effective one that could have been used with the news stories presented?*
>
> *3) After studying the use of television techniques in this script, reorganize and rewrite the radio script on pages 97-98 for television presentation, including the necessary video materials and directions.*

THE HUNTLEY-BRINKLEY REPORT

MAY 24, 1966

TIME		SUBJECT	AUDIO	VIDEO	CAMERA
1	6:30:00 (:10)	OPENING A) HUNTLEY B) BRINKLEY	6A WASH	6A WASH	
	6:30:10 (:10)	FM: HB TITLE & ANNCR	KILL SOF 6A. .ANNCR	35 COLOR R1-1P	
	6:30:20 (:10)	ANNCR & VIZ OR SL — OPEN BB DRISTAN TABLETS	6A. .ANNCR	6A. .VIZ OR SL "DRISTAN"	

SEGMENT I (NOTE N.Q.D. COMM #1)

2	6:30:30 (:45)	HUNTLEY (VIET POLITICAL)	6A	6A	
3	6:31:15 (3:45)	VTR (PRETAPED) OR LIVE "L.A. #1 — DANANG" (RON NESSEN)	SOT OR LA	VTO OR LA COLOR	

STANDBY — PRETAPED FM IF LA FAILS:

	(1:45)	VTR (PRETAPED) "SAIGON RIOTS" (DEAN BRELIS)	(16 COLOR SOF — INT) (RS— NS— ES)		
4	6:35:00 (:20)	HUNTLEY (INTRO)	6A	6A	
5	6:35:20 (1:45)	VTR (PRETAPED) OR LIVE "L.A. #2 — SAIGON" (DAVID BURRINGTON)	SOT OR LA	VTO OR LA COLOR	
6	6:37:05 (:05)	VIZMO H&B		6A. .VIZ H&B	
7	6:37:10 (1:00)	N.Q.D. FM COMM #1 CHEF/DRISTAN #14	SOF	35 COL (:30) 35 POS (:30) R1—1P	

SEGMENT II

8	6:38:10 (:40)	HUNTLEY & VIZ (MILITARY AND INTRO)	6A	6A. .VIZ MAP	
9	6:38:50 (2:05)	NY FM & SUPERS "U THANT"	SOF/INT TAPE RA	16 COLOR RA SUPERS: THANT AND ATLANTIC CITY	

SEGMENT IV

23	6:47:20 (:30)	HUNTLEY (INTRO)	6A	6A	
24	6:47:50 (4:00)	VTR (PRETAPED) "L.A. #3 — WATTS" (JOHN DANCEY)	SOT	VTO	
25	6:51:50 (:15)	HUNTLEY (AUTO SALES)	6A	6A	

26	6:52:05 (:30)	WASH #3 (PAD)	WASH	WASH
27	6:52:35 (1:15)	HUNTLEY & VIZS (PAD)	6A	6A..VIZS
28	6:53:50 (:15)	HUNTLEY & VIZ (CLOSE PAD)	6A	6A VIZ STOX
29	6:54:05 (1:00)	FM COMM #5 POLIDENT #PD—138—60	SOF	35 POS R1—R2

SEGMENT V

30	6:55:05 (2:30)	WASH #4 (CLOSE)	WASH	WASH
	6:57:35 (:05)	G'NIGHT DAVE & G'NIGHT FOR NBC NEWS	6A	6A
31	6:57:40 (:45)	FM COMM #6 AQUA VELVA LATHER/LOTION #SL—702—30—BW—REV/AV—219—15—BW—rev	SOF	35 POS R1—R2
32	6:58:25 (:09)	VIZ & MUSIC	6A..MUSIC	6A..VIZ HB RPT

OPENING

HUNTLEY:	Chet Huntley, NBC NEWS, New York
BRINKLEY:	And David Brinkley, NBC NEWS, Washington.
FM HB TITLE & ANNOUNCER VO: KILL SOF	and here is the news, assembled for television every weekday night by the world's largest and most comprehensive broadcast news organization and brought to you in NBC color by...

COMMERCIAL

	The city of Danang returned to normal today, but 55 miles to the north the citizens of Hue continued to broadcast defiance of the
VIZ: MAP	S. Vietnamese central government
	In Saigon, the ruling junta appeared before about 400 persons representing all groups of the country except the Buddhists who sent only observers. Premier Ky and the head of state, Lt. Gen. Van Thieu, told the conference that order had to be restored, that remaining dissidence would be put down with as little bloodshed as possible.
VIZ: GEN THIEU	Gen. Van Thieu said the junta is thinking of adding 5 civilians and he pledged that the election for the constitutional assembly will be held on September 11th. During the meeting a small band of Buddhists and students demonstrated in front of the American Embassy.
	United States military headquarters in Saigon announced today that the shot which killed a S. Vietnamese soldier yesterday was fired by an American after all.

HUNTLEY	In Da Nang, an estimated 80 people, mostly civilians, died in the 8 day struggle. Another 412 were injured. Ron Nesson reports on the last moments of the uprising:
LIVE SWITCH (3:45) "LOS ANGELES #1" (RON NESSEN)	
ENDS ...	This is Ron Nessen, NBC NEWS, at the Tin Hoi Pagoda in Danang."
HUNTLEY	During the past four days, Buddhists in Saigon have poured into the streets in one violent protest after another. In countermeasures, riot police, for the first time, marched to the gates of the Vin Wao Dao pagoda and fired teargas into the crowds. Today they sealed off the Buddhist Institute, center of Buddhist unrest. David Burrington reports:
LIVE SWITCH (1:45) "LOS ANGELES #2" (DAVID BURRINGTON)	
ENDS ...	David Burrington, NBC NEWS, Saigon."

* * *

INTO NEW ORLEANS	
HUNTLEY: VIZ: WEBER	Private Adam Weber, Jr., was inducted into the Army last November, assigned to the infantry, and sent to Vietnam.
	Weber, a former seminary student, now faces a court martial for refusal to bear arms. Weber says he is willing to serve but not to kill.
	In New Orleans, his father was interviewed by WDSU-TV.
VTR PRETAPE (:40) "NEW ORLEANS" (WEBER) (SOF)	
SOF ENDS...	"....I imagine that it put a strain on him and then, knowing that he would be inducted one day."
PRIMARIES	
HUNTLEY:	In Oregon today, Democratic voters went to the polls to choose between two senatorial candidates who represented opposing views on the war in Vietnam.
VIZ:M&D	Howard Morgan, a former State Democratic Chairman, said he opposed the war, and Representative Robert Duncan declared his full support for the Administration's policies.
	So far, voters have turned out in only moderate numbers.
VIZ:H&B	But in Florida, Democrats turned out in nearly record numbers to nominate a candidate for Governor in one of the bitterest political fights in the state's history. It was between Miami's liberal Mayor Robert King High and Haydon Burns, Florida's present conservative Governor.
WASH #2 (:30) (PAD)	
BRINKLEY ENDS. . . .	...and said the belief that if negroes move into a neighborhood the values go down is a myth and he said those opposed to open housing are either guilty of race bias or ignorance."

* * *

WASH #3 (:30)
(PAD)

BRINKLEY ENDS. . . .   "CHET"

CLOSE PAD
VIZ:STOX   Prices rose again today on the New York Stock Exchange. The
                             Dow Jones Industrial Average gained almost six points.

WASH #4 (2:30)
(DIRKSEN)   fm ends... let you see my operation?
                                              (APPLAUSE)

BRINKLEY ENDS. . . .   Goodnight Chet."

HUNTLEY: Goodnight David and goodnight for NBC NEWS.

SPORTS

Sports usually fall into the area of news and special events. The writing of sports material is similar to the writing of news material. If anything, the style for sports broadcasts must be even more precise, clearer and more direct than for news broadcasts. The language is more colloquial, and though technical terms are to be avoided, the writer of sports may use many more expressions relating to a specialized area than can the writer of news.

Types of Sports Programs

The straight sportscast concentrates on recapitulation of the results of sports events and on news relating to sports in general. Some sportscasts are oriented solely to summaries of results. These summaries may come from press service reports or private sources of the station. Material which is rewritten from newspaper accounts or which is taken from press service reports should be adapted to fit the purpose of the program and the personality of the broadcaster.

The sports feature program may include live or recorded (taped or filmed) interviews with sports personalities, anecdotes or dramatizations of events in sports, human interest or background stories on personalities or events, or remotes relating to sports but not in themselves an actual sporting event.

The sports program may amalgamate several individual types or, as in the case of the after-event critique or summary, may concentrate on one type alone.

The most popular sports broadcast is, of course, the on-the-spot broadcast of an event while it is taking place. In some instances economic, travel or legal factors prevent the direct broadcast of the event and it is reconstructed via telegraphed reports or, in the case of television, is shown on film or video tape some time after the event has taken place.

Organization

The formats for the sports broadcast parallel those of the news broadcast. The most common approach is to take the top sport of the season, give all the results and news of that sport, and work toward the least important sport. In such an organization the most important story of the most important sport is given first unless a special item from another area of sports overrides it. Within each sport the general pattern in this organization includes the results first, the general news (such as trades, injuries and so forth) next and future events last. The local sports scene is usually coordinated with the national sports news. There are, of course, variations of this format, with all the results of all sports sometimes presented first, and the general news following.

> ● *Note the breakdown of stories in the excerpts and topic statements of the 15-minute sports broadcast below. Compare the style of writing with that of the regular news broadcast, particularly the simplicity and informality, and the use of specialized language.*

(Opening: Monday, May 29)

Good evening, everyone. This is Stan Lomax with the day's doings in the world of sport. The holiday eve found a general lull as far as sports scheduling was concerned In baseball, there are three major league contests on the day's program: one this afternoon and two this evening. And by playing night games the Boston Red Sox and Los Angeles clubs are not permitted to play double headers tomorrow. In fact, the holiday—which in years past was automatically given over to double headers—will have six tomorrow, with two single daylight games and one night contest.

New York will be without baseball tomorrow—with the Yankees out of town in Boston. Jersey City has an afternoon double header with Charleston at Roosevelt stadium, 1:30, which gives over the city to soccer and horse racing.

We'll pick up the day's happenings in a minute—after this message from your GENERAL TIRE DEALER.

COMMERCIAL - LIVE

[Results of the Day's Baseball Game.]

(Follo Game)

And that was the complete picture as far as daylight competition in the major leagues was concerned. There are two games listed for this evening—one in each league. In Boston, the Yankees—who are having their troubles with pitching—are to play the Red Sox—a club beset by an inability to hit.

By splitting yesterday's long double header with the last place Chicago White Sox, the New Yorkers retained a half game lead over the Baltimore Orioles in their duel for third place. The Yanks are still one full game in back of second place Cleveland—and four and a half away from the pace setting Detroit Tigers.

Manager Ralph Houk—who has been more than patient with his starters—who seldom get past the fifth inning—admitted today that he was pondering a change in his pitching assignments. Apparently there will be no change in personnel—since no club will part with a reliable starter. And the farm system has no one ready to step in as anything more than a reliever. Which may mean that one—or two—of the men designated as starters will go to the bull pen. And a couple of the younger men will be promoted to starting berths.

Unlike July Fourth—which has the unreliable tradition that the leaders after the day's shooting will meet in the world series—Memorial Day carries no particular significance. As of yet no one in either league has shown overpowering class—and the races are still wide open. Even the White Sox—in last place—believe that they'll find the answer any day now and become a factor in the American League race.

Getting back to the Yankees—the delicate pitching situation has forced manager Houk to nominate left hander Whitey Ford to work in Fenway Park this evening—something that usually has been avoided in the past. That towering left field wall—so close to home plate—makes it rough for a left hander facing right handed pull hitters. But it's a matter of necessity, and Whitey will make one of his rare starts in Back Bay tonight.

[About 30 seconds on Ford and his opposing pitcher of the evening, including their records against the opposing clubs.]

The other clubs in the American League are not scheduled tonight. The program tomorrow has the Yanks and Red Sox playing a single game in Boston. Los Angeles and Washington play one in Washington. And the double headers will pair the Minnesota Twins and Cleveland Indians in Cleveland; Kansas City Athletics and Detroit Tigers in Detroit; Baltimore Orioles and Chicago White Sox in Chicago.

In the National League, the St. Louis Cardinals open a Pacific Coast trip in Los Angeles this evening. The Red Birds are still in sixth place—but only six and a half from the top. And a good trip against Los Angeles and San Francisco would give Solly Hemus' team a springboard to a move upward.

Larry Jackson—whose fractured jaw acquired in spring training caused him to get off to a woeful start, losing his first three decisions—is to work for the Red Birds tonight. Last week Larry won his first game of the season—and it was against Los Angeles in St. Louis. His over-all mark against the West Coasters is 15 and 6. Sandy Koufax—who is 5 and 1 this season—works for the home side and Sandy has one decision over the Cardinals this season. But his lifetime mark is 5 and 5.

The clubs will play their holiday engagement tomorrow night. Other schedules for tomorrow—all double headers—Milwaukee Braves and Philadelphia Phillies at Connie Mack Stadium, Philadelphia; Chicago Cubs and Pittsburgh Pirates in Pittsburgh; Cincinnati Redlegs and San Francisco Giants in San Francisco.

We'll have the boxing and other items of the day in a moment—after this word from BALLANTINE.

COMMERCIAL - TRANSCRIPTION

(College Baseball)

There was a story of interest to college baseball followers in this area—the announce-ment of the District 2 NCAA All-Star team. The group was named by a committee of five coaches representing the district, which takes in New York, New Jersey, Pennsylvania, Maryland and Delaware.

[About one minute containing the names of the players, their positions, schools, and some of their outstanding achievements.]

(Boxing.)

Picking up the boxing: there will be a world's welterweight tussle on the program which opens tonight—a meeting in Los Angeles on Saturday in which Emile Griffith of the Virgin Islands defends his 147 pound title against Gaspar Ortega of Mexico. That's the highlight of an undistinguished week—which also has a world's championship event of sorts in London tomorrow. That would be the European version of the world's bantam-weight championship in which Alphonse Halimi of Algiers meets John Caldwell of Northern Ireland. In this country the National Boxing Association claims Eder Jofre of Brazil is the bantamweight champion. Plans are afoot to have the winner of the bout in London meet Jofre to consolidate the title.

Tonight the St. Nicholas Arena offers a substitute junior welterweight bout in which Jose Stable of Havana opposes Sweet Pea Adams of Philadelphia. Originally, Stephan Redl of Passaic was signed to meet Stable, but Stephan bowed out last week and Adams was secured as his stand-in.

Sweet Pea was known as Sweet Side until a couple of months ago. Under his old knickname he won 16, lost two and had one draw. As Sweet Side he was knocked out by Kenny Lane last fall. Hence the change in names. Stable has won 15, lost one and had one draw, and is currently working on a six straight winning streak.

Wednesday night Flash Elorde of the Phillipines, holder of the Junior Lightweight title, meets Giordano Campari of Italy in Manila in a non-title bout. And the word is this match will draw 30,000 spectators.

110

Saturday night's bout in Los Angeles between Griffith and Ortega was originally scheduled for this past Saturday—but was put over one week when Griffith was forced to stop training by a virus infection. This will be his first title defense—he lifted the crown by knocking out Benny Kid Paret in Miami this past winter.

COMMERCIAL - LIVE

[The following story was taken from the Wire Service. Some of the wording was edited to fit the Broadcaster's style.]

In basketball, the Amateur National Basketball League, the backbone of Amateur Athletic Union (AAU) basketball, has folded.

League President George J. Kolowich of the Denver-Chicago entry announced that the League would suspend operations for one year. He blamed the current point-shaving scandal in college basketball for his league's suspension. But Kolowich said it was hoped the league would be able to resume operations by the 1962-63 season.

The National Basketball League has been on the brink of halting for several years, and the withdrawal of the Cleveland Pipers and the Seattle Bakers after last season didn't help matters.

The League has provided the strongest teams for the National AAU Tournament held in Denver each March. It was formerly known as the National Industrial Basketball League.

"The recent scandals have created a recruiting hazard for corporations in our League," Kolowich said in his announcement.

[About 30 seconds devoted to the scandals and their relationship to the suspension of League operations.]

(Soccer)

In soccer there will be a double header in the International League at the Polo Grounds tomorrow. In the first game the New York Americans are to play Bes-ik-tas of Turkey. And in the afterpiece it will be Kilmarnock of Scotland against Karlsruhe of Germany. The Americans have won two out of two so far—and a success tomorrow would put them in the league lead. Bes-ik-tas was swamped by Bangu of Brazil, the defending champions, yesterday.

In the second game Kilmarnock—winners of its division title last year and loser to Bangu in the playoffs—is favored over the German side—which blows hot and cold.

(Windup)

Now—before we turn back to the baseball for the customary last look at the day's schedule—here's the message from SALEM.

COMMERCIAL - TRANSCRIPTION

In baseball, one daylight game, NATIONAL LEAGUE. In San Francisco: SAN FRANCISCO GIANTS: 1, CINCINNATI REDLEGS: 5. Tonight—ST. LOUIS CARDINALS and LOS ANGELES in Los Angeles. Other clubs not scheduled.

In the AMERICAN LEAGUE—one game scheduled tonight: NEW YORK YANKEES—BOSTON RED SOX in Boston.

Other clubs not scheduled.

IN THE INTERNATIONAL LEAGUE:

JERSEY CITY at ROCHESTER

I'll be back tomorrow night with the day's doings in the world of sports. And until then this is Stan Lomax saying Good Night.

Courtesy of Stan Lomax, Sports Director, WOR.

111

Live Broadcasts

On-the-spot descriptions of events can be extremely exciting. On-the-spot broadcasts technically are special events, which are described in the next chapter. For the purposes of organization, however, an arbitrary differentiation is made here between the sports contest and the sports special event that is not a contest between two known principals. The former is included here, under live sports broadcasts, while the latter will be examined under special events.

Although the jobs of television and radio broadcasters differ, those of the continuity writers are essentially the same. In television the broadcasters are announcers and not narrators, as they are in radio. Even if they wanted to, the television broadcasters would find it difficult to keep up with the action as seen by the audience, except in slow games such as baseball. Since sports are visual to begin with, the less description by the television broadcaster the better. The television announcer is primarily an encyclopedia of background information. The radio announcer needs background information, too, but sometimes is too busy with narration to use very much of it.

The sports broadcaster must have filler material, that is, information relating to pre-event action and color, statistics, form charts, information on the site of the event, on the history of the event, about the participants, human interest stories and similar material which either heighten the audience's interest or help clarify the action to the audience. This material must be written up and must be available to the broadcaster to be used when needed, specifically during lulls in the action, and in pre-game and post-game opening and closing segments. At one time staff writers prepared this material. More recently, sports broadcasters have been hired as experts in their fields and often they are expected to know and provide their own filler material. The primary job of the continuity writer is to outline the format of the live sports event. The following standard outline is one that was used for professional hockey games televised by CBS. Note that the material includes not only the opening and closing format, but contains the commercial format so that the announcer knows when to break, and the lead-in script material for the commercial. Included for the broadcaster's reference is the sponsor schedule for the hockey telecasts. All other material usually is compiled by the broadcaster or broadcasting team. Each page of the opening and closing formats are set up so that after the first page the announcements of network sponsors or local co-op sponsors may be inserted without disrupting the continuity.

VIDEO	AUDIO
Up from black	Sneak theme
FILM	
PROFESSIONAL HOCKEY (Super)	ANNCR: Coming your way now is PROFESSIONAL HOCKEY, the fastest game in the world . . . .
SUPER (NAME OF TEAMS)	and BIG match it is ---- the _____ against the _____ . (Theme up and under)
CBS SPORTS (Super)	ANNCR: This is the _____ in a series of exciting matches that will be brought to you every Saturday afternoon during the season . . .
BEST IN SPORTS (Super)	As part of the continuing effort of CBS SPORTS to present the BEST IN SPORTS all the year around. (Theme up and under)
NATIONAL LEAGUE HOCKEY (Super)	ANNCR: This is an important regular season contest in the National Hockey League . . . hockey's MAJOR league . . .
NAME OF STADIUM (Super)	being brought to you direct from famed _____ in _____ (Theme up and under)
NAME OF TEAM	ANNCR: So now get ready to watch the match between the _____ and the _____ . . .
BUD PALMER and FRED CUSICK (Super)	with description by Bud Palmer and Fred Cusick. Now let's go to (Name of Stadium) _____ (Theme up and hold) By permission of CBS Television Sports.

CLOSING BILLBOARD

VIDEO	AUDIO
PROFESSIONAL HOCKEY	You have just seen a presentation of fast-moving PROFESSIONAL HOCKEY . . .
NATIONAL LEAGUE HOCKEY	one of the big regular season matches of the NATIONAL HOCKEY LEAGUE . . . the MAJOR league of hockey.
	(Theme up and under)
NAME OF TEAMS	Today's exciting contest was between the _____ and the _____ . . .
NAME OF STADIUM	Played on the _____ home ice, the famed _____ in _____ .
	(Theme up and under)
NEXT SATURDAY	We invite you to join us again NEXT Saturday afternoon for another big Professional Hockey Match . . .
NAME OF TEAMS	Next week's televised contest will bring together the (Name of Team) _____ and the (Name of team) _____ at the (Name of Stadium) _____ .
	(Theme up and under)
BUD PALMER AND FRED CUSICK	The description of today's match has been provided by BUD PALMER AND FRED CUSICK . . .
PROFESSIONAL HOCKEY is a CBS TELEVISION NETWORK Presentation PRODUCED BY CBS SPORTS	This presentation of PROFESSIONAL HOCKEY has been produced by CBS SPORTS.
	(Theme up and hold)
SYSTEM	

114

HOCKEY COMMERCIAL FORMAT

Before Opening Face-Off - "Very shortly play will be starting here at (name or arena) and we will have action for you."
(1 minute commercial)

First Period - During 1st period of play three 20 second commercials are to be inserted at the discretion of each co-op station. Audio Cue: "There's a whistle on the ice and the score is _____ & _____ ."

1st pause during play-by-play.	.20 seconds
2nd pause during play-by-play.	.20 seconds
3rd pause during play-by-play.	.20 seconds

End of First Period - "That is the end of the first period and the score is _____ & _____ ."
(1 minute commercial)

Middle First Intermission - "In just a moment, we are going to have more entertainment for you during this intermission."

Before Second Period Face-Off - "Very shortly, play will be starting in the second period at (name of arena) and we will have more action for you."
(1 minute commercial)

Second Period - During 2nd period of play three 20 second commercials are to be inserted at the discretion of each co-op station. Audio Cue: "There's a whistle on the ice and the score is _____ & _____ ."

1st pause during play-by-play.	.20 seconds
2nd pause during play-by-play.	.20 seconds
3rd pause during play-by-play.	.20 seconds

End of Second Period - "That's the end of the second period and the score is _____ & _____ ."
(1 minute commercial)

Middle Second Intermission - "In just a moment we are going to have more entertainment for you during this intermission."

Before Third Period Face-Off - "Very shortly play will be starting in the third period here at (name of arena) and we will have more action for you."
(1 minute commercial)

Third Period - During 3rd period of play three 20 second commercials are to be inserted at the discretion of each co-op station. Audio Cue: "There's a whistle on the ice and the score is _____ & _____ ."

1st pause during play-by-play.	.20 seconds
2nd pause during play-by-play.	.20 seconds
3rd pause during play-by-play.	.20 seconds

End of Third Period - "That is the end of the game and the score is _____ & _____ ."
(1 minute commercial)

Statistical Wrap-up

Before Closing Billboard - This wraps up another National Hockey League telecast. Final score _____ & _____ ."

			PERIOD	
DATE	GAME	FIRST	SECOND	THIRD
JAN. 4	– Boston at Rangers	R	C	M
11	– Chicago at Detroit	M	R	C
18	– Rangers at Chicago	C	M	R
25	– Detroit at Boston	R	C	M
FEB. 1	– Chicago at Rangers	M	R	C
8	– Rangers at Detroit	C	M	R
15	– Canadians at Boston	R	C	M
22	– Boston at Detroit	M	R	C
MAR. 1	– Boston at Chicago	C	M	R
8	– Detroit at Chicago	R	C	M
15	– Rangers at Boston	M	R	C
22	– Chicago at Detroit	C	M	R

R - Carling
C - Co-op
M - Marlboro

Stroh Brewing Company sponsor rotation will be the same as "C". Where two periods have been made available for co-op sale, Stroh, since their commercials are inserted locally, may arrange with stations for either period.

The following sports format technically belongs under special events, too. Inasmuch as it is a live presentation of a series of contests, it is presented here for the purpose of comparing the local on-the-spot sports broadcast with that of the network.

● *What significant differences, if any, are there in the preparation of the rundown sheet for a network sports event and for a local sports event?*

VIDEO	AUDIO
OPENING: LONG SHOT OF SPORTLAND:	(BOOTH ANN.) NOW LIVE FROM BEAUTI-FUL SPORTLAND ON U.S. 1 NORTH OF RALEIGH --- WRAL-TV PRESENTS . . .
CUE THE MUSIC—SUPER L-317-s	BOWLING FROM SPORTLAND . . . THE EXCITING NEW BOWLING SHOW WHERE
PAN SLOW RIGHT	EACH WEEK YOU'LL SEE THE TOP BOWLERS IN THIS AREA COMPETE FOR
CUT TO CU OF BOWLER	PRIZES AND THE TITLE OF KING OF THE HILL—PLUS A CHANCE TO WIN $10,000
ZOOM BACK SLOWLY	SHOULD THEY BOWL A PERFECT 300 GAME. NOW HERE'S YOUR BOWLING HOST, JIM HEAVNER.
DROP SUPER AND ZOOM IN ON JIM HEAVNER, FADING OUT THE MUSIC	(JIM) HELLO, LADIES AND GENTLEMEN, I'M JIM HEAVNER AND I'LL BE YOUR HOST . . (DOES WARM-UP) (INTRODUCES BOWLERS) (DOES THE INTERVIEW) (THEN RIGHT BEFORE THE START OF THE FIRST GAME) WE'LL START OUR FIRST GAME RIGHT AFTER THIS IMPORTANT MESSAGE.
CUT TO STUDIO FOR BREAK ONE:	(SIXTY SECONDS)
BACK LIVE:	(STARTS FIRST GAME) (AFTER FIRST GAME, WE WILL HAVE INTERVIEWS ONLY IF WE ARE INSIDE OF 0:15) (CUT TO SECOND BREAK WITH CUE—WE'LL START OUR SECOND GAME RIGHT AFTER THIS IMPORTANT MESSAGE.)
CUT TO STUDIO FOR BREAK TWO:	(SIXTY SECONDS)
BACK LIVE:	(START SECOND GAME) (WE SHOULD HAVE FINISHED SECOND GAME PRIOR TO 0:38) (IF WE'RE RUNNING NEAR OR OVER THIS KILL BREAK THREE) (TIME PERMITTING CUT TO THIRD BREAK WITH CUE—WE'LL START OUR THIRD GAME RIGHT AFTER THIS IMPORTANT MES-SAGE.)
CUT TO STUDIO FOR BREAK THREE:	(SIXTY SECONDS)
BACK LIVE:	(STARTS THIRD GAME) (AFTER GAME, TIME PERMITTING, HE INTERVIEWS WINNER AND LOSER HANDING THEM THEIR ENVELOPES) (IF WE NEED A PAD, HEAVNER BRINGS OUT CHARLIE BOSWELL FOR THE BOWLING TIP OF THE WEEK) (IF FURTHER PAD IS NEEDED USE FOURTH PROMO CUTAWAY) (CLOSE IS REVERSE OF THE OPENING—
PAN LEFT	HEAVNER BOWS OUT)
CUT TO LONG SHOT OF SPORTLAND WITH MUSIC	(BOOTH ANN.) LIVE FROM BEAUTIFUL SPORTLAND ON U.S. 1 NORTH OF RALEIGH WRAL-TV HAS PRESENTED
SUPER SLIDE: L-317-s AND CUE MUSIC	BOWLING FROM SPORTLAND . . . BE WITH US AGAIN NEXT WEEK WHEN TOP BOWLERS IN THIS AREA AGAIN COMPETE FOR PRIZES AND THE TITLE OF KING OF THE HILL—PLUS A CHANCE TO WIN $10,000 ON BOWLING FROM SPORTLAND—

117

SUPER SLIDE: L-207-s

SUPER SLIDE: L-307-s

SUPER SLIDE: L-317-s: MUSIC UP
AND OUT:

BLACK:

BOWLING FROM SPORTLAND WAS
DIRECTED BY ROSS SHAHEEN

By permission of Sportland, Inc.

FOR APPLICATION AND REVIEW

1. Clip out the front page stories from your daily newspaper and organize them for a radio news broadcast according to each of the following approaches: topical; geographical; international, national, local; from most to least important, regardless of category. Write the script for a 15-minute straight news broadcast for radio, using one of the organizations developed above.
2. Rewrite the radio broadcast you have developed in the exercise above for a television news program, utilizing photos, film, slides and other visuals.
3. Prepare the opening and closing continuity and the filler material for a live local broadcast — for television and radio both — of the next athletic event in your community. Rewrite your material as though the same event were to be broadcast over a national network.

5

SPECIAL EVENTS, FEATURES AND DOCUMENTARIES

SPECIAL EVENTS, special features and documentaries usually are under the direction of the news department of the television or radio station. These three types of programs all deal with news or information, some of it taking place at the moment of broadcast, some of it of a historical nature and some of it of an academic or cultural nature without necessarily being pertinent to an immediate or major issue of the day.

SPECIAL EVENTS

Special events are usually on-the-spot, remote broadcasts of a newsworthy nature. The announcer treats these special events, whether headline news, sports or the arts, as he does the live sports broadcast, narrating them on radio and announcing them on television. As with live sports broadcasts, the opening and closing material is provided by the writer, and the transition and filler material, when possible, is provided by the broadcaster assigned to the event. As much continuity as possible is prepared concerning the event, the personalities, and background, and even concerning probable or possible happenings. Most special events are more effective on television than on radio. They frequently are filmed or taped for subsequent presentation. The picture captures the action, and the commentary provides background and clarifying information. Films or tapes of special events usually are edited and sometimes carefully prepared beforehand in terms of format, transitions, introductions, and specific material to be recorded. In actuality, these special event films and tapes or, in the case of radio, tape recordings, sometimes become prepared special features rather than extemporaneous on-the-spot broadcasts. There is often only a fine line between the special feature and the special event, and any given program may be either one or a combination of both. The special feature — and its ultimate refinement, the documentary — will be discussed separately. Suffice to note now, in terms of difference between the two forms, that the special event is a broadcast which covers an actual happening that is part of the stream of life, while a special feature is a broadcast which is devised, developed and executed by the broadcaster or other producing organization.

Types

The special event ordinarily originates and is conducted outside of station supervision, and includes such happenings as parades, dedications, banquets, awards, the arrival of dignitaries, the opening of new supermarkets, fashion shows and even publicity stunts. More significant kinds of special events, perhaps, are political conventions and astronaut launchings. (Broadcasts of election returns may be considered special events, although they are, in essence, special features prepared by the individual network or station.) The tragic assassination of President John F. Kennedy in 1963 was an event covered fully by most television and radio stations in the country.

Styles of Writing

The writer should collect as much information as possible on the event, including news stories, maps, press releases, photographs and other material. Copy is prepared for all emergencies as well as for opening, closing, transition and filler material. Coverage in depth of a special event requires considerable preliminary work. Russ Tornabene, Director of News for NBC Radio, has stated:

"Extensive research goes into the preparation of material to be used as background for broadcasting special events. For example, the research document prepared for the 1964 Olympics ran to about 500 pages. The basic research continuity book for the Gemini 8 coverage in March, 1966, was about 400 pages long, with special tabbed sections for various categories, such as medicine, biographical material, the space capsule and so forth. The job of the writer, therefore, in preparing background material for special events is an important one. In addition, the correspondent doing the broadcast adds to the basic book with research, interviews and materials of his own."

Inasmuch as the form of the special event is extemporaneous, the prepared material must be simple, straightforward and informal. Frequently, only a detailed outline or "rundown" of the sequence of events may be prepared by the writer. The following was adapted from an actual network presentation.

RUNDOWN SHEET ON STADIUM REMOTE, FOOTBALL COACH TRIBUTE

Approx. 2:15 P.M.:	Panoramic view of Stadium. Super card: "Football Coach's Last Game." Announcer voice over.
Approx. 2:55 P.M.:	Panoramic view of half-time ceremonies at Stadium. Super card: "Football Coach's Last Game." Announcer voice over.
Approx. 4:50 P.M.:	Announcer introduction to closing minutes of football game. Feature scoreboard clock running out. Super card over action on field as gun sounds ending game. Interviewer describe closing moments of game.

1. Interviewer stations Football Coach on the field facing the field camera. Bands of the competing universities line up behind Football Coach and Interviewer.

2. Band music concludes and Interviewer thanks the bands on behalf of Football Coach. (Interviewer's mike should be fed into stadium public address system for any narration while on field.)

3. Football Coach and Interviewer walk up ramp to field house followed by special guests. At entrance to field house they are picked up by camera on dolly and led down the hall of the University dressing room. The University squad and the opposing team's captain follow closely.

4. Interviewer introduces some friends and former players of Football Coach, with brief comments from the guests and from Football Coach. It is hoped that the Presidents of both Universities can be present, and that the President of Football Coach's University can quote from letters written to Football Coach by prominent persons in government and in other fields. At some point during the proceedings an outstanding national football coach will talk to Football Coach from station studio via split screen.

5. At conclusion of program Interviewer presents Football Coach with award from Network.

6. Brief comment from Football Coach to his University alumni throughout the country.

In the foregoing illustration the network station participated in the planning and execution of the events that took place, although the characters and the event itself were real, behaving and taking place, respectively, as they would in the normal action of life and not contrived by the broadcaster. When the station does not participate at all in the actual action of the event — a concert or recital, for example — the writer's job is somewhat different. He may need to prepare only the opening and closing as in the following example. Note the detailed video directions. (SC refers to "studio card," or card bearing the indicated information.)

VIDEO	AUDIO
OPENING:	
Cover shot of Choral group	Channel five presents . . .
Super Slide: L-20	the INTERCOLLEGIATE CHORAL FESTIVAL . . .
	The festival, which was held last evening at William Neal Reynolds Coliseum, included choral groups from ten colleges throughout North Carolina . . . and a massed chorus of over 450 voices.
Super SC: Dr. Knud Anderson	The director is Dr. Knud Anderson of the New Orleans Opera House.
Super SC: Willa Fay Batts	Piano Soloist is Willa Fay Batts;
Super SC: Beatrice Donley	Alto Soloist, Beatrice Donley; and
Super SC: Mary Ida Hodge	Accompanist, Mary Ida Hodge. And now . . . the Premier INTERCOLLEGIATE CHORAL FESTIVAL OF NORTH CAROLINA:
CLOSING	
Super Slide: L-20	Channel Five has presented The Premier of THE INTERCOLLEGIATE CHORAL FESTIVAL OF North Carolina, directed by
Super SC: Dr. Knud Anderson	Dr. Knud Anderson.

Courtesy of WRAL-TV, Raleigh, N. C.

121

SPECIAL FEATURES

Only a thin line separates many special events from special features —
and vice versa. In most stations the two are not separated, but are put into the
same category for organizational and production purposes. Some differences
may be found, although not at all times or in all cases. The special feature is
planned more definitively and fully than is the special event. The broadcaster
usually has more control over the sequence of events in the special feature
than in the special event. The special event usually is live, while the special
feature frequently is filmed, taped, recorded, or produced live from a complete script. Special events usually are public presentations of some kind
which have been presented live before an audience. Special features usually
have been prepared solely for television or radio presentation and usually have
not been presented before an in-person audience. And, as noted earlier, the
special event is part of the stream of life while the special feature is designed
by a producing organization.

Types

The special feature usually is a 2-minute or 15-minute — and sometimes
longer — broadcast of a public service nature. Subjects for the special feature
might include a human interest broadcast such as a presentation of the work
of a social service group, an examination of the local school system or the local
firehouse operation, a trip to some point of interest, a how-to-do-it broadcast,
a behind-the-scenes broadcast, or even a review of a political, social or scien-
tific question. In the latter category the special feature takes on some of the
attributes of the documentary.

Writing Approach

The special feature is closer to the documentary form and is analyzed,
researched and written in more depth and in more detail than is the special
event. The writer of the special feature has greater opportunity for writing an
actual script or rundown sheet to which the producer and director will adhere.
Do not be afraid — dependent upon the subject matter, program time and desires of the station and/or agency — to aim for the high art of the documentary form.

The special feature rundown sheets that follow illustrate two program
types: a how-to-do-it presentation and a behind-the-scenes broadcast. In the
first one the writer shows a problem and then presents a method of solving it.
The approach is informational and educational. In the second the writer concentrates on the human interest aspect. The approach primarily is to stimulate
the audience's attitudes, with some informational and educational elements.

VIDEO	AUDIO
	THEME MUSIC
PROGRAM TITLE CARD	ANNOUNCER: Introduction . . . "and here is your County Extension Agent, John Roberts."
OPEN: CAMERA ON ROBERTS AT TABLE	"Good afternoon, friends. Today our topic is about cricket control."
CLOSEUP (CU) LIVE CRICKETS IN JARS	Makes brief comment on crickets as a household nuisance and fact that they damage fabrics and sometimes crops.
PAN TO CLOSEUP OF FIELD SPECIMEN OF CRICKET DAMAGE	"Let's look at some of the ways we can control these insects."
CLOSEUP (CU) WEATHER STRIPPING ON BOARD	Explains that proper weather stripping keeps insects outside the house.
CLOSEUP (CU) PIECE OF PIPE THROUGH LARGE HOLE IN BOARD	Explains that space around pipe should be sealed.
MEDIUM SHOT (MS) TO CLOSEUP (CU) DEMONSTRATION OF HOW TO SEAL PIPE	Describes method.
CLOSEUP (CU) ZIPPER BAG	Explains importance of proper storage of clothes.
	"Protection is fine, but we want to do away with these insects altogether."
MEDIUM SHOT (MS) OF THREE TYPES OF INSECTICIDES	"Here are three types of insecticides that can do the job."
CLOSEUP (CU) OF 1 - CAN OF DUSTING POWDER 2 - LIQUID PREPARATION 3 - BAG OF WETTABLE POWDER	Explains and shows how to apply insecticides to doorsills, foundations of buildings, etc.
CLOSEUP (CU) BULLETIN —THEN SHOW CARD	SUMMARY — Then tie-in for further information — Write for bulletin.
WRITE TO COUNTY AGENT, COURTHOUSE, ETC.	"That's our farm and home feature for today. See you next week, same time, same station." THEME MUSIC - STATION ANNOUNCER.

<u>U.S. Department of Agriculture Handbook for County Agents.</u>

VIDEO	AUDIO
SLIDE #1 TRI-STATE STORY	MUSIC: RECORD "RED CROSS SONG" IN AND OUT BEHIND STATION ANNOUNCER: As a public service, WEHT presents TRI- STATE STORY—a half hour prepared
SLIDE #2 RED CROSS EMBLEM	through the cooperation of the Springfield Chapter of the American Red Cross. Here to introduce our guests for this evening is Mr. John Smith, Director of Public Rela- tions for the Springfield Red Cross. Mr. Smith:
CAMERA ON SMITH	(MR. SMITH THANKS ANNOUNCER AND INTRODUCES TWO GUESTS, MR. HARVEY AND MR. JONES. THEN ASKS MR. HARVEY TO SPEAK)
CAMERA ON HARVEY CLOSEUP OF PHOTOS ON EASEL	(MR. HARVEY TELLS OF RECENT DISASTER WORK IN HARRISBURG AREA, SHOWING PHOTOGRAPHS OF SERVICE WORKERS. HE WILL RISE AND WALK TO THE EASEL.)
CAMERA ON SMITH AND JONES	(MR. SMITH INTRODUCES MR. JONES. THEY DISCUSS SUMMER SAFETY SCHOOL FOR SWIMMERS. JONES LEADS INTO FILM WITH FOLLOWING CUE: "Now I'd like our viewers to see a film that was made at Lake Roundwood during last year's Summer Safety School."
SPECIAL FILM	(8:35) (SILENT -- JONES LIVE VOICE-OVER)
CAMERA ON JONES	(JONES INTRODUCES ARTIFICIAL RES- PIRATION DEMONSTRATION.)
CAMERA ON TWO BOYS	(JONES DESCRIBES METHODS OFF CAMERA.)
CAMERA ON SMITH	(SMITH THANKS JONES AND HARVEY AND GIVES CONCLUDING REMARKS.)
SLIDE #3 TRI-STATE STORY	MUSIC: THEME IN AND UNDER STATION ANNOUNCER: Tri-State Story, a WEHT Public Service Presentation, is on the air each week at this time. Today's program was prepared through the cooperation of the Springfield Chapter of the American Red Cross. By permission of American National Red Cross.

Although the special feature is a public service presentation and often contains informational and educational content, it does not have to be purely factual or academic in nature. It may take the form of a variety show or a drama. It may combine these elements with news, speeches and discussions, or with any of the diverse television and radio program materials. Ordinarily, such a special feature will be oriented around a person or thing or situation. In the case of the following illustration the subject is a battleship. The writer has prepared a complete script, organized the material so that the program is entertainment as well as public service, and used an approach that tends toward the documentary.

> ● *As you study the "U.S.S. North Carolina" script determine whether 1) the organization of the guests' appearances is done effectively; 2) the transitions are logical and fresh; 3) the photo and description sequence of the "U.S.S. North Carolina" is presented well and is in the most effective place in the program; 4) the visuals are the best that might have been used; 5) the entire program is as potent in doing its persuasive job as would be a well-written commercial.*

U.S.S. NORTH CAROLINA

SILENT FILM . . . . BATTLESHIP BRING IN SUPER	MUSIC UP . . . ESTABLISH AND FADE UNDER FOR BOOTH INTRO: THIS IS THE SHOWBOAT . . . A PROUD SHIP MANNED BY PROUD MEN . . . THE PRIDE OF THE U.S. FLEET IN WORLD WAR II. . . . SHE EARNED BATTLE STARS FOR 12 MAJOR ENGAGEMENTS AND LED THE U.S. NAVY TO VICTORY IN THE PACIFIC. HER OFFICIAL NAME . . . THE U.S.S. NORTH CAROLINA. SHE FOUGHT THE GOOD FIGHT AGAINST ENEMY PLANES, SURFACE SHIPS AND SUBMARINES . . . SHE WITHSTOOD THE RIGORS OF THE VICIOUS STORMS OF THE PACIFIC OCEAN. HER PRESENT HOME IS THE NAVY YARD AT BAYONNE, NEW JERSEY . . . HER FUTURE HOME IS WILMINGTON, NORTH CAROLINA. THIS GREAT SHIP IS OURS FOR THE SAVING AND YOU CAN HELP. NOW, HERE IS RAY REEVE.
REEVE STUDIO SHOT	TONITE THE TELEVISION STATIONS OF NORTH CAROLINA HAVE COMBINED EFFORTS TO BRING YOU AN OUTSTANDING PROGRAM OF ENTERTAINMENT AND HISTORY. WE'LL HEAR FROM JANE MORGAN, DICK GROAT, ANDY GRIFFITH, DAVE BRINKLEY, SECRETARY OF COMMERCE LUTHER HODGES AND GOVERNOR OF NORTH CAROLINA TERRY SANFORD AND WE'LL MEET THE U.S.S. NORTH CAROLINA . . . IN WAR AND IN PEACE. THIS GREAT SHIP WAS SLATED FOR THE SCRAP HEAP BY THE U.S. NAVY UNTIL SEVERAL NORTH CAROLINIANS GOT TOGETHER AND DECIDED TO SAVE THE NORTH CAROLINA AND BRING HER HOME AS A STATE SHRINE. NOW WE CAN ALL HELP SAVE THE NORTH CAROLINA AND BRING HER HOME SO WE CAN PRESERVE FOREVER THE HERITAGE OF THIS GREAT SHIP. THE U.S.S. NORTH CAROLINA BATTLESHIP COMMISSION HAS SELECTED WILMINGTON AS THE SITE AND PERMANENT HOME OF THE SHIP. AND AS SOON AS A BERTH CAN BE DREDGED AND THE HUGE WARSHIP CAN BE TOWED FROM NEW JERSEY TO WILMINGTON, THE U.S.S. NORTH CAROLINA WILL BE FOREVER IN THE TAR HEEL STATE. BEFORE WE GO ANY FURTHER, LET'S MEET A NEW TAR HEEL . . . SONGSTRESS JANE MORGAN WHO SINGS HER NEWEST HIT RECORDING . . . "LOVE MAKES THE WORLD GO ROUND."

VIDEO TAPE JANE MORGAN 2:44

REEVE READ OVER FILM . . 60 SEC	SHE IS TWO CITY BLOCKS LONG AND 15 STORIES HIGH, THIS GIANT OF THE SEAS . . . THE U.S.S. NORTH CAROLINA. AT THE TIME SHE WAS COMMISSIONED IN 1941 AND FOR MANY YEARS AFTERWARD, THE U.S.S. NORTH CAROLINA WAS THE GREATEST SEA WEAPON EVER BUILT BY THE UNITED STATES. THE NORTH CAROLINA IS NOW MOORED AT THE NAVY BASE IN BAYONNE, NEW JERSEY, AND IS SCHEDULED TO BE DESTROYED FOR SCRAP ON JULY 1ST UNLESS MONEY IS RAISED TO SAVE HER. THE SAME ENGINEER WHO BERTHED THE BATTLESHIP TEXAS, CYRIL ADAMS OF HOUSTON, TEXAS, NOW SERVES AS ENGINEER FOR THE STATE OF NORTH CAROLINA IN PLANS TO ESTABLISH THE NORTH CAROLINA AS A MEMORIAL AT WILMINGTON. GOVERNOR TERRY SANFORD COMMISSIONED PRESIDENT KENNEDY THE FIRST AD-MIRAL IN NORTH CAROLINAS' NAVY TO OPEN THE DRIVE TO BRING THE NORTH CAROLINA HOME.
CAMERA TO AD- MIRAL CERTIFI- CATE CARD BATTLE- SHIP FUND CUT TO REEVE	COMMISSIONS IN THE NORTH CAROLINA NAVY FOR THE RANK OF ADMIRAL WILL BE PRESENTED TO EACH PERSON WHO CON-TRIBUTES AS MUCH AS $500 FOR THE BATTLESHIP FUND. YOU CAN SEND YOUR CONTRIBUTION TO THE BATTLESHIP FUND, GOVERNOR'S OFFICE, RALEIGH, N.C. ALL MONEY FOR THE U.S.S. NORTH CAROLINA WILL COME FROM YOU, THE CITIZENS OF NORTH CAROLINA. NO TAX MONEY WILL BE USED. THE SMALL ADMISSION CHARGE FOR PERSONS TOURING THE SHIP WILL ENABLE IT TO BE SELF-SUPPORTING. TONITE MARKS THE KICKOFF IN THE STATEWIDE DRIVE TO COLLECT $250,000 WHICH IS NECESSARY TO PREPARE THE SITE, TOW THE BATTLESHIP TO NORTH CAROLINA AND PREPARE HER FOR SHOWING TO THE PUBLIC. YOUR COUNTY CHAIRMAN AND MEM-BERS OF HIS COMMITTEE WILL CALL ON YOU WITHIN THE NEXT TWO WEEKS FOR YOUR CONTRIBUTION. THE MONEY MUST BE RAISED BY JUNE 15 TO ASSURE THE RETURN OF THE BATTLE-SHIP TO NORTH CAROLINA. NOW LET'S CALL IN ONE OF THE GREATEST ATHLETES IN THE HISTORY OF NORTH CAROLINA, AND THE CAPTAIN OF THE WORLD CHAMPION PITTSBURGH PIRATES, DICK GROAT;

GROAT VIDEOTAPE 2:03

REEVE READ OVER FILM . . . 42 SECS.	HER CREW TOOK GOOD CARE OF HER THEN. SHE WAS THE GREATEST WARSHIP EVER BUILT BY THE UNITED STATES . . . THE PRIDE OF OUR FLEET AND AFFECTIONATELY CALLED "THE SHOWBOAT." SHE DID MORE THAN HER SHARE OF THE FIGHTING AND AT THE END OF THE WAR HAD 12 BATTLE STARS FOR MAJOR ENGAGEMENTS. ONE OF HER BIG JOBS WAS IN CONVOYS PROVIDING PROTECTIVE COVER FOR OUR CARRIERS AND THEIR PLANES. SHE FOUGHT FOR US THEN AND WE CAN FIGHT FOR HER NOW. LET'S BRING THE NORTH CAROLINA HOME.
REEVE STUDIO SHOT	ONE OF NORTH CAROLINA'S MOST ILLUSTRIOUS NATIVES IS ANDY GRIFFITH . . . HERE HE IS SPEAKING TO US FROM CALIF-ORNIA WHERE HE'S MAKING A MOVIE.

GRIFFITH VIDEO TAPE 6:18

REEVE READ OVER FILM . . . 44 SECS.	COMBAT WAS ROUGH, AND SOMETIMES THE SEA WAS ROUGHER, BUT THE GREAT BATTLESHIP SURVIVED IT ALL. THE NORTH CAROLINA WAS A FIGHTING SHIP, MANNED BY FIGHTING MEN. SHE TOOK HER LUMPS IN THE FIERCE FIGHTING, BUT ALWAYS CAME BACK FOR MORE. AFTER VICTORY HAD BEEN WON IN THE PACIFIC, THE U.S.S. NORTH CAROLINA ENTERED THE PANAMA CANAL ON HER WAY HOME. THE ONE LAST LAP IN HER

JOURNEY IS NOW UP TO US. OUR DONATIONS WILL BRING HER BACK TO NORTH CAROLINA AND HER FINAL HOME.

REEVE
STUDIO SHOT

THE NORTH CAROLINA WILL BE ONE OF THE GREATEST TOURIST ATTRACTIONS IN THE STATE AND WILL MEAN MUCH TO "VARIETY VACATIONLAND." HER HISTORY WILL BE OF VALUE TO THE SCHOOL CHILDREN. NOW LET'S HEAR FROM TWO MORE WELL KNOWN TAR HEELS, WHO, INCIDENTALLY, ARE BOTH ADMIRALS IN THE NORTH CAROLINA NAVY. SEC. OF COMMERCE LUTHER HODGES AND NEWSCASTER DAVID BRINKLEY.

HODGES-BRINKLEY VIDEOTAPE 3:08

REEVE READ
OVER PHOTOS
(2 MIN.)
1.

THE U.S.S. NORTH CAROLINA WAS LAUNCHED JUNE 13, 1940, AND WAS THE FIRST SHIP TO HAVE 16 INCH GUNS FOLLOWING THE WASHINGTON NAVAL TREATY OF 1922. HER OVERALL LENGTH IS 729 FEET, MORE THAN TWO CITY BLOCKS AND SHE STANDS 155 FEET HIGH.

2.

GOING THRU THE PANAMA CANAL, HER WIDTH OF 108 FEET MADE IT A CLOSE CALL, BUT SHE SQUEEZED BY WITH A FEW INCHES TO SPARE ON EITHER SIDE.

3.

THE BIG 16 INCH GUNS WERE A CONSTANT MENACE TO THE ENEMY AND HELPED PROVIDE PROTECTION FOR THE VITAL AIRCRAFT CARRIERS. THESE GUNS DAMAGED MANY AN ENEMY SHIP AND SOFTENED UP MANY BEACHES FOR THE LANDING PARTIES PREPARING FOR INVASIONS OF ENEMY STRONGHOLDS.

4.

EVEN THE MIGHTIEST OF SHIPS NEEDED SUPPLIES AND THE NORTH CAROLINA REFUELED AND TOOK ON SUPPLIES FROM THE TANKERS AND SUPPLY SHIPS OF THE NAVY DURING A LULL IN THE FIGHTING.

5.

MAIL CALL GLADDENS THE HEART OF EVERY SERVICEMAN . . . AND THE FIGHTING MEN OF THE NORTH CAROLINA OFTEN GOT THEIR MAIL FAR OUT AT SEA AND TRANSFERRED FROM ANOTHER SHIP.

6.

A VERSATILE SHIP SHE WAS . . . A SEAPLANE TO SEEK OUT THE ENEMY . . . 16 INCH GUNS TO FIRE AT TARGETS MILES AWAY . . . AND A SPEED OF 27 KNOTS WHICH ENABLED HER TO MANEUVER QUICKLY AND MOVE INTO ACTION IN A HURRY.

7.

NOW THE BIG GUNS ARE SILENT . . . A REMINDER OF FIGHTING DAYS LEFT BEHIND. THE SHOWBOAT IS IN MOTHBALLS IN NEW JERSEY . . .

8.

ALONG WITH OTHER SHIPS OF THE NAVY. BUT WE WANT TO MOVE HER FROM THIS SITE TO

9.

THIS SITE . . . A PERMANENT HOME IN WILMINGTON FOR ALL NORTH CAROLINIANS. SHE'LL BE LOCATED ACROSS THE RIVER FROM DOWNTOWN WILMINGTON, EASILY ACCESSIBLE FROM SEVERAL HIGHWAYS AND OPEN FOR VISITORS.

REEVE
STUDIO SHOT

A WHILE BACK WE HEARD FROM ONE OF THE NEWEST, AND FAIREST, CITIZENS OF NORTH CAROLINA, JANE MORGAN. HERE SHE IS AGAIN, THIS TIME SINGING "THE DAY THAT THE RAINS CAME DOWN" . . .

JANE MORGAN VIDEO TAPE 2:56

127

REEVE STUDIO SHOT	THANK YOU JANE. NEW HANOVER COUNTY INITIATED THE FUND DRIVE IN THE STATE AND HAS ALREADY COLLECTED OVER $45,000. THIRTY THOUSAND DOLLARS WILL GO TO PURCHASE THE NECESSARY SITE, AND THE REMAINDER OF THE MONEY WILL GO TOWARD THE $250,000 NEEDED TO BRING THE NORTH CAROLINA HOME. THIS GIVES THE STATE A BIG START TOWARD RAISING THE NECESSARY MONEY. AND, AS ANDY GRIFFITH SAID EARLIER, ALL DONATIONS ARE TAX DEDUCTIBLE. TONITE'S PROGRAM WOULD NOT BE COMPLETE UNLESS WE HEARD FROM THE NUMBER 1 CITIZEN OF NORTH CAROLINA, OUR GOVERNOR, THE HONORABLE TERRY SANFORD. GOVERNOR SANFORD.

SANFORD VIDEOTAPE 1:30

REEVE STUDIO SHOT PICKUP MODEL OF SHIP	THIS IS A MODEL OF THE NORTH CAROLINA, AND A VERY IMPRESSIVE ONE. BELIEVE ME, IT TAKES A LOT OF PATIENCE AND A STEADY HAND TO PUT ONE OF THESE THINGS TOGETHER. THIS MODEL IS SOMETHING THAT REALLY APPEALS TO THE BOYS . . . BUT THE REAL NORTH CAROLINA IS SOMETHING THAT SHOULD APPEAL TO ALL OF US. ACTUALLY, THE U.S.S. NORTH CAROLINA IS PART OF OUR GREAT STATE. IT FOUGHT FOR OUR FREEDOM AND MANY TAR HEELS LOST THEIR LIVES WHILE SERVING ABOARD THE NORTH CAROLINA. TO LET HER BE CUT UP AND SOLD FOR SCRAP WOULD BE A TRAGEDY. SHE BELONGS HOME IN NORTH CAROLINA AND WITH YOUR HELP, SHE'LL COME HOME VERY SOON. IT'S BEEN A PLEASURE TO BE WITH YOU TONITE AND TO BE ABLE TO INTRODUCE SUCH AN OUTSTANDING GROUP OF NORTH CAROLINIANS WHO ARE BACKING THE BATTLESHIP MOVE. EVERY PERSON WHO APPEARED ON TONITE'S PROGRAM DONATED THEIR TIME AND EFFORT TO THE BATTLESHIP FUND. THIS IS RAY REEVE SPEAKING. GOOD NITE.

CLOSE:	
	(MUSIC UP, ESTABLISH, FADE UNDER FOR BOOTH CLOSE)
SILENT FILM BATTLESHIP	THE TELEVISION STATIONS OF NORTH CAROLINA, IN A SPIRIT OF COOPERATION FOR A GREATER NORTH CAROLINA, HAVE PRESENTED TONITE'S PROGRAM. WE HOPE YOU HAVE ENJOYED IT.
SUPER CARD	THE U.S.S. NORTH CAROLINA PROGRAM WAS PRODUCED IN THE STUDIOS OF WRAL-TV, RALEIGH, WRITTEN BY WAYNE JACKSON, DIRECTED BY NICK POND, AND PRODUCED BY GEORGE BRENHOLTZ.
	(MUSIC UP FOR 10 SECONDS)
SUPER CARD	SEND YOUR DONATION TO THE BATTLESHIP FUND, GOVERNOR'S OFFICE, RALEIGH, NORTH CAROLINA AND GIVE TO YOUR COUNTY COMMITTEE WHEN THEY CALL ON YOU.
SUPER CARD	WE WISH TO THANK THE MANY PERSONS WHO GAVE OF THEIR TIME AND EFFORTS TO MAKE THIS PROGRAM POSSIBLE. THIS PROGRAM WAS PRE-RECORDED FOR PRESENTATION AT THIS TIME.
	(MUSIC UP FOR PAD)
	THIS IS THE NORTH CAROLINA TELEVISION NETWORK.

Script by Wayne Jackson of WECT-TV, Wilmington, N. C.

THE DOCUMENTARY

It is sometimes said that next to the drama the documentary is the highest form of television and radio art. Some network news personnel will disagree and say that the documentary, combining as it does news, special event or special feature material, and drama, is the highest form. The documentary not only explores the present, but it interprets the past and sometimes even prognosticates the future. It not only presents the news — the documentary program usually falls under the news division of the station or network — but it presents it in highly dramatic form, combined with intellectual and emotional meaning.

Types

Robert Flaherty is considered the father of the modern documentary. His "Nanook of the North," completed in 1922, set a pattern for a special type of documentary film: that which went beneath the exterior of life, that which took an attitude toward man, and carefully selected the elements of society and man's relationship to those elements that dramatized the attitude. Flaherty eulogized the strength and nobility of man in a hostile or, at the very least, difficult environment. Pare Lorentz, noted for his productions of "The Plow That Broke the Plains" and "The River" under Franklin D. Roosevelt's administration in the 1930's, forwarded another type of documentary: the presentation of a problem affecting a large number of people and the ways in which that problem could be solved. Lorentz's type of documentary called for positive action on the part of the viewer to remedy an unfortunate or ugly situation. A third type of documentary is exemplified in the British film, "Night Mail," produced by innovator John Grierson. The details of ordinary, everyday existence — in this instance the delivery in Britain of the night mail — are presented in a dramatic, but non-sensational manner. In this type we see man as he really is; we receive factual information without a special attitude or point of view expressed or stimulated.

These types (the student of documentary writing is urged to view the films noted above) provide the bases for writing the television and radio documentary. The documentary for the mass media may use one of the three approaches or — and this frequently is the case — combine two or more of the types in varying degrees. This is so even when the documentary may not deal with an event, but with a person as, for example, in the "Biography in Sound" radio series presented by the National Broadcasting Company.

Form

Although the documentary is dramatic, it is not a drama in the sense of the fictional play. It is more or less a faithful representation of a true story. That is not to say that all documentaries are unimpeachably true. Editing can make any series of sequences seem other than what they really are. The documentary form itself is flexible. A semi-documentary or fictional documentary is based on reality, but in itself is not necessarily fact. It may take a basically true situation and group of characters and fictionalize them; it may take characters or an event and speculate, as authentically as possible, in order to fill in documentary gaps; it may take several situations and a number of varied characters and create a composite picture. On television the "Circle Theatre" has presented this semi-documentary approach very successfully, taking a real situation and using it as a base for a partially fictional dramatization.

The documentary deals with news — with issues, people, events — but it is not a news story. The difference may not relate so much to content as it does to the approach. A 30-minute news program on a murder in New York City may present fully all of the known factual material. A documentary on the same subject, in this instance CBS Radio's "Who Killed Michael Farmer?" (see page 138) goes much further in depth, exploring not only what happened but, as far as possible, the reasons for what happened, the attitudes and feelings, not previously made public, of the persons involved and of the experts, and the implications and significance of the event in terms of society and especially in terms of the lives of individual people. Where the news report is oriented toward objectivity, the documentary often presents a point of view; it editorializes.

Ostensibly, the documentary program should be put together in the field, with tape recorders and/or cameras. The very fact that the program may be done outside of the studio does not guarantee that it will be a good one. Sometimes small stations can't send out a crew for the time it takes to prepare the program effectively. Occasionally, a program of equivalent worth can be done by reading all the literature on the subject, writing a script, and then doing it in the studio with a narrator and selected tapes or films. Editing, in fact, is a crucial part of the making of a documentary. Radio station WBT, in Charlotte, North Carolina, won several awards with a documentary based on the taping of materials received in English from Radio Moscow, and then editing to insert within the Moscow reports comments which represented the point of view of the producer of the program. Educational radio station WUNC at the University of North Carolina created several documentaries utilizing already-recorded materials. In one, produced by former opera star Norman Cordon, the record albums "The Blue and Grey," containing songs of the Civil War, were used as bases for interviews, lectures and discussions on the events suggested by the songs. The participants were historians, scholars, military men and writers from the university and the Chapel Hill community.

Writing Procedure

Essentially, the documentary contains the real words of real persons (or their writings, published and unpublished, including letters if they are not living or cannot possibly be reached and there is no record of their voices), and the sounds and motion pictures (or photos, if films cannot be obtained) of the people and the event. These materials, sometimes seemingly unrelated, must be put together into a dramatic, cohesive whole and edited in terms of a script.

The script, obviously, cannot be created by the writer in the isolation of his back bedroom. First, the writer must have an idea. What subject of public interest is worthy of documentary treatment? Violence in Alabama? Protests for peace in Vietnam? The scenic pleasures of central California? When the writer finds an idea — which as likely will come from the producer or director of the documentary as from the writer — he must decide on purpose. Will he present an objective view of a community's traditions and customs? Will he support majority mob rule as a solution to a problem? Will he show the courage of a minority group in a hostile social environment? Will he present a chronological account of one day at a voter registration office? Will he show the attitudes and motivations of protesting college students as well as their political actions? Will his own orientation (or that of the producer or network or agency or sponsor) as a "hawk" or a "dove" have any bearing on program content? Will he try to persuade all people that the only way to find true rejuvenation of body and spirit is to spend all of their vacation time in Yosemite National Park? At this point the writer does as thorough research as possible. Libraries, personal visits to persons and places, and investigations of the availability of audio and visual materials already recorded will occupy much time. After the research is complete, the writer prepares an outline.

Sometimes that is as far as he can go pending the accumulation of materials that will later be edited into the final form of the program. He can, however, suggest the materials to be obtained and, to a degree, suggest the orientation or even the content of those materials. He can prepare preliminary narration. The writer's work will continue throughout the period of gathering materials. As the materials come in he will revise his detailed outline and begin to juxtapose concrete narration with tapes or films. After all the materials possible have been gathered, the writer can then concentrate on the final script which is used for the selection and organization of specific materials for the final taping or editing of the program. It is important to note that in a great many instances the writer serves also as producer of the documentary.

Sometimes an entire documentary may come from just a few minutes of audio tape or from a short piece of film which carries material available to no other reporter or station. The writer may decide that this material would make a good beginning or a good ending, and plan the rest of the program around it. For example, a network may have an exclusive film of a minute's duration of a secret meeting between the heads of two major world powers. From this short film, with the aid of newsreels, interviews and further filming not necessarily related directly to the event, a documentary program can be created.

Writing Technique

Even if you want only to give the facts of the matter, make them dramatic. Facts alone are not sufficient. Find the human interest element. If the subject is an inanimate object, such as a new mechanical invention, endow the machine with live attributes as, indeed, many machines seem to have, and use this as a base. The documentary uses many principles of dramatic writing. The material, at least in part, should be presented in a dramatized manner through the exploration of character, the introduction of a conflict, and the development of the conflict through complications until a crisis is reached. The human interest elements, the little things, are important. In sum, an inanimate object must be given a personality, a situation must be presented in terms of the people involved.

The documentary utilizes in its writing many production elements of the drama, including background music, special settings in television, narration, special effects and, in the semi- or fictionalized documentary, actors portraying real persons, living or dead. One of the finest of the latter form in any medium — a script well worth reading and studying — is Norman Corwin's "On A Note of Triumph."

A narrator is almost always used in the documentary. But it is important to use the narrator judiciously, for if he plays too great a role he will detract from the actual material.

In radio, the points should not be too drawn out, particularly taped statements and interviews. The writer should avoid the possibility that the program will sound like a series of lectures or interviews. Sometimes important material must be deleted from the presentations of the actual persons. In such cases the narrator can summarize in concise, crisp statements the material that cannot be presented.

The writer should be aware of the needs for and possibilities of editing the tapes and/or film. Although the director and producer will supervise the final editing, it might help the writer to know, for example, that he can combine sound from one source (say, a folk-singer in Tennessee) with film from another source (a flooded town in southern Illinois).

Application: Procedure

A radio documentary may be produced with virtually no budget and no equipment save two or three tape recorders and some tapes. One such documentary was prepared as as assignment in a radio production course of the Department of Radio, Television and Motion Pictures at the University of North Carolina. Let us examine the procedure followed. First, a subject was decided upon: the problems of the small farmer in the Piedmont region of North Carolina and the possible relationship of these problems to politics. The three major documentary types were combined in the purpose of the documentary: to present information in a straightforward, unbiased manner; to show by implication that there was a problem that had to be solved and to indicate several possible solutions; and to present the farmer as a persevering person in a difficult economic environment. It was decided that not only farmers, but experts from the university should be interviewed and their tapes edited in a sort of counterpoint fashion.

Research was the next step, with as much material as could be found on the problem gathered from an examination of all available literature and from preliminary talks with farmers and persons familiar with the farm problem. The subject and purpose were clarified further and, on the basis of the projected findings of the documentary, specific interviewees were chosen — farmers in terms of the size, location and crop of the farm, and experts in terms of their academic department and special area of study.

A careful distillation of material already gathered led to the formation of a series of pertinent and inter-related questions to be asked the farmers and the experts. After the interviews were completed, a script containing the narration and a description of the taped material to be inserted was developed from all the material available, including tapes, library research and personal interviews. An analysis of the script indicated places that were weak, some because of the lack of material and others because of the superfluity of material. Further field work and the addition and pruning of material resulted in a final script, ready for the editing process.

The following is a composite of the script and a verbatim transcription of the program. The final script is shown in capitals; the material in parentheses is that actually recorded and incorporated into the program with the narration. Note here the use of numbers indicating the tape and cut to be used, with notations of the first and last words of each cut to help the editor. The program, the recipient of a national award for public service reporting, was broadcast over radio station WUNC.

> ● One criticism of this script may be that it tries to cover too many subjects. Another may be that it is not sufficiently dramatic. If you find any validity to these criticisms, take the material contained in the script, plus other material that you can get through your personal research, and rewrite this documentary in outline form, improving on it as you think necessary.

THE PIEDMONT NORTH CAROLINA FARMER AND POLITICS, 1961

OPEN COLD: TAPE #1, CUT 1, DUPREE SMITH: "I WOULD LIKE VERY MUCH . . . BEST PLACE TO WORK."

(I would like very much to spend my entire life here on the farm because I feel like being near the land and being near the soil and seeing the operation of God on this earth is the best place to live and the best place to work.)

MUSIC: IN, UP, AND UNDER

NARRATOR: THIS IS THE SMALL FARMER IN THE PIEDMONT OF NORTH CAROLINA.

MUSIC: UP AND OUT

NARRATOR: YOU ARE LISTENING TO THE "PIEDMONT, NORTH CAROLINA, FARMER AND POLITICS, 1961." THE VOICE YOU JUST HEARD WAS THAT OF DUPREE SMITH, A FARMER IN PIEDMONT, NORTH CAROLINA. IN RURAL AMERICA A CENTURY AGO THE FARM PROBLEM WAS AN INDIVIDUAL ONE OF DIGGING A LIVING OUT OF THE LAND. EACH FARMER SOLVED HIS OWN INDIVIDUAL PROBLEMS WITHOUT GOVERNMENT AID. NEARLY EVERYONE

FARMED. TODAY, BECAUSE OF INCREASING COST OF MAIN -
TAINING CROPS, LARGER SURPLUSES, HEAVIER STORAGE COSTS
AND LOWER FARM INCOME, THE SMALL FARMER IN NORTH
CAROLINA, AS WELL AS ACROSS THE NATION, HAS BEEN UNABLE
TO DEPEND ON HIS LAND FOR A LIVING. PRODUCTION CON-
TINUED TO GROW. SURPLUSES MOUNTED. FARM INCOMES FELL
AND THE GOVERNMENT SUBSIDIES NECESSARILY GREW.

PROFESSOR
KOVENOCK: TAPE #2, CUT 1: "THE COMMON PROBLEMS . . . ARE THESE."

(The common problems shared by almost all national farmers today
and, at the same time, most North Carolina farmers, are these.)

NARRATOR: YOU ARE LISTENING TO PROFESSOR DAVID KOVENOCK OF THE
POLITICAL SCIENCE DEPARTMENT OF THE UNIVERSITY OF
NORTH CAROLINA.

KOVENOCK: TAPE #2, CUT 2: "FIRST OF ALL . . . SHELTER FOR HIS
FAMILY."

(First of all, a decline in the income going to the farmer—a problem
of—this is particularly for, let us say, the marginal farmer, the
farmer with a small operation in North Carolina and the rest of
the country—the problem of obtaining employment off the farm, that
is, some relatively attractive alternative to continuing an operation
on the farm that is becoming insufficient for feeding, clothing, and
buying shelter for his family.)

NARRATOR: THIS IS DUPREE SMITH'S PROBLEM.

SMITH: TAPE #1, CUT 2: "YES, THAT WAS MY DESIRE . . . PART TIME
AND WORKING."

(Yes, that was my desire after returning from service, was to go
back to nature and live and raise a family where I felt that I would
enjoy living to the fullest. For several years, on this same amount
of land, I was able to support my family and myself adequately. For
the last year or two, this has been on the decrease. The decline has
been to such extent, that I've had to go into other fields—my wife
helping part time and working.)

NARRATOR: WHAT SPECIFICALLY ARE DUPREE SMITH'S PROBLEMS?

KOVENOCK: TAPE #2, CUT 3: "THE COMMON PROBLEM . . . OCCUPATIONAL
PURSUIT?"

(The common problem shared by the North Carolina farmer and by
the national farmer would be, first of all, the condition of agriculture, the relationship of the supply of agricultural commodities to
the demand and, of course, consequently, the price that the farmer
receives which, of course, now is somewhat depressed. The second
major problem is the condition of the rest of the economy as a whole—
that is, is it sufficiently good so that the farmer has some alternatives to continuing his, currently, rather unsatisfactory occupational
pursuit?)

NARRATOR: FARMERS ARE MARKETING MORE, BUT ARE RECEIVING LOWER
PRICES FOR THEIR CROPS AND PRODUCE. DR. PHILLIPS
RUSSELL, A FORMER COLLEGE PROFESSOR AND RETIRED
FARMER, HAS THIS TO SAY:

PHILLIPS
RUSSELL: TAPE #3, CUT 1: "THE FARMER HAS BEEN LOSING . . . IN AN
UNPROTECTED MARKET."

(The farmer has been losing out everywhere, because he has to buy the things that he needs in a protected market and he has to sell in an unprotected market.)

NARRATOR: WHAT IS THE FARMER'S ANSWER TO THIS PROBLEM? FARMING HAS BECOME A BUSINESS INSTEAD OF A WAY OF LIFE. THE FARMER IS FORCED TO CURTAIL HIS ACTIVITIES ON THE FARM IN ORDER TO SUPPORT HIS FAMILY. DR. RUSSELL SAYS:

RUSSELL: TAPE #3, CUT 2: "THAT'S THE ONLY WAY . . . 24-HOUR FARMER."

(That's the only way that a man can continue in farming—is to make some extra money in town to spend it out in the country because he's losing everywhere as a 24-hour farmer.)

NARRATOR: FARMER HARRY WOODS COMMENTS:

HARRY
WOODS: TAPE #4, CUT 1: "I WOULD HATE . . . AT THIS TIME."

(I would hate to have to try—let's put it that way—right at this time.)

INTERVIEWER: TAPE #1: CUT 1 (CONT.): "WOULD YOU LIKE . . . IT FULL TIME?"

(Would you like to be able to work it full time?)

WOODS: TAPE #4, CUT 1 (CONT.): "WELL, I ENJOY . . . IT'S PRETTY ROUGH."

(Well, I enjoy farming. I enjoy it, but as far as actually making a living out of it, I would hate to think that I had to do it, because it's pretty rough.)

NARRATOR: MANY BELIEVE THAT THE BASIS FOR SOLVING THE PROBLEM LIES AT THE FEDERAL GOVERNMENT LEVEL. HARDEST HIT IS THE FARMER WHO CAN LEAST AFFORD IT, THE SMALL COM-MERCIAL FARMERS WORKING INFERIOR LAND. THEY LACK ADEQUATE CAPITAL TO IMPROVE THEIR HOMES. MUCH OF THEIR EFFORT GOES INTO PRODUCING THEIR OWN FOOD. OFTEN. THEY DON'T HAVE THE MECHANICAL AIDS TO MAKE THEM MORE EFFICIENT. THEY ALSO GET LITTLE BENEFIT FROM THE SUBSIDIES AND HIGH SUPPORTS BECAUSE THEIR YIELD IS LOW AND THEY CAN'T AFFORD TO STORE UNTIL THE GOVERN-MENT MAKES PAYMENT.

RUSSELL: TAPE #3, CUT 3: "IF FARMING . . . THAT'D BE FATAL."

(If farming is to be continued, and the country still has to rely on the farms for three very important things: food, feed, and fiber, and if the farming system collapses, we won't have enough fiber, and in case of war, that'd be fatal.)

INTERVIEWER: TAPE #3, CUT 3 (CONT.): "DO YOU THINK . . . ADMINISTRATIONS?"

(Do you think that during the last past eight years, under the Repub-lican administration, that farming has suffered more than it had under the Truman and Roosevelt administrations?)

RUSSELL: TAPE #3, CUT 3 (CONT.): "NOT NECESSARILY MORE . . . NOT OF AGRICULTURE."

(Not necessarily more, but the momentum on decline became faster because under the Eisenhower administration the interest was on the promotion of the welfare of industry, not of agriculture.)

INTERVIEWER: TAPE #3, CUT 3 (CONT.): "DO YOU THINK . . . IN AGRICULTURE?"

(Do you think, now, with the Democratic administration coming in once again that perhaps it will return to some of the New Deal type of policy used in agriculture?)

RUSSELL: TAPE #3, CUT 3 (CONT.): "WELL, I THINK . . . IN CONGRESS THEN."

(Well, I think that would have to be considered. I was always an advocate, or rather, supporter of the Brannan Plan that was discussed under the Truman administration, but never adopted as opposed by Congress, particularly by Southern representatives in Congress then.)

NARRATOR: BESIDES PRICE SUPPORTS, STORAGE AND SOIL BANKS, THE GOVERNMENT SPENDS SOME TWO AND A HALF BILLION DOLLARS TO OPERATE ITS OTHER FUNCTIONS FOR THE IMPROVEMENT OF FARMING. THERE IS LITTLE AGREEMENT AS TO JUST WHAT ROLE GOVERNMENT SHOULD PLAY IN ASSISTING THE FARMER. FARMER HARRY WOODS HAD THIS TO SAY ABOUT THE RETIRING REPUBLICAN ADMINISTRATION:

WOODS: TAPE #4, CUT 2: "THE FARM PROBLEM . . . TO HAVE THEM."

(The farm problem has been with us ever since I've known anything about the farm, and there have been both sides in, and it's never been solved yet. Until they really get down to business and want to solve it, why, it never will be. Now, you said something about politics, why, you know, and I think that everybody else realizes that there is politics in the farm program as they are administered. By the time that they go into the Contress and come out, you know what happens, and, it's difficult to ever work out something that, well, that is workable. But, as far as Republicans or Democrats, why, we've had farm problems under both parties, and I think we'll continue to have them.)

KOVENOCK: TAPE #2, CUT 4: "THERE'S COMMON AGREEMENT . . . THIRTY-EIGHT CENTS."

(There's common agreement, common ground for agreement, that during the last seven or eight years, the Republican administration since 1952, that farm income has gone down roughly twenty-five per cent. The farm purchasing power is at the lowest point since sometime during the 1930's. Further, we have relatively great social dislocations among farmers and non-farmers in rural America due to the relative decline of the position of the farmer in the eonomic sphere. There's common agreement, I think, that the Department of Agriculture has spent more money in the last seven years than all preceding Secretaries of Agriculture have spent in the 9-year period prior to 1952. We now have more employees in the Department of Agriculture than we've ever had before, and, of course, they are serving fewer farmers. The size of the surplus is, of course, grounds for common agreement. It's multiplied six or seven times since the last Democratic administration—now worth, roughly, seven billion dollars. And, of course, the farmer's share of the dollar that we spend in the grocery store has declined now to a low point of thirty-eight cents.)

NARRATOR: DR. PHILLIPS RUSSELL HAD THIS TO SAY WHEN ASKED IF HE THOUGHT THAT FARMING HAD SUFFERED UNDER THE REPUBLICAN ADMINISTRATION:

RUSSELL: TAPE #3, CUT 4: "NOT NECESSARILY MORE . . . NOT OF AGRICULTURE."

(Not necessarily more, but the momentum of decline became faster because, under the Eisenhower Administration, the emphasis was mostly on the welfare of industry, not of agriculture.)

NARRATOR: AS TO THE PROSPECTS FOR KENNEDY'S NEW FRONTIER, DR. KOVENOCK SAID THIS:

KOVENOCK: TAPE #2, CUT 5: "I'M CERTAIN . . . BY GOVERNMENT."

	(I'm certain that the new administration will produce no cure-all. There will be no sudden change in upturn in the position of the farmer here in North Carolina or in the nation as a whole, because many of the problems of agriculture are quite beyond quick manipulation by government.)
NARRATOR:	DUPREE SMITH HAD AN OPINION WITH A SOMEWHAT LIGHTER VIEW:
SMITH:	TAPE #1, CUT 3: "I DON'T THINK . . . I DON'T KNOW."
	(I don't think that Mr. Kennedy will go into raising any chickens, (LAUGHTER) to run any competition with us poultry farmers, so I think, maybe, we might get just a little help; I don't know.)
MUSIC:	IN AND UNDER
NARRATOR:	THESE ARE THE PROBLEMS.
MUSIC:	FADE OUT
NARRATOR:	THE ANSWERS ARE NOT APPARENT. THE FARM INCOME DILEMMA SPELLS TROUBLE, NOT ONLY FOR THE FARMERS, BUT FOR THE PEOPLE WHO DO BUSINESS WITH THEM, POLITICIANS, GOVERNMENT OFFICIALS AND TAX PAYERS ALIKE. WHAT DOES THE FARMER, AS A MEMBER OF THE AMERICAN SOCIETY, DESERVE? PROFESSOR S. H. HOBBS OF THE SOCIOLOGY DEPARTMENT OF THE UNIVERSITY OF NORTH CAROLINA HAD THIS TO DAY:
HOBBS:	TAPE #5, CUT 1: "ONE IS THE PROBLEM . . . ECONOMIC SYSTEM."
	(One is the problem of maintaining income adequate to maintain a level of living comparable with other groups. This does not mean that farmers deserve an income equal to that of any other group, but he does deserve to have an income that enables him to live comfortably in the American economic system.)
NARRATOR:	IN A REGULATED, PROTECTED, AND PARTIALLY SUBSIDIZED ECONOMY SUCH AS OURS, THE FARMER REQUIRES CONSIDERABLE PROTECTION. THE TASK IS TO DEVISE NEW METHODS WHICH WILL PROVIDE HIM WITH AN ADEQUATE INCOME FOR THE VITAL FOOD WHICH HE PRODUCES.
SMITH:	TAPE #1, CUT 1: "I WOULD LIKE . . . PLACE TO WORK."
	(I would like very much to spend my entire life here on the farm because I feel like being near the land and being near the soil and seeing the operation of God on this earth is the best place to live and the best place to work.)
MUSIC:	IN, UP, HOLD, UNDER.
NARRATOR:	YOU HAVE BEEN LISTENING TO "THE PIEDMONT, NORTH CAROLINA, FARMER AND POLITICS, 1961." THIS PROGRAM WAS A STUDENT PRODUCTION OF THE RADIO PRODUCTION CLASS IN THE DEPARTMENT OF RADIO, TELEVISION AND MOTION PICTURES OF THE UNIVERSITY OF NORTH CAROLINA. ASSOCIATED WITH THE PRODUCTION WERE: BUD CARTER, YOSHI CHINEN, JIM CLARK, WILLIAM GAY, ROGER KOONCE, JOHN MOORE, ANITA ROSEFIELD, ALEX WARREN, ANNE WILLIAMS, STEVE SILVERSTEIN AS ENGINEER, AND WAYNE UPCHURCH, YOUR ANNOUNCER.
MUSIC:	UP AND OUT.

Application: Organization

One of the finest documentaries of radio or television was CBS Radio's "Who Killed Michael Farmer?," an exploration in depth of a murder, the murderers and their environment. Part of the documentary is presented here, with comments noting the organizational approach and some of the techniques used.

"WHO KILLED MICHAEL FARMER?"

OPENS COLD:

MURROW: This is Ed Murrow. Here is how a mother and a father remember their son — Michael Farmer.

ET: MR. AND MRS. FARMER:

MRS. FARMER: Michael was tall and very good looking. He had blond hair and blue eyes. Maybe I'm prejudiced as a mother, but I thought he had a saintly face.

MR. FARMER: He was always laughing and joking. He was a very courageous and spirited boy. He was athletic, even though he walked with a limp from an attack of polio when he was ten years old. He was an excellent student who had great plans for his future. It's a hard thing to realize that there is no future any longer.

MURROW: Michael Farmer died on the night of July 30, 1957. He was fifteen years old. He was stabbed and beaten to death in a New York City park. Boys in a teenage street gang were arrested for this crime. Ten gang members — under fifteen years of age — were convicted of juvenile delinquency and committed to state training schools. Seven other boys — fifteen to eighteen — stood trial for first degree murder . . . were defended by twenty-seven court-appointed lawyers. Their trial lasted ninety-three days; ended last Tuesday. This was the verdict of an all male, blue ribbon jury.

ET: JUROR:

We found Louis Alvarez and Charles Horton guilty of murder in the second degree, and we also found Lencio de Leon and Leroy Birch guilty of manslaughter in the second degree. We found Richard Hills and George Melendez not guilty because we believe these boys were forced to go along with the gang the night of the murder. We also found John McCarthy not guilty because we were convinced, beyond a reasonable doubt, that this boy was mentally sick and didn't know what was going on at any time.

MURROW: It would seem that this case now is closed. All that remains is for a judge to pass sentence. Under the law, the gang alone is guilty of the murder of Michael Farmer. But there is more to be said. More is involved here, than one act of violence, committed on one summer night. The roots of this crime go back a long ways. In the next hour — you will hear the voices of boys and adults involved in the case. This is not a dramatization.

The tragedy first became news on the night of July 30, 1957. At 6:30 on this steaming summer evening in New York City, the Egyptian Kings and Dragons gang began to assemble. They met outside a neighborhood hangout — a candy story at 152nd Street and Broadway, in Manhattan's upper West Side. They came from a twenty-block area . . . from teeming tenements, rooming houses and housing projects. One of their leaders remembers the number of boys present this night.

"WHO KILLED MICHAEL FARMER?"
❍ Columbia Broadcasting System, Inc. 1962. Written and produced by Jay L. McMullen.

A standard method of effectively opening a radio documentary is to select carefully cut of the mass of taped material several short statements by persons involved and present them immediately in order to get the audience attention and interest as well as to tell, sharply and concretely, what the program is about. This is especially effective here in the opening statements of Mr. and Mrs. Farmer. The stark nature of the beginning of the program — it opens cold, no introduction, no music — lends force to the opening. Short opening quotes are not usually sufficient, however, to provide enough background information. The narrator condenses and states in terse terms the necessary additional material. The type of documentary is suggested close to the beginning. The statement: "But there is more to be said. More is involved here . . . the roots of crime go back a long ways" indicates the line of development: not only will the event and the people involved be explored in depth, but a problem will be presented and solutions will be sought.

ET: GANG MEMBER:

We had a lot o' little kids, big kids, we had at least seventy-five — then a lot of 'em had to go home before nine o'clock; we was supposed to leave at nine o'clock but then we changed our plans to ten o'clock, you know. So I told a lot o' little kids I don't wanna see them get into trouble, you know, nice guys, so I told them they could go home. So they went home. That left us with around twenty-one kids.

MORROW: People sitting on the stoops and garbage cans along this street watched them . . . grouped together, talking excitedly. They called each other by their nicknames: Magician, Big Man, Little King, Boppo. No one bothered to ask what they were talking about. This boy remembers.

ET: GANG MEMBER:

They were talking about what they were going to do and everything. They were going to fight and everything. But they'd never planned nothing. They just said we were gonna go to the fight and we were just gonna get some guys for revenge. They said we ain't gonna let these Jesters beat up any of our guys no more.

MURROW: The Jesters are a street gang in an adjoining neighborhood — Washington Heights, where Michael Farmer lived. The two gangs were feuding. Boys on both sides had been beaten and stabbed. There is evidence that this night the gang planned to surprise and attack any Jesters they could find. They came prepared for a fight.

ET: GANG MEMBER:

Some picked a stick and some had got some knives and chains out of their houses and everything. One had a bayonette. No, a machete.

MURROW: Holding these weapons they lingered on the corner of a brightly lit street in the heart of a great city. A police station was one block away. One gang leader went to a candy store . . . telephoned the President of a brother gang . . . requested guns and cars for the night's activity . . . was told: "We can't join you. We have troubles of our own tonight." Shortly after nine PM, the gang walked to a nearby park . . . was followed there by some girl friends. A gang member, 14 years old, continues the story.

ET: GANG MEMBER:

We went down to the park and sat around for a while. Then we started drinking and we drank whiskey and wine and we was drunk. Then we started talkin' about girls. We started sayin' to the girls that if they get us to bring us some roses an' all that — that if we get caught to write to us and all this.

MURROW: In one hour, Michael Farmer would be dead. The gang prepared to move out. Some had doubts.

Suspense is an important ingredient of the documentary. But it is not the suspense of finding out what is going to happen. The documentary is based on fact: we already know. The suspense is in learning the motivations, the inner feelings, the attitudes of the persons involved even as the actual event is retold. This is implied in the narrator's previous speech.

ET:	GANG MEMBER:

I didn't wanna go at first, but they said come on. So then all the big guys forced me to go. I was scared. I was worried. I realized like what I was doing I'd probably get in trouble.

MURROW: They left the park and headed for trouble at about ten PM. They walked uptown toward the neighborhood of the rival gang — the Jesters. They walked in two's and three's to avoid attention. Along the way, they met, by chance, this boy.

ET: GANG MEMBER:

I was walkin' uptown with a couple of friends and we ran into Magician and them there. They asked us if we wanted to go to a fight, and we said yes. When they asked me if I wanted to go to a fight, I couldn't say no. I mean I could say no, but for old-times sake, I said yes.

MURROW: He was a former member of the gang—just went along this night, "For Old-times Sake." Next stop: Highbridge Park . . . within the territory of the Jesters. Michael Farmer lived one block from the park. In the summer, the Egyptian Kings and Dragons fought the Jesters at the park swimming pool. This pool is closed at ten PM but not drained. Boys in the neighborhood frequently slip through a breach in the gate to swim here late at night. The Egyptian Kings and Dragons regrouped near the pool. Two gang members continue the story.

ET: GANG MEMBERS:

FIRST BOY: We were waiting over there, in the grass. Then two guys went down to see if there were a lot of the Jesters down there. To check. I was kind of nervous; felt kind of cold inside.

SECOND BOY: They sent three guys around the block. We walked around the block to see how strong the club was we was gonna fight. To see if they had lots of guys and what-not. What we saw, they had lots of big guys. I'd say about nineteen, twenty or eighteen, like that. And we figured it out so we kept on walking around the block.

MURROW: While their scouts prowled the neighborhood, Michael Farmer and his friend, sixteen year old Roger McShane, were in Mike Farmer's apartment . . . listening to rock 'n' roll records. This is Mrs. Farmer.

We can see the use here of D. W. Griffith's technique of dynamic cutting: switching back and forth between two or more settings and two or more persons or groups of people who are following a parallel course in time and in action. The actions of the gang have been presented in chronological order. Now time is moved back and the actions of Michael Farmer and Roger McShane will catch up in time and place.

ET: MRS. FARMER:

They stayed in his room playin' these new records that they had bought and Michael came out to the kitchen, just as I asked my husband what time it was, to set the clock. It was then five after ten. He asked for a glass of milk and as he walked from the kitchen, he asked, "I'm going to walk Roger home." And that was the last time I saw him.

MURROW: Both boys had been warned by their parents to stay out of Highbridge Park at night. But, as they walked along the street on this steaming July evening, they decided to sneak a swim in the park pool. At this pool, the Egyptian Kings and Dragons were waiting for their scouts to return. Here is what happened next; first in the words of Roger McShane; then in words of the gang members.

ET: McSHANE AND EGYPTIAN KINGS:

McSHANE: It was ten-thirty when we entered the park;
we saw couples on the benches, in the back of the pool, and they all
stared at us, and I guess they must 'ave saw the gang there — I don't
think they were fifty or sixty feet away. When we reached the front
of the stairs, we looked up and there was two of their gang members
on top of the stairs. They were two smaller ones, and they had
garrison belts wrapped around their hands. They didn't say nothin'
to us, they looked kind of scared.

FIRST BOY: I was scared. I knew they were gonna jump
them, an' everythin' and I was scared. When they were comin' up,
they all were separatin' and everything like that.

McSHANE: I saw the main body of the gang slowly walk
out of the bushes, on my right. I turned around fast, to see what
Michael was going to do, and this kid came runnin' at me with the
belts. Then I ran, myself, and told Michael to run.

SECOND BOY: He couldn't run anyway, cause we were all
around him. So then I said, "You're a Jester," and he said "Yeah,"
and I punched him in the face. And then somebody hit him with a bat
over the head. And then I kept punchin' him. Some of them were too
scared to do anything. They were just standin' there, lookin'.

THIRD BOY: I was watchin' him. I didn't wanna hit him,
at first. Then I kicked him twice. He was layin' on the ground,
lookin' up at us. I kicked him on the jaw, or some place; then I
kicked him in the stomach. That was the least I could do, was kick
'im.

FOURTH BOY: I was aimin' to hit him, but I didn't get a
chance to hit him. There was so many guys on him — I got scared
when I saw the knife go into the guy, and I ran right there. After
everybody ran, this guy stayed, and started hittin' him with a machete.

MURROW: The rest of the gang pursued Roger McShane.

ET: McSHANE:

I ran down the hill and there was three more of the gang members
down at the bottom of the hill, in the baseball field; and the kids
chased me down hill, yelling to them to get me.

MURROW: Members of the gang remember.

ET: EGYPTIAN KINGS AND McSHANE:

FIRST BOY: Somebody yelled out, "Grab him. He's a
Jester." So then they grabbed him. Mission grabbed him, he turned
around and stabbed him in the back. I was . . . I was stunned. I
couldn't do nuthin'. And then Mission — he went like that and he
pulled : . . he had a switch blade and he said, "you're gonna hit him
with the bat or I'll stab you." So I just hit him lightly with the bat.

SECOND BOY: Mission stabbed him and the guy he . . . like
hunched over. He's standin' up and I knock him down. Then he was
down on the ground, everybody was kickin' him, stompin' him,
punchin' him, stabbin' him so he tried to get back up and I knock him
down again. Then the guy stabbed him in the back with a bread knife.

THIRD BOY: I just went like that, and I stabbed him with the
bread knife. You know, I was drunk so I just stabbed him. (LAUGHS)
He was screamin' like a dog. He was screamin' there. And then I
took the knife out and I told the other guys to run. So I ran and then
the rest of the guys ran with me. They wanted to stay there and keep
on doin' it, so I said, "No, come on. Don't kill the guy." And we ran.

ET: FOURTH BOY: The guy that stabbed him in the back with the
bread knife, he told me that when he took the knife out o' his back, he
said, "Thank you."

McSHANE: They got up fast right after they stabbed me.
And I just lay there on my stomach and there was five of them as
they walked away. And as they walked away they . . . this other big
kid came down with a machete or some large knife of some sort, and
he wanted to stab me too with it. And they told him, "No, come on.
We got him. We messed him up already. Come on." And they took
off up the hill and they all walked up the hill and right after that they
all of 'em turned their heads and looked back at me. I got up and
staggered into the street to get a cab. And I got in a taxi and I asked
him to take me to the Medical Center and get my friend and I blacked
out.

MURROW: The gang scattered and fled from the park. This boy believes he is
the last gang member who saw Michael Farmer this night.

ET: GANG MEMBER:

While I was runnin' up the footpath, I saw somebody staggering in the
bushes and I just looked and turned around, looked up and kept on
runnin'. I think that was the Farmer boy, he was staggerin' in the
bushes.

The suspense has been built and a climax reached. The selection and editing of taped
materials to tell the story of the assault and murder are done magnificently. Excerpts from
the taped interviews were selected to follow a chronological pattern and to present the
actions, feelings and attitudes of the gang members in terms of increasing tempo and
violence. Various physical and emotional viewpoints are presented, all relating to one
another and building the suspense into an ultimate explosion. The documentary should be
dramatic. Is there any doubt about the existence of drama in the preceding sequence?
The audience is put into the center of the action, feeling it perhaps even more strongly than
if the incident were fictionalized and presented, as such incidents frequently are, on a
"private-eye" series. Could any line of a play be more dramatic than, in context, "That
was the least I could do, was kick 'im," or "(LAUGHS) He was screamin' like a dog," or
"The guy that stabbed him in the back with the bread knife, he told me that when he took
the knife out o' his back, he said 'Thank you'." ?

MURROW: He left behind a boy nearly dead . . . continued home . . . had a glass
of milk . . . went to bed. But then.

ET: GANG MEMBER:

I couldn't sleep that night or nuthin' cause I used to fall asleep for about
half an hour. Wake up again during the middle of the night. My
mother said, "What was the matter with you? Looks like something
is wrong." I said, "Nothin'."

MURROW: That boy used a baseball bat in the attack. This boy used a bread
knife.

ET: GANG MEMBER:

First I went to the river to throw my knife away and then I went home.
An' then I couldn't sleep. I was in bed. My mother kept on askin' me
where was I and I . . . I told her, you know, that I was in the movies.
I was worried about them two boys. If they would die . . . I knew I
was gonna get caught.

MURROW: At Presbyterian Medical Center, Roger McShane was on the critical
list. Before undergoing major surgery that saved his life, he told
about the attack in Highbridge Park. The official police record reveals what happened next. The speaker: New York City's Deputy
Police Commissioner, Walter Arm.

142

ET: COMMISSIONER ARM:

A member of the hospital staff notified the police and patrolmen of the 34th precinct arrived at the hospital a few minutes afterwards and learned from the McShane boy that his friend Michael Farmer was still in the part, under attack. The patrolmen rushed to the park, where they found the Farmer boy just before eleven PM. He was lying on the ground off the footpath and moaning in pain. The policemen were soon joined by detectives and young Farmer told them, "The Egyptian Kings got me." The Farmer boy made this comment as he was being rushed to the hospital at 11:05 PM. The parents of the boy were notified.

MURROW: Mr. and Mrs. Farmer continue the story.

ET: MR. AND MRS. FARMER:

MR. FARMER: The Sergeant from the 34th Precinct called us, and asked who I was, and was I the father of Michael Farmer. I said I was, and he said, "Well, your boy is in Mother Cabrini Hospital, in serious condition." I identified myself further, as a fireman in this area, and he said, "Oh, I'll come right down and give you a lift down to the hospital." So this sergeant drove us down to the hospital; as we walked in, the officer who was on duty there called the sergeant, and he said the boy had died fifteen minutes earlier.

MRS. FARMER: And the sister there in the hospital, took us downstairs to identify the body. He had an expression as though he was just calling for help.

MR. FARMER: Well, it was real bad . . . he was my number one boy.

MURROW: This boy had never been in trouble with the police. Several Egyptian Kings and Dragons claim they often saw him with the Jesters; assumed he was a member. The Jesters say neither Farmer nor McShane belonged to their gang . . . and according to police, there is no evidence to the contrary. From the Jesters, police learned which boys might have been involved in the assault at Highbridge Park. At 6:30 AM, this gang member heard somebody knocking at the door of his apartment in a housing project.

ET: GANG MEMBER:

I hear this knockin' on the door. I didn't think it was the police, you know. 'Cause, you know, I thought I wasn't gonna get caught, so I was layin' in bed and told my mother, "Mommie, I think that's the milkman knockin' on the door or somebody." She said, "Why don't you answer it," and I said, "No, I'm in my underwear." So she says, "OK, I'll go." She opened the door and my mother comes over, "You get in any trouble last night?" And I says, "No, Mommie, I didn't get in no trouble last night." And then she says, "Well, there's a policeman over here, wants to see you." And I says, "What for," and he says, "Somethin' that happened last night," and I says, "OK," then, I started thinkin' of trying, you know, runnin' away from the house, so I put on my clothes and acted innocent, you know. He said to me, "You know what happened last night?" I say, "No, No. I don't know a thing that happened last night. I was in the car from ten on." He says, "Oh, if that's the truth, you have nothin' to worry about. You like to come down to the police station with us?" And I said, "OK."

MURROW: Another gang member spent the morning in Children's Court, pleading innocent to a robbery committed two weeks earlier. He was released, pending a hearing. When he returned home, police were waiting to question him about the murder of Michael Farmer. This is the boy who used a bread knife in the assault at Highbridge park.

143

ET: GANG MEMBER:

Well, when we was goin' to the . . . to the paddy wagon, the detective,
he kept wipin' his feet on my suit. So I told him to cut it out, and he
still won't cut it out. So then, then the Sergeant says, "Cut it out," so
then he said, "Why don't you mind your business," and he kept on doin'
it. He kept on wipin' his feet on my suit, and I just got the suit out of
the cleaners, that's all. I told him, "I just got the suit out of the
cleaners," and he says to me, "That's just too bad. That suit belongs
in the garbage can." So he kept on wipin' his feet on my suit, and he
kept on sayin', "You murderer" and all this. They kept on sayin',
"You're gonna get the electric chair, you're gonna get the electric
chair." He kept on sayin' that to me; he made me mad. If I had a gun,
I would have shot them all.

MURROW: He told us, "I hate cops." The police say his story of what happened in
that paddy wagon is fantasy. They also deny threatening another gang
member who explains why he wanted to be caught.

ET: GANG MEMBER:

I was crackin' up 'cause I wanted them to hurry up and come and get
me and get it over with, so when I got picked up, I felt safe then. We
went in the car and then they threatened me. I mean, not exactly a
threat, but they told me what was goin' to happen: I'd get beat up if I
didn't talk. So I told them, "Tell me, who was the guy that squealed?"
They told me, "Who do you think you are, Dillinger or somebody —
ya gonna get even with the guy?" I said, "No, I just wanted to know."
They said, "No." So they took me to the Precinct; it made me laugh
to see all the guys sitting there in the . . . in the . . . when I walked
in, everybody said, "Ha ha, " and started laughin' so I felt all right
with the fellas then. My girl was sitting there anyway, and she . . .
she had the knives.

MURROW: Police found two hunting knives hidden in the bureau drawer of a
fifteen-year-old girl-friend of the gang. Two gang members admitted
that they gave these knives to the girl after the assault at Highbridge
Park. The police record continues.

ET: COMMISSIONER ARM:

The search of the gang during their interrogation yielded five knives,
several garrison belts and a heavy length of chain. All of the young
men arrested made full admissions to police officers and to representatives from the staff of District Attorney Hogan. At 8:00 PM the
following day, seven of the boys were charged with homicide, two
others were charged with attempted homicide, and ten others were
charged with juvenile delinquency.

MURROW: Police said, "This is the largest group of boys ever arrested for a
New York City killing." Statistically, they were among 58 youths in
the city arrested in 1957 for murder and non-negligent manslaughter
. . . among more than three thousand youths under twenty-one arrested
in the nation last year for crimes of major violence . . . and among
an estimated one million youths arrested for crimes of all kinds.
The father of Michael Farmer attended the preliminary court hearing
of the gang members later indicted for the murder of his son. As he
watched them arraigned before a judge, he made a judgment of his
own.

ET: MR. FARMER:

They are monsters — in my mind I classify them as savage animals.
That's all. I don't think that they have any civilization in them. I
think they're just two-legged animals. They haven't any concept of
living with other people, outside of to show that they can do something
worse than the other or to claim any sort of notoriety. These boys
didn't even hang their heads, most of them, when they came to court.

144

They stood erect and looked around the court for their relatives. And so forth. One of them had a small smirk when they looked in our direction. They should be put away, and kept away. Or if the penalty is death, to be executed. Certainly they set themselves up in the form of a judge, jury and execution squad in the case of my son. All in the matter of minutes. This is pure jungle activity.

Thus far the script has told what happened. In the material dealing with actions and attitudes after the crime was committed, the script begins to imply that there is more to the story than what happened, that the persons involved are not the two dimensional characters of the television fiction series. Yet, the act was so grievous and wanton that it is not too difficult to come to the same conclusion as Mr. Farmer. This speech indicates a division in the script. Can we simply leave the story there—this is a jungle and the only solution is to destroy the animals therein? The script begins to explore motivation, begins to get behind the problem.

MURROW: Two detectives told the judge at the gang's arraignment, "These boys showed no remorse and gave us little cooperation." At their murder trial, some of the boys testified that police beat and frightened them into making confessions. The police officers accused, denied this under oath. First reports on this crime suggested that at least one gang member had stabbed for thrills. Police said the fourteen-year-old boy who used a bread knife in the attack told them, "I always wanted to know what it would feel like to stick a knife through human bone." This same boy denied to us that he said that; gave us three other reasons for his crime. First.

ET: GANG MEMBER:

I told you I didn't know what I was doing, I was drunk. I went out, you know, I . . . you know, I was drunk, I just went like that, and I stabbed him.

MURROW: We asked him, "Did you know the boy you stabbed?" Answer: "No, but I thought he was a Jester." Question: "Had the Jesters ever done anything to you?" Answer:

ET: GANG MEMBER:

They kept on callin' me a Spick. They kept on saying, "You dirty Spick, get out of this block." Every time I go in the pool, they said to me the same thing. I don't bother them, 'cause, you know, I don't want to get into no trouble with them, but one day they beat me up. You know, there was about five of them, and they wouldn't leave me alone. They beat me up, and I had to take a chance to get the boys so we could beat them up.

MURROW: He said his third reason for stabbing a boy he did not know involved his fear of gang discipline.

ET: GANG MEMBER:

See, because we say before, if anybody don't beat up somebody, when we get back, he's gonna get beat up. So I say, "OK." They got special guys, you know, to keep their eyes on the boys. Anyone who don't swing out is gonna get it when we come back. They got to pass through a line; they got about fifteen boys over here, and fifteen boys over there, and you know, in a straight line, like that. They got to pass through there and they all got belts in their hand.

MURROW: So far, we have heard that a boy was killed because other boys — most of them under fifteen —got drunk, wanted revenge, feared gang discipline. Only one boy charged with murder pleaded not guilty on grounds of insanity. He was declared legally sane. But a psychiatrist testified in court that this boy was epileptic and "incapable of premeditating and deliberating." Court-appointed defense council did not request psychiatric examination of the other six boys on trial for their lives. The jury that convicted some of them heard very little

145

about their mental and emotional make-up. Our reporter tried to get psychiatric reports on the other gang members too young to be tried for murder. He questioned Marion Cohen, head of the treatment service, New York City Youth House. She told him.

ET:

MISS COHEN AND REPORTER:

COHEN: We see our function as holding boys remanded temporarily by Children's Court until disposition of their case is made by a judge. While the boy is here, we try to study and diagnose his problem.

REPORTER: Well, now, the younger members of the gang that killed Michael Farmer were brought here. Did you study the individual boys; make reports on them for the judge who was going to try them?

COHEN: No, we did not.

REPORTER: Why not?

COHEN: Because the judge did not request it.

REPORTER: Is this usual practice?

COHEN: No, in most cases, judges are interested in finding out as much as they can about the individual boy's problems, in order to differentiate his needs.

REPORTER: But in this case, nothing was found out about the mental make-up or the individual needs of these boys. Is that right?

COHEN: Yes.

REPORTER: Do you usually wait for the court to request such studies?

COHEN: No, when we are fully staffed, we do a study on every boy who is here for more than a week.

REPORTER: Why didn't you study these boys then?

COHEN: Because we are two-thirds under-staffed. We have only four case-workers for three-hundred boys.

MURROW: The New York City Youth House is a brand-new five-million-dollar building. It has a swimming pool, self-service elevators — the most modern equipment. But there are only four case-workers for three-hundred boys. Reason: low pay and a shortage of trained personnel. Our reporter continues his conversation with Marion Cohen.

ET:

MISS COHEN AND REPORTER:

REPORTER: Can you make any generalizations about the gang members you have studied?

COHEN: Yes, these are kids who essentially feel in themselves weak and inadequate . . . and have to present a tough facade to others. Of course, most adolescents feel insecure. But these boys have a distorted idea of what real adequacy is. They become easy prey for leaders whose sole drive is aggressive. They are egged on by their peers to establish a tough reputation . . . each kid daring the other to go one step farther. They have to compete on a level of violence.

146

MURROW: It would seem that members of the Egyptian Kings and Dragons gang
            fit the pattern. Consider the statement of this fourteen-year-old gang
            member who participated in the assault at Highbridge Park.

The interviews with the experts may be considered transition material. It is established that there is a problem. Some of the reasons for the problem are tentatively suggested. The audience now is ready for exploration of the problem and a clarification of
the reasons.

ET: GANG MEMBER:

            I didn't want to be like . . . you know, different from the other guys.
            Like they hit him, I hit him. In other words, I didn't want to show
            myself as a punk. You know, ya always talkin', "Oh man, when I catch
            a guy, I'll beat him up," and all of that, you know. So after you go out
            and you catch a guy, and you don't do nothin', they say, "Oh man, he
            can't belong to no gang, because he ain't gonna do nothin'."

MURROW: Are we to believe that a boy is dead — murdered — because those who
            killed him fear being called "punks"? Another gang member says he
            acted to protect his reputation. He calls it "rep."

ET: GANG MEMBER:

            Momentarily, I started to thinking about it inside: did I have my mind
            made up I'm not going to be in no gang. Then I go on inside. Some-
            thing comes up den here come all my friends coming to me. Like I
            said before, I'm intelligent and so forth. They be coming to me —
            then they talk to me about what they gonna do. Like, "Man, we'll go
            out here and kill this guy." I say, "Yeah." They kept on talkin' and
            talkin'. I said, "Man, I just gotta go with you." Myself, I don't want
            to go, but when they start talkin' about what they gonna do, I say,
            "So, he isn't gonna take over my rep. I ain't gonna let him be known
            more than me." And I go ahead just for selfishness. I go ahead, and
            get caught or something; sometimes I get caught, sometimes I don't.
            I'm in some trouble there.

MURROW: That boy admits that he kicked and punched Roger McShane during
            the attack at Highbridge Park . . . didn't stab him because he didn't
            have a knife. We asked, "Suppose you had a knife; would you have
            used it? Answer:

ET: GANG MEMBER:

            If I would of got the knife, I would have stabbed him. That would have
            gave me more of a build-up. People would have respected me for
            what I've done and things like that. They would say, "There goes a
            cold killer."

MURROW: He wants people to say, "There goes a cold killer." He is only
            fourteen years old — the same age as the boy who used a bread knife
            in the Highbridge Park attack . . . and who told us why he too wants
            to be known as a "cold killer."

ET: GANG MEMBER:

            It makes you feel like a big shot. You know some guys think they're
            big shots and all that. They think, you know, they got the power to do
            everything they feel like doing. They say, like, "I wanna stab a guy."
            and then the other guy say, "Oh, I wouldn't dare to do that." You
            know, he thinks I'm acting like a big shot. That's the way he feels.
            He probably thinks in his mind, "Oh, he probably won't do that."
            Then, when we go to a fight, you know, he finds out what I do.

MURROW: Some gang members told police that they bragged to each other about
            beating and stabbing Farmer and McShane . . . wanted to make cer-
            tain they would be known as "tough guys." According to the official
            police record, this was the reaction of their parents.

ET: COMMISSIONER ARM:

During the hours that the boys were rounded up and brought to the police station, many of their parents came to the scene. They expressed shock and bewilderment and disbelief over the fact that their boys were being questioned by police and might have had a part in this hideous crime. When they finally realized that this was true, they still couldn't believe it.

MURROW: One mother told our reporter.

ET: MOTHER OF GANG MEMBER AND REPORTER:

MOTHER: I had absolutely no problems with him. Everyone in the neighborhood can vouch for that. When I walked out there this morning, all my store-keepers and everythin' just can't believe that my son is mixed up in anything like this. (SIGH) I have no idea what I can do for him right now. I doubt if there is anything we can do for him right now.

REPORTER: Do you plan to go over to see him?

MOTHER: Of course I have to go to see my child. (SOBBING) I can't let him down now. Even though he was wrong, I still can't just turn my back on him. (SOBBING)

MURROW: Parents went to see their sons in jail; and how did they react when they saw them? One boy said:

ET: GANG MEMBER:

My mother said she was ashamed of me, and everything, and I told her that it wasn't my fault and I couldn't help it. My father wanted to kill me at first, and after I explained to him what happened he was still. . . he was still like . . . felt bad about it, ashamed to walk the streets after somethin' like that, but then you know, he wouldn't touch me then, after I told him what happened.

MURROW: The statement of another gang member.

ET: GANG MEMBER:

My father understood. He didn't actually understand, but you know, he didn't take it as hard as my mother. My mother . . . it came out in the newspapers, she had a heart attack. It's a lucky thing she's alive today.

MURROW: One mother talked to her son in the presence of the other boys arrested. Here is what she said, according to this gang member present.

ET: GANG MEMBER:

When she sees him she says to him, "How did it feel when you did that to Farmer? It was good, eh?" You know, jokin' around with the kid. So we told her, "You know what your son did?" I says, "He stabbed him in the back." She says, she just went like that, shrugged her, you know, shoulders. Then we didn't pay any attention to her, because ya know, you don't like to see a mother actin' like that with a kid ya know.

MURROW: What is known about the mental and emotional make-up of parents whose children commit crimes? Dr. Marjorie Rittwagen, staff psychiatrist for New York Children's Courts, gave us some statistics.

148

ET: DR. RITTWAGEN:

We find that some seventy-five to eighty per cent of parents of
children who are brought into this court are emotionally ill or have
severe personality or character disorders. They include sociopathic
personality disorders, alcoholics and the like. And about ten per cent
of this seventy-five to eighty per cent are commitably psychotic — in
fact, some parents go completely berserk in Court, threaten judges
and are sent to psychiatric wards for observation. Most of these
parents are so overwhelmed with their own problems, that they ignore
their children. Kids feel not so much rejected as nonentities. Usually,
in these homes, there are no fathers.

MURROW: There are no fathers in the homes of five of the seven gang members
tried for the murder of Michael Farmer. Four of these boys live with
their mothers; one with his grandparents. His mother told our reporter why she left her son.

ET: MOTHER OF GANG MEMBER AND REPORTER:

MOTHER: He has lived with my mother all his life from
birth. (SOBS) I lived there up to two, three years ago. It seems like
since I left my child everything has happened. (SOBS) Not that I just
walked out on him, but when I planned to get married I spoke to him.
He said, "Well, go ahead, you have to have some happiness; you
can't just stay with me all the time." So I said, "Will you be willing
to come with me?" He said, "No, I don't want to leave my grandparents." (SOB)

REPORTER: Do you think that it would have been important
if he had stayed with you?

MOTHER: I think it would have been important had I
stayed with him and not leave him at the age of fifteen. I wouldn't
advise that to anyone who has a boy, or any other child. (SOBS)

MURROW: Eleven of the eighteen boys arrested in the Farmer case come from
homes broken by desertion, divorce or death. Children's Court
psychiatrist Marjorie Rittwagen says this is the pattern.

ET: DR. RITTWAGEN:

Some seventy to eighty per cent of our children come from homes
broken by desertion or divorce. Most of the children stay with their
mothers. At critical times in their lives they are left in a fatherless
home. They're almost afraid to relate too closely to their mothers,
and are often driven into the streets to seek companionship with a
gang. They find the superficial group relationship more comfortable
than individual ones. In fact, difficulty in relating to people is one of
their big handicaps. They don't talk out their problems, they act
them out.

MURROW: Example: this thirteen year old boy. He lives with a mother married
and divorced three times. She works to support him . . . cannot
spend much time with him. Her son has plenty of problems, but she
doesn't know about them.

ET: GANG MEMBER:

I never tell her about my problems. One reason is that if I tell her
my problems, like some guys were beating me up, she would keep
me in the house . . . and wouldn't let me go out. Or if I tell her I'm
doing badly in school, she'll probably hit me. Or if I tell her I had
an argument with a teacher, or something like that, she'd probably hit
me. She don't give me a chance to explain, you know. She just comes
out, and pow, she hits me. I don't tell her anything.

149

MURROW: He doesn't talk out his problems; he acts them out — sometimes by firing a beebee gun at adults.

ET: GANG MEMBER:

Tell you the truth, I used to shoot people myself. Sometimes I would shoot the people I don't like too much, you know. (LAUGHS) I would be up on the roof and they would be walkin' by with packages or something — and Pow, I would shoot them.

MURROW: Violence is all around him, he says.

ET: GANG MEMBER:

Usually I go for horror pictures like "Frankenstein and the Mummy" or things like that. I like it when he goes and kills the guy or rips a guy in half or something like that. (LAUGHS) Or when he throws somebody off a cliff. You know, all them exciting things.

MURROW: Next: the gang member who used a bread knife in the Highbridge Park attack. He lived with his mother and step-father; told us he often quarreled with his mother; wanted his step-father to spend more time with him.

ET: GANG MEMBER:

I'll ask him to take me boat-riding, fishing, or some place like that, ball game. He'll say, "No." He don't go no place. The only place where he goes, he goes to the bar. And from the bar, he goes home. Sleep, that's about all he do. I don't talk to my parents a lot of times. I don't hardly talk to them — there's nothing to talk about. There's nothing to discuss about. They can't help me.

MURROW: They can't help me! What he wants, he says, is to be like his favorite comic book hero.

ET: GANG MEMBER:

Mighty Mouse — he's a mouse — he's dressed up like Superman. He's got little pants — they're red. The shirt is yellow. You know, and then he helps out the mouse. Everytime the cats try to get the mouse, Mighty Mouse comes and helps the mouse, just like Superman. He's stronger than the cats. Nothing can hurt him.

MURROW: Another boy told us: "My father doesn't want to hear my troubles. They make him mad." Reason:

ET: .   GANG MEMBER:

He wants me to be better than my other brother. That's why every time he comes to me and say, "You see, you gonna be like your brother. The one that's in the Tombs. If you keep on doing wrong, you gonna be like him." He kept on telling me that, so I said, "Well, if he wants me to be like him, I'm gonna be like him." So I started doing wrong things. And then he says to me, "I don't wanna catch you in trouble." Well, in one way he should have got me in trouble before, because he found a gun that I had . . . you know, I had a home-made. And he found it, and he didn't say nothin', he just broke it up and threw it away and kept me in the house for one day. He should have took it to the police or somethin', and told them that I had it. Maybe I would have been sent to the Youth House or someplace, before, and I wouldn't have gotten into so much trouble, and I would have learned my lesson.

150

MURROW: This was his first arrest. But ten of the eighteen boys involved in the Farmer case had previous records as juvenile offenders; some for such minor offenses as trespassing or chalking names on buildings; others for serious crimes, including assault, burglary and attempted grand larceny. Three gang members were under the supervision of probation officers. But how much supervision does a boy on probation get, in New York City? Clarence Leeds is Chief Probation Officer at Children's Court.

The script is now fully into the problem as it concerns the characters of the story. The transitions, through selecting and editing, are excellent, moving logically, yet not obviously, from the boys to the parents. The statements of the boys and the parents all follow a pattern, validating the diagnosis of the sociologist and the psychiatrist. Now the documentary can attempt an investigation of the solutions to the problem, those attempted and those still to come.

ET: CLARENCE LEEDS:

Our probation officers have minimum case loads of between sixty and seventy delinquent boys apiece. This means that at best they can talk to each boy perhaps once a month. And you can't give a child the guidance and help he needs by seeing him that infrequently. We are doing just about double the number of case loads and investigations that we're equipped to handle and possibly as a consequence of this, about thirty per cent of the boys on probation commit new offenses which will bring them to the attention of the court once again.

MURROW: Three Egyptian Dragons on probation participated in the murder of Michael Farmer. Another member of this gang had served one year in a state training school for juvenile delinquents . . . was diagnosed as a "dangerous psychopath" . . . but received no psychotherapy. Reason: there are 500 boys in this institution; only one psychiatrist and one psychologist to treat them. Five months after this "dangerous psychopath" was released from the institution, he stabbed Roger McShane at Highbridge Park. Who is to blame? John Warren Hill, Chief Justice of New York's Children's Court, told us why many very disturbed children are released quickly by state institutions.

ET: JUDGE HILL:

It is a shocking fact that children committed to state institutions by this court often are discharged from these institutions within four to six months without having received any real treatment or help. Why? Because our state facilities for the long term care of delinquent children are so shockingly inadequate that our state institutions must make these discharges quickly in order to make room for new court commitments. For while the rate of delinquency has increased in New York City, since 1951 through 1956, by 83 per cent, as revealed by our own court statistics, there's not been a single additional bed provided in our state institutions for delinquent children, aside from some few which the city made available for use by the state. But that was a bare nothing compared to the great need which has developed increasingly in this area.

MURROW: Children released from New York institutions are put on parole. The Egyptian Dragon diagnosed as a "dangerous psychopath" was assigned to a youth parole worker . . . was under the supervision of this worker at the time of the Farmer murder. But how closely was he watched? Joseph Linda is in charge of youth parole workers, New York City area.

ET: JOSEPH LINDA:

Each of our youth parole workers supervises about 80 boys, and in some cases, about 100 boys, because of staff shortage. This means that they may see these boys as infrequently as once every two months.

151

MURROW:	Youth parole and probation agencies are non-existent in half the counties of this nation. In most of the other counties, they are under-staffed, according to a survey by the National Probation and Parole Association. Some responsibility for supervising problem children often is shifted to the schools by the courts. This happened in the case of several Egyptian Kings and Dragons brought to court prior to the murder of Michael Farmer. The speaker, Murray Sachs, court liaison officer, Board of Education, New York City.
ET:	MURRAY SACHS:
	The courts had made a number of requests in the helping of these youngsters. The unfortunate thing about these children was this: they would refuse to come to school. Not coming to school, they wouldn't be doing the things that we think are constructive and helpful. Those, we know, have such deep-rooted behavior problems must be dealt with on that basis by specialists who are equipped to handle it, and, for heaven's sake, our community, our citizens should not expect the school to do that. It seems that the only one that might help them would be the institution where they might be placed, and given indi-vidualized and controlled assistance, of one kind or another. Again we're faced with the serious problem of there's just no place for them.
MURROW:	In the richest state of the nation, long-term institutional care is not available for eighty per cent of delinquent children under twelve years of age. No state institution for these children exists. The few private institutions are jammed. One gang member involved in the Farmer case committed five offenses before he was twelve years old. Within a week or two after each arrest, he was set free in the community. At twelve, children are eligible for state training schools. But even then it is difficult to place them because of overcrowding. John Warren Hill, Chief Justice of New York's Children's Court, sums up the result.
ET:	JUDGE HILL:
	In a great number of cases of very disturbed children, children who should be removed from the community, this court has been unable to find any placement for the child and our only alternative has been to place these children on probation, which, of course, means their return to the community.
MURROW:	They are sent back to the streets — unhelped, unsupervised. Set free in the community, what do they do with their time? Listen to one boy describe a typical summer day in his neighborhood of brick tenements in Manhattan's upper west side.
ET:	GANG MEMBER:
	I usually get up at 11 or 12 o'clock, you know, I sleep late. And then I will go out and see the guys, sitting on the stoop, you know, doing nothin'. I would sit there with them, and sometimes they will say, "Let's split and go to a movie," so I would go to the movie with them. Or sometimes we would try and get a game of stickball or somethin' like that. Our block is crowded, we didn't hardly have a chance to play because the busses kept going back and forth, back and forth. We couldn't do nothin'. So that we just sit, then when it got to night-time, well, you know, we would go around, and say, "Come on, man, let's go break windows for some excitement" or "Come on man, let's go boppin'." Then we would go and look for guys, to beat 'em up. Then we would come back. And then, (LAUGHS) we would sit on the stoop, man, and we'd hear a cop car outside and we would all fly up to the roof, or somethin' like that. Then, we just come down and start talkin' and talkin'.
MURROW:	Consider the day of another boy, sixteen years old. He makes the rounds of schools, pool halls, and candy store hangouts. He works for a syndicate . . . sells marijuana cigarettes to other children and smokes them himself.

ET: GANG MEMBER:

I'd get the dough by sellin' it. I'd take about four or five a day. It keeps me goin'. All depends . . . when I get up in the morning I take one or two; three hours later take another one. If I ain't got nothin' to do, I just feel like goofin', crackin' up and everythin'. I just take another one. Go to a dance, take two or three. If you don't get it easy, you try all kinds of — not violence, but you see an easy dollar to rob, you rob it. You see somethin' to pawn, you pawn it.

MURROW:

Boys troubled and adrift in the community formed the gang that killed Michael Farmer. Sociologists call gangs of this breed "anti-social groups" or "fighting gangs." They exist in most of our large cities. According to police estimates there are 134 of these gangs in Los Angeles County; 24 in Miami; 110 in New York, including the Egyptian Kings and Dragons.

You have read about two-thirds of the documentary script. The voices and sounds of realism have been presented. The thoughts and feelings of as many different and varied persons as might be found in a Shakespearean tragedy have been explored. "What" happened moved into "why" it happened into the evolution of a problem that demands a solution. Much as do the films of Pare Lorentz, "Who killed Michael Farmer?" then examines the possible solutions to the problem. The final few pages of the documentary script sum up:

ET: GREENHILL REPORT:

Residents trace the origin of juvenile crime to parents' inability to control their children, racial issues, newcomers in the area, lack of police protection, intimidation of teachers and policemen by youth gangs, and a lack of restrictive measures in Highbridge Park. Persons interviewed reported 16 major incidents leading to death or hospitalization in the last three years. Ten of them in the last two weeks. Most of the incidents had not been reported to police for fear of gang retaliation. Among the population in general, there were attitudes of hopelessness and fear. A large number of people expect gang retaliation after the present crisis has quieted down. They are cynical and see no way of preventing retaliation for it has always occurred in the past. About 40 per cent of children between the ages of 3 and 16 reacted immediately with a variety of physical and emotional symptoms. For the first time, some children began to carry knives for their own protection.

MURROW:

One boy in the neighborhood who fears for his life is Michael Farmer's friend, Roger McShane — a State's witness at the murder trial of the Egyptian Kings and Dragons. During the trial, McShane received two death threats in the mail. One letter said: "You are alive. But if them guys get the chair, we will kill you." That threat possibly came from a crank. But no one can be sure — least of all Roger McShane.

ET: Mc SHANE:

There's nothing you can do except protect yourself. It's just gonna get wilder and wilder. I mean, it's just gonna get worse. You can't have a policeman walking around with every boy or girl that leaves his house at night. And follow him to the store if he has to go to the store or follow him up to the show or you can't have a policeman follow each individual all around the neighborhood just so they can be protected.

MURROW: The parents of Michael Farmer.

ET: MR. AND MRS. FARMER:

MR. FARMER: I'm very much afraid for my son Rayme. Rayme's 14. Who knows the rest of these Egyptian Kings won't come up looking for him, or trying to extend their activities; make themselves a little bit more infamous. You can't reason with the type of minds that they have. You don't know what they'll come up with next.

153

MRS. FARMER: I'm worried about all of us. There was a time when I'd run down at night for milk, or to mail a letter, now I wouldn't go down the street after nine o'clock. I just have that terrible feeling that something is lurking there in the dark.

MURROW: Fear remains in this community. A new summer approaches . . . and according to one volunteer youth worker in the area already there are danger signals.

ET: YOUTH WORKER:

The situation is beginning to look critical once again. We find that one of the Egyptian Kings apparently not involved in the Michael Farmer killing is now trying to reorganize a gang and is recruiting in the area. Unless something is done very quickly with this particular gang, we are definitely going to run into the same situation in a very short time. You can't say whether that will be six months or a year from now, but if this gang is allowed to reorganize again, there may be more killings and something had better be done, fast, if we are interested in saving other children from the fate of Michael Farmer.

MURROW: What has been solved by the verdict of a jury and the commitment of 15 boys to institutions which are ill-equipped to re-habilitate them; and because of overcrowding, may soon return them to the community? The problem of juvenile crime continues. The experts may list all sorts of causes. But they agree on one answer to why these conditions continue to exist: We permit them to. This is Ed Murrow. Good Night.

The Television Documentary

The basic approaches and techniques are essentially the same for the television and radio documentary. The most important difference is the obvious use of visuals in television. Where the radio documentary gathers words and sounds, the television documentary must add film, photos and graphics. Where the radio program must use dialogue and/or narration to describe something, the television program needs only the picture itself. Television has the advantage of the motion picture's "visual writing," the ability to tell a story more concisely and sometimes more meaningfully through showing instead of telling.

The picture may be the primary element in any given sequence in the television documentary, with the narration and taped dialogue secondary. The people and their actions may be actually seen and thus understood, rather than being imagined through verbal descriptions of what they did and saw. On the other hand, the words of the people and the narrator may be the prime movers, with the pictures merely filling in visually what is being described in words. Visual techniques could not substitute for the verbal inner revelations of the gang members in "Who Killed Michael Farmer?"

"The Twentieth Century" has been one of the most successful documentary series on television. Its techniques vary: it deals with people, with places, with events, with inanimate objects, with ideas — each subject frequently requiring a special visual approach. In some instances the writer has prepared a script on the basis of old film clips of an historical nature. Programs on Nazism, for example, have utilized this approach to a large extent. In other instances the writer has relied on recent or current stock film. In most cases it is necessary for a production team to go out and get fresh filmed material as dictated by the needs of the script. In the following opening sequences from "The Twentieth Century" two-part presentation of "Sweden: Trouble in Paradise," the interview technique was combined with the travelogue to present an analysis of the country, of its theoretical as well as physical institutions, through the opinion of its citizens. Note the ways in which the narrative unfolding of this program differs from that of "Who Killed Michael Farmer?"

CRONKITE:

I'm Walter Cronkite — and this is Stockholm. What is it like to live in the world's most highly developed welfare state? Today in democratic Sweden — a unique experiment is going on. Social benefits extend literally from the cradle to the grave. Some call it a paradise on earth. Others see it as beset with problems — juvenile delinquency, alcoholism, suicide Today we present the first of two episodes filmed by THE TWENTIETH CENTURY in this land of many paradoxes — "Sweden" — Is there trouble in Paradise? as The Prudential Insurance Company of America presents THE TWENTIETH CENTURY.

(MAIN TITLE)

(COMMERCIAL)

CRONKITE:

Town hall	Stockholm — a city built on islands and spanned by bridges — sometimes called the Venice of the North. This is the capital of the Swedish Welfare State — the center of a homogeneous nation of seven and a half million people who enjoy the highest standard of living in Europe today.
Train thru countryside	Here, old tradition lives side by side with the development of one of the most progressive societies in the world — under a government which has delivered to its people an ever increasing number of social benefits that have aroused both skepticism and envy throughout the world. (BEAT) Stockholm is overcrowded and many of its one million inhabitants commute daily from suburban centers. Prosperous,
People in train	well fed, well clothed — the Swedes are well provided for — by a benevolent, paternalistic, democratic government — aiming to banish poverty and provide a sense of security for all the people.

THE TWENTIETH CENTURY — Sweden: Trouble in Paradise? Part I. ⊙Columbia Broadcasting System, Inc. 1962. Written by Wilfrid Fleisher.

People in street	What is it like to live in the Welfare State — where few are wealthy and fewer are poor — where practically every basic need is anticipated by the State? Does the levelling of society and all this security lead to the loss of incentive and initiative? We asked the Swedes themselves.
Bergmann	A worker.

MR. BERGMANN:

"I need not worry so much about my parents and relatives as I had to do under other circumstances. I need not fear from being ruined by sickness and unemployment. When I am old and cannot work any longer, I know I have a pension I can live on. This gives me real liberty."

CRONKITE:

Browaldh	A banker.

BROWALDH:

"Well, I've heard a lot about this problem about what makes Sammy run, I mean, what is the incentive for me and other executives to work as hard as we undoubtedly do — running around in a square wheel in fact. And I don't believe that Swedish executives have such pronounced economic incentives as maybe our American colleagues or our English colleagues. I and my generation of executives, we feel that being an executive in charge of a very interesting job is sort of reward enough."

CRONKITE:

Heckscher	A Conservative leader.

HECKSCHER:

"In many respects I think public life in Sweden and even private life is becoming a bit dreary. You do everything by organization. You live in a house which is established by one organization. You buy your food in a coop established by another organization. Your salary, your wages, are fixed by collective contract. You take your pleasures in a society which is again part of a large organization and the only unorganized thing is sleep."

CRONKITE:

People	Despite divergent opinions the fact remains that the people of the Welfare State have lived under the same Social Democratic, or Labor Government, almost continuously for the past 29 years — repeatedly endorsing it in parliamentary and municipal elections.
Govt House	In the Chancery — Government House — we spoke with Sweden's Prime Minister for the past 15 years — Tage Erlander.

CRONKITE:

Erlander	Mr. Prime Minister, what is the ultimate objective of the democratic government? Are you striving for total state ownership of the means of production and of real property?

156

"Now, the ultimate goal is the happiness of the citizens and the nationalization cannot be more than a means to reach that goal. We have in Sweden a mixed economy. I should think that only 10% is owned by the government, by the State, and 90% are private industry."

CRONKITE:

Ballbearing plant   Sweden's modern industry goes largely into exports,which makes the welfare program possible. No poor nation could afford it. Although the State operates most public services — the railways, telegraph, telephone, nearly half the bus lines, and is part owner in the air lines — Sweden is not a Socialist State. About 90% of Swedish industry — including its timber products, steel, and most of its iron ore — remains in private hands.

Government and industry, needing each other, have worked out a unique relationship which extends from the top level to the worker. The worker's main protection is in his labor union. Every worker must join a union and thereby becomes automatically a member of the Social Democratic Party.

The program on Sweden was a combination of the three classical approaches: the presentation of a problem of society; the special analysis of the life of a man or of a people; the showing of the everyday, ordinary existence of a part of the world.

Television documentaries have varied: some have dealt with current, controversial issues, important to the everyday existence and even the life or death of the viewing public. Most have avoided controversy. Many, artistically excellent, present historical subjects. Television commentator Howard K. Smith, in an address in 1965, stated: "I was a judge for the Emmy Awards this year. I sat through six solid hours of watching what were called documentaries. They were all very elaborate, and in beautiful color and must have cost a fortune to produce. But not one dealt with the untidy but fascinating world we live in. Most were a good two or three safe centuries away from today. I protested that I had been given no documentaries to judge. I was told there weren't any." Mr. Smith added that "objectivity does not mean what present documentarians think it does: balancing each thought or statement with its opposite . . . a careful mutual cancellation of facts and views signifying, in the end, nothing." The documentaries in the mid-1960's most directly meeting current controversy head-on were produced by National Educational Television.

The following sports documentary — perhaps, in part, a feature rather than entirely a documentary — utilizes a sophisticated adaptation of the Flaherty approach: the presentation of the tribulations of an individual man and his fight for success. This documentary is of necessity oriented toward the human interest element. However, even a documentary which concentrates on an inanimate object — a town or city, for example — should incorporate the human interest element, endowing the non-live subject with live qualities, if necessary.

● *Preceding the following excerpts from "A Jockey's World" is an earlier step in the writer's work — the outline. 1) As you read the outline and the excerpts determine to what extent the script concretely reflects the outline plan, and to what extent the script departs from the outline. How valuable was the outline in this writing assignment? 2) In terms of the outline, are there any sections of the excerpted material that you would have written in a different way? 3) List the various visual techniques employed and evaluate their effectiveness.*

Tentative Outline for "A Jockey's World" with Eddie Arcaro.

1. The horses are moving into the starting gate. The color and excitement of the track just before the race.

2. Super opening billboard.

3. The race—from start to finish. It makes no difference who wins. If Arcaro, so much the better.

4. At the scale as the jocks dismount. Palmer introduces himself and the show.

5. Arcaro in front of his locker with Palmer. He's relaxing now between races, smoking and talking with anyone who drops by.
   TALK—a chance for the viewer to get a good, close look at this man.

6. The facilities at the track. What does a jockey's "office" look like?
   a. The sweat room.
   b. The sleep room.
   c. The valets.
   d. The game room and snack bar.

7. The new generation of jockeys: we meet Leonard and Yother at TV set.

8. What were the early days like for Arcaro? How did he get into this business?
   TALK.

9. Montage of some of Arcaro's greatest races.

10. The tricks of the trade. Seated on a horse and equipped with a wireless mike, Arcaro gives us an insight into the art of winning races.

11. Arcaro starts getting dressed for next race.
    TALK: how you make a living in racing.
    a. Working for a stable.
    b. Free lancing.
    c. The function of an agent.

12. The hazards of the trade. A montage of track footage showing some of the most exciting spills and accidents through the years.

13. Build-up to next race.
    a. Arcaro finishes dressing.
    b. The scales.
    c. The owner-trainer.
    d. The paddock parade.

14. The race—from start to finish. Again, it doesn't matter who wins, but this time we stay as tight as possible on Arcaro.

15. The wrap-up: Palmer and Arcaro.

"A Jockey's World" with Eddie Arcaro

VIDEO	AUDIO
ESTAB. SHOT OF TRACK, THE HORSES ARE ABOUT 50 FEET FROM THE START-ING GATE.	CROWD NOISE
MED. SHOT TRACK. THE HORSES ARE CLOSER TO THE STARTING GATE.	TRACK ANNCR. (VOICE OVER) The horses are approaching the starting gate. PALMER (V.O.) CBS Television presents . . . The Summer Sports Spectacular . . . "A Jockey's World" with . . .
CU ARCARO ON HORSE.	Eddie Arcaro
MCU STARTING GATE. THE HORSES ARE ONLY A FEW FEET AWAY.	Brought to you by . . . (NAME OF PRODUCT)
CU STARTING GATE. NOW THE HORSES ARE BEING PUT IN THEIR STALLS.	(NATURAL SOUND: THE STARTER, HIS ASSISTANTS, THE JOCKEYS, AND THE HORSES.)
CU AS HORSES BREAK FROM THE GATE.	(CROWD ROAR.)
	TRACK ANNCR. (V.O.) They're off!
FOLLOW ENTIRE RACE.	TRACK ANNCR. (V.O.) (CALLS RACE AS HE NORMALLY WOULD.)
HORSES CROSS FINISH LINE.	TRACK ANNCR. (V.O.) (ANNOUNCES WIN, PLACE AND SHOW HORSES.)
CU FACES IN CROWD FOR REACTIONS TO OUTCOME OF RACE.	(CROWD NOISE: THE EXCITED HUM THAT ALWAYS ACCOMPANIES THE END OF A RACE.)
CU ARCARO HEADING FOR THE WEIGH-ING-IN AREA. HE IS STANDING UP IN THE STIRRUPS.	PALMER (V.O.) This is Eddie Arcaro—businessman. His business is racing horses. He's been in this line of work for almost thirty years. To say that he's been a success at it would be somewhat of an understatement. By almost any standard he is the outstand-ing jockey in the world today.
ARCARO ON SCALE.	Arcaro's actual working time during a day is very short—perhaps a total of fifteen minutes. But the strain is great, and it shows on his face.

"SUMMER SPORTS SPECTACULAR: Eddie Arcaro — Little Giant," a production of CBS Television Sports, written by Craig Gilbert. © Columbia Broadcasting System, Inc. 1962.

ARCARO WALKS THROUGH RUNWAY TO PADDOCK.	A champion in any sport has special problems and Arcaro is no exception.
	But for him there is an extra hazard. When he boots home a winner, the fans love him. When he loses, he has cost them money.
CU CROWD LEANING OVER PADDOCK RAILING REACTING TO ARCARO.	CROWD (COMMENTS DIRECTED AT ARCARO.)
MS PALMER IN HIGH LIMBO AREA OVERLOOKING TRACK. HE HAS BEEN WATCHING PROCEEDINGS WITH BINOCULARS. NOW HE LOWERS THEM AND TURNS TO CAMERA.	Hi, I'm Bud Palmer. Eddie Arcaro is 45 years old. At an age when most other athletes have long since retired, Arcaro seems to be at the peak of his powers. His specialized skills have never been sharper, his reputation never greater. Most of a jockey's life, like the proverbial seven-eighths of an iceberg, is hidden from public view.

The script next covers outline points 5 and 6. The following is a part of the end of 6 and most of 7:

JOCKS AT TABLE IN RECREATION ROOM PLAYING CARDS.	PALMER (V.O.) One of the best ways to kill the time between races is a card game. In a jockey's world the favorites are gin or knock rummy.
	(NATURAL SOUND: CONVERSATION OF JOCKS PLAYING CARDS.)
JOCKS PLAYING POOL OR BILLIARDS.	PALMER (V.O.) Some jockeys prefer pool or billiards.
	(NATURAL SOUND: CONVERSATION OF JOCKEYS PLAYING POOL OR BILLIARDS.)
JOCKEYS WATCHING TELEVISION.	PALMER (V.O.) Jockeys are among the most avid watchers of daytime television. More often than not they are reduced to watching vintage horse operas.
	(NATURAL SOUND: THE ACTUAL SOUND COMING FROM THE SET. TALK, COMMENTS OF THE JOCKS AS THEY WATCH.)
PAN UP TO CLOSED-CIRCUIT TV SET.	TRACK ANNCR. (V.O.) The horses are at the starting gate.
	PALMER (V.O.) For those jockeys not in a particular race, closed-circuit television enables them to watch the proceedings.
JOCKS WATCH RACE ON TV.	(NATURAL SOUND: THE TRACK ANNOUNCER AS HE CALLS THE RACE AND THE COMMENTS OF THE JOCKS AS THEY WATCH.)

The script counterpart of item 8 of the outline includes film clips of sports events and heroes of Arcaro's youth. Item 10 is deleted from the final script. Items 9 and 12 are combined into one continuous sequence in which Arcaro, ostensibly in the process of getting ready for his next race, narrates most of the material, voice over stock and special film clips of tracks where he has raced, races in which accidents occurred and Kentucky Derby races. An excerpt from this sequence follows:

DISSOLVE TO: STOCK FOOTAGE: BAINBRIDGE TRACK IN OHIO.	ARCARO (V.O.) The date of my first race was May 18, 1931. I was fifteen years old. The place was Bainbridge, Ohio and the horse's name was Golden Bu. It would be nice to report that I won, but the charts don't lie. Down in black and white it says I finished sixth. All I remember is that I borrowed the equipment from the other jocks. I lost my cap and finished with the tails of the silks hanging out of my pants. And I remember one more thing. I remember coming back to the jock's room and the others kidding me.
STOCK FOOTAGE: EARLY RACING AT AGUA CALIENTE.	The kidding—or at least that kind of kidding—stopped on January 14, 1932, the day I rode my first winner at Agua Caliente. The horse's name was Eagle Bird and he flew home with me bouncing up and down on him grinning from ear to ear.
DISSOLVE TO: ARCARO IN FRONT OF HIS LOCKER.	ARCARO Winning that first race was quite a thrill. For a while there my head really swelled up and I lived in a dream world. Then, as I got to ride in more races, I came back to earth in a hurry. I suddenly realized that I was a 16 year-old kid riding against a bunch of race-hardened old pros who had been taught to fight—and I mean fight—for every inch of ground.

In the final script item 12 is followed by parts of item 11 and by item 13:

JOCKEYS WALK THROUGH TUNNEL TO PADDOCK.	PALMER (V.O.) (NARRATION IF NEEDED.) (JOCKS SELDOM BET ON RACES.) (HOW JOCKS ARE PAID.)
FOLLOW ARCARO TO WHERE TRAINER AND OWNER ARE STANDING.	(NATURAL SOUND: CONVERSATION BETWEEN TRAINER, OWNER AND ARCARO.)
	PALMER (V.O.) (NARRATION IF NEEDED.)
STABLE BOYS WALK HORSES AROUND PADDOCK. THE CROWD HANGS OVER THE RAILING AND WATCHES INTENTLY.	(NATURAL SOUND: THE SOUNDS OF THE CROWD AND THE PADDOCKS.)

STABLE BOYS LEAD HORSES INTO
MOUNTING STALLS. ARCARO AND
TRAINER ARE STANDING BY THEIR
STALL.

(NATURAL SOUND: TRAINER GIVES
ARCARO LAST MINUTE INSTRUCTIONS.)

PALMER (V.O.)
(NARRATION IF NEEDED.)
(WHAT THESE LAST MINUTE INSTRUC-
TIONS MIGHT CONSIST OF.)

ARCARO MOUNTS HORSE. THE PARADE
ONTO THE TRACK STARTS.

(NATURAL SOUND: TRUMPET FLOURISH.)

TRACK ANNCR. (V.O.)
The horses are on the track.

The script ends with the running of the race.

ARCARO CROSSES FINISH LINE. TIGHT
ON HIM WIN OR LOSE.

(NATURAL SOUND: THE ROAR OF THE
CROWD.)

THE CROWD: FACES

ARCARO ON HORSE JOGS BACK TO
WEIGHING OUT AREA.

PALMER (V.O.)
(STARTS FINAL STATEMENT.)

ARCARO DISMOUNTS.

ARCARO WEIGHS IN.

ARCARO WALKS THROUGH PADDOCK.

ARCARO LOOKS UP AT CROWD. HIS
FACE FILLS THE SCREEN, AND WE
FREEZE THE FRAME.

PALMER (V.O.)
(COMPLETES FINAL STATEMENT.)

REFERENCE BOOKS ON TELEVISION PUBLIC AFFAIRS
AND DOCUMENTARY PROGRAMS
Two recent works of special interest to the writer are:
A. William Bluem, *Documentary in American Television* (New York: Hastings House, 1965).
Norman Swallow, *Factual Television* (New York: Hastings House, 1966).

FOR APPLICATION AND REVIEW

1. Find out what special event, worthy of news coverage, will take place in your community in the near future. The event may be a speech, a concert or a more dramatic occurence such as an election. Prepare the opening and closing, transition and filler material for this event for radio broadcast. Include, if possible, an interview with one or more personalities taking part in the event. Revise the material you prepared for radio, for television broadcast.

2. Write the routine sheet for a how-to-do-it radio special feature. The subject should be one of importance to a large professional group in your community.

3. Write the full script for a behind-the-scenes, human interest television special feature. The purpose should be to persuade as well as to inform. A public health or social welfare subject should be used.

4. Write a documentary script for television or radio, using one or a combination of the basic documentary types. The subject should be one that is vital to the welfare and continued existence of mankind.

5. Write a documentary script for the medium not used in 4), above, using a documentary type not used in 4). The subject should be one which is relatively unimportant and which is not of vital interest to humanity.

6

TALKS PROGRAMS

THE TERM "talks" is all-inclusive here, and covers interview programs, discussion programs, quiz, panel, audience participation shows and speeches. Some of these shows may have prepared scripts. Most do not, however, but are outlined on rundown or on routine sheets, prepared as fully as possible through consultation or rehearsal with guests or participants, and then done extemporaneously or, to varying degrees, ad-lib. The writer must be aware that even in the program that appears to be completely ad-lib, as much of the actual script and as many of the ad-libs as possible are prepared. The reason for such preparation is obvious: why take a chance with an unprepared word or sequence when you can have better chance of success with prepared material?

THE RUNDOWN SHEET AND ROUTINE SHEET

The rundown sheet has been mentioned in previous chapters. Inasmuch as it is sometimes the only prepared material in some forms of talks programs, it deserves special consideration here. The basic rundown sheet is a standard part of all programming and consists of a detailed listing of every sequence in a given program, with the elapsed time for each item. Because broadcasting operates on a split-second schedule, the rundown sheet not only is necessary in planning, but the final version must be adhered to in the actual performance. Examine the interview show rundown sheet on page 166, the debate program outline and proposed rundown on pages 185 and 186, and also the two variety show rundown sheets on pages 212-213. For some shows for which there is no script a "routine sheet" is used. It is more detailed than the rundown sheet and consists of as much of the dialogue and action as can be prepared. Examine the routine sheets for extemporaneous-type shows on pages 188-194.

THE INTERVIEW

The interview on radio or television may be prepared completely, with a finished script for interviewer and interviewee; it may be oriented around an outline, where the general line of questioning and answering is prepared, but the exact words to be used are extemporaneous; it may be completely unprepared, or ad-lib. Very rarely are interviews either completely ad-lib or completely scripted. The unprepared interview is too risky, with the interviewee likely to be either too garrulous, embarrassing or embarrassed, or just plain dull and the interviewer likely to be faced with the almost impossible task of organizing, preparing and thinking of appropriate questions on the spot. The prepared script usually results in a stilted, monotonous presentation except when both the interviewer and interviewee are skilled performers or actors who can make a written line sound extemporaneous, a situation not often likely to occur.

Approach

Most interviews are set up in outline form. A broad outline of the purpose and form of questioning is prepared by the interviewer and staff and, on the basis of knowledge or research concerning the interviewee, a number of questions are prepared. In order to be ready to ask questions in a logical order, the interviewer must have an idea of the possible answers to the major questions already developed. For this purpose a preliminary conference or pre-interview, if possible, is held with the interviewee who is briefed, sometimes lightly, sometimes fully, on the questions to be asked. The interviewee indicates the general line of answering. On the basis of this conference the interviewer is able to develop follow-up and probing questions and arrange the general line of questioning in its most effective order.

The written material for the extemporaneous type of interview or, for that matter, discussion program, usually consists of the rundown and/or routine sheet which should contain a detailed step-by-step outline of the program, opening and closing continuity, introductory material for each section of the program, and list of questions and content of the answers as determined in the pre-interview session. The following material is the rundown sheet and the first half of the complete script from one of the "Tex and Jinx" programs. Although the program is no longer on the air, these rundown and routine sheets are illustrative not only of the interview show, but (note use of a jury for questions and subsequent general discussion) of the format for the discussion and extemporaneous talks programs as well. The questions and answers, though perhaps more than could be used on the program, provide sufficient material for lengthy interviewing, if necessary, and guarantee smooth continuity for questioning.

1:00:00   OPEN & BILLBOARD: "DOES A NEW HAT OR A NEW DRESS DO MORE FOR A WOMAN'S MORALE?"
SALLY VICTOR
ADELE SIMPSON

1:04:00   NEWS

1:05:00   VOGUE PATTERNS

1:06:00   INTRO JURY: LILLY DACHE; PRINCESS BORGHESE; EUGENIA SHEPPARD; BARBARA LOLLEY.

1:08:00   SHOW SALLY'S HATS (CHOSEN AS BEST BOOSTERS OF WOMAN'S MORALE)
JINX INTERVIEW SALLY

1:16:00   COMMERCIALS: TROPICANA (LIVE)
GIMBELS (2:00 SOF)

1:19:10   BRING ON MODEL WEARING ADELE SIMPSON DRESS (BEST MORALE BOOSTER)
TEX INTERVIEW ADELE SIMPSON

1:27:00   COMMERCIALS: SAVARIN (LIVE)
LESTOIL (SOF)

1:29:10   JURY QUESTIONS

1:40:00   SHORT STORY: "SAM" WITH CHARLES COBURN AND PHYLLIS JOYCE

1:42:00   COMMERCIALS: SULFOAM (LIVE)
DOVE (:10 SOF)
ROBERT HALL (SOF)

1:44:10   HILTON PLUG
CONTINUE JURY QUESTIONS

1:50:00   COMMERCIALS: DOESKIN (SOF & LIVE TAG)
BETTY CROCKER (LIVE)

1:52:00   JURY LINE QUESTIONS (JUST A FEW)

1:55:00   VERDICT FROM JURY

1:58:30   THANX: BILLBOARD THURSDAY. MRS. NORMAN VINCENT PEALE AND THEO BIKEL. "HAVE EASTER AND PASSOVER LOST THEIR MEANING IN THE MISSILE AGE?"

ROUTINE SHEET

OPEN ON CU OF HAND STRIKING GONG, W/THEME

PULL BACK FOR T & J; (JINX HAS BLOWUPS OF LABELS)

TEX: GOOD AFTERNOON . . . THIS IS TEX McCRARY IN PEACOCK ALLEY OF THE WALDORF.

JINX: AND THIS IS JINX . . . WITH ANOTHER SESSION OF THE TEX AND JINX JURY
. . . AND THE ISSUE BEFORE THE JURY TODAY IS ONE WHICH MAKES WOMEN SIT UP
AND TAKE SIDES . . . AS STRONGLY AS BASEBALL INTERESTS THE MEN IN THE
AUDIENCE . . . TODAY'S TOPIC——"DOES A NEW HAT OR A NEW DRESS DO MORE
FOR A WOMAN'S MORALE?"*********THERE'S NO DOUBT WHICH SIDE OF THE ISSUE
EACH OF OUR STAR WITNESSES IS ON TODAY . . . BUT, FOR THE RECORD . . . LET'S
GET THE OPENING STATEMENT OF THE WOMAN BEHIND THIS LABEL . . . WHICH
APPEARS IN THE HATS WORN BY THE FIRST LADY OF THE LAND, MAMIE EISEN-
HOWER . . . AND OTHER FASHION LEADERS:

SALLY VICTOR:

> (DS THRU CU OF VICTOR LABEL TO CU OF
> SALLY, FOR OPENING STATEMENT)

> (CUT TO CU OF SIMPSON LABEL)

JINX: (VOICE-OVER) OUR SECOND STAR WITNESS IS THE DESIGNER BEHIND THIS
FAMOUS LABEL . . . ALTHOUGH SHE'S PETITE ENOUGH TO STAND LESS THAN FIVE
FEET TALL . . . SHE'S ONE OF THE GIANTS OF THE FASHION WORLD:

ADELE SIMPSON:

> (DS THRU LABEL TO ADELE FOR STATEMENT)
> CUT TO TEX

TEX: WE'LL BE BACK TO INTRODUCE OUR JURY . . . (WHICH IS DISTINGUISHED BY
THE PRESENCE OF ANOTHER GREAT FASHION NAME, LILLY DACHE) . . . AND
WE'LL BEGIN ROUND ONE . . . RIGHT AFTER THE LATEST NEWS FROM NBC.

JINX QUESTIONS FOR SALLY VICTOR

1) LAST WEEK . . . THIS HAT YOU MADE FOR MRS. EISENHOWER HIT THE FRONT
PAGES. BUT DOESN'T THIS PROVE . . . YOUR HATS GIVE THAT SPECIAL LIFT TO
A WOMAN'S MORALE . . . BUT ONLY TO THE SPECIAL FEW WHO CAN AFFORD THEM?

> (JINX SHOW MAMIE HAT. AND N.Y. TIMES FRONT PAGE)

2) SHOULDN'T A WOMAN FEEL BOTH BETTER AND MORE BUSINESSLIKE . . .
BUYING A BASIC DRESS THAT'S GOOD FOR SEVERAL SEASONS . . . INSTEAD OF A
HAT THAT'S GOOD FOR ONLY ONE SEASON?

3) IF ONE OF YOUR CUSTOMERS WANTED TO BOOST HER LOW SPIRITS . . . BY
BUYING A HAT THAT LOOKED FOOLISH ON HER . . . ISN'T IT TRUE THAT YOU
WOULDN'T LET HER BUY IT . . . EVEN THOUGH IT MIGHT MAKE HER FEEL BETTER?

4) DOESN'T A NEW HAT CHANGE FROM A MORALE-BOOSTER TO A MORALE-
BUSTER . . . WHEN A HUSBAND FOLLOWS THE OLD AMERICAN CUSTOM OF LAUGH-
ING AT HIS WIFE'S NEW SPRING BONNET?

5) WHEN WOMEN IMPULSIVELY BUY NEW HATS TO BOOST THEIR SPIRITS AT
EASTERTIME . . . AREN'T THEY OFTEN IN DANGER OF PAYING GOOD MONEY FOR
FADS . . . INSTEAD OF FASHIONS?

6) TO MOST WOMEN . . . EASTER MEANS ENDING THE GLOOM OF WINTER WITH A
BRIGHT NEW HAT. BUT SHOULDN'T THE HAT INDUSTRY BE CRITICIZED AT
EASTERTIME . . . FOR MAKING HATS MEAN MORE TO WOMEN'S MORALE . . . THAN
PRAYERS?

1) No. Sally emphasizes that no matter how many front-page celebrities she may have on her rolls, there are many, many women who simply like Sally's hats but can't afford to buy a carload. So they save their pennies and get a marvelous hat, perfect in size, color, styling, etc. This is better than getting a cheaper hat that isn't as great as a Sally hat. And nothing gives a woman a greater lift than knowing she's wearing a good hat that looks beautiful and draws comment.

2) The other way round. It's precisely because a woman can wear a basic good dress for several seasons that she should get her greatest lift in buying a new hat every year. The basic dress is just that — basic. No one can see your dress when you're sitting down or hemmed in at a cocktail party. It's the hat they see. If you want a lift, get it where people see you most: your head & shoulders.

3) Darned right I wouldn't let her buy it. Sally explains how and why she may occasionally bully a customer, if needs be. Her main job is fitting the best hat to the faces and needs of her customers. Sally is objective about the way the hat looks; women get their hats because they care about how others will look at them. Since no woman is ever objective in looking at herself in a milliner's mirror, it's up to the Sallies of this world to bully the customers into making the right choice — the choice the customer will not regret ever.

4) Men don't understand hats — maybe because hats mean so little to them. They spend 10 dollars for a hat — and wonder why wifey doesn't do the same, and why she needs a new hat every year when he doesn't. Sally points out that hubby fails to realize that if he checks his hat once a week in a checkroom, a $10.00 hat has cost him $23.00 over a year. Failing to recognize what he himself is paying for a hat, how can he understand his wife's necessities in millinery?

5) Sally draws a sharp line between fads and fashions. Fashion is that quality that makes a woman magically prettier than she actually is. Hats aren't practical — they don't keep colds away — they're meant to frame the face and complement the ensemble. Fashion does all this in a hat. Fad means, to Sally, using whatever is momentary or bizarre — making a hat out of context with the general silhouette a woman is wearing. She'll draw examples of fads.

6) Sally detests commercialization of hats-for-Easter. Even though this is the time for new hats, at the end of dark winter, one should never use Easter as an excuse for bringing out wild and bizarre head coverings. Anyway, why push hats at Eastertime at all? The hat is as much a part of Spring as spring cleaning. Don't push it — and don't make horse's-heads, flower pots, etc. into hats and then use the word "Easter" with it; it isn't right.

Courtesy of J. R. McCrary, Seven Arts

One of the best interview programs of the mid-1960's combining personality, informational and opinion materials with people prominent and/or important in varied fields is Duncan MacDonald's on WQXR, New York. Here is an example of the routine sheet-outline script, omitting the formal opening and closing, from one of her 30-minute programs:

Twenty years ago the United Nations Charter was signed in San Francisco. In observance of this anniversary our guest today is Dr. Rodolphe L. Coigney, Director of the World Health Organization liaison office with the UN in New York City.

Dr. Coigney was born and educated in Paris. His career in international health began in 1944. In 1947 he became director of health for the International Refugee Organization. In his present post at the UN he represents WHO—the World Health Organization —at Economic and Social Council meetings, the Committee of the UN General Assembly, and other bodies of the UN.

1) Dr. Coigney, as one of the 10 specialized agencies of the UN, what is WHO's specific function?
   a) Is it included in the Charter of the UN?

b) Active/passive purpose?

c) Is WHO affected by various crises within UN?
Financial/political? Your own crises in health?

d) Do you have specific long term goals, or do you respond only to crises in health? Earthquakes/Floods/Epidemics?

2) How does the work of WHO tie in with other UN organizations?
UNICEF/ILO/Food and Agriculture/UNESCO/International Civil Aviation/International Bank/Reconstruction and Development/International Monetary Fund/Universal Postal/International Communications/World Meteorological.

3) Background of WHO.
a) How started? Switzerland?

b) Headquarters for all international organizations?

4) How much would the work of WHO differ in a country medically advanced, such as Sweden, as opposed to developing countries: Africa, Far East?
a) Religious or social taboos? b) Witch doctors? c) Birth control?

5) Can you give an example of a decision made at Headquarters and then carried out in some remote area of the world?

6) What do you consider WHO's greatest success story in fighting a specific disease: malaria, yaws?
a) Ramifications of disease? Economic/Disability for work?

7) Your secretary mentioned on the phone that you were going to Latin America. What specifically takes you there now?

8) How does a country get WHO assistance?
a) Invited? b) Matching funds?

9) We are aware of the shortage of doctors and nurses in the United States. What is the situation world-wide?
a) Do you think Public Health is an important career for young people? Now? For the future?

Courtesy of Duncan MacDonald, radio commentator on WQXR—the
radio station of The New York Times.

Sometimes, of course, the interviewee will not be available for a conference before the interview, and the interviewer and staff must guess at the probable answers to their questions. In other cases, the interviewee is not only available for a conference, but appears at the studio for a rehearsal of the program before it actually goes on the air, thus solidifying the show while retaining its extemporaneous quality.

In all interviews — prepared, extemporaneous or ad-lib — the writer must set up at least the opening and closing continuity, including introductory material about the interviewee. The closing continuity should be of different lengths in case the program runs shorter or longer than expected. The writer must make sure that in all interviews the proper introductions are made and the background of the guest is clearly presented. Except where the person being interviewed is well known, it is wise, in outlining the order of questions, to begin with questions of a human interest nature so that the audience gets to know a bit of the informal personality of the guest before the interview is too far along. One exception to this approach is the informational, news-type interview.

The following is an excerpt, including all the material into the first question and all the material from the final answer, from the "Meet the Press" news-type interview program. It is assumed that the reporters present had some of their questions prepared and adjusted their questioning as the interview moved into certain channels.

M E E T   T H E   P R E S S

Produced by Lawrence E. Spivak

- - -

MODERATOR: Ned Brooks

GUEST: James H. Smith, Jr.
                       Director, International Cooperation
                          Administration

PANEL: Jack Bell, Associated Press
                       Peter Lisagor, Chicago Daily News Service
                       Robert McCormick, NBC News
                       Lawrence E. Spivak

- - -

THE ANNOUNCER: Our guest, ladies and gentlemen, is the head of the Mutual Security Program, James H. Smith, Jr., Director of the International Cooperation Administration.

In just a moment, Mr. Smith will MEET THE PRESS.

(Commercial)

THE ANNOUNCER: Now MEET THE PRESS, the prize-winning program produced by Lawrence E. Spivak.

Ready for this spontaneous, unrehearsed conference are four of America's top reporters. Please remember their questions do not necessarily reflect their point of view. It is their way of getting behind the headlines.

Here is the Moderator of MEET THE PRESS, Mr. Ned Brooks.

MR. BROOKS: Welcome once again to MEET THE PRESS. One of the controversial measures now before Congress is the foreign aid program. Our guest is the man who directs it, Mr. James H. Smith, the head of the International Cooperation Administration.

In the weeks ahead he faces the task of convincing Congress that an appropriation of nearly four billion dollars is a wise investment in our future security. On the other side it is being argued that foreign spending has made enemies. Opposition to the program has been intensified by demands that the government give first priority to measures for meeting the business recession here at home.

Mr. Smith took over the directorship of the ICA last November. Over the past 20 years he has had wide experience in international negotiations and in the development of free world security.

In World War II he served as a navy pilot and a member of the staff of Admiral Arthur Radford. He is a lawyer. His most recent government position was Assistant Secretary of the Navy for Air, a position that he held for three years.

And now seated around the press table ready to interview Mr. Smith are Jack Bell of the Associated Press, Robert McCormick of NBC News, Peter Lisagor of the Chicago Daily News, and Lawrence E. Spivak, our regular member of the MEET THE PRESS panel.

Now Mr. Smith, if you are ready, we will start the questions with Mr. Spivak.

MR. BROOKS: I am sorry I will have to interrupt, Mr. Smith, I see our time is up.

Thank you very much Mr. Smith for being with us.

And now here is our announcer.

(Commercial)

THE ANNOUNCER: Good bye for Mr. James H. Smith, Jr. and MEET THE PRESS. For a printed copy of today's discussion send 10 cents in coin and a stamped, self-addressed envelope to the National Publishing Company, Washington 2, D. C.

MEET THE PRESS is produced by Lawrence E. Spivak, Associate Producers Helen Johnson and Betty Cole. Directed by Frank Slingland. Technical Director, Leon Cromack. Production Supervisor, Doris Corwith.

Next week MEET THE PRESS will have as its guest Governor Robert Meyner of the State of New Jersey.

This is Jack Roney speaking. MEET THE PRESS came to you from the Sheraton Park Hotel in Washington, D. C.

<u>Courtesy of NBC'S MEET THE PRESS</u>

Television Techniques

Although the interview may be a simple question-and-answer process between two people, in television some movement should be injected into the program. The movement may be of an entirely subjective nature, with the camera probing the facial expressions and bodily gestures of the interviewee in response to certain questions. The visual effect may be broader and more objective, with film clips or slides or photographs of places, experiences, or personalities referred to by the interviewee. For example, an interview with a college professor might have film clips of the institution where he teaches. An interview with a doctor might have visual material concerning the hospital where he works or experiments for which he is famous. Films or photographs of an interviewee's home town are sometimes effective.

Because television is visual, the interviewer must be cautioned about misleading the audience, even unintentionally. There is the frequently-told story of the television interviewer who made much in pre-program publicity of his forthcoming interview with a famous burlesque strip-teaser. Although the public should have known better, many people were quite disappointed that she didn't do what she obviously couldn't do on television.

Types of Interviews

There are three major interview types: the opinion interview, the information interview and the personality interview. Any given interview can combine elements of all three.

The Opinion Interview. The opinion interview is best exemplified by the "man-in-the-street" program. Any interview that concentrates on the beliefs of an individual, whether produced in or out of the studio, may be an opinion interview. However, inasmuch as many of the studio interviews of this nature

171

are with prominent people, usually experts in their fields, such interviews are not only opinion but, to a great extent, information and even personality types. Even in the man-in-the-street completely ad-lib program, the interviewer must have an introduction, a question, and follow-up questions developed in the light of possible answers. If the interview is to be on tape, the interviewee may be briefed before actually recording the interview. In the live, man-in-the-street interview, prospective interviewees may be gathered and briefed before the program goes on the air.

The Information Interview. The information interview is of the public service type. The information may be delivered by a relatively unknown figure or by a prominent person in the field. Since the main object is the communication of information, sometimes a complete script may be prepared. The interviewee may provide direct factual material, may deliver information oriented toward a cause or purpose, or may combine information with personal belief. If a script is written, the personality of the speaker should be kept in mind. If the interviewee is not likely to be a performer, that is, a good "reader," then it is better to prepare a detailed outline and rehearse the program as an extemporaneous presentation.

The 5-minute interview below indicates a generalized approach — a script that is flexible enough to fit every situation, every occasion and, hopefully, every interviewee.

> (THE QUESTIONS ARE FOR YOUR REGULAR ANNOUNCER.
> THE ANSWERS FOR ANOTHER ANNOUNCER, OR IF POSSIBLE,
> SOMEBODY FROM YOUR COMMUNITY AGENCY FOR THE
> BLIND, OR FROM THE LION'S CLUB OR SOME OTHER ORGAN-
> IZATION. THIS IS, OF COURSE, ONLY SUGGESTED. THE
> FOLLOWING QUESTIONS CAN BE ALTERED TO FIT ANY
> OCCASION.)

ANNCR: I've been looking forward to this particular interview because it deals with a subject of which most of us know practically nothing. <u>Blindness</u>. Come to think of it, I suppose there is a reason for that. Blindness is not one of the <u>scare</u> topics . . . it doesn't kill! In fact, blind people are often so unobtrusive and seem so well adjusted that we perhaps feel we can disregard them with a good conscience . . . Or perhaps it affects you just the <u>other</u> way when you see a blind person . . . perhaps you keep staring at him with deep pity in your heart? Well, I don't think either approach is the right one. Let's chat a little today with Mr. (NAME OF GUEST) who has come to our microphone to give us a few minutes of his (HER) time. Mr. (GIVE NAME), we're glad to have you.

GUEST: Naturally I'm pleased and happy that I have the privilege to be here. You know, blind people are very ardent radio fans.

ANNCR: Good . . . Now, it's obviously impossible for us to discuss the entire field of blindness in the United States. It would take us twenty years to do that. Have you any idea how we can narrow down this field?

GUEST: If I may make a suggestion, there is one thing that causes those of us who work with the blind more trouble than anything else — the popular misconceptions about blindness.

ANNCR: I don't think I quite follow you, Mr. (NAME).

GUEST: Let me put it this way, and ask you — do you believe that blind people have a sixth sense?

ANNCR: A sixth sense?

GUEST: Yes. Haven't you heard people say that the minute a person becomes blind there is some sort of compensation and that he is granted some sort of sixth sense which is supposed to make up for his loss of sight?

ANNCR: (BRIGHTENING) You know, now that I think of it, I have. I really have. And that is one of the misconceptions you are thinking of?

GUEST: Yes, indeed. There is, of course, no such thing as a sixth sense.

ANNCR: But isn't it true that blind people do manage to get around better than sighted people who have their eyes bandaged, for instance?

GUEST: Yes. That's because blind people have learned to use their other senses with more assurance. They have trained their hearing so they detect sounds most of us pass up. Their sense of touch has been trained. I know of some blind people who have developed their senses of touch and hearing to such an extent that when they pass an object, airwaves and echoes of sounds tell them where it is.

ANNCR: Very interesting. I understand that we're not to call the achievements of blind people amazing, since they don't want to consider themselves objects of amazement.

GUEST: Correct. All that well-adjusted blind people want is the privilege of leading the normal lives all other people lead.

ANNCR: Now, let me think . . . Let me see if I can remember another misconception about blindness which might fit into this conversation. Let's see . . . not so easy . . .

GUEST: May I help a bit?

ANNCR: Yes, you'd better.

GUEST: Suppose I mention two names. Homer and Milton.

ANNCR: I get it. The misconception that all blind people are geniuses — either poets or musicians or something. Not true, eh?

GUEST: Not true. There are, of course, good blind musicians. Often, if a blind person has a good ear and musical ability, he can develop it very well indeed — because usually he has fewer distractions when practicing, for instance. But he's not a good musician just because he happens to be blind. And certainly blind people are no better poets than the sighted. Although we do have some remarkable blind — even deaf-blind — poets and authors. Helen Keller, of course, is an author, and she has a way with words that is amazing. Excuse me, now I am using the word "amazing." And there is Richard Kinney, who recently graduated from college with a scholarship from the American Foundation for the Blind. He has published several books of poetry. And — you may wonder at this — the critics praised him for his perception of color & sound.

ANNCR: Color which he can't see.

GUEST: And sound which he can't hear . . . Because, you see, Richard Kinney is both deaf and blind . . .

ANNCR: Amazing! . . . Pardon me . . . Very interesting. Now, let's see. If I remember my history, blind people in ancient times were either killed off, or at best they were allowed to beg. But I seem to remember that in a few cases they were considered to be holy men.

GUEST: Yes, that happened in Egypt occasionally. Blind people were considered prophets, and they went around as holy men. Of course, some of them may have been exploiting their blindness just as some of our blind beggars today exploit their blindness.

173

ANNCR: Ah, there's another misconception! All that blind people can do is to beg. Is that what you are hinting at?

GUEST: Precisely. As a matter of fact, all well-adjusted blind people, and those of us who work with them, writhe inwardly whenever we see blind beggars go down a city street making all sorts of noises with a heavy white cane whining "Help the blind." They are doing blind people more of a disservice than a service.

ANNCR: Well, we've covered a lot of ground on misconceptions about the blind.

GUEST: (LAUGHS) Your saying that reminds me of one more misconception. I've been guilty of this one myself. Using the word THE blind — as if blind people were one big herd of buffalos or some other queer animal, crowding together for shelter and protection.

ANNCR: I never thought of that. That's not good, calling blind people THE blind?

GUEST: It's not terribly bad, IF you know what you mean when you say it. But certainly there is no such thing as THE blind. There are blind individuals. and blind individuals differ as much from each other as sighted differ from each other. In other words, here in America we like to think that the individual is sacred. And so he is. And this sacredness of the individual must of course be extended to blind people. For each blind person is an individual.

ANNCR: You know, Mr. (OR MRS. — NAME), I think we had a misconception about this program when we began. We thought we could cover a lot more ground than our five minutes permitted. So I'm sorry, but I have to interrupt. But I wish to thank you most sincerely for coming up to our studio and chatting about misconceptions concerning blind people. Thank you, Mr. (NAME). This is station _____

Courtesy of The American Foundation for the Blind.

The news interview such as "Meet the Press" falls into the category of the information interview. Where important personalities are the subjects, the information necessarily is mixed with opinion, although what might be called opinion by some might be called fact by others. "Face the Nation" also achieved its popularity through the information-news approach. Examine the opening as indicated on the routine sheet, below, including the video directions. It is assumed that the reporters were prepared with questions.

FACE THE NATION

Sunday, 4:00-4:30 PM EST, Washington, D. C.

VIDEO	AUDIO
#2 ON PHOTO BLOW-UP OF CAM TUR-RET--PRE-SET SUPER SLIDE "CBS TELEVISION PRESENTS" S-150	BEAT!
	ANNCR: Paul M. Butler . . . (BEAT) . . .
	ANNCR: 'FACE THE NATION"
	MUSIC STRINGS 4 SECS AND UNDER
CUT TO #3 GUEST	ANNCR: You are about to see the Chairman of the Democratic National Committee, Paul M. Butler. . .

"FACE THE NATION," Telecast February 2, 1958. © Columbia Broadcasting System, Inc. 1962.

CUT TO #1 WS PANEL	with questions from veteran correspondents representing the nation's press:
CUT TO #2 CU'S OF PANEL, PAN RT TO LEFT, KEEP PANNING TO MODERATOR	Robert J. Donovan, Chief of the Washington Bureau of the New York Herald Tribune;
	Wells Church of CBS News; and John Madigan, Assistant Editor of the Chicago American.
	And now from CBS News . . . the moderator of FACE THE NATION . . . Stuart Novins.
	NOVINS:
CUT TO #3 GUEST	
CUT TO #1 WS, ZOOM IN	And now with the first question,
CUT TO #2 CU PANELIST	Mr. Madigan.
	MADIGAN:

The Personality Interview. This is the human interest, feature story kind of interview. The format of the program may be oriented toward one purpose — to probe or to embarrass or to flatter — or it may be flexible, combining and interweaving these various facets. The most successful personality interview programs of recent years seem to be oriented toward a combination of probing for personal attitudes and revelation of personal beliefs and actions. To prepare pertinent questions for the personality interview, full background information on the interviewee must be obtained. The questions must be outlined and the interviewee must be talked with before the program in order to prepare the depth questions and the logical order of questioning. The rundown sheet usually contains the opening, closing, background and introductory information on the personality, and a series of questions to be used during the interview. Examine the excerpts below from the transcript of the Mike Wallace "personality" interview with Mrs. Eleanor Roosevelt. Although this particular program is dated and the series is no longer on the air, this interview show was quite popular and set several patterns for the probing, personal interview approach. Note, at the very beginning, how the lack of sufficient preparation resulted in an error on the interviewer's part concerning Mrs. Roosevelt's acquaintance with Mahatma Gandhi. Note, also, the interviewer's good use of quotations and other materials prepared for certain specific subject areas and for follow-up questions relating to general areas of answers.

> ● *Keep in mind the fact that the following excerpts are from a transcript of what occurred on the program, not from a script prepared before the program. Make lists of the following items: 1) any questions and answers you believe were prepared before the program went on the air; 2) any questions and answers you believe were not adequately prepared and which should have been to guarantee a better show; 3) any questions and answers that seem to be too well prepared and which detract from the spontaneity of the program.*

GUEST: ELEANOR ROOSEVELT

WALLACE: Good evening. Tonight my guest is a woman who has been called the
"First Lady of the World." She is Mrs. Eleanor Roosevelt. I shall ask
Mrs. Roosevelt to talk about Dwight Eisenhower, Nikita Khrushchev,
Westbrook Pegler, and garlic pills. What you're about to see is unre-
hearsed, uncensored, my name is Mike Wallace, the cigarette is Philip
Morris.

(COMMERCIAL)

WALLACE: And now to our story. At the age of seventy-four Eleanor Roosevelt has
seen a lot of the world and the world has seen a lot of her. Tonight I
shall ask Mrs. Roosevelt about some of the most pressing world issues,
about America's leadership or lack of it, about the Soviet menace and
indications that we may be losing our strength as a nation to resist it.
Later in the program we'll talk with Mrs. Roosevelt about her code of
values and her family life. Mrs. Roosevelt, first of all let me ask you
this: You've seen great leaders like Winston Churchill, Mahatma Gandhi,
your own husband. I wonder if in capsule fashion you can tell me what
qualities enabled these men to shape the course of history as they did,
what did they have that made them the leaders they were?

ROOSEVELT: I never met Mahatma Gandhi, — but, I think everyone felt they knew him
even if they hadn't met him. I think one thing they had in common, all
these men, was great courage, both spiritual, mental and physical courage.
Mahatma Gandhi I would say had perhaps a greater spiritual quality
whereas Winston Churchill had besides the courage, ability and above
everything else, the ability to put into words what his people felt so that
he could always lead them. And my own husband I think had great patience,
which you need in a democracy because you have to come to do fundamental
things, you have to have the patience to have people educated; and then I
think he had a deep interest in human beings as human beings.

WALLACE: . . . What about intellectual capacity and physical vigor? How important
do you think those two qualities were in these people?

ROOSEVELT: . . . I think it's important to have both . . .

* * *

WALLACE: . . . I ask you this — what I'm trying to do now is to find out about our
present leadership. President Eisenhower in two or three years now will
no longer be our President. Can you name for me, Mrs. Roosevelt, any
leading Democrats or Republicans who are in the same league with a
Churchill or a Gandhi or a Roosevelt, who have the stature to lead our
free world against the threat of Communism?

ROOSEVELT: Well, at the present time I don't think it would be fair to name any
particular people because . . . it is very often the opportunity which brings
out the qualities in a man and most of the leaders on the Democratic side
have not had the opportunity to meet the responsibilities and to show us
whether they have the leadership qualities that are needed at the present

176

ROOSEVELT: time. Many of them have shown ability and certain different qualities but
(CONT.) we have not yet seen, I don't think, anyone in a position . . .

WALLACE: uhmmmmm.mmm. . .

ROOSEVELT: . . .and to show whether they had full leadership quality that the present
day seems to require. Now on the Republican side of course the only one
who stands out is Mr. Nixon, and he has made no mistakes of late. He's
been extremely careful. I would say he had ability, how much conviction
is another question.

WALLACE: Well, you mentioned Mr. Nixon in your column in McCalls magazine in
January of Nineteen fifty-six. You wrote about Republican leaders and
about Mr. Nixon you said the following: "Richard Nixon would be the least
attractive. I know that given — that given great responsibility, men sometimes change" — which in a sense is what you're just saying. You say,
"I know that given great responsibility men sometimes change, but
Mr. Nixon's Presidency would worry me," you said. Why do you reserve
this special criticism for Mr. Nixon?

ROOSEVELT: Because I think that in great crises you need to have deep rooted convictions and I have a feeling from the kind of campaigns that I have watched
Mr. Nixon in in the past that his convictions are not very strong.

***

WALLACE: Is it possible, Mrs. Roosevelt, that Communism, State Socialism anyway,
is the wave of the future and that Capitalism is on its way out?

ROOSEVELT: Well, that is what Mr. Khrushchev says. I don't know much about Capitalism, but I do know about Democracy and freedom, and if Capitalism
may change in many, many ways, I'm not really very much interested in
Capitalism. I'm enormously interested in freedom and retaining the right
to have whatever economy we want and to shape it as we want and a —
having sufficient Democracy so that the people — actually hold their
Government in their own hands.

WALLACE: Then you do not think — if we wanted it that it would be a catastrophe if
Socialism came peacefully to the United States as it has come to other
nations in the world?

ROOSEVELT: To a certain extent I don't see any real need for socialism in the United
States immediately, but things change and it may be that there will come
a need for partial changes in our economy. I don't know. I'm not an eco-
nomist and I'm not a financier. But I — I'm not worried by that side of it.
I'm intensely anxious to preserve the freedom that gives you the right to
think and to act and to talk as you please. That I think is essential to happiness and the life of the people.

WALLACE: Mrs. Roosevelt, in just a moment I'd like to get your reaction to the
charges made by perhaps your most severe critic, Westbrook Pegler. He
once wrote this about you, he said, "this woman is a political force of
enormous ambitions. I believe she is a menace, unscrupulous as to truth,
vain and cynical—all with a pretense of exaggerated kindness and human
feeling which deceives millions of gullible persons." In a moment I would
like to get your opinion, your reaction to Westbrook Pegler's charge and
your opinion of Mr. Pegler, and we'll get the answers to those questions
in just a minute.

(COMMERCIAL)

WALLACE: Now then, Mrs. Roosevelt, your reaction to that charge by Westbrook
Pegler, I don't feel that it's necessary to repeat it, I'm sure that you heard
it the first time around.

177

ROOSEVELT: Well, it seems to me a little exaggerated let us say, no one could be quite as bad as all that, and—uh—as far as—as—uh—political ambition goes I think that's rather answered itself because I've never run for office and I've never asked for an office of any kind. So I can't have much political ambition, but—uh—I can see—uh—that Mr. Pegler probably—uh—probably believes all these things and ah — I'm not — I suppose one does things unconsciously that makes you seem like that, and perhaps I do seem like that to him, and I think it must be terrible to hate as many things as Mr. Pegler hates, and I — I would be unhappy, I think, and therefore I am afraid that he's unhappy, and I'm sorry for him, because after all, we all grow older and we all have to live with ourselves, and I think that must sometimes be difficult for Mr. Pegler.

***

WALLACE: One of the things the press leaped on last year was the fact that your son, Franklin, acted as legal representative in the United States for the Dominican Dictator Trujillo. As a crusader for Democracy and for freedom yourself, how did you feel about your son's working for Trujillo?

ROOSEVELT: Well, I asked my son about a — what he was doing, and he told me he was representing the Government, not Mr. Trujillo personally; that he felt that it was a legitimate thing for him to do as a lawyer and that he was not doing it for any political reasons but for pure business reasons as a lawyer. I do not, as a rule, interfere, and I did not feel that I was a — entitled to interfere in this case with my children. I leave them to do, after they are grown, what they think right, as I think all young people have a right to do.

WALLACE: Do I detect then, that you would have been just as happy had he not represented Trujillo?

ROOSEVELT: As it turned out, I think it might have been wiser, yes, but that is not — I — I do not hold my judgment above his, he was doing what he felt was legitimate to do and I think he had a right to make his own mind up on that subject.

WALLACE: And now the final question, the one that I promised at the beginning that I was going to ask, and that is about Garlic Pills.

ROOSEVELT: (LAUGHS)

WALLACE: I understand, that you — I don't know if you do still, but at one time in the not too distant past you ate Garlic Pills and I'd like to know why and how they worked out.

ROOSEVELT: My doctor told me to take them to help my memory. It doesn't help my memory much, but nevertheless that is what I was given them for.

WALLACE: And do you still?

ROOSEVELT: Oh, yes.

WALLACE: In spite of the fact, that it hasn't helped your memory?

ROOSEVELT: Well, that's of course age. You gave me one more year and at my age, ah - - ah - - you don't like to add to your years, because they come too quickly anyway . . .

WALLACE: It's only 73?

ROOSEVELT: I'm really only 73.

WALLACE: Only 73? I beg your pardon.

ROOSEVELT: But, that doesn't matter in many ways, only that they go so fast when you get to be my age and I suppose that it's that that gives poor memory, not the Garlic Pills.

178

WALLACE:	Mrs. Roosevelt, I thank you for taking the time for coming and talking with us this evening.
ROOSEVELT:	Thank you.
WALLACE:	Because she will fight courageously for what she believes, Eleanor Roosevelt has had to pay a certain price, bitter criticism, a lack of privacy, the infighting of partisan politics, but Eleanor Roosevelt has also reaped what must be the most satisfying of all rewards, the respect and with it the affection of hundreds of millions of persons around the world.
	I'll bring you a rundown on next week's interview with a well-known television personality in just a moment.

(COMMERCIAL)

***

Mike Wallace's interview of Mrs. Eleanor Roosevelt appeared on the American Broadcasting Company television network on November 23, 1957.

DISCUSSION PROGRAMS

The discussion program is oriented toward the exchange of opinions and information and, to some degree, the arriving at solutions, actual or implied, on important questions or problems. The term discussion frequently is applied incorrectly to television interview programs such as "Meet the Press."

Approach

Sometimes complete scripts, written by a writer in collaboration with the participants, are prepared for discussion programs. To achieve spontaneity, however, it is better to plan only an outline, indicating the general form and organization of the discussion. This outline should be given to all participants so that they may plan their own contributions in accordance with the general format. The writer should indicate in the format the issues to be discussed, the order in which the discussion will take place, and the time allotted for each point or each participant. If possible, the participants, in consultation with the writer, should prepare a statement of their general views so that there can be a pre-performance exchange of ideas and a coordination of all participants' contributions toward a smooth, well-integrated program. Just as too much preparation can result in a dull program, too little preparation may result in the participants being unable to cope with the split-second needs of a spontaneous program. In addition, without pre-planning among participants, there may be an unnecessary duplication of material.

A decision must be made in the early stages of planning whether to use a controversial topic, certainly the best approach for achieving vitality and excitement in the program, and whether to promote or avoid disagreement among the participants. The topics should be presented as questions, thus provoking investigation and thought. In addition, the topics should be broadly oriented, preferably in terms of general policy, and should not be so narrow that they can be answered with a yes or no response or with obvious statements of fact.

In the extemporaneous discussion program the same principles apply as in the interview. Opening and closing remarks and introductions should be written out. If possible, general summaries should be prepared for the moderator or master of ceremonies. In some instances, a brief outline or routine sheet consisting of a summary of the action of the program and a listing of the topics to be covered, or a rundown sheet may be sufficient.

In television visual elements should be incorporated. The setting should, if possible, relate to the topic. Although the visual element may be relatively simple, it should help to convey a feeling of excitement and challenge in terms of the topic under consideration.

Types

There are several major types of discussion programs: the symposium; the panel; the group discussion; and the debate.

Symposium. The symposium presents several persons who have prepared individual solutions to a given problem. Each of the participants is given an equal period of time in which to present his or her ideas. First, each participant presents, with the same time limit for each, a prepared statement on the question. The question should be one which has at least two distinct sides, such as "Should the Fifth Amendment of the Constitution Be Repealed?" After the participants have presented their prepared talks, members of the audience may direct questions to any or all members of the symposium. During this question period the participants sometimes cross-question each other and exchange ideas. After a specified time period, the questions from the audience are ended and each participant is permitted an equal amount of time for summing up his or her viewpoint. "America's Town Meeting of the Air," on radio for many years, was an outstanding example of the symposium. The routine sheet or outline contains the moderator's opening remarks, the introduction of the participants, set time limits for the prepared statements, audience question period and summaries, and the closing for the program.

Panel. The panel discussion is more unstructured than the symposium. In the panel discussion several people in a round-table situation present their ideas concerning a problem. There is no set time limit for individual contributions and sometimes no limitation of the matters to be discussed. The participants are not required to have prepared statements and, if they wish, need not be prepared at all but may discuss the problem "off the tops of their heads." A moderator, who usually does not participate in the discussion, attempts to guide it and see that it does not get out of hand or too far from the topic. The approach is very informal, with the participants offering their personal comments and evaluations at will. No solution to the problem necessarily is reached, although the moderator frequently summarizes in order to clarify the point at which the panelists have arrived. A routine sheet will consist of the moderator's opening remarks, the introduction of the panel members, a statement of the problem, a flexible outline of subtopics to be discussed under the main topic (the outline to be given to each panel member sometime prior to the program), and the closing for the program.

• Examine the following materials in terms of the principles of good preparation for the panel discussion program. Determine whether the topic and the manner in which the questions are phrased provide the essentials for good discussion. Is the development of the topic too limited, or is there opportunity for the clear presentation of varied opinions, attitudes and information? Does the organization of the program move logically toward a climax? Is there a logical interrelationship between the various parts of the discussion? Are the participants properly introduced?

WUNC "CAROLINA ROUNDTABLE"

"The Berlin Crisis"

Thursday, 7-8 P.M.

MODERATOR (GEORGE HALL): (OPEN COLD) West Berlin—to be or not to be? This question has been reiterated thousands of times by the peoples of the world. With the erection of physical barricades between the Eastern and Western zones of Berlin, conflict between the East and West German regimes has become one on which may very well hang the future of the entire world.

This is your Moderator, George Hall, welcoming you to another "Carolina Roundtable."

All of us are by now fearfully aware of the critical importance of West Berlin. Most of us recognize that the East Berlin limitations on inter-city travel and the West Berlin opposition to negotiation with and recognition of the East have created an impasse that demands a response from both sides. What is that response to be—not only that of the West and of the United States, but that of the Communist East and of the Soviet Union? How will the choice of a course of action determine not only the fate of both Berlins, but of mankind? Are there any areas of compromise that would be satisfactory to all parties?

This evening, with the aid of our guests, we will attempt to seek answers to these questions.

Dr. Charles B. Robson is a professor of Political Science at the University of North Carolina and an authority on Germany. Dr. Robson teaches in the fields of German government and in modern political theory. He recently spent a year in Germany studying that country's political affairs. Good evening, Dr. Robson.

ROBSON: (RESPONSE)

MODERATOR: Dr. Leopold B. Koziebrodzki is an associate professor of Economics and History at the University of North Carolina. His special field is Russian foreign relations in the twentieth century, and he has observed first-hand governmental policies of eastern European countries in relation to the Soviet Union. Good evening, Dr. Koziebrodzki.

KOZIEBRODZKI: (RESPONSE)

MODERATOR: Dr. Samuel Shepard Jones is Burton Craige Professor of Political Science at the University of North Carolina. His area of specialization is United States foreign policy and international politics. He has served as cultural attache with the U.S. State Department, and has lectured before the National War College. Good evening, Dr. Jones.

JONES: (RESPONSE)

MODERATOR: I'd like to remind you gentlemen, and our listeners, that questions are encouraged from our listening audience. Any one having a question, for any or all of our panel members, is invited to phone the WUNC studios at 942-3172. Your question will be taped and played back for our panel to answer at the first opportunity. The number, again, is 942-3172.

        Now, gentlemen, with the East German government having seized the political offensive, it seems as if the next step is up to the West. In view of the growing power and influence of the small and uncommitted countries in the United Nations, what concessions, if any, should the West be prepared to make in the interest of peace in Berlin? Dr. Jones, would you start the discussion on this matter?

(BRING IN OTHER PANELISTS ON THIS QUESTION. THROUGH PRE-DISCUSSION, DETERMINE TENTATIVE AGREEMENT ON SOME AREAS, AS BELOW.)

(SUB-TOPICS, AS NEEDED)

1. Berlin to be a free city under U.N. jurisdiction, as proposed by Soviet Union?

2. Limited recognition of East German government?

3. Demilitarization of West Berlin, with most Western troops withdrawn?

4. Eventual admission of East Germany into U.N.?

MODERATOR: (REMINDER TO AUDIENCE ON PHONE CALLS)

        Presuming that some of these concessions, in whole or in part, are granted, might this not result in East Germany effectively controlling West Berlin, at least in relation to the vital avenues of traffic into and out of the city? And, if so, might this not lead to sufficient pressure from the Communist allies to achieve a disintegration of West Berlin as an ally of the western powers? Dr. Koziebrodzki, what is your evaluation of this possibility?

        (BRING IN OTHER PANELISTS ON THIS QUESTION.)

        (SUB-TOPICS, AS NEEDED)

1. Discrimination between Western air traffic and civilian traffic from West Germany?

2. Economic and/or political pressures on West Berlin and on West Germany?

3. Effect on prestige and political power of West Germany? Effect on prestige and political power of East Germany?

4. Role of Soviet Union and other communist countries?

MODERATOR: (REMINDER TO AUDIENCE ON PHONE CALLS)

        A meeting between West Germany's Dr. Konrad Adenauer and President Kennedy is expected shortly. What is likely to be the stand of West Germany on this issue? Dr. Robson, do you believe that Adenauer will be prepared to offer any conciliations to East Germany and to the Soviet Union? What role will West Germany ask the United States to play in this situation?

(BRING IN OTHER PANELISTS.)

(SUB-TOPICS, AS NEEDED)

1. West German agreement to permit a demilitarized Berlin under U.N.?

2. Assurances needed by West Germany regarding free access to and from Berlin?

3. West German recognition of and/or negotiation with East Germany.

MODERATOR: (IF ABOVE TOPICS NOT CONCLUDED BY 8 MINUTES BEFORE THE END OF THE PROGRAM, SKIP TO FOLLOWING:) Of all of the possibilities discussed on the program, which, if any, do you think have the most chance of acceptance?

(IF FEW OR NONE, ASK ABOUT ALTERNATIVES AND POSSIBILITIES OF WAR.)

MODERATOR: (SUMMARY AT 3-MINUTE MARK.)

1. Possible concessions by West.

2. Attitudes and actions of East Germany and the East.

3. Attitudes and actions of West Germany.

4. Future of Berlin.

5. Chances of war.

MODERATOR: (AT 1-MINUTE MARK) Dr. Charles Robson, Dr. Leopold Koziebrodzki, and Dr. Shepard Jones of the University of North Carolina, we thank you for being our guests this evening on this "Carolina Roundtable" discussion of the possible solutions to the Berlin problem.

GUESTS: (MASS RESPONSE OF GOOD NIGHT, ETC.)

MODERATOR: We thank you all for listening, and invite you to join us next week at this same time when "Carolina Roundtable's" guests, _____, _____, and _____ will discuss _____ .

This has been a presentation of WUNC, the FM radio station of the Department of Radio, Television and Motion Pictures, in the Communication Center of the University of North Carolina. Continuity was written by Gilbert File, and the program was directed by Reno Bailey. Your moderator has been George Hall.

In many instances the station itself may have little more to do with the panel discussion than to arrange for time and provide production personnel. The actual planning of the discussion may be under the direction of a moderator or of an outside organization. The writer connected with the station may be responsible only for the opening and closing material, as illustrated in the following continuity sheet. (The letters SC in the video directions stand for "studio card," equivalent here to title cards prepared for superimposures.)

VIDEO	AUDIO
OPENING: Long shot of panel	Channel Five presents . . .
Super SC: "Untying the Apron Strings"	UNTYING THE APRON STRINGS . . . the first in a series of panel discussions concerning the family and young people,
Super Slide: L-154	presented by the Raleigh Parent-Youth League. The Parent-Youth League was organized two years ago for the purpose of encouraging better understanding between parents and young people.
MCU of Rev. Wooldridge Super SC: Rev. Wooldridge	Our moderator for today's program is the reverend Oscar Wooldridge, co-ordinator of religious affairs at North Carolina State College. Rev. Wooldridge:
2-SHOT DOWN PANEL, INTRO. OF OTHER MEMBERS.	

CLOSING:

Super SC: "Untying . . . "

Slide: L-

Channel Five, in co-operation with the Raleigh Parent-Youth League has presented "Untying the Apron Strings." Next week our program is entitled "Spring: Proms . . . Beach Parties." The League invites your comments on this series. Mail them to the Raleigh Parent-Youth League, WRAL-Television, Raleigh.

This has been a Studio Five presentation directed by Paul Oughton.

Courtesy of WRAL-TV, Raleigh, N.C.

Group Discussion.   Group discussion differs from most other forms of discussion in that it attempts to solve a problem by employing the objective, cooperative thinking and research of all the participants. The participants do not attempt to impose their own viewpoints and do not take opposing positions, but attempt to examine all materials in an unbiased manner and, in common investigation and unanimous decision, reach a solution acceptable to and best for the entire group. A moderator, who does not participate, guides the discussion and sees that it remains objective, that all group members participate and that none dominates, and that the discussion does not go off the track. A basic organizational approach for a group discussion would be a definition and limitation of the problem, a determination of the causes of the problem through objective research, and a determination of solutions based on the causes. Ideally, each participant is prepared with an outline containing facts pertinent to each step in the discussion process. The question itself should be a broad one, not answerable by a "yes" or a "no," such as "Should Juvenile Delinquents Be Sent to Work Camps?," but necessitating analysis, such as "What Should Be Done About Juvenile Delinquency?" The prepared material most often would be only an outline containing the opening, the introduction of the participants, some basic factual information under each step of the process, and the closing.

Debate.   A debate consists of two distinctly opposite sides of a question, one side taking the affirmative, the other side the negative. Debate should not be confused with panel or symposium, where participants may take opposite stands, but are not required to. In the debate the participants devote all of their energies to disputing each other, to building up their own arguments and destroying those of the opponent. The debaters may be individuals or may be in teams of two or more on a side. The debate itself has a number of distinct forms of organization. In all forms, however, there are just two sides, and each side is given a specified time for presentation of an initial argument, for rebuttal of the opponent's argument, and for summary. Some forms utilize direct confrontation and cross-examination. The prepared continuity need be only the opening, introduction of participants, introduction and time limits for each phase of the debate, explanations and interviews, if desired, and closing.

● *Following are a summary, outline and rundown sheets for a proposed discussion series using the debate approach. These materials would be submitted to a station, network or agency for consideration. 1) After you examine them determine a) other debate techniques that might be used within the same basic format; b) the potentials of this format for an audience participation program. 2) Prepare a routine sheet based on one of the rundown sheets above.*

DEBATE

A proposed television series.

The series is patterned after the collegiate debate.
The ideal program time would be one hour. The factors of entertainment and commercial responsibilities suggest a program time of one-half hour.

The program shall consist of two teams of two debaters each.
The questions to be debated shall be controversial, such as:
1. Communist China Should Be Admitted to the United Nations.
2. Congress Should Declare Organized Baseball A Monopoly.
3. Capital Punishment Should Be Abolished.
The questions chosen for debate must have at least two diametrically opposing views.

It would be excellent to have the debating teams composed of prominent people. The necessity for taking a clear stand on the issue and the need for some preparation for the debate may make it difficult to obtain such participants. In lieu of prominent people, the teams would consist of debating teams representing colleges and universities within the effective range of the television station.

(Note: It also would be possible to approach the program from the light, humorous side, using an audience participation-quiz show technique. Audience participants, either singly or in teams of two, could engage in short debates, lasting only several minutes apiece, on largely humorous subjects. The winners would be decided either by a team of judges or by audience response as measured by applause meters. The winners would be rewarded with prizes. Such debates could go beyond the audience participation phase and be oriented toward a mature quiz show type of approach, with individual or team winners receiving large monetary awards and continuing on succeeding programs against challengers, the winners to be decided by unimpeachable, prominent people acting as judges.)

The collegiate debate approach would be the basic form. The position each team takes is determined by a flip of a coin as part of the opening billboard for each show. (In college debate tournaments the teams do not know until the last moments before the debate which side they will take. The teams are informed of the topic beforehand, however, and prepare themselves on all facets of the question.)

Each team will have an equal time to speak. The order of speaking shall be:

Affirmative Argument:	4 minutes
Negative Argument :	4 minutes
Affirmative Rebuttal :	3 minutes
Negative Rebuttal :	3 minutes
Negative Summary :	3 minutes
Affirmative Summary :	3 minutes

(The above time limitations — see rundown sheet — are predicated on the insertion of commercials; if the program is sustaining, the speaking times may be extended.)

A team of three judges, composed of prominent people or college faculty members, will judge the debate on its merits and decide upon a winner at the conclusion of each debate. The winning team will remain on the program the following week and will be challenged by a team from another college, or elimination tournament procedure will be followed.

Awards shall be made in the form of prizes to the winning team, consolation awards to the losing team, and an award (such as a debating scholarship) shall be given to the college represented by the winning team. Honorariums shall be given to the judges.

Rundown Sheet

Program time: 29:30   Time

1. Opening billboard, explanation of debate procedure, tossing of coin to determine sides
2. Commercial   2:00
3. Introduction of Debaters   3:30
4. Affirmative and Negative Arguments   5:30
5. Commercial   13:30
6. Affirmative and Negative Rebuttals   15:00
7. Negative and Affirmative Summaries   21:00
8. Commercial   27:00
9. Decision; announcement of next week's teams; Closing Billboard   28:30

The following rundown sheet is from a series presented on WUNC-TV, Chapel Hill, North Carolina. A detailed routine sheet was also prepared for each program.

DEBATE TONIGHT!

AIR TIME: Monday, October 30, 9:30 P.M.

UNIVERSITY OF NORTH CAROLINA VS. DUKE UNIVERSITY

Topic.   Resolved: That labor organizations should be under the jurisdiction of anti-trust legislation.

RUNDOWN SHEET
Opening. Super titles.
Moderator: explanation of debate procedure   0:15
Moderator: introduction of Duke team members and coach   2:00
Moderator: introduction of North Carolina team members and coach   5:00
First Affirmative Constructive speaker   8:00
Cross Examination by Second Negative speaker   13:00
First Negative Constructive speaker   16:00
Cross Examination by First Affirmative speaker   21:00
Second Affirmative Constructive speaker   24:00
Cross Examination by First Negative speaker   29:00
Second Negative Constructive speaker   32:00
Cross Examination by Second Affirmative speaker   37:00
Moderator: introduction of judges   40:00
Third Negative speaker, Rebuttal and Summary   42:00
Third Affirmative speaker, Rebuttal and Summary   47:00
Moderator: explanation of judging procedure; interview with coaches   52:00
Decision of judges   56:00
Moderator: recap of names of participants and schools; names   57:00
             of teams to meet on next program; topic for next
             debate
Closing.   Super credits.   58:00
Black   59:00

Programs such as the above and those following are frequently "idea" programs. That is, they are not necessarily part of standard station or network formats, as is the d.j. show or the straight news broadcast, but they are developed and presented for station or network consideration by an individual or group not necessarily associated with the broadcasting organization. It is important for the creator of a program or series to be careful about such submissions, especially if he has a proposal of value. For example, the debate format and idea above were presented to one of the major networks. The series was considered worthwhile, but not "commercial" enough. A little more than two years after the submission the network produced a debate series, neither giving acknowledgment to the person who had proposed such a series, nor answering several letters from the writer inquiring about his earlier proposal and the eventual production of the series.

QUIZ, PANEL, AND AUDIENCE PARTICIPATION SHOWS

Actually, all of these types fall into the "quiz" category. Someone is expected to be able to solve some problem if they are to achieve the specific goal of the program, whether it is to stump a panel of experts, answer extremely complicated or extremely elementary questions about some subject, or hit one's spouse in the face three out of five times with a custard pie.

Approach

These programs are invariably of the spontaneous type. The script is prepared as fully as it can be; the opening and closing continuity, the introductions (when possible), the presumably ad-lib jokes (when possible), the questions and similar material are written out beforehand. This is the "routine sheet." The material, however, must be flexible and adaptable in terms of the situations themselves, which can be, to a greater or lesser degree, spontaneous. The prepared material must be designed to fit the personality of the master of ceremonies and should be developed in consultation with him or her. For example, in the audience participation show as much of the dialogue as possible is written out except that which will be given by the participants, and in many instances even the participants' supposedly ad-lib dialogue is written out or indicated in general form. This, of course, implies an orientation or rehearsal session before the show. The routine sheet should include the continuity preceding each stunt or gag or question or act. If specific stunts are used, they must be timed accurately beforehand so that the script fits into the required time length. Extra material often must be prepared to fill in case the show runs short. (Note "if third contestant" and "mail plug" in the "What's My Line" routine sheet on page 189.)

If the program begins with material that sets the tone and mood of the show, then the continuation of that feeling is not too different to achieve — provided the continuity material is available and there is a good master of ceremonies or panel.

Television Techniques

The radio and television forms are essentially the same, except that in television the emphasis should be on the visual elements: complicated stunts, charts, slides, drawings, film, costumes, visual aspects of personalities and so forth. In making the situation visual for television, the approach itself may be a simple one. Think back to the quiz shows of recent years. How elementary and yet how effective was the format of an individual grimacing and sweating in the confines of a glamorized telephone booth with tens of thousands of dollars seemingly hanging on his answer to a question!

On the following pages are excerpts from the panel-quiz game, "What's My Line?," and from the audience-participation show, "Truth or Consequences." These examples illustrate the basic formats and routine sheets for these kinds of programs. Note the overriding factor in both of these scripts: a "gimmick."

> ● *1) One of the most important aspects of the quiz show-audience participation program type is to involve the listening and viewing audience in the proceedings. Select the elements in these scripts that contribute to this goal. 2) Analyze these materials in terms of the fact that although these programs are presented as if they were completely extemporaneous or ad-lib, as much of the continuity as feasible is prepared beforehand.*

"WHAT'S MY LINE?" #813
SUNDAY, APRIL 24, 1966
10:30 — 11:00 PM STUDIO #52

WML PROGRAM ASTRO OP BB FILM

VIDEO	AUDIO
ANIMATION CARTOON	MUSIC — SOUND ON FILM
	JOHNNY OLSON: (LIVE)
	"WHAT'S MY LINE?" . . . brought to you by . . .
CUT TO: COMMERCIAL	
CUT TO FILM:	Now let's all play
CLOSING ANIMATION	"WHAT'S MY LINE?"
	SOUND EFFECT: SHOT
	APPLAUSE

APPLAUSE
<u>JOHNNY OLSON</u>: (LIVE)   And now live from New York, let's meet our "WHAT'S MY
                              LINE?" panel. FIRST, the delightful star of stage, and televi-
                              sion . . .

CAMERA TO NEWMAN   <u>MISS PHYLLIS NEWMAN</u>
NEWMAN: On my left—(AD LIBS)
CAMERA TO USTINOV   <u>PETER USTINOV</u>
USTINOV: On my left—(AD LIBS)
CAMERA TO FRANCIS   <u>ARLENE FRANCIS</u>
FRANCIS: On my left—(AD LIBS)
CAMERA TO CERF   <u>BENNETT CERF</u>:
CERF: And may I present our distinguished MC and moderator—MR.
                          JOHN DALY.

<u>DALY</u>:   Good evening, ladies and gentlemen. Welcome to "WHAT'S
                          MY LINE?" Once again tonight we're going to put our camera
                          close up on a few people from some varied and, perhaps, un-
                          expected occupations, here to baffle our panel to the happy end
                          they can carry home some prize money! We will also have a
                          famous mystery guest before our panel a little later in the
                          show. . .
                          Right now we'll meet our first contestant. Will you sign in,
                          please.

(FIRST CONTESTANT
PLAY GAME—EXIT)
(APPLAUSE)

<u>DALY</u>:   We'll have another contestant for you in just a moment, after
                          this word.

COMMERCIAL

<u>DALY</u>:   And now we'll meet our next contestant. Will you sign in,
                          please.

(SECOND CONTESTANT
PLAY GAME—EXIT)
(APPLAUSE)

<u>DALY</u>:   We'll meet tonight's Mystery Guest in just a moment, but
                          first this message.

COMMERCIAL

<u>DALY</u>:   Now we come to the special feature of our program—the ap-
                          pearance of our MYSTERY GUEST. And because our panel
                          would recognize our guest by sight, we have provided them
                          with blindfolds. Are the blindfolds all in place? All right, will
                          you come in, MYSTERY CHALLENGER and sign in please.
                          As you know, each panelist will get ONLY ONE QUESTION AT
                          A TIME.
                          All set? And now we'll start with - - - - - - - - - - - - - .

<u>DALY</u>:   You've done very well (not very well) so far tonight, panel,
(IF THIRD CONTESTANT)   and we'll have another contestant after this word.

<u>DALY</u>:   You've (not) done very well tonight, panel. (Congratulations)
(IF NO THIRD)   We'll all be back after this word.

COMMERCIAL

<u>MAIL PLUG</u>

189

DALY:	If you'd like to appear on "WHAT'S MY LINE?" and try to puzzle our panel with your occupation—simply send us a picture we can keep and your occupation. Send them to: "WHAT'S MY LINE?" CBS, 51 WEST 52nd STREET, NEW YORK, NEW YORK, 10019. Sorry, no pictures returned.

And now, until next week, this is John Daly saying goodnight, Phyllis. . .

CAMERA PANS ACROSS
PANEL

NEWMAN:	Goodnight, Peter.
USTINOV:	Goodnight, Arlene.
FRANCIS:	Goodnight, Bennett.
CERF:	Goodnight, John.
DALY:	And goodnight, ladies and gentlemen, and thanks for being with us on "WHAT'S MY LINE?"

DALY FACES CAMERA

MUSIC: (RECORD)

APPLAUSE

―――――

SLIDE LINE-UP

1. "WHAT'S MY LINE?"
   (DETECTIVE)

   JOHNNY OLSON: (LIVE) "WHAT'S MY LINE?" is a CBS Television Network Production in association with Mark Goodson and Bill Todman.

2. A CBS TELEVISION NETWORK
   PRODUCTION

3. MARK GOODSON — BILL TODMAN

4. EXECUTIVE PRODUCER
   GIL FATES

5. DIRECTED BY
   FRANKLIN HELLER

6. ASSOCIATE PRODUCERS

7. SCENIC DESIGN

8. ASSOCIATE DIRECTOR
   PRODUCTION SUPERVISOR

9. TECHNICAL DIRECTOR
   AUDIO
   LIGHTING DIRECTOR

Ed Bailey, producer of "Truth or Consequences," has stated that this show is based on "a spontaneous, ad-libbed format, and thus the script merely outlines the stunt or consequence. Our Master of Ceremonies, Bob Barker, is very quick-witted and glib, and on the basis of the script outline of the consequence, improvises the entire show." In terms of this statement, note in the following excerpt that most of the sequence is designated by only one item, number 10, and that the fully-scripted material the writer has prepared is of an introductory and transitional nature.

<u>"TRUTH OR CONSEQUENCES"</u>

<u>BOB BARKER</u>

1. Bring on contestants.

2. Interview and question.

3. Now, I know it probably never happens in your family, but every once in a while you hear about some member of a family putting a little money away for a rainy day, so to speak . . . and the interesting thing about some of these deposits is that only the person who put the money away knows where it is.

4. Tell me, Mrs. _____, do you think your husband has a few bills tucked away that you know nothing about?

(HEH HEH)

And, M . _____, do you think that Mrs. _____ might have a dollar or two hidden in a teapot that you know nothing about?

(ANSWER)

5. In any event, when such a thing does
   happen the money is put in a secret
   place known only to the one who put it
   there. Now, today we want to conduct
   a little experiment.

6. Reveal table and props.

   (WE NEED ONLY THREE PROPS . . .
   A COOKIE JAR . . . A PIGGY BANK,
   AND A COPY OF PLAYBOY FOR THE
   COFFEE TABLE)

7. I want you to notice that we have on
   display a cookie jar . . . a piggy
   bank . . . and there on the table, a
   man's type magazine.

8. Now, here's what's going to happen.
   Mrs. _____, I want you to
   take these bills.
   You'll note there is a one dollar bill . . .
   a five dollar bill, and a one hundred
   dollar bill.

9. Now, Mrs. _____, I want you
   to hide one of these bills in the cookie
   jar . . . one in the piggy bank, and one
   in the magazine. We'll close the curtains
   so not even the studio audience will
   know where you put the money. The
   first one Mr. _____picks
   is the bill you take home.

10. Play act.

11. Award winnings and consolation, if necessary.

   A variation of the audience participation sequence may be noted in the following excerpt from a "Truth and Consequences" program of an earlier format. Here the
script preparation is a little more detailed.

STEVE DUNNE

And now, ladies and gentlemen — as you
can probably well imagine, TRUTH OR
CONSEQUENCES is not exactly what you
might call a well rehearsed show. In fact,
we very rarely have any idea of what's
going to happen right up to and including
the time we go on the air. Well, tonight is
no exception. During our pre-show warmup,
I met one of the cutest young fellows we've
ever had in our studio audience. Anyway —
I thought you folks at home might get as much
of a kick out of seeing this youngster as I
did. And so, I'm going to ask that same
youngster along with his mother and grandmother to come down here on our stage if
they will, please.

(TURN ON HOUSE LIGHTS AND FOLLOW
 FAMILY DOWN ON STAGE)

1. Establish that mother's reason for bringing child to show tonight is that she couldn't get a baby sitter.

2. Ask camera to get closeup of baby.

3. Comment on the fact that there are three generations.

Well — it's certainly been nice talking to you folks, but like I say — we really had no consequence in mind for you when we asked you to come down on stage.

STEVE

(AS IF SUDDEN THOUGHT)

Wait a minute! I may have an idea. You couldn't get a baby sitter — right? (ANS) And we have 20,000,000 possible baby sitters watching us tonight — right?   (ANS)

(CALLS)

Ed Bailey — will you please bring me a telephone!   (DOES)

Okay, you folks at home — here's your chance to help out this young lady with a baby sitter problem. If you are available for baby sitting, please call immediately to this number. (LOOKS AT PHONE) Hollywood _____.   Now then, let's see what happens. Who knows — we might end up with enough baby sitters to take care of you for a full year, Mrs. Vianchi.

(PHONE RINGS AND STEVE PICKS IT UP)

Hello? Are you calling regarding doing some baby sitting for Mrs. Vianchi? (YES)

SUPER: "THIS IS THE BABY'S GREAT GRANDMOTHER FLOWN IN FROM TEXAS FOR THIS FAMILY REUNION."

And where are you calling from? (SAN ANGELO, TEXAS)

And may I have your name? (MRS. GRACE HEATH)

(PLAY REACTION OF PIGEON ON STAGE)

Well, Mrs. Heath, I'm sure Mrs. Vianchi would love to have you be her baby sitter, but how long would it take you to get to California from Texas?

(I'LL BE THERE JUST AS SOON AS I CAN)

(GREAT-GRANDMOTHER WALKS ON STAGE)

(REACTION)

(DURING THIS REUNION, PHONE RINGS AGAIN. STEVE PICKS IT UP.)

Hello — I'm sorry, the position has already been filled.

SUPER: "THIS IS THE BABY'S GREAT GREAT GRANDMOTHER ALSO FIOWN IN FOR THIS FAMILY REUNION"

Just the same, I <u>would</u> like to know your name, if I may.

(MRS. JOSIE DAVIS)

(PLAY REACTION OF PIGEON)

And how soon can you be in California?

(RIGHT AWAY)

(GREAT GREAT GRANDMOTHER ENTERS)

(REACTION)

<u>STEVE</u>

1. Comment on five generations being together at one time.

2. Well, TRUTH OR CONSEQUENCES is mighty happy to have had a part in bringing about this most unusual family reunion and we hope you will all enjoy the short visit here in California at our expense.

   Thanks for joining us tonight and God bless you all.

   ***

Courtesy of Ralph Edwards Productions, presented on NBC-TV.

SPEECHES

Ordinarily, there is little the continuity writer has to prepare in relation to a speech except the opening and closing material for the station announcer and, possibly, introductory material relating to the speaker. When an introduction of this kind is written, a good rule to remember is that the better known the speaker is, the less there has to be said about him.

If the speech is prepared by the speaker or his writers, the station writer or producer or director has a few things to check. First, the speech is usually gone over to see that it is compatible with station policy and F.C.C. rules. Next, the speech itself should be an effective one, from the point of view of information, or entertainment or persuasion. The speaker often is willing and even eager to accept advice from the station writer as to how to improve the speech in terms of the television and radio media and audience. Finally, and most important, the speech must be checked for time. Speakers unfamiliar with television and radio techniques frequently do not realize the necessity for split-second scheduling of programs, and their speeches may run short or, worse, too long and have to be cut off.

These needs, except for that of time, are bypassed in relation to political speeches or speeches by figures of importance. No one would suggest to the President of the United States, except his own advisers, that his speech should be changed to conform to arbitrary policy or media potentials. Only a reminder of the time available is necessary.

If the speech is prepared by the writer in the station, then the writer must do it in collaboration with the speaker. First, the format should be determined. Will it be a straight speech? Will there be a panel or interviewer present? Will there be questions from the audience? The speech may be written out and read on radio or placed on a TelePrompTer for television. At all times the speech should fit the personality of the speaker.

The lecture or sermon is a speech-type often found on television and radio. Alfred C. Reinert, Business Manager of The Evangelical Foundation, Inc., wrote of the procedure used by the late Dr. Donald Grey Barnhouse when he prepared his transcribed half-hour radio sermons:

> "Dr. Barnhouse wrote the script himself, keeping to a set marginal depth and page length, which figured out at eight typewritten pages including the question and answer.
>
> "However, while recording, Dr. Barnhouse was quite apt to ad-lib. . . . After the recording had been made, the radio technician ran off the tape and timed it. He then turned the script over to our editor who cut sections until she brought the script within the prescribed time limit. While doing this, she had to keep in mind not only logical transition, but the fact that Dr. Barnhouse's voice must be cut at just the point where it would sound like a natural ending."

Occasionally, the speech on television may be developed into more than a simple verbal presentation and may include film clips, slides and other visual material. Such speeches are, essentially, illustrated talks or lectures, and are prepared as special features.

FOR APPLICATION AND REVIEW

1. Prepare an outline, rundown sheet and routine sheet for:
   an opinion interview; a personality interview; an information
   interview. Each interview should be with a *different person* of
   local importance, such as a noted athlete or a prominent university faculty member.
2. Do the same exercise, using the *same person* as the subject for
   all three interview types.
3. Prepare an outline, rundown sheet and routine sheet for a discussion program on a highly controversial subject. If possible,
   select participants and produce the program. (The program
   may be for television or radio.)
4. Devise formats for a panel-quiz, a games or an audience participation show that may be produced, a) on an educational
   television and/or radio station, b) on a network television and/
   or radio station.
5. Develop the format for one of the shows you planned in 4),
   above, into a routine sheet for production on television. What
   are the special visual techniques you used that you would not
   have applied if the same program were to be produced for radio?
6. Watch a network panel discussion television program. Taking
   the basic form of that program, prepare an outline, rundown
   sheet and routine sheet for a similar program to be done over
   a local educational or community television station.

7

MUSIC AND
VARIETY PROGRAMS

MUSIC PROGRAMS

MUSIC COMPRISES the bulk of radio programming today. Independent stations rely primarily on music for program content, and even network affiliates devote most of their non-network time to music shows. In the last three decades, since Martin Block made famous the concept of a radio announcer playing records separated by comment and commercial, the disc jockey has become a national institution. Before television drew so much of the live talent away from radio, live studio musical programs featuring symphony orchestras, popular singers, jazz bands, opera stars, and other musical soloists and groups were popular. Such live programming has, to a great degree, disappeared, although some standard programs, such as the Texaco Opera Series, the Telephone and Firestone programs, individual popular stars, and special programs of a high quality on stations such as New York's WNYC, continued on radio for a long time in the age of television.

Television has not utilized the musical program to the degree that radio did. There have been some good special programs, some successful orchestras such as Lawrence Welk's, a few personalities such as Liberace, and several successful attempts at adapting the radio disc jockey program, such as the Dick Clark show. But, by and large, the musical content on television is oriented toward individual performances on variety shows. Popular entertainers such as Perry Como, who are primarily singers, have variety, not musical shows. Frank Sinatra, who might be expected to be as popular as anyone with a straight musical program, was unsuccessful with a television series.

The job for the scriptwriter in the area of music is primarily in the writing of continuity for the music-variety TV show, the radio magazine — which combines music, variety, news and talks — and for some — usually classical — disc jockey programs.

Approach and Format

A musical program, live or recorded, must have organic continuity. That is, there must be a central program idea, a focal point around which all the

197

material is organized and from which the program grows and develops. No program can be haphazard. There are some disc jockeys who are clever enough to grab a batch of records at the last minute and spontaneously organize them somehow into a good program. Most often such a program reflects the inferiority of its planning.

The musical program may have a central theme developed around a personality, an event, a type of music, a locality — around almost anything that can give it unity. The writer can find ideas for central themes in many places: special days, national holidays, the anniversary of a composer's birth, a new film by a popular singing star, a national or international event that suggests a certain theme such as love, war, the jungle, adventure and so forth. The musical selections themselves should have a clear relationship to each other, and the non-musical script continuity transitions between numbers should indicate this relationship.

The following program, one of a series sent to RCA Victor subscriber stations, is illustrative of continuity for the classical recorded music program built around a theme. Note that a listing of records according to RCA catalogue number and according to playing time precedes the script, thus providing a simple rundown sheet.

<u>MUSIC YOU WANT</u>

LM-6026   Catalani: LORELEI: DANCE OF THE WATER NYMPHS
             NBC Symphony Orchestra, Arturo Toscanini, conductor

SIDE 3:   Band 4   6:23

LM-1913   Delibes: COPPELIA: EXCERPTS
             Boston Symphony Orchestra, Pierre Monteux, conductor

SIDE 2:   Entire   25:31

LM-2150   Stravinsky: SONG OF THE NIGHTINGALE
             Chicago Symphony Orchestra, Fritz Reiner, conductor

SIDE 2:   Entire   22:13

* *

G07L-0783   AIR FOR G STRING (fading after 20 seconds)

ANNCR: (Sponsor or) His Master's Voice is on the air with THE MUSIC YOU
             WANT WHEN YOU WANT IT, a program of RCA Victor High Fidelity Red
             Seal records.

G07L-0783   AIR FOR G STRING (Up 5 seconds and fade out)

ANNCR: Today's program is devoted to musical works that deal with the super-
             natural. One of the three selections is from an opera, one is a suite from
             a ballet, and the third — from a new RCA Victor album — is a symphonic
             poem, later used for a ballet.

             The supernatural has always had a strong hold on the imagination of man.
             The unknown and the unusual, with the laws of nature in a distorted or
             suspended state, has occupied story-tellers from their earliest days. It
             is only natural that this strong impulse, throughout time and all races,
             should attract composers as suitable subject matter. Our three works
             today deal with three separate types of the supernatural: mythological

creatures who are portents of evil for mankind — a mechanical doll with complete but superficial resemblance to living beings — and animals with human characteristics and traits.

We open with a selection from Catalani's opera Lorelei. The opera deals with maidens who inhabit a rock in the middle of the Rhine River and lure sailors to destruction. We hear the Dance of the Water Nymphs, in a performance by Arturo Toscanini and the NBC Symphony Orchestra.

LM-6026
SIDE 3:
Band 4   Catalani: LORELEI: DANCE OF THE WATER NYMPHS   8:05

ANNCR: We have opened today's program with the Dance of the Water Nymphs from the opera, Lorelei by Catalani, Arturo Toscanini led the NBC Symphony Orchestra in our performance.

Our second selection devoted to the supernatural in music is the suite from the ballet, Coppelia (Coe-pay-lyah), or the Girl with the Enamel Eyes, by Leo Delibes (Lay-oh Duh-leeb). Coppelia, one of the most popular of all evening-length ballets, had its first performance at the Paris Opera in May, 1870. The dominant figure in the story is Coppelia, an almost human mechanical doll. The youth Frantz falls in love with her, much to the chagrin of his lively fiancee Swanhilde. But all ends happily, and in the final act the betrothal of Frantz and Swanhilde is celebrated.

The selections we are to hear from Coppelia are as follows: Prelude — Swanhilde's Scene and Waltz — Czardas — The Doll's Scene and Waltz — Ballade — and Slavic theme and variations. We hear Coppelia in a performance by members of the Boston Symphony Orchestra under the direction of the veteran French conductor, Pierre Monteux. Selections from the ballet, Coppelia by Leo Delibes.

LM-1913
SIDE 2:
Entire   Delibes: COPPELIA   34:52

ANNCR: Members of the Boston Symphony Orchestra under the direction of Pierre Monteux have just been heard in selections from the ballet Coppelia by Leo Delibes.

Animals with human traits and emotions are at least as old as Aesop. Igor Stravinsky, before composing his ballet, The Firebird, wrote the first act of an opera, The Nightingale, which — for a number of years — remained unfinished. The opera was to deal with a nightingale who, moved by pity, returns to save the life of a man who previously rejected it. Stravinsky was prevailed upon to finish his score after the composition of his revolutionary Le Sacre du Printemps. Naturally, he was a different composer at that time, disparities of musical style resulted, and Stravinsky remained dissatisfied with the opera. He took the later sections of The Nightingale and turned them into a symphonic poem, changing the title to The Song of the Nightingale. Like most of his works, this symphonic poem became the basis for a ballet.

The Song of the Nightingale concerns the Emperor of China who shifts his affection from a live nightingale to a mechanical one, a present from the Emperor of Japan. He falls ill and is on his deathbed. The real nightingale, contrite at having deserted the Emperor after his change-of-heart, returns to sing to him and restores him to health.

The Song of the Nightingale, a symphonic Poem by Igor Stravinsky, in a new RCA Victor recording by Fritz Reiner and the Chicago Symphony Orchestra.

LM-2150
SIDE 2:
Entire   Stravinsky: THE SONG OF THE NIGHTINGALE   58:33

ANNCR: Fritz Reiner and the Chicago Symphony Orchestra have just played
Stravinsky's Song of the Nightingale, a new RCA Victor recording. The
other side of this album, Prokofieff's Lieutenant Kije (Kee-gee), will be
played at a later date.

STANDARD CLOSE

Next Program (Premiere): - Monteux interprets Tchaikovsky's
Sleeping Beauty ballet.

G07L-0783   THEME UP TO END OF BROADCAST PERIOD.

Examples of further types of central themes are evident in the following
excerpts:

ANNCR: The three greatest masters of the Viennese classical school
are Ludwig von Beethoven, Wolfgang Amadeus Mozart and Franz Joseph
Hayden. Today we will hear works by each of these three masters.

ANNCR: Our program today offers Russian music of the 19th century.
We open with Borodin's atmospheric orchestral sketch, "On the Steppes
of Central Asia." Leopold Stokowski leads his orchestra in this performance.

The format of the musical program should reflect the elements of any
good entertainment program. It should open with something that gets the
attention of the audience. Then it may relax a bit — not so as to fall to
mediocrity, but by presenting something that may not be on so exciting a plane
as the initial number. The program should build from there, continuing from
one high point to another until the climax of the program is reached with the
final number. The building to a climax should be neither boring nor repetitious,
however. The writer can avoid this by creating variety within the organization
of the program, offering the listener a change of pace throughout, after each
high point giving the audience a rest and then moving on to a higher point.

There are a number of general considerations the writer must keep in
mind in planning the program format and choosing the kind of music and
specific musical numbers to be presented. On the network live musical show
a musical director usually will choose the music, but in other circumstances
the writer (or disc jockey) may perform this function. He should make sure
that the program content fits the personalities of the performers, whether they
are live orchestras, vocalists or disc jockeys. The writer must analyze the
potential audience for the program and, while giving them something that is
popular — that is, something they want to hear — should not play down to
them. No matter what type of music it is, pop or classical, the best of that
type should be presented. In this same vein, remember that an audience tunes
in a particular program because that program has established a certain kind of
musical format or approach. The writer must adhere to the purpose of the
program. The audience may listen for relaxation, for thinking, for education,
for dancing or for one of many other purposes. This implies, too, an adherence to

a single type of music. Although there are exceptions, the mixing of Beethoven and "Bop" or of "rock and roll" and waltzes likely would not be the best way to build an audience.

The writing itself should be fresh. In the disc jockey program especially, we seem to hear the same phraseology over and over. Orchestras always "render," singers always give "vocal renditions of," and pianists always play "on the eighty-eight." The announcer's language overflows with phrases such as "ever-popular," "inimitable," "scintillating," and "impromptu meanderings." Transitions and lead-ins provide another problem. The trite joke or play on words has become an over-used device for introducing a number. Phrases such as "For our next number," "Our next record," and "Next on the turntable," have long ceased to serve a worthwhile purpose in musical continuity. Perhaps that doesn't leave the writer with very much choice. If it is impossible to think of something new and fresh and not trite, the best approach is to keep it simple.

Because music itself makes up the bulk of the program content, the script continuity is short compared with that of other program types. The writer can learn just how much continuity he will have to provide by first outlining the show, noting the musical selections to be presented and determining the time for each. In the disc jockey show he will find that each record or transcription will have a specific time length indicated. In the live show the performer or musical director will be able to provide the timing. The writer need not worry too much about the exact timing on the live show, for the director will always adjust minor time problems during rehearsals.

Program Types

The Disc Jockey Program. Both in the smaller stations, where there is lack of time and/or personnel, and in the larger stations, where there may be personalities who can at one and the same time recall, organize, interrelate and present ideas correlated with musical numbers with speed and fluency, ad-lib programs are predominant. Unfortunately, unless one has the latter ability in high degree, ad-libbing tends to become boring and repetitious, as well as extremely trite. Even the best ad-lib comedians make certain they get the best available writers to prepare their ad-lib remarks. An astounding number of disc jockeys attempt to give the impression that their shows consist entirely of unprepared ad libs. Successful D.J.'s rarely take a chance with complete ad-libbing. Why be half-safe when you can make sure with some script preparation? Formats of programs, general introductions to numbers, openings and closings and the order of musical selections are helpful continuity items.

The music library is of great importance to the radio station. The continuity writer should know the content of the music library. Records, when received, should be auditioned, timed and catalogued. Cross-indexing is desirable, with separate indices for theme, performer, composer and any other area which may be the determinant in the preparation of a program.

Just as with the editing of the news, the preparation of continuity in terms of informality, interest, language level and so forth should be oriented toward the personality of the disc jockey and the form and purpose of his show.

Harold Green, Program Manager of WMAL radio, Washington, D.C., states the following about the disc jockey and the D.J. program:

The day of the "limited" announcer is about over. Just a beautiful voice, or just a snappy, witty or attractive personality is not enough for today's successful radio station. All the tricks, gimmicks, formats, points of view have been tried in one form or another. Some are quite successful in a limited way. The danger that the individual suffers is the strong possibility that he will remain submerged or anonymous. This is particularly true in a station that depends strongly on a particular "format." We feel that the stations that matter in the community don't limit themselves to a format or other gimmick. The key is community involvement — information with a purpose — and a continuity of sound (in music and personality) that will continually serve, and please, the audience that particular station has cultivated.

Our announcers go on the air each day with a thick folder of clippings, personal observations, letters from listeners, and tears from all the news and sports wires. By the time a man actually goes on the air each day, he is fully briefed on all that is happening that is significant in the news, in sports, special events in the community, special broadcasts of more than routine interest scheduled for that day and week, or anything else that amounts to information *with a purpose*. He has spent a minimum of two hours in the music library. Generally, each day's music preparation time amounts to approximately 50% of air time. A 4-hour program requires about two hours to prepare musically. This is for one who is thoroughly familiar with the library. Otherwise it becomes a 1:1 ratio, or even longer. This is because the music list must reflect variety and balance: up-tempo music, boy vocal, lush orchestral, girl vocal, combo or variety, group vocal, and back around again. Specialty, novelty, or other types that break the pattern must be showcased by the D.J. There must be a reason for playing these "extras," and it must be explained.

It is safe to say that when a man does a smooth, informative, professional 4-hour show — and one that teased the imagination and piqued the curiosity — he did an equal four hours of preparation. If he doesn't, he'll know it in about an hour, I'll know it in about an hour and a half, and the listener will know it before noon the next day. Without preparation, background, genuine interest in the world around him, and diligent attention to getting informed and staying informed, a broadcaster sinks instantly into mediocrity. He is then relying on tricks . . . he is ordinary . . . he is short-changing his audience.

He won't last long.

The "Pop" Program. In addition to fulfilling all the needs indicated above, the "pop" music program must be highly conscious of fads and fancies. Catering mostly to young people, popular music and its values are constantly vacillating. An Elvis Presley style may become a Beatles style which may in turn become a Sammy Davis, Jr. style in a matter of months, weeks or even days. It is not suggested that the pop program cater to the lowest common denominator of what may be chronologically, as well as intellectually, the twelve-year-old level. The disc jockey, in great degree, molds and determines the tastes in popular music. Popular music covers a vast area and includes not only current favorites, as exemplified in the 1940's by "swing" and in the 1950's and 1960's by "rock and roll," but in a broad sense also may include music from the theatre, semi-classical ballads, the different varieties of jazz, background music from films, foreign songs, novelty numbers, old favorites and even folk songs. Since, for the most part, programs tend not to mix these various categories too frequently, any given program or segment of a program usually will contain similar types of material. This creates difficulty in preparation — in finding different ways of introducing the numbers in order to achieve variety in continuity.

The Classical Program. The writer of the classical music program must be more of an "expert" than the writer of the pop music program. The educational and intellectual levels of the listener of the classical music show are likely to be above those of the average listener of the pop music show, and our classical music audience is likely to be more critical of the written material presented. The audience expects more than a cursory introduction, and more continuity is needed than in the pop program. The "expert" analysis must be presented thoroughly. It is not sufficient to say "This is the finest example of chamber music written in the twentieth century." The writer should give the reasons why.

Classical music continuity may be oriented toward special areas. There may be a concentration on symphonies, or on chamber music, or on operatic excerpts and so forth. Note how the program on pages 198-200 dealing with the "supernatural" is able to combine, within its central theme, opera, symphony and ballet.

Examine the following scripts for examples of continuity in another classical music area, the complete opera. Note that each program is an hour in length, the continuity for each program overshadowed by the length of the opera itself. Had there been more program time, the continuity could have been more detailed.

● *Determine the degree to which the continuity presents "expert" information, as well as serves the other requirements of the good musical program.*

MUSIC YOU WANT

LM-6025   Beethoven: FIDELIO: ACT ONE
           Bampton, Steber, sops.; Laderoute, ten.; NBC Symphony Orchestra,
           Arturo Toscanini, conductor

SIDES 1
 and 2:   Entire   58:09

* *

G07L-0783 AIR FOR G STRING (fading after 20 seconds)

ANNCR: (Sponsor or) His Master's Voice is on the air with THE MUSIC YOU WANT
           WHEN YOU WANT IT, a program of RCA Victor High Fidelity Red Seal
           records.

G07L-0783 AIR FOR G STRING (Up 5 seconds and fade out)

ANNCR: We are to hear today and tomorrow Beethoven's opera Fidelio, interpreted
           by Arturo Toscanini. The story of Act One, which we hear today, concerns
           Florestan, a political prisoner unjustly imprisoned by his enemy Pizarro,
           governor of the state prison. Florestan's wife, Leonora, disguises herself
           as a boy and --- using the name of Fidelio --- becomes assistant to the
           jailer Rocco. Pizarro decides to kill Florestan upon learning that the
           Prime Minister is to visit the prison, and bids Rocco dig a grave. Rocco
           balks, however, at murder and Pizarro decides personally to kill Florestan.
           Rocco allows the prisoners access to the courtyard, but Leonora, scanning
           the faces, is unable to find Florestan. She rejoices when she finds she is to
           accompany Rocco to the dungeon.

           Arturo Toscanini conducts the NBC Symphony and the following soloists: Rose
           Bampton --- Leonora; Herbert Janssen --- Pizarro; Sidor Belarsky ---
           Rocco; Eleanor Steber --- Rocco's daughter; and Joseph Laderoute ---
           Rocco's assistant. The Overture and Act I of Beethoven's Fidelio.

LM-6025
SIDES 1
 and 2:
 Entire   Beethoven: FIDELIO, ACT I   59:38

ANNCR: You have just heard Act I of Beethoven's Fidelio, in a rendition conducted by
           Toscanini. Listen tomorrow at this same time for the conclusion of Fidelio.

           STANDARD CLOSE.

MUSIC YOU WANT

LM-6025   Beethoven: FIDELIO: ACT TWO
           Bampton, Steber, sops.; Laderoute, ten.; NBC Symphony Orchestra,
           Arturo Toscanini, conductor

SIDES 3
 and 4:   Entire   53:54

* *

G07L-0783   AIR FOR G STRING (fading after 20 seconds)

ANNCR: (Sponsor or) His Master's Voice is on the air with THE MUSIC YOU WANT
WHEN YOU WANT IT, a program of RCA Victor High Fidelity Red Seal
records.

G07L-0783   AIR FOR G STRING (Up 5 seconds and fade out)

ANNCR: Yesterday we brought you the Overture and Act One of Fidelio, an opera by
Ludwig van Beethoven. We conclude our playing today of this RCA Victor
complete opera recording, an album taken from Arturo Toscanini's NBC
Symphony broadcasts for December 10th and 17th, 1944. Our artists include
Jan Peerce, Rose Bampton, Nicola Moscona, Eleanor Steber and Herbert
Janssen.

Beethoven had long wanted to write an opera because --- more than any other
musical medium --- opera was an art of and for the people. He also knew it
was lucrative --- a consideration one should never rule out in Beethoven's
case. He searched for a suitable libretto for many years. Finally he decided
on an old French story and hired a German versifier to make a libretto of
it. The original title was "Leonora, or Conjugal Love."

The German composer's efforts on his opera were titanic, even for him. His
sketch-books reveal no fewer than eighteen different beginnings for Florestan'
second act aria, and ten for the final triumphant chorus.

Similar uncountable revisions figure throughout the score. Perhaps the
quintessence of this desire for perfection is illustrated by the four overtures
Beethoven wrote in his obsession to find just the proper mood with which to
begin his opera. Because the opera was originally entitled Leonora, the
first three overtures retain that title. The lighter, less heroic Fidelio
Overture was finally chosen by Beethoven as being more in keeping with the
emotional mood of the opera's opening scene.

The premier of Fidelio took place in 1805. It was a failure. Beethoven,
prevailed upon by friends, compressed the opera into two acts and cut three
whole numbers from the opening parts of the score. The second production
was on its way to becoming a success when Beethoven, in one of his typical,
unreasonable rages, withdrew Fidelio from the boards. The opera's third
production, in May of 1814, was the last during Beethoven's lifetime.

The story of the second --- and last --- act of Fidelio is as follows:
Florestan, the husband of Leonora (now disguised in man's attire as Fidelio,
the jailer's assistant), is chained to a wall in the prison dungeon. He sings
of his miserable plight. Leonora and Rocco, the jailer, appear. Upon seeing
her husband, whom she recognizes with difficulty, she says nothing and as-
sists Rocco to dig the grave, intended for Florestan and ordered by Pizarro,
governor of the state prison. Pizarro appears and tries to stab the defense-
less prisoner. Leonora rushes to shield Florestan. "Kill his wife first,"
she cries out. Enraged, Pizarro attempts to kill them both; Leonora defends
herself and Florestan with a concealed pistol. At this point the long awaited
Prime Minister arrives and releases all the political prisoners unjustly
held by Pizarro, who is arrested and led away.

The cast includes Jan Peerce as Florestan --- Rose Bampton as Leonora ---
Nicola Moscona as Don Fernando, the Prime Minister --- Herbert Janssen
as Pizzaro --- Sidor Belarsky as Rocco, chief jailer --- Eleanor Steber as
Marcellina, Rocco's daughter --- and Joseph Laderoute as Jacquino, Rocco's
assistant, in love with Marcellina. The choral director is Peter Wilhousky and
Arturo Toscanini conducts the NBC Symphony Orchestra. Act Two of
Beethoven's opera, Fidelio.

```
LM-6025
SIDES 3
  and 4:
   Entire    Beethoven: FIDELIO: ACT TWO                               57:35
```

ANNCR: We have just brought you the second act of Beethoven's opera, Fidelio, as recorded from Arturo Toscanini's NBC broadcasts for December 10th and 17th, 1944. Yesterday we brought you Act One of this score, Beethoven's only opera. Included in our cast were Rose Bampton as Leonora --- Jan Peerce, Florestan --- Nicola Moscona, the Prime Minister --- Herbert Janssen, Pizarro --- Sidor Belarsky, Rocco --- Eleanor Steber, Marcellina --- and Joseph Lauderoute, Jacquino.

STANDARD CLOSE

Next Program (premiere): Presenting Tozzi (TOT-see), a program of nine bass arias by Mozart and Verdi by Giorgio Tozzi, the sensational American basso of the Metropolitan Opera.

G07L-0783   THEME UP TO END OF BROADCAST PERIOD

The Live Program. The live musical program frequently concentrates on a type of performance. Physical types include vocalists, either singly or in groups; single or dual instruments (twin-piano teams often are heard); pianist-vocalist combined in a single person; combinations (or, to use the appropriate term, "combos") consisting of band-vocalist personnel; novelty groups; instrumental groups, including salon, chamber and string ensembles; orchestras, including concert, symphony, band or dance orchestras; and choral groups.

Writing the live show is basically the same as writing the show consisting of recorded material, except that in the live situation the writer can include material that reflects the elements of the variety show by inserting the live personalities in the dialogue portion of the script. Instead of relying solely upon narration by a disc jockey, the writer can incorporate elements of the interview. The approach to the live show usually centers around a musical event, orchestra or individual. One of the most popular live musical shows for many years was "The Voice of Firestone." The following script from this program illustrates the concentration on a featured musical personality. The performer is also included in the continuity and introduces the program's central theme, which is developed throughout and clearly forwarded through the transitions.

> ● As you study the following script, do you think the featured performer could or should have been included in more of the non-musical portion? Is there a theme? Freshness? The proper amount of written continuity?

(Opening Theme - "If I Could Tell You")

James: Good evening, ladies and gentlemen. Firestone, the name that stands for highest quality in tires and tubes, and in hundreds of other products for cars and trucks; as well as for outstanding values in products for home and farm and for work and recreation; manufacturer of Foamex, the foamed rubber cushioning widely used for mattresses, furniture, footwear and transportation seating; and Velon, the quality plastic used in rainwear, luggage, venetian blind tapes, self-sticking decorative films and outdoor-indoor furniture; presents the Voice of Firestone, the program that brings you familiar favorites featuring Howard Barlow and the Firestone Orchestra and Chorus, and the mezzo-soprano star of the Metropolitan Opera and concert stage, Mildred Miller.

(End Theme)

Miller: There's a fabled part of this world of ours where music is master. It's here
(Live)   that people sing friendly, familiar songs. Here are the birthplaces of such musical giants as Wagner, Beethoven, Mozart, Strauss, Brahms, Bach and ever so many more. It is a world of old castles along the Rhine, ancient walled cities, cathedrals which have been standing for centuries, snow-capped Alps, the Black Forest. It is the land of the polka and the waltz. Let's make a quick trip there, shall we? Hugh James, will you be our guide?

James: Thank you, Miss Miller. Perhaps one of the most treasured memories of people who have traveled through this fabulous land is Bavaria where the Alps lift their heads above puffy, white clouds; where dark forests and ancient castles lend enchantment to the breathtaking scenery. This is the home of painters, of sculptors, of musicians! Here the heart is always happy and always young.

("Explosions Polka" - Orchestra)

("While Hearts Are Singing" - Chorus)

("The Lorelei" - Miller)

James: However small the village, however remote from the modern autobahns and express trains, the Gasthaus welcomes all who pass that way, whether it be in Oberammergau, in Bayreuth, in Darmstadt or on the purple heath of Luneberg. Along the famous Weinstrasse during the autumn, the evergreen is hoisted above the door to herald the arrival of the new wine. Here is the center of the town's society, the hub of political discussions, the forum of opinion, the very embodiment of all that is "Gemutlichkeit."

(Medley: "Du Du Liebst Mir Im Herzen"

             "Mein Hut Hast Drei Ecken"

             "Lili Marlene" - Charlie Magnante, Miller, Chorus and Orchestra)

("Stars in My Eyes" - Miller)

James: Thank you, Miss Miller.

(COMMERCIAL ANNOUNCEMENT)

James: No river in the world boasts as many legends as the Rhine. Stories tell of gold that is buried beneath its waters, of the Lorelei Rock where beautiful maidens lured men to their doom. As it flows along the French Border and continues through Western Germany and The Netherlands, it passes the age-old castles which rise in proud and stately beauty. Within their walls you hear the happy sounds of laughter and music <u>when</u> there is a celebration going on, and the melodies of today are intermingled with the songs of yesteryear.

207

("Voi Che Sapete" - Miller)

(Excerpt from "Die Meistersinger" - Orchestra)

James: Thank you, Mr. Barlow.

(SECOND COMMERCIAL ANNOUNCEMENT

James: This lively heart of Europe beats in tempo to wonderful music -- especially
           in three-quarter time to the colorful sweep of the waltz. Its rhythm brings
           to mind the native costumes of the Tyrol and melodic voices echoed by the
           snow-covered Alps -- Salzburg where Beethoven wrote the "Eroica" and
           where not far from his home, you find the houses of Strauss and Schubert and
           Haydn. During the sunny, warm months of July and August, Salzburg becomes
           the festival city and the music of Mozart is gloriously performed . . . as
           well as the music of other immortal composers.

("Merry Widow Waltz" - Miller and Chorus)

(Closing Theme - "In My Garden")

James: We are happy to have had you with us this evening and we invite you to tune
           in again next Monday at the same time when the Voice of Firestone will
           present the bass-baritone star of the Metropolitan Opera and concert stage,
           Cesare Siepi. On January 27, our artists will be Lisa Della Casa and Cesare
           Valletti. In February our artists will be Giuseppe Campora, Jerome Hines,
           Richard Tucker and Thomas L. Thomas. So be sure to listen to the Voice
           of Firestone every Monday evening to hear these world-famous artists and
           the exciting musical arrangements of the Firestone Orchestra and Chorus
           under the direction of Howard Barlow.

(End Theme)

(Applause)

James: This is Hugh James saying thank you and good evening for Firestone.

By permission of The Firestone Tire and Rubber Company.

Since the demise of most live musical shows in network radio broadcasting, the combination live-disc jockey program sometimes has been presented.
In order to capitalize on the attraction of a personality and still save on the
costs of a full musical production, the network or large station presents the
personality combining live songs with recorded and transcribed material. In
addition, RCA provides a script-record service in which the D.J., live, questions
a personality whose answers and songs have been pre-recorded.

Television Considerations. One of the reasons that musical programs
have not been especially popular or successful on television is that music, obviously enough, is not a visual art form. Attempts to make visual action the
focal point of musical programs on television often have defeated the purposes
of musical presentation and have resulted in unfulfilled goals, both aurally and
visually. The action must remain secondary to the sound. Yet, the action must
be of sufficient interest to make worthwhile the audience's full attention and
time to the television screen. Otherwise, the listener might just as well hear the
music on radio or on a phonograph.

There are several approaches in supplementing the musical program on
television with live action. The first thing the writer must ask is: "What will the

picture add to the sound?" The writer should avoid gimmicks, strange angles and bizarre shots which may be exciting in themselves, but which have no integral relationship to the music. If the writer first develops a central theme, such as a relationship to a locale, an interpretation or representation of a situation, or the conveying of a mood, it will be easier for him to find the specific visual elements for the program.

The most common approach, and in its simplicity perhaps the most effective, is the direct presentation of the performers on camera. This is the principal form of the disc jockey show on television, where the disc jockey, the guest performer, or a studio audience of youngsters dancing to the music is the usual visual ingredient. In the live musical performance the writer prepares audio and video continuity that deals not only with the material being played, but with how it is played.

Different sections or members of the orchestra, band or other musical group may be the focal points. This permits a visual concentration on and an examination of the different aspects of the performance, such as the brass section, the first violinist, the drummer or the conductor. The same approach may be used with vocalists. Elements of the variety show may be incorporated with this visual emphasis on the performers. For example, the antics of a hillbilly band in costume may provide effective visual action.

Abstract representations also may be used effectively. These abstractions, or visual symbols conveying the meaning and mood of the music, may be drawings or paintings, free forms, architectural compositions, or a kaleidoscope of any of the elements of the plastic arts. Color combinations can be used to great advantage.

Other art forms, specifically pantomime and dance, may provide interpretive visualizations of the music. Inanimate objects and forms, such as photographs, paintings, slides and film, can also illustrate realistic and non-realistic interpretations. Landscapes, people, places, actions and events may be shown, indicating various environmental and psychological meanings and moods of the music.

VARIETY PROGRAMS

Reading a chapter of a book, or even a dozen books, will not give a writer the craft of comedy of a Fred Allen or a Goodman Ace. This book does not provide techniques for comedy writing. It does, however, provide some basic approaches to the organization of the variety show, which includes elements of comedy, situation, suspense and music.

Program Types

The term, variety show, implies a combination of two or more elements of entertainment and art. A musical number, an acrobat, a puppeteer, a dancer, a pianist, a comic, a Shakespearean actor, a ventriloquist, a singer: if all of these were thrown together on a stage and all went through their individual acts in the space of a half-hour, an hour, or more, we would have a variety show. But the variety show is not a haphazard conglomeration of different actions, although this seems to be the case too frequently on some television programs. Different types and formats, developed through the American and European stages, have found their place on television. The basic types are the vaudeville show, the music hall variety, the revue, the comic-dominated show, the personality program with guests and the musical comedy approach.

Vaudeville and music hall variety are basically the same, oriented around specialty acts such as acrobats and ventriloquists and, in American television, frequently including performers in music and dance. The revue is organized primarily in terms of music and dance numbers, with comedians frequently providing the continuity.

The comic-dominated show may consist of a comedian as the central performer, with various guests and/or standard acts, as in the Bob Hope and Milton Berle approaches; or it may be oriented almost exclusively around the talents of the comic, with occasional special acts, as in the Danny Kaye approach.

A personality, such as Sammy Davis, Jr., may mix his own songs with contributions from guests, making what is in essence a revue centered around one performer. When such shows have a thread of continuity, no matter how thin, they then become musical revues. The thread may be any kind of a theme: the songs of a particular composer, a national holiday, an historical happening, the biography of a famous entertainer, a locale and many others.

When more than a thread, but a plot line (even a meager one) is used, we have the makings of a musical comedy. Rodgers and Hammerstein's adaptation of "Cinderella" is an example of television musical comedy. Some musical comedies on television pretend to that category in name only, however, and may be little more than a thinly connected series of songs and dances by popular entertainers.

Vaudeville variety, as exemplified by the Ed Sullivan show, has been successful in American television. Of the other types of variety shows, either music or comedy seems to be the main ingredient. Comedy will dominate, alternating with musical numbers and specialty acts, or music will dominate, alternating with comedy and specialty routines. In all of the variety shows there is a master of ceremonies. The MC may be a non-performer, such as Ed Sullivan who rarely participates in any routines and has different guest acts each week, a performer such as Steve Allen who participated in many of the acts in his show, or host-performers like Jack Paar and Johnny Carson who participate in some of the routines in their programs. Rundown sheets of the Ed Sullivan and the Johnny Carson "Tonight" shows are on pages 212-313.

As already implied, though not specifically stated, there may be combinations of various types of performances and variety techniques. Situation comedy has become an important element in many variety shows. Jackie Gleason, whose early programs were essentially series of variety acts and comedy routines, gradually developed sketches of a situation comedy nature until these sketches became an important and successful part of his program.

Approach and Organization

The most important thing for the writer of the variety show to remember is that there must be a peg on which to hang the show. The writer must develop a clear, central theme, capable of being organized into a sound structure, with a unity that holds all the parts of the program together. Otherwise, each number will be a number in itself, and unless the audience especially wants to watch a specific upcoming act, it could feel free at any time to tune in another station at the end of an act. The theme could be a distinct one, as indicated earlier under program types, or the continuity factor could simply be the personality of the master of ceremonies (as with Ed Sullivan) or comedian (as with Danny Kaye). The exception to the need for strong continuity is the vaudeville-music hall type of presentation. In these shows, as implied above, the audience is held by frequent reminders of the special acts still to come.

Within each separate type of variety show there are distinct orientations that must be determined by the writer. Will the musical portions stress popular or novelty numbers? Will the dances be classical in style? Modern? Presentational? Representational? Interpretive? The comedy must be written to fit the personality of the comic, and it must contain a sufficient amount of ad-lib material to forward the public concept of the comic's spontaneous talents. What kind of comedy will be emphasized? Simple good humor? Wit? Satire? Slapstick? Will it combine elements of several types? Will it go into special areas of farce, of sophisticated humor, of irrelevancy, or irreverance? The comedy material for a Jackie Gleason, for example, would be oriented toward broad, physical gags. The comedy for a Sid Caesar or a Nichols and May would be oriented toward the more sophisticated wit, the intellectual approach, the irreverent type of satire.

This kind of questioning is necessary when preparing all types of variety shows. In addition to the general and specific approaches, the intrinsic meaning of the term "variety" must be considered — the word defines its own organization. There must be a differentiation between each number and among the various segments of a given program. Contrast is important — not too great a contrast to disturb the viewers, but enough so that there can be no feeling of sameness, a feeling too easily transferred into boredom. Musical number should not follow musical number, comedy routine should not follow comedy routine. The suspense created by a juggler who balances an unbelievable number of fiery hoops on the end of his nose should not be directly followed by the similar suspense of a group of acrobats balancing one another on each other's noses. The effect upon the audience of these acts is too much the same.

In some variety programs each individual act prepares its own material. Only the basic continuity is prepared by the staff writer. A rundown sheet indicating the exact order and times of all of the acts is prepared. Transitional continuity may be put on a TelePrompTer. Some variety shows, such as the Ed Sullivan Show, do not employ a script in the true sense of the word. John R. McGeehan, associate producer of the Sullivan program, has stated that because it is a variety show "our acts and specialties are in the vast majority of cases unrelated . . . there is little if any preparatory material written for such introductions and transitions . . . Our show goes through an extensive preparation and rehearsal period prior to air time . . . Mr. Sullivan prefers to turn away from the prepared script and rely almost completely upon his own spontaneous remarks during air time."

The final number or act on the television variety program should have two versions, a short and a long one, so that the proper version will be called for, depending on the time remaining when that act begins.

On some variety shows a complete script is prepared at one source.

● *Compare and contrast the following rundown sheets for the Ed Sullivan and "Tonight" shows. 1) Are the acts so arranged that there is enough variety in each succeeding one? 2) Is there a preponderance, either in number of appearances or in allotted time, of any one type of act? 3) Are the commercials placed as well as they could be? 4) What are the similarities as well as the differences between the two programs?*

THE ED SULLIVAN SHOW
AIR: MAY 8, 1966   AIR TIMING SHEET

1.	OPENING	1:55		2:00
2.	1st CX — WISH-BONE (FILM)	1:00	1:55	3:55
3.	SALUTE TO IRVING BERLIN	1:55	2:55	4:55
4.	AUDIENCE INTRO — Capt. Maplen	:45	4:50	6:50
5.	CBS-TV AFFILIATES MENTION	:30	5:35	7:35
6.	HARRY JAMES & BAND — "Sunday Morning"	2:55	6:05	8:05
7.	2nd CX — BURLINGTON (FILM)	1:10	9:00	11:00
8.	HENNY YOUNGMAN	6:00	10:10	12:10
9.	AUDIENCE INTRO- Ky. Derby Winner	:30	16:10	18:10
10.	McGUIRE SISTERS	4:30	16:40	18:40
11.	3rd CX — RINSO (FILM)	1:10	21:10	23:10
12.	TOPO GIGIO (TAPE)	4:00	22:20	24:20
13.	SERENDIPITY SINGERS	3:30	26:20	28:20
14.	4th CX — ANACIN (FILM)	1:10	29:50	31:50
15.	JOHN BYNER	5:30	31:00	33:00
16.	McGUIRE SISTERS & HARRY JAMES	3:45	36:30	38:30
17.	5th CX — KENT (FILM)	1:10	40:15	42:15
18.	JEAN CARROLL	6:00	41:25	43:25

19.	GORDON & SHEILA MACRAE	6:30	47:25	49:25
20.	6th CX — NEWPORT (FILM)	1:10	53:55	55:55
21.	TRAILER & GOODNIGHT	:45	55:05	57:05
22.	BB/CREDITS	1:14	55:50	57:50
			57:04	59:04

Courtesy of CBS Television.

THE TONIGHT SHOW
WEDNESDAY, MAY 18, 1966

GUESTS: EDDY ARNOLD (RUDY)
TOM SMOTHERS (BR)
DOC SEVERINSEN AND HIS
SEXTET (SK)
ANNA MOFFO (SY)

HOST: JOHNNY CARSON
ANNCR: ED MCMAHON
COND: SKITCH HENDERSON

_____ 6:30 (11:15) _____

1:00	1.	THEME AND OPENING (SLIDE)
5:15	2.	SKITCH AND ED AND ORCH
1:00	3.	PROMO
1:00	4.	PUBLIC SERVICE
3:00	5.	JOE WILLIAMS (SONG)
2:30	6.	SKITCH AND ED
1:15	7.	NI-STATION BREAK

_____ 6:45 (11:30) _____

1:00	8.	THEME AND OPENING (SLIDE)
1:30	9.	COMML: SUNBEAM (Ed [iron] to film)
6:00	10.	JOHNNY-MONOLOGUE
1:30	11.	COMML: CHESTERFIELD (John to film) (C)
4:30	12.	MATERIAL
1:30	13.	COMML: DENTU CREME (John to film)
6:00	14.	ANNA MOFFO
2:05	15.	NETWORK FILL
5:20	16.	ANNA MOFFO
1:15	17.	NI-STATION BREAK

_____ 7:15 (12:00) _____

:10	18.	THEME AND ORCH
1:30	19.	COMML: HOTPOINT (John [kit. Model] to Film to Ed live tag) (C)
6:00	20.	TOM SMOTHERS
1:30	21.	COMML: BUDWEISER (John [bottle] to Ed live with slide) (C)
5:00	22.	TOM SMOTHERS
1:30	23.	COMML: JAYMAR (John [sign] to Ed live with slides) (C)
5:40	24.	TOM SMOTHERS
2:05	25.	NETWORK FILL
6:00	26.	DOC SEVERINSEN (2 NOS)
1:15	27.	NI-STATION BREAK

_____ 7:45 (12:30) _____

:15	28.	THEME AND LIVE AUD PAN
1:30	29.	COMML: SUNBEAM (John [iron] to film)
6:00	30.	EDDY ARNOLD
1:30	31.	COMML: CHESTERFIELD (John to film) (C)
6:00	32.	EDDY ARNOLD
1:30	33.	COMM: DENTU CREME (John to film)
6:00	34.	JOE WILLIAMS (SONG)
2:05	35.	NETWORK FILL
5:15	36.	PANEL

GOODNIGHT AND BILLBOARD
PRE-RECORDED ANNOUNCE

:35	37.	NI-STATION BREAK

Courtesy of the NBC Television Network

213

THE RADIO MAGAZINE

One of the interesting experiments of post-television radio has been the magazine format, in which a continuous stream of different kinds of materials — music, news, interviews, discussions, human interest features, sports, special events, skits and a voluminously interspersed series of commercials — is presented over a given, extended time period. This format seems oriented toward the person on-the-go, the listener who may be occupied primarily in other things and who will listen with one ear most of the time and with both ears some of the time and who can be held with a well-produced, interesting variety of short program segments.

The writer's job is two-fold: research and organization. He must prepare a routine sheet which clearly delineates the time length for each presentation and which accurately schedules the commercial announcements. He must provide accurate background material for introduction to the differing sections of the program, and he sometimes writes complete script material where a prepared and rehearsed segment is used at the pilot studio. Other scripting is done by local people in the "field," for most of the material on the program is usually "remote." Perhaps the most difficult job is total arrangement of the program, over many hours, to provide both continuity and variety in subject matter and length at the same time.

Probably the most successful of such programs has been the National Broadcasting Company's *Monitor*. Examine the following excerpt from one of its routine sheets (more akin to the "rundown" sheets described earlier) and the accompanying script for the same time period.

M O N I T O R   PAGE 8
ROUTINE SHEET   DATE FEB 5, '66
                     TIME 10:46:30

TIME	RADIO CENTRAL		NEMO
	BEEPER		
10:44:50	RAYBURN & CARTRIDGE: INTRO ON STAGE	(:30)	
10:45:20	TAPE: ON STAGE *BROOKS & REINER	(2:40)	
	ARTIST*COFFEEHOUSE		
	OPENS: I WOULD LIKE TO		
	CLOSES: GIVE IT TO YOU FOR $40.00		
	(applause & laughter- :03)		
10:48:00	RAYBURN: OUTRO	(0:05)	
10:48:05	CARTRIDGE & RAYBURN: MONITOR TIP	(:25)	
10:48:30	RAYBURN & CARTRIDGE: K2R COMMERCIAL	(1:00)	
10:49:30	RAYBURN: INTRO	(:10)	
10:49:40	DISC: (45) 1,2,3 - J. JONES RUNS	(1:58)	
	210 sneak 12	fades	
10:51:45	CARTRIDGE: RING SOUNDER	(0:05)	
10:51:50	RAYBURN: INTRO RING	(0:10)	
10:52:00	CARTRIDGE: STATE FARM COMMERCIAL	(1:00)	(23)
10:53:00	RAYBURN: REINTRO	(0:05)	
10:53:05)	TAPE: RING AROUND THE WORLD	(2:30)	
		approx.	
	SEE SCRIPT FOR CUES		
10:55:35	CARTRIDGE: RING SOUNDER	(0:05)	
10:55:40	RAYBURN: RING TAG	(0:05)	
10:55:45	CARTRIDGE: LUDEN'S COMMERCIAL	(0:30)	(5)
10:56:15	DISC: HARD DAY'S NIGHT - NO D.P.	(2:15)	
	(45) runs (2:50)		
10:58:25	RAYBURN: OUTRO	(:15)	

10:58:40   STAFF ANNCR: COMPANY CUE

BEEPER:

RAYBURN: Once again, it's MONITOR...Gene Rayburn, your host...and the
                         next order of business is ... "MONITOR, ONSTAGE!"

CART: THEME (UNDER ON CUE)

RAYBURN:	...Star performances, recorded live, at leading theatres, night-clubs, and concert halls throughout the world.
	Our stars right now are Carl Reiner and Mel Brooks as a beatnick artist. The scene: a coffee house.
TAPE:	MONITOR ONSTAGE (REINER-BROOKS) 2:40
	OPEN: "I WOULD LIKE TO....
	CLOSE: ...GIVE IT TO YOU FOR $40! (LAUGHTER AND APP. :03)
RAYBURN:	"MONITOR, ONSTAGE!" ...And that was Carl Reiner and Mel Brooks.
CART:	TIP SOUNDER (UNDER ON CUE)
RAYBURN:	Next...a MONITOR TIP...for the housewife. Going to a group activity with the children this weekend? Why not take a large shopping bag along and stow all the caps, mittens, and scarves in it as they're removed. When it's time to leave, there'll be no frantic last-minute panic search for missing articles. Listen for useful information on MONITOR TIPS... ...throughout every weekend. Here's another tip:
CART AND RAYBURN:	K2R (NEXT PAGE) 1:00
RAYBURN:	Jack Jones sings for the "In" crowd. That's not an editorial comment, but the title of Jack Jones' latest album. And this is one of the high-flying songs from it: "One, Two, Three."
DISC:	ONE, TWO, THREE, (SNEAK :12) 1:58 (FADES)
CART:	RING SOUNDER (UNDER ON CUE)
RAYBURN:	MONITOR'S "Ring Around The World"...a closeup of people and events both at home and abroad. "President Johnson's week leading up to his decision for the Hawaiian Conference on Vietnam." That story, in one minute, from Ray Scherer, NBC NEWS, White House Correspondent ....
	........brought to you by STATE FARM MUTUAL, the world's largest car insurance company.
CART:	STATE FARM 1:00
RAYBURN:	NOW .... Ray Scherer, NBC NEWS, White House Correspondent.
TAPE:	RING (WASH.) 2:27
	OPEN: "PRESIDENT JOHNSON'S WEEK ....
	CLOSE: .....WHITE HOUSE CORRESPONDENT."
CART:	RING SOUNDER (UNDER ON CUE)
RAYBURN:	"Ring Around The World" ...another in our weekend series of closeups of people and events in other countries.
	Now, here's Jonathan Winters for LUDEN'S:
CART:	LUDEN'S :30

DISC:	HARD DAY'S NIGHT (<u>NOT</u> A DEADPOT)
RAYBURN:	You can credit the Ramsey Lewis Trio for that arrangement of "A Hard Day's Night."
	Credit NBC with the best and most complete coverage of the news around the nation and the world. For proof of that claim, just stay tuned now for NBC-MONITOR News On The Hour... coming up, immediately. This is Gene Rayburn.
BEEPER:	
ANNCR:	
SYSTEM:	

<u>Courtesy of NBC Radio Network.</u>

FOR APPLICATION AND REVIEW

1. Write a rundown sheet and a basic outline — not a script — of opening, closing and record introductions for a local disc jockey pop music radio show.
2. Write the complete script for a half-hour radio classical music record show, to be distributed on a national basis to local stations.
3. Write a 15-minute script for a live music show to be mc'd by a major personality over a radio network.
4. Watch a television variety show. Analyze and evaluate the following: theme, if any; organization of the acts; general approach to the material (kinds of dances, comedy, music); freshness of writing; special use of visual techniques.
5. Prepare rundown sheets and outlines for the following types of television variety shows: vaudeville; personality with guests; comic-dominated.
   State a) your central theme for the show, b) the special organization of the material, the reasons for the placement of each act, and the reasons for the length of each act, c) the reasons for the approaches used in the dance, music, and comedy sequences.
6. If you are in a position to work with one or more other persons, prepare, with them, a complete half-hour variety show for television, each member of the writing team concentrating on a special part of the program, and all cooperating in the over-all planning of the show. With the same or another group prepare the rundown, routine sheets and script for a radio magazine format.

8

WOMEN'S AND CHILDREN'S PROGRAMS

WOMEN'S AND CHILDREN'S programs frequently are grouped together in one chapter in works on broadcasting. This phenomenon does not imply that all other programs are chauvinistically for men only. Actually, a contrary form of classification is valid. Women's and children's programs are the only major types that appeal to specialized groups, over and above the general mass audience. Though many men undoubtedly do enjoy these program types, the programs have specific orientations. In many instances, the individual women's or children's program makes a contribution not duplicated by any other program of a radio or television station or network.

WOMEN'S PROGRAMS

There are many program types — such as the afternoon quiz or audience participation show, the drama as represented in the soap opera, and the feature film — which, because of the hour of presentation, attract primarily an audience of women. The women's program, as discussed here, refers to the presentation which carries content that is of interest primarily to women, regardless of the time of day it is watched or heard.

The women's program may range in content from announcements of club meetings to cooking lessons to examinations of juvenile delinquency. These programs are particularly effective on small, independent stations, where matters of a social and civic interest are of a more personal nature than in the larger community. The local women's show usually concentrates on local news, local fashions, local personalities, and local social and civic events and problems. The local women's program also can make important educational contributions because of, rather than in spite of, its limited coverage. Many such shows have reinforced civic campaigns of interest to the housewife, such as promoting higher budgets for the schools or improvements in municipal services. It is said that the women's program is the only program type that can do a good public educational job while being commercial at the same time.

In the program which includes a number of subject areas such as fashions, food and interior decoration, there rarely is a dearth of advertisers. A sponsor usually may be found for the portion of the program dealing with his particular product or service. This "magazinc" format is commercially effective. Individual programs dealing with cooking or gardening often require a single sponsor for the entire time portion. The latter approach is found more often on the network and large station than on the small local station.

Although there is no reason why a male writer cannot prepare the continuity for the women's program, it is usual for a female writer to be assigned to the job. In addition, the program almost always is conducted by female personalities. Some exceptions might include a gardening program or a program segment containing marketing news, but in almost all other areas the material and presentation belong to the woman.

The writer of the women's show on the local station usually is the person who conducts the program. Network women's programs use regular writing staffs. (However, we are not concerned here so much with the network shows, which are few and far between, principally because they frequently encompass more than material designed especially for women and often include material of a variety nature.) In some instances the program may be oriented around one facet, such as cooking. Demonstration is the keynote in such programs; it would be wise to let the demonstrator dictate the organization of any script used, with the writer merely filling in the blank spaces with speakable introductory, filler and closing material. In effect, the writer would not prepare a script but a routine sheet for the demonstration-type program.

The women's program on the local station commonly includes several segments such as civic affairs, fashion news, an interview and market reports, all well interspersed with commercials. The program should be informal and chatty, but it should never condescend or talk down to its audience.

Following are headings, descriptions and a few selected excerpts from the script of a one-hour program for women. The script was written for a local radio station in a city of about 200,000 people. It was prepared as one of the assignments for a television and radio writing class. The program is entitled "The Ruth Morrison Show." The writer's approach was to center the material around the woman in the home. The program presents domestic information and includes a daily feature: an interview or a panel discussion. The format is informal and music is used occasionally. Listeners are invited to participate in the program, either through the mail or in person through special invitation.

> ● *Keeping in mind the principles pertaining to a good women's program, how would you correct and grade this assignment? Be specific in your evaluations and criticisms. What degree of success would this program have on commercial radio?*

THEME: In, up, and under.

RUTH: Good afternoon, ladies. This is Ruth Morrison once again, hoping to spend the next hour at home with you. And what features we have on today's program! You'll learn the best way to choose that wallpaper you've been thinking of getting, how to make the children's lunches more interesting and many more items of help to you. The special treat for today is an interview with Sally Steindler, the famous champion of physical fitness. Shall we get started? My first message for you today is from the Beauty Bar.

Ladies, if you haven't been to the Beauty Bar yet . . . I have never seen such a complete collection of cosmetics . . . (description of cosmetics) . . . To give you some idea of the kind of work he does, Mr. Jack from the Beauty Bar has the following tips for you ladies:

To keep your hairdo perfect: Pin up any straggling curls before you start your make-up, spray them . . .

Smooth in foundation twice as long as you think is necessary to make sure . . .

(Further beauty tips follow.)

Thanks so much, Mr. Jack . . . I know all of you will want to stop in at the Beauty Bar. For appointments with Mr. Jack, simply call . . .

Beauty in the home, though, is just as important as facial glamour. In the home department today we have a very special feature which should be of great use to many of you. If you're in the midst of decorating . . .

(Several suggestions for redecorating follow.)

If your room is small do select plain or small-patterned wallpaper, whereas in a big room . . .

A handy trick to widen a long, narrow room is to . . .

(After several more suggestions, this section of the program is brought to a close:)

And a last reminder—don't use exciting colors in rooms you want to be relaxing.

(Information on a selected paperback library is presented.)

In the kitchen corner today we are featuring the latest in prepared desserts. Betty Crocker makes available Chiffon Cake Mixes which make cakes with the lightness of angel food and the moist richness of butter cake. Two eggs and water are all you need add. These General Mills mixes . . .

The Swanson Company announces that there is now a wider choice of frozen pies . . .

And here's a Two-in-One dessert. You'll find a newcomer in the pudding and cake mix field in Pillsbury Mills Orange Pudding Cake Mix . . .

With these conveniences it certainly isn't any trouble to prepare a delicious dessert on short notice. And with the warm weather coming along, wouldn't it be a good idea to prepare some of these desserts for family picnics and church socials?

(Ruth Morrison reads letters from mothers giving solutions to problems in raising children.)

And now it's time for that special part of the program where we meet and talk to interesting and often famous people. Our featured guest today is a young woman who seems to be leading the crusade for physical fitness which is sweeping the country. That young woman is Sally Steindler, nationally noted and admired by millions--by way of television, radio, the magazines, and lecture platforms.

(A descriptive background of the guest follows. The writer includes at this point a highly detailed interview outline, in which all the possible questions and probable answers are written down for the interviewer's guidance. The interview covers the guest's personal life, marriage, the concept of physical fitness, human interest stories about people the guest worked with, formulas for fitness, and the guest's goals in her work. The interviewer closes with the following:)

Sally Steindler has become an institution. She has not let her personal life disappear under the avalanche of her professional triumphs. She is surely a perfect example of a woman who successfully has combined her role as a housewife with her business activities. I want to thank you so much for taking time out to visit with us today, Sally. It really was a pleasure.

(A discussion of special gifts for special occasions is sponsored by a gift shop.)

(A series of recipes and suggestions for making food interesting is given.)

(A list of civic, social, church and club events is presented.)

(Ruth Morrison answers home and garden questions sent in by listeners.)

Before I go off the air for today, I'd like to leave you with some definitions of marriage, given by four very famous people. Said Henrick Ibsen: "Marriage is a thing you've got to give your whole mind to." "By its best title, it's a monopoly," wrote Charles Lamb. And said the famous novelist George Eliot, it's "a relation of either sympathy or conquest." But the one that's my favorite is by John Ray: "Marriage is one year of joy, one of comfort, and all the rest of content."

Till tomorrow, ladies, this is Ruth Morrison hoping you have a wonderful day.

MUSIC: Theme, up and out.

Written by Susan Goldstein.

A highly successful women's show, the winner of Peabody, NET and Emmy Awards among others, is educational television's "The French Chef." The initial script includes a detailed equipment layout, which is used as one would stage directions. The following excerpts are from the working outline, which is changed and developed into a final script during the single rehearsal in which personality Julia Child creates an extemporaneous quality for the program.

THE FRENCH CHEF

(Show #96, 6/24, Boeuf Bourguignon—Beef in Red Wine)

OPENING (WORK TOP)

(READY STEW ON PLATTER)
This is a Boeuf Bourguignon, the most famous beef stew there is, in a rich winey-dark sauce flavored with onions and mushrooms. How good it smells. We're doing Beef in Red Wine today on "The French Chef."

CREDITS

PUT PLATTER IN OVEN; GET RID OF CASSEROLE; START PEELING ONIONS

INTRODUCTION (COOK TOP)

#1 Burner on high.
Welcome to "The French Chef." I'm Julia Child. These are little onions I'm getting ready for Beef in Red Wine. Really plain stew. Most famous. Ingredients very simple. (LIST.) It's how the French combine them that gives special taste.

221

WATER IN BLUE SKILLET

1/3 inch.
These small peeled onions (INTO PAN), 1 diameter, 3-4 per person. One later, if more,
2 pans. Butter, salt, cover, 20-30 mins. How peel. White braised. Cook separately/why.
(SET LOWER RT. BURNER.)

MUSHROOMS

Oil in no-stick pan. Butter in. Describe mushrooms. About 1 lb. — 2 c. Butter foam talk.
Pan talk. (SET #2 BURNER. HEAT LL. to 4.)

BACON TALK

3rd element—bacon done—mushrooms—onions. Bacon important/why. Plain or smoked,
French unsmoked. "Lardons." (CUT LARDONS—SHOW.) Can order or butt (SHOW). Can
smoked/salt (SHOW). If smoked/out—why. If salt/out—why.

* * *

DRAIN MEAT

Drain onions. Onion juice in sauce.

SAUCE TALK

Degrease. Taste.

BEURRE MANIÉ

3 tb. flour. 3 tb. butter. (MAKE—DESCRIBE. INTO SAUCE.)

ASSEMBLE BEEF (FAST)

Salt mushrooms. Vegetables in casserole.

SAUCE OVER MEAT

Simmer. Shake to blend.

ONTO PLATTER

Decorate. Parsley.

20 SEC. LEFT—AHEAD TALK

(TOWEL OFF.)

DINING ROOM

SERVE: potatoes, noodles or rice. Just big chunks bread. Sop gravy. Strong young red
wine (POUR). Beaujolais, Mt. Red—same as cooked with. FOLLOW: tossed green salad,
cheese, fruit.

20 SEC. CUE

Now you've seen famous Boeuf Bourguignon. Really simple stew, every day ingredients:
beef, red wine, onions, mushrooms, herbs. But what a marvelous dish. Really—best beef
ever stewed.

10 SEC. CUE

That's all for today on "The French Chef." This is Julia Child. Bon Appetit.

CREDITS

Written by Julia Child and Ruth Lockwood for WGBH-TV, Channel 2, Boston, Mass.

Another women's program worth studying, "Calendar," was developed
in the early 1960's for weekday morning presentation. Although it presented
material informally and in an entertaining manner, it respected the viewers'

ability and maturity. Its content usually was of serious importance not only to women, but to citizens in general, and it presented problems and situations about which the listener was prompted to think and perhaps even do something. The following excerpts are from a typical program.

CALENDAR

(TELOP)

STUDIO SHOT

#1 BILL GILLIAND VO

TAKE SUPER TELOP:	DAY
" " "	DATE
" " "	CALENDAR
" " "	REASONER
" " "	FICKETT

Tuesday, November 7th, 1961 live from New York, the CBS Television Network presents CALENDAR -- with Harry Reasoner and Mary Fickett.

REASONER

Good morning.

MARY

Good morning.

REASONER

This is Tuesday, November 7th, Election Day if you hadn't heard - which seems improbable. Today on CALENDAR you'll meet best-selling author Theodore H. White, Debby Drake, a woman who's interested in women's figures, and you'll hear from a man whose opinion I respect highly, who thinks cats are dumb.

MARY

On this date in 1940, the third largest suspension bridge in the world, linking Tacoma, Washington with the Olympic Peninsula, collapsed during a windstorm.

REASONER

I remember that . . . as a matter of fact, ever since I've thought they shouldn't collect bridge tolls until you reach the opposite side. I'd be mad as a wet hen if I paid a quarter and the bridge collapsed before I got my money's worth.

MARY

There are lots of CALENDAR items for today.

Marie Curie, discoverer of radium was born today in 1867.

General William Harrison defeated Tecumseh's Shawnee Indians at Tippecanoe in 1811, and President Roosevelt was elected for a record fourth term in 1944.

REASONER

Who was his vice president?

MARY

Wasn't it Harry Truman?

#2 LEAD IN AND PROMO

MARY

I'll be back in one minute with exercise
expert, Debby Drake.

(PROMO)

#3 WORLD OF SERVICE

BILL GILLIAND VO

TELOP: SERVICE   Calendar's World of Service!

#4 DEBBIE DRAKE - (MARY)

MARY

If Harry is a little bit jealous today -- it's
because he couldn't get to interview our
next guest.

She's a young lady by the name of Debbie
Drake -- and in this weight-conscious nation
of ours -- she's one of television's best-
known exercise instructors.

We all know that weight control has become
a big business in this country. There are
thousands of reducing salons of one kind
or another doing business right now. Of
course, Debbie's students don't go to her.
She comes to them, over Station W-I-S-H,
in Indianapolis, on a program syndicated to
80 additional stations around the country.
As one gal who religiously attends a daily
exercise class -- I'm really happy to
welcome Debbie to CALENDAR:

(NOTE FOR PROMPTER)

SUGGESTED QUESTIONS

- Is it true there have been changing weight
  standards for women during the past few
  years?

- Why do women get overweight in the
  first place?

- Are women less active now? Don't they
  exercise as much as they used to?

- What are some exercises a woman can
  do around the house without having to slip
  into a leotard or other special clothing?

- What about exercises for men?

- We always hear about pregnant women
  becoming overweight. Are there special
  exercises one can do during pregnancy?

224

(CONTINUE PROMPTER)

#5 LEAD IN & COMMERCIAL - REXALL

MARY

Thank you so much Debby Drake for being here with us on CALENDAR.

I think every woman likes to get advice on how she can improve her figure. I never seem to do anything about it but I like to get it anyway.

Harry Reasoner will be back with author Theodore H. White after this message.

(COMMERCIAL)

#6 WORLD OF SERVICE

BILL GILLIAND VO

TELOP: SERVICE

Calendar's World of Service!

#7 TED WHITE & HARRY - (BALLOT
                                        INTRO)

(REASONER AT NEWS AREA)

REASONER

One of the best reasons for cherishing democracy is that, despite its faults, it assumes people are smart enough in the long run to decide what's good for them.

Election Day is traditionally the time they make a lot of decisions.

DENVER

As you can see from these election ballots, it's becoming increasingly more complicated.

Here's the ballot citizens of Denver, Colorado were expected to fill out intelligently last year. There were 95 candidates running for 45 offices and they had seven constitutional amendments couched in legal terms that weren't easy to understand.

LOS ANGELES

Here's a Los Angeles ballot we got hold of for 1954. It took nine minutes just to read this ballot and people outside the booth begin shuffling their feet after you've been in there thirty seconds.

WAYNE COUNTY

In Wayne County - that's Detroit - voters had to choose from among 153 candidates to fill 53 offices.

That was 1959. It's probably worse this year.

NEW YORK

In New York City the current ballot lists nine political parties with candidates running for various offices.

STARTS WALK TO INTERVIEW AREA

All these complications tend to discourage people from voting in an off-year if there isn't some broad, clear-cut issue like whether to extend city sewage beyond where the trolley tracks used to end when there were trolleys.

The disturbing thing is that in off-year elections -- years when we aren't electing a president -- the individual's vote is apt to be more decisive than in a presidential year. In 1959, for example, in Rose Creek, Minnesota, the mayor was out of town and didn't vote. When he got back he found he'd lost the election 82 to 81.

Despite our faith in the elective system, most of us are pretty fuzzy about the details of how it works. Our guest this morning is Mr. Theodore H. White, known to his friends in the newspaper business as "Teddy."

Teddy White has a knack for becoming an expert on things. He is the author of several books on China; last year he wrote the best-selling novel "The View From the Fortieth Floor" and now he has established himself as an expert on elections with his most recent book "The Making of The President 1960."

Welcome to CALENDAR, Teddy.

#8 LEAD IN AND PROMO

REASONER - (TEDDY WHITE OUTRO)

Thank you for being with us on CALENDAR, and lots of success with your book "The Making of The President 1960."

I'll be back with the news after this message.

(PROMO)

#9 WORLD OF FACT

BILL GILLIAND VO

TELOP: FACT

Calendar's World of Fact! And now, here's Harry Reasoner with the news.

#10 REASONER NEWS

#11 LEAD IN & COMMERCIAL -
        ARMSTRONG

REASONER (NEWS OUTRO)

That's the news. In just one minute you'll hear from a man who lives with a dumb cat.

#12 WORLD OF LIVING

226

BILL GILLIAND VO

Calendar's World of Living!

* #13 CATS - (HARRY)

REASONER

* (CATS COMING)

#14 LEAD IN & COMMERCIAL -
        EXCEDRIN

REASONER (CATS OUTRO)

Please address any complaints you have
about my attitude towards cats to Mary
Fickett.

We'll be back after this commercial
message.

* * *

Tomorrow on CALENDAR, we'll be talking with Delores Durkin, Associate Professor at Columbia University's Teachers
College.

The subject is a timely one: what is the
right age for pre-school children to learn
to read?

#16 COMMERCIAL

#17 CREDITS

BILL GILLIAND VO

SUPER TELOPS:

CALENDAR
REASONER

FICKETT
CALENDAR

CALENDAR, with Harry Reasoner and
Mary Fickett was presented live from New
York.

Courtesy of CBS News.

CHILDREN'S PROGRAMS

Imagination is the key word in the preparation and writing of programs
for children. The imaginations of children are broad, exciting, stimulating. It
is only when we approach adulthood that we begin to conform, to restrict our
minds and thoughts, to dry up that most precious of creative potentials.

A young friend of mine, when three years old, one day placed strips of transparent tape across the dials of his family's television set, stepped back to look at what he had done, and then seriously observed, "Now I control the world."

And in a sense, he was right. For it is through television that much of the world first makes itself known to the small child. Writing for children offers an excellent opportunity for creativity, for they are open and willing to receive what the world has to offer. At the same time, because what comes to them through the TV set has such meaning and importance, they are not willing to accept commercial television's usual narcotizing program content as easily as are most of their parents.

This does not imply that children will believe anything. They will not be fooled. Because their imaginations are so sharp, they are sometimes more critical than adults. They can release themselves to be led into almost any fantasy, *provided there has been a valid, believable base to begin with*. In this manner, the children's program approximates the approach to writing the adult farce-comedy. As long as characters, situation and environment are initially believable, and as long as what has been established is developed logically and in terms of the characters' motivations, the subsequent actions and events will be accepted within the context of the play.

General Approaches

Many so-called children's shows attempt to capture the interest of parents and other assorted adults. This is fine, if it is not done for an ulterior reason. Indeed, in some cases the term "children's program" is a misnomer because many of these supposedly bi-oriented shows really are aimed at adults almost exclusively. In some instances the parents are brought in because it is the parent, after all, who will decide on whether or not a product is to be purchased.

The writer must be consistent in the format and execution of his program idea. The writer can judge his own work for children by putting himself in the place of an adult — a task of some proportion for some writers, judging by many of the programs on television and radio. If an adult watching a children's program finds it dull and tasteless and not worth his time, then quite likely that program is not going to enrich his child's day, develop his taste or be worth his time. One must differentiate between audience ratings and value to the child. The child may "love" the program. But that is not the only criterion of its value, entertainment-wise or otherwise. The child may "love" candy, too, but a responsible parent — and writer — will not allow him to subsist on it during all his waking hours. The child may release some of his aggressiveness by throwing mud pies in the park, but the responsible parent — and writer — will not permit him to be exposed to continuous participation in or observation of aggressive violence.

Grace Stanistreet, one of the country's leading teachers of creative arts and drama for children, has written about some of the responsibilities of children's theatre that may be applied just as validly to children's television:

"In judging plays that are good for children, adults too often remain spectators. Actors and adult audience accept the fact that the play may not jar the adult out of the spectator role. If you accept the statement that any play should create life on stage and stimulate the audience to play its role then we have discovered one standard by which to judge what is good for children. Many people with the responsibility of selecting programs for the young, watch the child at the children's play and take his reaction to it as the best recommendation. Would they take a child's word about what to include in the week's menus? Or what the family should wear, or when they should go to the dentist? But these things are fundamental for good living they may protest. Is theatre different? Isn't exposure to cultural experience fundamental to good living?

"A child has no standards for judgment and evaluation. He is in the process of acquiring good habits, appetites, taste, standards, by association, example, influence. The wise parent knows the part he must play in developing these in his child. He must select the exposures, the images, the experiences out of his greater knowledge of the child's needs and what will serve these needs. He does not impose his will, desires, purpose, taste but refers and defers at times to the child's purpose, desires and abilities. He makes decisions based on both, not solely on one or the other."[1]

Content

The content of programs for children has been one of the broadcasting industry's most vulnerable areas of neglect, perhaps by commission even more than omission. The National Association of Broadcasters' standards of good practice for television and radio indicate the necessity of elements of realism which will provide a valid impression of the world at large in children's programs. Note the following excerpts from the sections on "Responsibility Toward Children" in the Television and Radio Codes. These rules concerning content certainly seem to be good ones.

"Programs specifically designed for listening by children shall be based upon sound social concepts and should reflect respect for parents, law and order, clean living, high morals, fair play and honorable behavior."

". . . violence and sex shall be presented without undue emphasis. . ."

Programs should avoid "material which is excessively violent or would create morbid suspense, or other undesirable reactions in children."

Programs "shall contribute to the healthy development of personality and character."

The most ardent television and radio fan would be hard-pressed to find a program either ostensibly for children or watched by children that did not violate at least one of the principles in the NAB Codes. Acts of violence are common in children's programs, and often are presented as heroic deeds. Murder is commonplace and, if performed by the "good guy," frequently is considered ethical. Even many programs of a cartoon nature for pre-school ages stress violence and various forms of prejudice. Perhaps the NAB Codes are too vague and require specific definitions of terms and clarifications for positive approaches to programming. The fact that the Codes are continually violated, even by many who subscribe to them, is common knowledge.

The Codes are not enforced; there is no authority or compunction upon the producers and the writers to present material of a beneficial — or non-harmful — nature to our children. Except in infrequent instances of gross and well-publicized violations of decency in regard to the molding of children's minds, morals, and personalities, ethical program content depends entirely on the integrity of the individual sponsor, producer and writer.

The Format

Age levels have been used as primary determinants in the approach to individual programs for children. Given programs of intellectual and emotional stimulation on a high plane, children of certain age levels (if we may use broad generalities) will respond in a positive manner to certain approaches. For the pre-school child the activity program featuring some elements of fantasy, such as Mother Goose rhymes, as well as the use of things familiar to the child's world, is common. The child in the first few grades of elementary school can be appealed to with material containing beginning elements of logical thinking, such as simple plots, fairy tale stories and even basic action, in activity or in drama. The child over eight or nine years of age responds more readily to the activities and accounts of the outside world, such as adventure stories, individual action, and some elements of accurate — though not disturbing — reality. In this latter category are some of the educational programs involving visits to interesting places, such as ABC-TV's "Discovery," or how-to programs, such as NBC-TV's "Mr. Wizard."

The best children's program, however, is not that which is written exclusively for a certain age level. Though the specific format of the program may appeal more to one age level than another, the good program can be enjoyed by all ages on different levels. For example, the elementary science program may be too advanced for the pre-schooler; the pre-schooler's program must be on a different plane. However, if the pre-schooler's program seems silly to the elementary school child and vulgar to the adult, it is not because it is below their level of understanding. It probably is because it *is* silly and vulgar. A dramatization of *Winnie the Pooh,* for example, can be seen by the pre-schooler, the elementary school child and the adult, and if it is a well-done program it will appeal to all three groups, although on different levels.

During the Federal Communication Commission's hearings on television in the fall of 1961, Melvin Helitzer, the advertising director of a toy manufacturer that spends 90% of its advertising budget on television, stated that one of the reasons for the failure of some shows written for children was that "the intelligence level of the writing was below that of the children." He said that "children are more intelligent than most adults believe," and that a program produced by people "who have no respect for children" was doomed to failure.

Specific Writing Techniques

The child should be reached in a direct manner. The presentational approach is most effective, with the narrator or character, if it is a dramatic piece, relating to the viewer candidly. The children must be able to understand the ideas presented. Be simple and be clear. This does not imply that children should be talked down to. On the contrary, avoid patronizing children; they are only too aware when this is happening. Too much dialogue is not advisable, either in a dramatic or non-dramatic program. Action and vivid, colorful presentation of ideas are most effective. This implies an adherence to a simplified plot in the dramatic story. Too much shouldn't be presented at one time and the story should not be drawn out; children have neither the ability to hold too many ideas at once nor the sitting patience of adults. Material of a light nature should be featured on children's programs or, if the material is serious in content, it should not be tragic or morbid and it should not contain the psychological probing often found in the better adult programs. This is especially true of programs oriented primarily for younger children. The resolutions should not be ambiguous and the characters, though not necessarily real, should be believable.

The child identifies to an extraordinary degree with those dramatic elements which are within his own realm of experience and understanding. The success of the "Lassie" type program is not accidental. The zeal of Marshall Dillon — or his writers — to murder as many bad guys as possible in the course of a half-hour or hour may stimulate latent tendencies toward violence and sadism in the child, but the story and characters may have no appreciable lasting effect on the well-adjusted child. "Lassie," however, to almost all children, is the "dog-next-door"!

If the writer wishes to present a program of an educational nature, he should avoid the simple repetition of material that children viewing the program may have gotten in school. Known material may be used in the educational program, but it should be used to stimulate the child to participate in the program through thinking and applying the knowledge already learned toward learning more. The writer should not pad the children's program. Determine the purpose of the program and stick to it. Don't try to fool or confuse the child, hoping that he won't notice a bad piece of writing. If a moral is to be presented, make it definite and clear, at the same time stimulating the child to think more about it.

Several techniques have been especially successful in the story or drama for the child audience. First, there must be suspense. Children, like adults, should be caught up in a conflict, no matter how simplified, and should want to know what is going to happen. Children should be let in on a secret that certain characters in the play do not know. And, finally, children always love a good "chase" no less than the adults who assiduously followed the "Keystone Cops" in silent films and who follow the westerns and mysteries on television today.

One of the finest children's programs on television has been National Educational Television's "What's New." The following excerpt is from the beginning of "Potomac Adventure," in which the viewer, through the eyes of two 11-year olds, are taken on a tour of Washington, D.C. by way of the historic Potomac River.

VIDEO	AUDIO
	(NARRATOR:)
(MS, PAN) Small stream trickling over rocks	The Indians named it Potomac. It begins high in the mountains. Small streams like this one feed it as it tumbles through the Appalachians.
(LS) Wide River with trees and Hillsides	It becomes wider as it meanders through the beautiful Maryland and Virginia countryside.
(LS) Great Falls and its rushing waters	At Great Falls, its waters cascade sharply across jagged rocks.
(MS, PAN) closer view of Falls	The River gains new force for its long trip to the Chesapeake Bay and the open sea. On its way, though, it will pass <u>Washington</u>, the nation's "Capital City."
	(MUSIC)
(LS) View of Georgetown and river from George Washington Parkway	The Potomac first meets the Old Georgetown section of Washington.
(MS) Georgetown "typical" street showing restored 18th Century homes	Georgetown was a bustling 18th Century town long before the adjoining Washington became the Federal City...That's a beautiful street, isn't it—preserved almost as it was, nearly 200 years ago.
(MS) C & O Canal lock, water spilling through	Here is one of the many locks along the C & O Canal, which runs beside the Potomac up into the mountains.
(ZOOM IN TO) Ducks on canal	For almost 100 years, mules plodded along the tow-paths pulling barges loaded with people and freight to and from Old Georgetown. The Canal finally ceased operation in 1924. The entire Canal is now a National Park.
(LS) Georgetown landing, Comdr. Slye waiting with young boy and girl	Say—See. That man waiting on the Georgetown landing over there, probably knows more about the Potomac than any man alive. His name is Commander Walter C. Slye. He was born and raised on the river, the son of a steamboat captain!

© 1965 <u>National Educational Television</u>

The television script that follows is one of a series, "The Adventures of Jack and Jill." The format of the series is to take a nursery rhyme or fairy tale and develop the implications of the piece past the point of its original conclusion. For example, this script, "Mary Had a Little Lamb," dramatizes what happens when the lamb actually follows Mary to school. This series utilizes a combination of live characters and puppets or marionettes. The incorporation of simplified plot and familiar nursery rhyme with action and adventure and concepts of reality (school and learning) makes this series one which can appeal to a broad age range. Note the use of suspense relative to what will actually happen to the lamb and, near the end, to Mary. Note, too, the use of the chase in the classroom and the letting in of the audience on a secret not known by the teacher when the lamb sneaks into the room. The action is made compact and, though many ideas are possible in the script, the content is simplified and the language clear and direct, at the same time avoiding the too frequently used "baby talk."

● *As you examine this program, note the following: the combination of education and entertainment in the format; the moral of the story presented clearly; the minor educational ideas indicated in the story itself and in the introduction and ending, in which direct identification is made between the performers and the audience.*

THE ADVENTURES OF JACK AND JILL

"MARY HAD A LITTLE LAMB"

<table>
<tr><td align="center">VIDEO</td><td align="center">AUDIO</td></tr>
<tr>
<td valign="top">OPEN: MUSIC UNDER, UP THROUGH OPENING. "THE ADVENTURES OF JACK AND JILL" SUPERIMPOSED ON MOVING COUNTRYSIDE OF FAIRYLAND SCENES, MOTHER GOOSE BACKGROUNDS. DISSOLVE TO TITLES.
DISSOLVE TO JACK AND JILL (THEY CAN BE PUPPETS OR LIVE ACTORS) LYING ON THE FLOOR OF LIVING ROOM OF THEIR HOUSE, NEAR EDGE OF THE PUPPET STAGE, READING FAIRY TALE BOOKS.</td>
<td valign="top">

MOTHER'S VOICE
(OFF) Jack and Jill, it's eight o'clock, time to go to bed.

JACK
(GETTING UP) Oh, it's time to go to bed again.

JILL
We can never stay up late and have any fun.

MOTHER
(OFF) Jack and Jill, did you hear me?

JILL
We may as well go, Jack.

JACK
All right, only I thought Uncle Will was coming with another bed-time story. (CALLS) Mother!
</td>
</tr>
</table>

The children ready for bed and the mother's problem in getting them to bed create an identification between the viewers and the characters.

MOTHER
(OFF) What is it, Jack?

JACK
Is Uncle Will coming tonight?

MOTHER
I almost forgot. Yes, he should have been here by now.

JILL
Can we wait up for him?

MOTHER
You can wait up for him for a little while, but if he doesn't come soon, you'll have to go to bed.

JACK
And if he does come?

MOTHER
(OFF) Then you can listen to his story, but you'll have to go to sleep the minute it's over.

JILL

Yes, Mummy.

JACK

We will.

UNCLE WILL

(OFF, CLOSE) Hello, children.

JACK AND JILL

Uncle Will!

PAN TO LIVE ACTOR, IN FRONT OF THE
PUPPET STAGE, WITH A FAIRY TALE
BOOK IN HIS HAND.

Uncle Will represents the "big brother" or "father" or "older friend," thus giving a feeling of security as well as friendliness to the viewer. At the same time, since he is not the disciplining father or mother, he creates a feeling of adventure or excitement.

WILL

How are you this evening, children?

JILL

Oh, we're just fine, Uncle Will.

JACK

We were waiting for you.

JILL

Do you have a story for us tonight?

JACK

What is it about?

WILL

Whoa! One at a time.
(HE PULLS UP A CHAIR TO THE EDGE
OF THE PUPPET STAGE, WHERE JACK
AND JILL HAVE GOTTEN AS CLOSE AS
POSSIBLE TO HIM.) Did mother say you
could stay up and watch me tell a story
tonight?

JACK AND JILL

Yes. She did.

WILL

All right, then. I'll tell you one. But
there's something you have to promise me.

JACK AND JILL

What's that?

WILL

That you'll go to bed the minute I'm
finished.

JACK AND JILL

We will.

Uncle Will carries forward the necessary discipline of the household by arranging, in a friendly manner, for a proper bedtime. This is an educational factor carried over to the child-viewer. The discussion that follows about the specific story to be told creates suspense.

WILL

Okay. Now, what story would you like to
hear today?

JILL
Little Red Riding Hood.

JACK
Aw, I like Jack and the Beanstalk.

JILL
How about Little Boy Blue?

JACK
We've heard that.

JILL
You tell us what story it is, Uncle Will.

WILL
Well, all the boys and girls have written
in asking for their favorite story, and
guess which one they picked for today?

The further direct involvement of the viewer with the program is indicated when Uncle
Will states that the story has been chosen by viewers who wrote in requesting their
favorite story.

JACK AND JILL
Tell us. Which one?

WILL
Mary and Her Little Lamb. Would you
like that?

JILL
That's a good one.

JACK
Aw, it's not so hot. Nothing happens.

WILL
Oh, but a great deal does happen, especially
after the Lamb gets to school. You remember the rhyme: Mary had a little lamb, its
fleece was white as snow.

JILL
And everywhere that Mary went the lamb
was sure to go. It followed her to school
one day, which was against the rule. . .

JACK
. . . It made the children laugh and play to
see a lamb at school.

The reciting of the nursery rhyme further involves the viewer. The child hearing the
rhyme knows it, and is likely to say it even as the characters do.

WILL
That's right! Now, would you like to hear
it?

JACK
Yes, we would.
(THEY LIE DOWN ON THE CARPET OF
THE LIVING ROOM FLOOR AND TURN TO
THE "MARY HAD A LITTLE LAMB"
RHYME IN THEIR FAIRY TALE BOOK, A
BOOK LIKE THE ONE CARRIED BY UNCLE
WILL.)

                                        WILL
                                Don't get your clothes dirty.

                                        JACK AND JILL
                                We'll be very careful.

                                        WILL
                                (HE PICKS UP HIS MOTHER GOOSE
                                FAIRY TALE BOOK AND BEGINS TO
                                READ.)

(AS WILL BEGINS TO READ, DOLLY IN
ON THE LETTERS ON THE PAGE, AND
FOLLOW EACH WORD WITH HIM:
"MARY HAD A LITTLE LAMB, ITS
FLEECE WAS WHITE AS SNOW, AND
EVERYWHERE THAT MARY WENT THE
LAMB WAS SURE TO GO."
(CUT TO JACK AND JILL, WHO FOLLOW   WILL (VOICE OVER)
ALONG IN THEIR BOOK.)   It followed her to school one day, which
(CLOSEUP ON PICTURE IN BOOK, OF   was against the rule . . . . .
MARY WALKING TO SCHOOL WITH LAMB
TRAILING BEHIND HER.)

A "training" device which would please the parent is the acknowledgment not to get one's
clothes dirty. The children's simultaneous reading of words in their books as Uncle Will
reads out loud from his book is an important educational device. (A promotional plan for
this program could include the distribution of books to the child viewer so that he could
practice reading in the same manner.)

DISSOLVE INTO SAME SET AS THE
PICTURE IN THE BOOK, WITH MARY
WALKING ALONG AND THE LAMB
FOLLOWING HER.

                                (JACK AND JILL ARE ON THE SIDE,
                                SEEING THE ACTION, BUT ARE NOT
                                OBSERVED BY MARY AND THE LAMB.)

                                (JACK AND JILL'S DIALOGUE THROUGH
                                THE REMAINDER OF THE "FAIRY TALE"
                                ACTION IS SOTTO VOCE.)

                                        JILL
                                Look, Jack, that must be Mary.

                                        JACK
                                And that must be her lamb.

The use of Jack and Jill as observers of the action creates another means of direct
involvement of the viewer with the action of the story.

                                        JILL
                                Just like in the story that Uncle Will was
                                telling us.

                                        JACK
                                Ssh . . . let's get a little closer and see if
                                they're really going to school.

                                        MARY
                                (TURNING TO THE LAMB) I'm sorry,
                                little lamb, but you know the rule. I'd
                                like to have you come with me, but you'll
                                have to wait here until I come back from
                                school.

                                        236

(MARY PATS THE LAMB SADLY; THE
LAMB SADLY SHAKES ITS HEAD, UNDER-
STANDING. MARY STARTS OFF AGAIN
AND THE LAMB SLYLY TIPTOES AFTER
HER. MARY SUDDENLY TURNS AND THE
LAMB STOPS SHORT. ACTING INNOCENT
AS IF IT HAD DONE NOTHING.)

MARY

You needn't act innocent. I know you're
trying to follow me to school. (LAMB
SHAKES ITS HEAD "NO.") Don't tell me
you aren't, when I know you are. It's not
nice for a little lamb not to tell the truth.
(HE HANGS HIS HEAD.) So you just stay
here as I say . . . (SHE WALKS OFF A
FEW STEPS, THEN TURNS) It's not my
fault . . . it's just the rules. (SHE GOES
AND THE LAMB SITS DOWN AND BEGINS
TO CRY.

JACK

(JACK AND JILL ARE NOT SOTTO VOCE
IN THE FOLLOWING SCENE, WITH THE
LAMB.)
(TO JILL) I don't know why the lamb
should cry, especially because of not
having to go to school.

LAMB

(CRYING, OVERHEARS JACK)
But I want to go to school.

JACK

Did you say something?

LAMB

Yes, I said I'd like to go to school.

JILL

You talked.

LAMB

Of course. You do, don't you?

JILL

Yes.

LAMB

Then why shouldn't I?

JACK

But you're a lamb.

The acceptance of the nursery rhyme makes possible the logical development of the Lamb
into a speaking character. Yet, realistically, Jack (with whom the viewer identifies) is
surprised to hear the lamb talk. The lamb explains this, below, and makes an
important educational point about imagination.

JILL

And who ever heard a lamb talk before?

LAMB

Lot's of people.

JILL

I haven't.

237

LAMB

That's because you've never been in animal faryland before. In your own real
world you never heard animals talk . . .
just as people in fairyland never hear me
talk . . . even Mary never heard me talk.

JILL

But how come we can hear you now?

LAMB

Because you're in fairyland. When boys
and girls and grownups look beneath their
own world and into the world of make-
believe they find so many things more wonderful than they could ever find in their
own world. If Mary were to dream about
our world, she might hear our animals
talk. All you have to do is look with your
imagination.

JACK

Oh, I don't think an imagination can make
things that wonderful.

LAMB

Oh? But I am talking, you see.

JACK

That's right, you are.

JILL

Yes, you are. I do see.

JACK

But I still don't understand why you
want to go to school.

LAMB

I've never gone to school. And children
have so much fun there. But there's
another reason.

JACK

Another reason?

LAMB

I'm almost six years old, and I don't know
how to read or write at all, at all. I want
to go to school because I don't want to be
a poor little lamb all my life and grow up
and not know anything. (THE LAMB BE-
GINS TO CRY AGAIN.)

Another important educational point is the lamb's explanation of why it wants to go to
school.

JILL

(PATTING THE LAMB) You musn't cry,
Mr. Lamb.

LAMB

I just can't help it.

JILL

But if you cry you'll get all sad under your
eyes and you won't look pretty.

238

                    LAMB
(WIPING HIS EYES) Yes, you're right.
Thank you, you're so kind.

                    JILL
We'd like to help you if we can.

                    LAMB
Would you?

                    JACK
If we can.

                    LAMB
Maybe, you would . . . ? (HESITATES)
No, I don't think I should ask you.

The hesitancy and discussion about whether or not the lamb should ask Jack and Jill to
do something creates suspense.

                    JACK
Ask us what?

                    LAMB
Maybe you would . . . ? No, I'd better not.

                    JILL
You can ask us.

                    LAMB
May I?

                    JACK
Yes.

                    LAMB
Well . . . .

                    JACK AND JILL
Well . . . ?

                    LAMB
(IN ONE BREATH) Would you take me to
school?

                    JILL
(AFTER A MOMENT) We'd like to . . . .

                    JACK
. . . . but we can't.

                    JILL
Because we're not real fairyland people.
We couldn't get into the fairyland school.

                    LAMB
That's right. I forgot. (SITS DOWN
SADLY.) Oh well, thank you anyway. I
knew it wouldn't work.

                    JACK
Why don't you just go?

                    LAMB
It's against the rules.

239

JILL

Well, since it's for a good purpose, maybe
this time it will be all right. And, after
all, you do want to become smart, don't
you?

LAMB

Yes, that's right.

JACK

Maybe you could walk in without anybody
seeing; and no one will even know you're
there.

LAMB

I would so much like to go.

JILL

Then why don't you, Mr. Lamb?

LAMB

(STANDING UP WITH DETERMINATION)
I think I will!

Expectation of something to come, suspense, and the beginning of letting the audience in
on something the other characters (Mary and the schoolteacher) do not know are encompassed in the lamb's decision to go off to school, although it's against the rules. Inasmuch as Jack and Jill were the convincing factors, the members of the audience (identifying with Jack and Jill) have a personal stake in the lamb's adventures.

JACK

Good for you.

LAMB

(JUMPING) I'm off to school.
(HE STARTS OUT.)

JILL

Goodbye, Mr. Lamb.

LAMB

Goodbye, and thank you.

JACK

Good luck.

LAMB

(GOING OFF SINGING) Mary had a little
lamb, little lamb, little lamb . . .

(JACK AND JILL STAND FOR A MOMENT
AND WATCH THE LAMB GO OFF.)

JILL

(TAKING JACK BY THE HAND.) Let's
follow him to school, Jack.

JACK

Why, Jill?

JILL

Nobody knows the lamb is going to school
except us.

JACK

So?

240

                                        JILL
                    Everybody will be so surprised. The
                    teacher, the pupils. It'll be such fun to
                    see the children laugh and play to see a
                    lamb at school.

                                        JACK
                    Yes, let's go, Jill. (AS THEY GO OFF)
                    Oh, what fun we're going to have. I can
                    hardly wait.

FADE OUT, END OF PART I,
"Mary Had A Little Lamb"

Part I ends with further suspense. The audience, through Jack and Jill, are going to see
the action, which now has been suggested clearly and simply. The audience, as observers,
will be able to look on, and know and see something that the characters will not.

          PART II.

FADE IN ON SCHOOL ROOM, WITH THE
TEACHER, MARY, LITTLE BOY BLUE,
LITTLE JACK HORNER, LITTLE MISS
MUFFET. THE CHILDREN ARE AT
THEIR DESKS. THE TEACHER IS IN
FRONT OF THE ROOM AT HER DESK
WITH A RULER-POINTER IN HER HAND.

The characters in the schoolroom are familiar to the audience.

                                        TEACHER
                    All right, who can tell me how to spell
                    dog? (POINTING) Little Boy Blue.

                                   LITTLE BOY BLUE
                    D-o-g.

                                        TEACHER
                    That's right.

                    (LAMB APPEARS IN DOORWAY BACK OF
                    TEACHER)

                                        LAMB
                    (TO AUDIENCE AND SELF) They're in
                    the middle of the lesson. I wonder if I
                    could go in?

                                        TEACHER
                    Who can spell cat?

                    (LITTLE MISS MUFFET RAISES HER
                    HAND)

                                        TEACHER
                    Little Miss Muffet.

                                   LITTLE MISS MUFFET
                    C-a-t.

                                        TEACHER
                    That's correct.

The spelling of dog and cat are, in themselves, educational contributions, no matter how
slight. A friendly classroom atmosphere is an important contribution to the thinking of
pre-school agers.

                                        241

LAMB
(STILL NOT SEEN BY ANYONE) I would so
very much like to be in school. (TO
CAMERA) Do you think I should?

TEACHER
Mary, you tell us how to spell lamb.

MARY
Lamb?

TEACHER
Lamb; like the little lamb you want to
bring to school with you. Even though
you know it's against the rule.

MARY
(ALMOST TEARFULLY) Lamb. L-a-m-b.

LAMB
Poor Mary. She's crying.

MARY
Oh, I wish he were here with me.

LAMB
I feel so sad. (BRUSHES AWAY A TEAR.)
(TO AUDIENCE) If you were me would you
go in. (AFTER A MOMENT) Would you?
(AFTER ANOTHER MOMENT IN WHICH
AUDIENCE REACTION PRESUMABLY HAS
BEEN POSITIVE.) All right, then, I'll
do it!

The presentational approach and direct involvement of the audience in the action is used
to the highest degree here. In effect, the audience decides the actions of the characters.
The involvement is complete.

(THE LAMB GOES INSIDE, STANDS IN
BACK OF THE TEACHER. SHE DOES NOT
SEE HIM. THE CHILDREN DO AND
BEGIN TO LAUGH. JACK AND JILL COME
TO THE DOOR AND LOOK IN.)

JILL
I hope we're not too late.

JACK
(POINTING) No, we're not too late -- there's
Mr. Lamb now.

JILL
Listen to the children laughing.

JACK
The teacher doesn't know he's there yet.
Let's watch.

JILL
This is such fun.

(THE LAMB STANDS BEHIND THE
TEACHER AND SMILES BROADLY AT
THE CHILDREN. THEY LAUGH HAPPILY.)

TEACHER
All right, children. What are you laughing
at?

242

(THERE IS NO ANSWER. THE TEACHER
TURNS AROUND TO SEE WHAT IT IS,
AND AS SHE DOES SO THE LAMB MOVES
WITH HER, STAYING IN BACK OF HER SO
SHE DOESN'T SEE HIM, STILL REMAINING
HIDDEN. THE CHILDREN LAUGH EVEN
MORE HILARIOUSLY.)

Gentle satire of adult behavior (which should not be carried too far in this case because
of the respect due the teacher-figure) is evident here. The audience is in on something
that the adult figure does not know. The psychological superiority conveyed is an important factor in pleasing the child.

TEACHER
There is something here. I know it. What
is it? (NO ANSWER) If you don't tell
me what you are laughing at, I'm going to
keep you all after school.

LITTLE JACK HORNER
(GETTING UP) I don't want to stay after
school; it's . . . (HE IS PULLED BACK
DOWN INTO HIS SEAT BY LITTLE BOY
BLUE, WHO IS SITTING BEHIND HIM.)

TEACHER
If no one will tell me, then I'll find out my-
self. (SHE PUTS THE POINTER ON THE
DESK, BEGINS TO WALK IN A CIRCLE
AROUND THE DESK, LOOKING. AS SHE
WALKS, THE LAMB TROTS BEHIND HER,
STAYING OUT OF HER SIGHT. EVERY
TIME SHE TURNS QUICKLY TO SEE IF
ANYONE IS BEHIND HER, THE LAMB
TURNS JUST AS QUICKLY TO GET
BEHIND HER AND IS NOT SEEN. SHE
FINISHES THE CIRCLE OF THE ROOM,
COMES IN FRONT OF THE DESK AGAIN
TO FACE THE CLASS.)

The beginning of physical action--the movement of the lamb--is introduced.

MCU LAMB TAKING THE POINTER
FROM THE TOP OF THE DESK AND
SITTING ON FLOOR BACK OF THE
DESK WITH IT.

(TEACHER TURNS TO GET THE POINTER,
FINDS IT IS GONE, TURNS BACK TO
CLASS.

TEACHER
Who took my pointer? (NO ANSWER)
Mary, did you take it?

MARY
No, I didn't.

TEACHER
Little Boy Blue, was it you?

LITTLE BOY BLUE
It wasn't me.

TEACHER
Little Jack Horner?

243

LITTLE JACK HORNER
No.

TEACHER
Miss Muffet, do you have it?

MISS MUFFET
I don't have it.

TEACHER
Well someone must have it. It couldn't
just disappear.

The continuation of action and the knowing of something that the adult character
does not know are coupled with further physical, comic action.

LS LAMB BEHIND DESK, LAUGHING,
AND TEACHER ON OTHER SIDE OF DESK,
LOOKING AT TOP OF POINTER. LAMB
BEGINS TO MOVE TOWARD THE FAR
END OF THE DESK TO PEEK AT
TEACHER, WHILE TEACHER, NOTICING
EDGE OF POINTER MOVING ALONG,
MOVES TOWARD SAME SIDE OF DESK.
BOTH MOVE SLOWLY.

CU LAMB'S FACE SMILING AS HE GETS
ALMOST TO EDGE OF DESK.

CU TEACHER'S FACE SMILING IN
SATISFACTION AS SHE GETS ALMOST
TO END.

THEY BOTH MEET SIMULTANEOUSLY.

(LAMB JUMPS IN SURPRISE.)

TEACHER
(LOUDLY)   Oh!

(LAMB TURNS, DROPS POINTER AND
BEGINS TO RUN THROUGH THE CLASS
ROOM.)

TEACHER
(RUNNING AFTER HIM)   So, it was
Mary's Little Lamb . . . Come back here . . .
stop . . . stop this instant.

(THE TEACHER CHASES THE LAMB
THROUGH THE CLASSROOM, AROUND
THE DESKS, PAST THE CHILDREN, WITH
DESKS, CHILDREN, BOOKS GETTING IN
THE WAY.   AT SEVERAL POINTS THE
TEACHER ALMOST HAS THE LAMB IN
HER GRASP, BUT TRIPS ON A BOOK, OR
A CHILD GETS IN THE WAY, OR THE
LAMB SCOOTS QUICKLY TO ONE SIDE
AND AWAY. THE CHILDREN JUMP AND
LAUGH AS THIS IS GOING ON, THE
TEACHER REPEATEDLY CALLING FOR
THE LAMB TO STOP. FINALLY, THE
LAMB IS PUSHED INTO A CORNER OF
THE ROOM AND THE TEACHER HAS HIM
TRAPPED. STANDING IN FRONT OF
HIM, SHE GRABS FOR HIM, BUT HE
DARTS AROUND HER AS SHE LUNGES.
THE CHASE CONTINUES FOR ANOTHER
THIRTY SECONDS OR MORE, WHEN AT
LAST THE LAMB IS AGAIN CORNERED.

244

THIS TIME THE TEACHER CATCHES HIM.
DURING THE CHASE THE TEACHER'S
PITFALLS MUST BE VALID AND PROBA-
BLE. SHE MUST NOT LOSE DIGNITY OR
BECOME A COMIC CHARACTER.)

The chase is one of the most important and entertaining elements in a children's program.
It ends with continued suspense: will the lamb remain or be ejected?

TEACHER

(OUT OF BREATH) Well, you ought to be
ashamed of yourself. (THE LAMB HANGS
HIS HEAD.) All of this disturbance. I'm
going to put you right out of school. (THE
LAMB IS SAD. SHE STARTS TO PUT HIM
OUT.) Come on. (THE LAMB GOES
SADLY, OF HIS OWN WILL, WALKING
SLOWLY.)

MARY

Please teacher, don't make him go. He
didn't mean anything wrong.

LITTLE BOY BLUE

Yes, teacher, please let him stay.

MISS MUFFET

He is such fun. Let him stay.

LITTLE JACK HORNER

We all want him to stay.

TEACHER

Well . . . if you promise to be good. (THEY
ALL CLAP AND TALK HAPPILY.) But
I'm still not decided. (THEY GROAN. TO
LAMB) Are you sorry for what you did?

(LAMB NODS HIS HEAD "YES.")

TEACHER

Why did you come here? Just to make the
children laugh and play?

(LAMB SHAKES HIS HEAD "NO.")

TEACHER

Did you come to school because you want
to be smart like the other boys and girls?

(LAMB NODS HIS HEAD "YES.")

TEACHER

Well, in that case, and because the pupils
want you here, I might let you stay.
(LAMB SMILES HAPPILY.) But ... I'm not
sure. (HE IS SAD AGAIN.) (TO AUDIENCE)
Well, boys and girls, shall I let Mr. Lamb
stay in school? (AFTER A MOMENT,
SMILING) All right, Mr. Lamb, you can
stay in school.

Liking and respect for the teacher, and the educational values of the program (desire to
learn, in this instance) are reaffirmed with the explanation of the lamb and the decision
of the teacher. Note how the entire story progresses on a very simple, direct plane.
The plot is uncomplicated and the presentation of all ideas is clear.

(LAMB AND PUPILS ALL SMILE HAP-
PILY, LAUGHING. THE TEACHER GETS
UP IN FRONT OF THE CLASS.)

245

JACK AND JILL SMILE HAPPILY, LOOK
AT LAMB.

CU LAMB AS HE LOOKS AT JACK AND
JILL.

JACK AND JILL LOOK AT LAMB. CU
LAMB AS HE WINKS AT THEM HAPPILY.

SONG CONTINUES, DISSOLVE INTO
PICTURE BOOK.

CAMERA DOLLIES OUT TO UNCLE
WILL. THEN OUT FURTHER TO
INCLUDE JACK AND JILL.

MARY
Thank you, teacher.

OTHER PUPILS
Thank you.

(THEY ALL TAKE THEIR SEATS, LAMB
COMES AND SITS BY MARY, WHO PETS
HIM.)

TEACHER
All together now, boys and girls.

ALL
(SINGING) Mary had a little lamb, little
lamb, etc.

(UNCLE WILL'S HANDS SLOWLY CLOSE
THE BOOK.)

WILL
Wake up, Jack and Jill, wake up. You've
fallen asleep.

(JACK AND JILL LOOK UP.)

WILL
Why, I bet you haven't heard a word I've
said.

JILL
Oh, we have.

JACK
It was a wonderful story.

WILL
But you were sleeping.

JACK
Maybe it looked like we were.

Jill
But we really weren't.

JACK AND JILL
We were in fairyland.

The thin line between reality and imagination is suggested by the implication that perhaps
Jack and Jill had been asleep.

WILL
Did you like the story?

JACK AND JILL
Very much.

MOTHER (OFF)
Jack and Jill, it's time to go to bed now.

WILL

That's mother calling. You'd better go.

JILL

Yes, Uncle Will. (SHE TAKES JACK BY THE HAND.) C'mon, Jack.

Another training device: there is no argument when mother calls Jack and Jill to bed. Below, suspense for the next program is created by a discussion of what the story will be.

JACK

Will you be back with another story for us on Thursday, Uncle Will?

WILL

I certainly will.

JILL

What story are you going to tell us then?

WILL

That depends on which one you would like.

JACK

Jack and the Beanstalk this time?

JILL

Little Miss Muffet was so cute in school; I'd like one about her.

JACK

Which one is it going to be, Uncle Will?

WILL

That will have to be decided by the boys and girls who write in telling me which story they would like best. Whatever one they want, I'll tell. Is that fair?

The direct involvement of the viewers is reemphasized with the invitation for them to write in their suggestions for stories to be presented on future programs.

JACK AND JILL

Yes.

JILL

I hope they write in some good ones.

JACK

Me, too.

WILL

I'm sure they will.

JACK AND JILL

Good night. (TO AUDIENCE) Good night.

WILL

Good night ... see you on Thursday. (TO AUDIENCE) Good night.

CU BOOK WITH MOTHER GOOSE PICTURE THAT UNCLE WILL IS HOLDING. MUSIC UNDER AND UP AS DISSOLVE INTO MOVING COUNTRYSIDE OF FAIRYLAND SCENES WITH TITLES, CREDITS SUPER-IMPOSED. COMMERCIAL. FADEOUT.

Television Techniques

The visual element of television can be exploited very effectively in the children's program. On any show, in any format, the writer may add puppets, marionettes, live actors, film, tape, standard electronic devices and, particularly enjoyable for children, special electronic tricks. The presentational approach was mentioned previously: on television the performer can play directly to the camera and the children, although this should not be overdone because children seem to know when the performer is fawning on them. Television is particularly effective in illustrating visual elements and in involving children in some kind of activity. Pre-school shows use this approach frequently, emphasizing painting, paper construction, little dances and similar visual-action games. The visual element also permits television effectively to introduce new ideas and sights beyond the immediate games or art activities, such as visits to a museum, a demonstration by an artist, an inside view of a fire station and so forth. The drama, however, continues to dominate the children's market — unfortunately in the form of old movies, cowboys and cartoons. Undoubtedly, these are more effective on television than on radio, although it might be said that the child's greater use of personal imagination with a radio program more easily might permit his own upbringing to decide to what degree violence is necessary and good, while with a television program the imprint is made with the child finding it more difficult to screen out undesirable factors. If television drama for children were of a higher quality this problem would not be so great.

Radio Techniques

With their orientation to the visual element of television and the need to bring almost nothing to much of the entertainment they receive, children who have grown up in the second half of the twentieth century have not exercised the disciplines of imagination or concentration developed by those a bit older who grew up with radio. The radio writer today must consider this lack of concentration and short attention span. At the same time he should be aware of the need — and opportunity — to rejuvenate the creative imaginations of our children. There should be frequent breaks, both in sound and music, in radio programs. Sounds themselves, the essence of radio, should be realistic. If no realistic sounds are available, it is better to let children use their imaginations entirely and to use no sound rather than to present an unsatisfactory facsimile.

The Manuscript

Many children's shows are written out completely. That is, the complete dialogue and directions are presented, as in "The Adventures of Jack and Jill" script. In many situations, particularly for non-dramatic presentations and for programs that are offered on a three- to six-times a week basis, it is difficult to prepare complete scripts. Usually, detailed outlines or routine sheets are written, from which the performers are able to develop extemporaneously the informal content. The following excerpts are from the combination script and routine sheet of "Captain Kangaroo," television's most successful, high quality, long-running children's show.

> ● As you examine this script, analyze it in terms of the principles for good children's program writing. Discuss the following, evaluating the reasons for your answers.
>
> 1) Is the action simple and clear?
> 2) Is there sufficient action?
> 3) Are there elements of comedy slapstick? Of a chase?
> 4) Is the presentational approach used effectively?
> 5) Does the show build, with suspense for individual sequences as well as for the program as a whole?
> 6) Are there educational values in the script?
> 7) Does the production make use of special visual elements?
> 8) Does the program attempt to raise the viewers' standards of artistic and cultural appreciation?

CAPTAIN KANGAROO — February 12

ITEM	PROPS AND MISC.
1. OPENING "CK" Telop.	gobo
2. OPERA BIT (TBA) Bob dances off the gobo and turns off theme at the desk. Greeting. He asks the boys and girls if they would like to hear a story. "There are many ways to tell a story, this is one way (takes book from pocket). Ballet is a story told in dance. Opera is a story told in song. This morning Mr. GJ, Mr. Moose and I are going to tell a story in song, we're going to present an Opera. The name of our Opera is, 'The Happy Magic Of Mr. Moose', and it's all about a King who learns that everyone in his Kingdom is happy all day long. The King is delighted that his people are so happy but he can't help wondering what has made them so. He thinks perhaps his Court Jester has gone thru the streets making everyone happy and gay, and as the Opera begins the King is in his castle waiting for his Court Jester. Mr. GJ plays the Jester, Mr. Moose plays himself and I play the King." DISSOLVE TO CURTAIN TELOP, "TBA" CLASSICAL UNDER. DISSOLVE FROM TELOP to Bob wearing crown and robe, he is pacing the floor in deep thought. "TBA"-OUT. Bob paces, stops and sings:	Book, cue cards for lyrics, Moose flower cart COSTUME: King's crown & robe (Bob), Court Jester costume (GJ), Robin Hood hat (Moose) MISC: curtain telop "the end" telop

"This news is grand!" (He paces then stops)
"Throughout my land!" (He paces then stops)
"Everyone is happy and gay
But what has made them that way?-" (He paces floor).

(GJ enters wearing Court Jester costume. Bob goes to him and sings:)

BOB: (TUNE: "THE MUFFIN MAN")

"Oh have you heard the latest news
The latest news, the latest news
Oh have you heard the latest news
Thank you Jester mine"

GJ:
"Oh yes I heard the latest news
The latest news, the latest news
Oh yes I heard the latest news
But thank good Mister Moose"

(Bob delivers an "aside" to camera: "A Moose? Did he say a Moose?")

BOB:
"Oh did you say thank Mister Moose
Thank Mister Moose, thank Mister Moose
Oh did you say thank Mister Moose
For this our Happy Land?"

The song continues for several verses.

(Bob and GJ join hands and dance in circle as they sing:)

"Yes yes we found the Magic Moose
Yes yes we found the Magic Moose
Yes yes we found the Magic Moose
Hurry with us if you care"

(Bob and GJ tiptoe to garden where GJ points out the flower cart)

(Bob tiptoes to the cart and inspects it carefully before giving this aside:
"My Jester has done his job well for the Magic Moose lives here
And perhaps the Moose will tell us the secret of spreading good cheer")

(The Moose pops up CUT TIGHT on him as he says:
"Magic? ... Me a Magic Moose?
I spread good cheer without magic I fear
But lend an ear and my secret you'll hear")

MOOSE: (TUNE: "LONDON BRIDGE")

"Be-ing nice to every-one, every-one, every-one
Be-ing nice to every-one is my secret

Be-ing kind to every-one, every-one, every-one
Be-ing kind to every-one is my secret

Be-ing good to every-one, every-one, every-one
Be-ing good to every-one is my secret (Moose Call)."

(Bob gives this aside: "Here is a lesson we must learn well
Join in the singing, the whole world we'll tell!")

Verse is repeated.

DISSOLVE TO TELOP: "THE END," "TBA" MUSIC UP & UNDER

3. TAG OPERA BIT (LEADS CARTOON)
DISSOLVE TO BOB AT DESK sans costume. Bob: "And so
the 'Happy Magic of Mr. Moose' was nothing more than being
nice to everyone and only those who have tried this magic
know how well it really works." Bob leads cartoon per content.

4. CARTOON

5. POCKETS (LEADS "BLING BLING")   3 mechanical toys
Bob empties pockets at desk. As he
finishes playing the last pocket prop   SOUND:
(SE: AXE CHOPPING WOOD).   axe chopping wood
Bob: "That's Mr. GJ, he's splitting some
logs to make a new fence, in the old days
that's the way they used to make the houses.
They'd split the logs and then pile them on
top of one another until they had a log cabin.
Do you know a log splitter who later became
the President of the United States? . . .
Abe Lincoln, that's right. Did you know that
today is his birthday? Mr. GJ and I are going
to talk about President Lincoln in just a little
while but right now let's pretend we've split
a whole pile of logs and we're going to build
a log cabin." HIT RECORD

6. RECORD: "BLING BLANG BUILD A HOUSE FOR BABY"   Lincoln logs sprayed
Bob panto's while a log cabin, in three sections, is with UV
matted from limbo (GUS). Lincoln logs are sprayed
with UV.

7. LINCOLN EXHIBIT   covered wagon (oxdrawn
On hand RESEARCH gives short incidents covering   if possible), log cabin,
Abe's kindness, his home, his education, his honesty one room school house,
and his first law book. Extended RESEARCH to cover 1/2 lb. of tea, 6 pennies,
dates of office, birth, death, etc. As "Bling Blang" law book (Blackstone's
tags GJ enters with a picture of Lincoln and puts it on "Commentaries" if
Goat. Bob invites the boys and girls to the Goat where possible), a picture of
the exhibit is set. They sollow his life from cabin to Lincoln, model Capital
President.   building

8. and 9.:
Lead in and Record, "Swinging on a Star."

10. PLAYTIME   shirt cardboard,
Bob makes a log cabin from shirt cardboard. Cut   scissors, pencil, tape
strip of shirt cardboard approx. 4 inches wide,
fold three times to shape of house and tape. Add
cardboard roof. Draw on logs.

11. CLOCK "KNOCK KNOCK" BIT
The sequence involves the studio audience and the viewers.

251

12. DRUM BIT (LEADS "NOISY FAMILY")
GJ comes in with bass drum strapped to his back.
Grange Hall Parade next week. Bob asks if the drum
is easier to play with it strapped on the back. GJ:
"You know I was wondering about that Captain, I only
put it there so I could see where I'm going." Bob suggests
GJ try to hit the drum with the drumsticks. GJ tries
but can't. Bob tries to loosen the strap but it won't
come off. "That's a shame Mr. GJ, I thought maybe
we could march around the T.H. and play the drum."
GJ suggests that Bob take the drumsticks and follow
him around. Bob agrees and panto's blowing whistle
(SE: POLICE WHISTLE). Bob: "Fooowarrd maaarrch!"
HIT RECORD.

large bass drum (straps)
and drumsticks

SOUND:
police whistle

COSTUME:
2 Shako hats

13. RECORD: "THE NOISY FAMILY"
Bob and GJ march around the T.H.
Relief shots in limbo of the various musical
instruments are supered into drum.

small bass drum, toy
snare drum, cymbals,
triangle, and striker

14. BAND BIT-TBA
At tag of record GJ still cannot remove drum from
his back.
The sequence involves playing of record.

2 tablespoons,
2 whisk brooms,
toy piano

15. LEAD IN TO CARTOON
Per content.

16. CARTOON

17. HIDE AND SEEK BIT
Sequence in which Bob tries unsuccessfully to
find Bunny Rabbit.

two dinner bells,
two carrots

18. LEAD IN TO "WINTER WONDERLAND"
Bob comes to sandbox where model houses, trees
and cars are set. Bob "asks" the boys and girls about
the placement of buildings etc. as he makes a village.
GO TIGHT on village when it is finished. Bob drops
snow on it saying, "Now if we drop some "Wonder Snow"
on our town what will be have? ... That's right, a Winter
Wonderland." HIT RECORD, DISSOLVE TO LIMBO.

houses, cars, trees,
large box of "snow"

19. RECORD: "WINTER WONDERLAND"
Limbo. Entire table is set as a snow covered
village (end to end). Table is covered with snow and
has snowmen and candy canes strewn about. Snow crawl.

entire plasticville town,
2 small snowmen, 6
candy canes, large box
of "snow"

MISC:
snow crawl

20. CLOSING CREDITS

21. SONGTIME: "MARY HAD A LITTLE LAMB"
Bob does songtime to allow GJ time for costume
change. Bob at desk tells the boys and girls the song
he is going to sing and calls BR "so he can act as
the lamb." BR is not to be found. The Moose pops
up at door and Bob asks him to play the part. Moose
agrees. HIT RECORD. Moose keeps giving his call
instead of Lamb imitation. At tag Bob explains
and demonstrates lamb's "Baaa" to Moose. Moose
catches on. Bob: "Now say goodbye to the boys and
girls." Moose: "Baaa baaoys aan girls, basa you
tomorrow."

22. SIGN OFF

Sources

The sources for children's program material are limitless. The best and most direct source is children's literature. A visit to the library will disclose thousands of books of stories, fairy tales and poems written especially for children. Even some adult literature, such as folk tales, provide good material. Adaptations of plays for children are good for special programs. Children's games, as found in books dealing with playground and party entertainment, also may be used advantageously. Although sponsors so far have been unwilling to venture into truly creative children's programming, creative dramatics can provide excellent source material.

NOTES TO CHAPTER 8

[1] *Showcase,* a pamphlet by Grace M. Stanistreet, Director of the Children's Centre for Creative Arts, Adelphi College, written for the Children's Theatre Conference, March, 1958.

FOR APPLICATION AND REVIEW

1. Write a 15-minute script for a women's program to be presented over your local station. The program should have a broad orientation and cover several areas, similar to the sample programs in this chapter.
2. Write a 15-minute script for a women's program to be presented over a television network. The program should be devoted to one subject only, such as cooking or fashions.
3. Write a script or a detailed routine sheet (such as that for "Captain Kangaroo") for a half-hour children's program to be presented over your local television station. The program should not be a play. Determine the age group you wish to reach and plan the program accordingly. At the same time determine whether the program will appeal, on different levels, to those outside of that age group.

9

THE PLAY

BRANDER MATTHEWS, who was one of the theatre's leading critics, wrote in his *The Development of the Drama* that

". . . dramaturgic principles are not mere rules laid down by theoretical critics, who have rarely any acquaintance with the actual theatre; they are laws, inherent in the nature of the art itself, standing eternal, as immitigable today as when Sophocles was alive, or Shakespeare, or Moliere."[1]

The rules of playwriting are universal. They apply generally to the structure of the play written for the stage, film, television or radio. The rules are modified in their specific applications by the special requirements of the particular medium.

It is not to be assumed, however, that playwriting can be taught. At least, the genius and inspiration cannot be taught, for playwriting is an art on a plane of creativity far above the mechanical facets of some of the phases of continuity writing. America's first and foremost playwriting teacher, George Pierce Baker, stated that what can be done, however, is to show the potential playwright how to apply whatever genius and dramatic insight he may have, through an understanding of the basic rules of dramaturgy. That is all that can be done, and that is all that will be attempted here.

Yet, even this cannot be taught in one chapter or in several chapters. Any full discussion of playwriting technique requires at least a complete book in itself. It would be a deception to imply otherwise. What will be presented here is a summary of the rules of playwriting and some new concepts of playwriting in terms of the special needs of the television and radio media. One who seriously wishes to write television and radio drama is strongly urged first to explore as thoroughly as possible the techniques of writing the play for the stage. Only then will he have a sound basis for television and playwriting. Among the better works on dramaturgy are George Pierce Baker's *Dramatic Technique,* Kenneth Thorpe Rowe's *Write That Play,* and John Howard Lawson's *Theory and Technique of Playwriting and Screenwriting.*

Before the actual techniques of writing can be applied, the writer must be able to recognize and exploit the sources out of which he can develop the ideas for his play.

SOURCES

The writer may find the motivating ingredient for his play in an event or happening, in a theme, in a character or characters, or in a background.

Many times a playwright has witnessed or experienced an incident or series of incidents that contain the fundamentals for good drama. From this event or happening the playwright can build character, situation, theme and background. The writer must remember, however, that what is exciting in life is not necessarily good drama. Drama is heightened life. It is a compression of the most important elements of a situation and requires a rearrangement, revision and condensation of life to make it drama and not merely human interest reporting. It is difficult for the beginning playwright to understand this, particularly when he has been a participant in or an observer of an interesting life-situation. What may seem to be the most tragic, most humorous, most exciting thing that has ever happened to the writer may actually be hackneyed, dull and undramatic in play form. Because something seems dramatic in real life does not mean that it will be dramatic if put into a play. Such transposition requires imagination, skill and, to no small degree, the indefinable genius of playwriting. For example, many of us have seen a situation where a destitute maiden aunt has come to live with a sister and brother-in-law, and in her psychological need has become somewhat of a disturbing factor in the marriage. To the participants, or even to a close observer, such a situation might have provocative and electrifying undertones. To someone not connected with the situation, it appears, and understandably so, dull and uninspiring. To the imaginative playwright, in this case to Tennessee Williams, it could become "A Streetcar Named Desire."

The writer may initiate the preliminary thinking about the play from a theme or an idea. Although censorship often prevents the television and radio playwright from saying what he would like, the writer can orient concepts such as loyalty, independence, self-realization, into motivating factors upon which to develop a drama. Note what Paddy Chayefsky did with the theme of loneliness in the television play, later a motion picture, "Marty." The theme must be translated into specific and full-blown people and concrete situations. Under the theme of loyalty, for example, there is the ever-present son who won't marry because his psychologically-motivated notion of loyalty is one which says that he cannot leave his mother. Under independence, there are any number of variations of the wife who leaves her husband because she is not accorded the freedom or respect she feels she needs. Under self-realization, there is an endless supply of potential plays oriented around the artist who prefers to live on bread and beans in a cold-water flat rather than accept the lucrative advertising agency job. The writer must be wary of attempting to develop a play around a theme alone. As can be seen from the examples above, the result can be uninteresting and trite. The theme serves merely as the germ of the idea for the play.

Another source for the play may lie in a background. The backgrounds of war, of high society, of a slum environment, of the business world, have provided the settings and motivations for many plays. The college student could do worse that to use the background of his own environment of the campus as an initiating factor for his play.

A final source for the play may come from a character or several characters, either as a group or rolled into one. In modern dramaturgy, character motivates action; that is, the plot develops out of the characters. For this reason, the choice of character as a source provides a potentially stronger foundation for the play than do the other sources. The writer must be cautious, however, in using this source independently of the others; it is difficult to build a play solely around a character or combination of characters taken from real life. For example, how undramatic is the idea of a salesman getting fired from a job because he is getting old and cannot make as many sales as he once did! Even if his character is enlarged by adding pride, self-deception and despondency leading to suicide, the dramatic potential is not yet fully realized. But work on the character, develop his many facets, beliefs, psychological needs, physical capabilities, relationships to other people, clarify a theme and background, and one might eventually get to Willy Loman of Arthur Miller's "Death of A Salesman" — brilliant on TV as well as on the stage.

The sources of the play — situation, theme, background and character — individually are only germs of ideas. To be valuable to the initial development of the play, each of these factors must be explored, expanded, revised, then developed in relationship to the other sources, and finally re-examined in its complete form to determine if the idea has any dramatic value at all. If it has, then the playwright is ready for the next step. Too many beginning writers think that once the source, the motivating factor, is clarified, the play can be written. Inexperienced writers — and lazy writers — sometimes believe that all they have to do is to have a pretty good idea of where they are going, and then sit down and write the play. Unfortunately, this is not the case. The actual writing of the play is the dessert of the playwright's art. The hard work is devoted to the planning of the play and, later, to the revisions of the manuscript. After the writer decides on the theme, situation, character or background as a base for the play, he must begin to clarify in his mind and on paper the various elements that develop from the base. For instance, if he chooses to work from a background, he must then determine the characters, the situation and the theme to go with that background.

The writer should, ideally, write out of his own experiences or out of something he knows so that the play may have a valid foundation. However, if the writer is too close, either emotionally or in terms of time, to the life-ingredients of the play, he will find it difficult to heighten and condense and dramatize — he will tend to be a reporter rather than a dramatist. The playwright should never be part of the play, but should be able to write it objectively. He should feel and understand every moment of it, but should do so as a third person. He should not use the play as personal therapy. It is a good idea to be several years and several emotional fathoms away from the play when one starts to write it.

PLAY STRUCTURE

Until the 18th century, with the exception of works by only a few play-wrights (notably Shakespeare), plot or action was the dominant element in the play. The plot line was the most important factor, and the characters and dialogue were fitted into the movement of the action. Modern drama has em-phasized character as most important. The actions which determine the plot are those the characters must take because of their particular personalities and psychological motivations. The dialogue is that which the characters must speak for the same reasons. The three major elements in the play structure — — character, plot and dialogue — all must be coordinated into a consistent and clear theme. This coordination of all elements toward a common end re-sults in the unity of the piece, a unity of impression. The characters' actions and the events are not arbitrary, and the audience must be prepared for the occurrence of these actions and events in a logical and valid manner. "Prepara-tion" is the term given to the material which thus prepares the audience. The background and situation also must be presented; this is the "exposition." Another element the playwright must consider is the "setting," which the play-wright describes in order to create a valid physical background and environ-ment for his characters.

After the writer is certain that he understands and can be objective about the characters, theme, situation and background, he can begin to create each of them in depth. He should do as much research as necessary — or, perhaps, as much as possible — to acquaint himself fully with the potentials of his play.

Each character should be literally psychoanalyzed by the writer. This should be done on paper, so the writer has the characters' complete histories and motivations in front of him at all times. The writer must develop a back-ground for each character, not only for the duration of the action of the play, but extending back much before the opening of the play (even going back to ancestors who may not appear in the play but who would have had some in-fluence on the character's personality). A complete analysis of the character also will provide an indication of the kind and form of dialogue the character should use. The writer should test out the dialogue on paper, putting the char-acter into hypothetical situations with other characters. It cannot be repeated too often that dialogue is not an approximation of real life speech; dialogue must be heightened and condensed from that of real life.

After the characters have been created, the writer is ready to create the situation, or plot line. This should be done in skeletonized form. The writer needs, first, a conflict. The conflict is between the protagonist of the play and some other character or force. A conflict may be between two individuals, an individual and a group, between two groups, between an individual or indi-viduals and nature, between an individual or individuals and some unknown force, or between an individual and his inner self. The nature of the conflict will be determined largely by the kinds of characters involved. After the con-flict has been decided upon, the plot moves inexorably toward a climax, the point at which one of the forces in conflict wins over the other. The play reaches the climax through a series of complications. Each complication is, in itself, a small conflict and climax. Each succeeding complication literally complicates the situation to a greater and greater degree until the final complication makes it impossible for the struggle to be heightened any longer. Something has to give. The climax must occur. The complications are not arbitrary. The characters themselves determine the events and the complications because the actions they take are those, and only those, they must take because of their particular motivations and personalities.

George Pierce Baker, in his *Dramatic Technique,* has written that

> ". . . situation exists because one is what he is and so has inner conflict, or clashes with another person, or with his environment. Change his character a little and the situation must change. Involve more people in it, and immediately their very presence, affecting the people originally in the scene, will change the situation."[2]

British playwright Terrence Rattigan has written similarly in an article, "The Characters Make the Play":

> "A play is born — for me, at any rate — in a character, in a background or setting, in a period or in a theme, never in a plot. I believe that in the process of a play's preliminary construction during that long and difficult period of gestation before a line is put on paper, the plot is the last of the vital organs to take shape.
>
> "If the characters are correctly fashioned — by which I do not mean accurately representing living people but correctly conceived in their relationship to each other — the play will grow out of them. A number of firmly and definitely imagined characters will act — must act — in a firm and definite way. This gives you your plot. If it does not, your characters are wrongly conceived and you must start again."[3]

Once the preliminary planning, gestation, research and analysis are completed, the writer is ready. But not for writing the play. Not yet. Next comes the scenario or detailed outline. The writer who has been conscientious up to now will learn from the scenario whether or not he has a potentially good play, if any play at all. Through careful construction and analysis of the scenario, the writer may eliminate the bad points and strengthen the good points of the play even before it is written.

Before writing a detailed scenario, however, the writer must have a knowledge of the concepts of dramaturgy — of the basic rules for the play regardless of whatever medium it is written for, and of the modified rules for the television and radio play, concepts determined by the special characteristics of these media.

CONCEPTS OF PLAYWRITING

Unity

One of the essentials that applies to all plays, regardless of type or style of production, is the unity of action or impression. There should be no elements within the play that do not relate in thorough and consistent fashion to all the other elements, moving toward a realization of the purpose of the playwright. Not a single extraneous element may detract from the unified totality of impression received by the audience. The so-called unities of time and of place, erroneously attributed to Aristotle, are completely flexible in modern dramaturgy.

Plot

The plot structure of a play is based on a complication arising out of the individual's or group's relationships to some other force. This is the conflict, the point when the two or more forces come into opposition. The conflict must be presented as soon as possible in the play, for the rest of the play structure follows and is built upon this element. Next come a series of complications or crises, each one creating further difficulty in relation to the major conflict, and each building in a rising crescendo so that the entire play moves toward a final crisis or climax. The climax occurs at the instant the conflicting forces meet head on and a change occurs to or in at least one of them. This is the turning point. One force wins and the other loses. The play may end at this moment. There may, however, be a final clarification of what happens, as a result of the climax, to the characters or forces involved. This remaining plot structure is called the "resolution."

The elementary plot structure of the play may be diagrammed as follows:

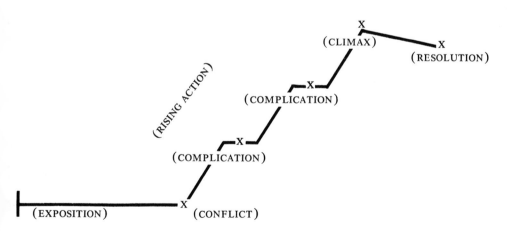

Character

Character, plot and dialogue comprise the three primary ingredients of the play. All must be completely and consistently integrated. In modern dramaturgical theory character is the prime mover of the action, and determines plot and dialogue. The character does not conform to a plot structure. The qualities of the character determine the action. The character must be revealed through the action; that is, through what he does and what he says, and not through arbitrary description or exposition. Character is delineated most effectively by what the individual does at moments of crisis. This does not imply physical action alone, but includes the concept of inner or psychological action. The character must be consistent throughout the play in everything he does and says, and must be plausible in terms of life and reality. This does not mean that characters are copies of real life persons; they must be dramatically heightened interpretations of reality.

Dialogue

There is some difference of opinion as to whether dialogue should be realistic or poetic. It must, however, be "dramatic." Inasmuch as the play does not duplicate real people or the exact action of real life, but heightens and condenses these elements, the dialogue also has to be heightened and condensed rather than duplicated. The dialogue must truly conform to the personality of the character speaking it, it must be completely consistent with the character and with itself throughout the play, and it must forward the situation, the showing of the character and the movement of the plot.

Exposition

Exposition, the revelation of the background of the characters and situation and the clarification of the present circumstances, must not be obvious or come through some device, such as the telephone conversation, the servant or the next-door neighbor. It must come out as the action carries the play forward and must be a natural part of the action. The exposition should be presented as early as possible in the play.

Preparation

Preparation, too, must be made subtly. Preparation, or foreshadowing, is the unobtrusive planting, through action or dialogue, of material which prepares the audience for subsequent events, making their occurrence logical and not arbitrary. Proper preparation validates subsequent actions of the characters; it is presented throughout the play.

Setting

Setting is determined by the form of the play and the physical and mechanical needs of the play structure. Setting serves as locale, background and environment for the characters of the play; it is a psychological and aesthetic presentation of the purpose of the play and of the author.

It should be noted again that the above is only a summary of the rules of dramaturgy, presented here solely as a very elementary introduction to the techniques of writing the play for television and radio.

THE RADIO PLAY

The writer of the radio play must interrelate the basic rules of dramaturgy with the special characteristics of the radio medium. A review of the basic elements and technical aspects of the radio medium in Chapters 1 and 2 would be helpful at this point.

Radio rightly has been called the "theatre of the imagination." There are absolutely no limitations except those of the human mind. The radio playwright has no restrictions on place, setting, number of characters, kinds of actions or movement of time. In radio, the writer can take the audience anywhere and make his characters do anything. He can create mental images of infinite variations, as long as these images are within the realm of the imagination of his listeners. The special characteristics of the radio medium, as indicated in Chapters 1 and 2, result in the following modifications of the basic rules of dramaturgy in writing the radio play.

Unity

There are no unities of time and place in radio. The radio script may take us 20,000 years into the future and in the twinkling of a sound effect transport us to an age 20,000 years in the past. Radio may present a character in his living room and in a split second place the same character (and place us, the audience, who are in the position and place of the characters who are "on mike") in his office in another part of town. Radio may move us from a polar ice cap to the moon to a battlefield to a jungle to the depths of Hades, creating without restriction the settings for our imaginations. Radio has no visual limitations. The writer must remember *not* to restrict his own imagination by what he can "see." Radio has no physical space limitations. We can have one battlefield with tens of thousands of soldiers or, within seconds, a dozen similar battlefields with as many more characters.

What must not be forgotten is that no matter how loose the unities of time and place, the radio play must have a unity of action; that is, it must have a consistency and wholeness of purpose and development within the script. Each sequence must be integrated thoroughly with every other sequence, all contributing to the total goal or effect the writer wishes to create.

Plot

The plot structure of the radio play is essentially the same as that for the stage play. Exposition, a conflict, complications, a climax and, if necessary, a resolution must be set forth clearly. The radio play must have a rising action which creates suspense and holds the interest of the audience. The limitation of time modifies some of the rules concerning these elements. Exposition may be revealed as the action is progressing, with the presentation of the conflict at the very opening of the drama. The limitation of time also makes it necessary for the writer to concentrate on only one simple plot line and to avoid all sub-plots.

Character

The characters in the radio play must be as valid as those in the stage play, and the rules for their creation and development apply just as fully to radio as to theatre. The time limitation of radio makes it impossible, however, to deal with the characters, even the most important ones, in depth. In much radio drama, therefore, character is not the motivating force; plot is. The writer should attempt to develop a concomitant effect of one upon the other. The characters must be consistent with themselves and appropriate with reality, although heightened from real life. It might be expected that the lack of visual perception in radio would change the revelation of a character from what he says and does solely to what he says. This is not so. Character is revealed through what the character does; the difference between radio and the stage and television is that, in radio, what he does is not shown visually, but the actions are presented through sound and dialogue. Because too many voices may become confusing to a radio audience, the number of roles in the play should be limited. For the same reason, the writer should limit the number of characters in any one scene.

Dialogue

Dialogue in the radio play must be consistent with itself and with the characters; it must be appropriate with the situation and the characters; and it must be dramatically heightened. Even more than on the stage or in television, dialogue in radio serves to forward the situation, reveal character and uncover the plot line. Everything on radio is conveyed through dialogue, sound effects, music or silence. The use of sound and music is more important in radio than in other media. The use of dialogue similarly is more important. Dialogue must clearly indicate all of the action taking place. Dialogue must clearly introduce the characters; presented naturally, such dialogue not only must tell who the people are, but must describe them and, if possible, tell something about them. Dialogue often may be used to describe movement and places of action, but not in an obvious manner. For example, nothing is so trite as a character saying, "Now, if you'll excuse me, I'll push back this chair I'm sitting on, and go. My coat is hanging on that clothes tree right inside the front door, isn't it? I can get it. It's only a few steps from this room." Or: "Now that we're in my sixth floor bachelor apartment with the etchings on the wall, the hi-fi set in the corner by the window, and the green plush carpet on the floor . . ."

Exposition

As noted above, exposition is difficult in radio because it must be presented solely through dialogue and sound. Exposition, because of the short time for the play, should be presented as soon as possible, but preferably through the action, not through description. Inasmuch as the audience can't see the characters or the settings, the writer must clarify these elements of the play before any important action takes place. To solve this problem, radio has employed a technique used much less frequently in the other media: the narrator. The narrator can either be divorced entirely from the play or can be an integral part of it.

Preparation

Preparation functions in the radio play in the same way as in the stage play. It must be valid and it must be made subtly. Because the radio writer cannot present the preparation visually, with all the subtle nuances of the visual element, he must be certain that just because he knows what the character motivations are he does not fail to give the audience sufficient preparation. If anything, the radio play requires an overabundance of preparation rather than too little.

Setting

Radio offers the writer limitations and advantages in the matter of setting. One drawback is that the writer cannot present a visual setting which, at one glance, can provide an environment and atmosphere for his characters. He has to do it all through dialogue and sound. On the other hand, the radio writer is limited only by the imaginative potential of the audience; he can put the audience into almost any setting he wishes. The radio writer should be wary of using this facility too freely, however. He should not be tempted into creating an imaginary setting that is invalid. The mental picture he creates for the audience must be the right one for the play. The locale and environment must be believable for the characters and the situation, and must forward the psychological and aesthetic purposes of the author.

Movement from setting to setting may be accomplished through silence, fading, narration, a music bridge or sound effects.

As indicated in Chapter 1, one of the great advantages the radio playwright has over the stage playwright is that the former can control and direct the attention of the audience much more effectively than can the latter. The radio audience cannot select the elements of the play by which they are to be stimulated; the theatre audience can pick out any part of the action on the stage it desires. Radio permits a much greater subjective response, and the writer can deal with elements that strike close to the emotional needs and desires of the audience. He can, in turn, use these emotional stimuli to activate the intellectual concerns of the audience. If he uses his medium correctly he can hold a tight grip on the feelings and minds of his listeners.

In creating the play for radio, the writer must keep several special technical considerations in mind. He should not skimp on sound effects or music, for he needs these elements to clarify movement, setting and action. While not overdoing it, he should be certain that he has used sound effectively and sufficiently for the purposes of his play. He should be certain that his script contains the proper devices for transitions of time and place and has enough music, fulfilling all the needs indicated in Chapter 2. The exits and entrances of characters should be made clear through sound. The sound effects and music should be integrated with the action of the play, and each of these effects should be indicated clearly in relation to the specific need of the script at the precise moment the effect is used.

The play should be of a proper length for the time period, and within the play the scenes should be neither so short as to be lacking in clarity, nor so long as to be repetitious and boring. Nor should individual speeches of characters be too long. In any play, character development should be revealed through action, though the soliloquy may be effective in certain kinds of plays. An examination of several of the radio verse plays of Archibald MacLeish will indicate some of the possibilities for the use of long speeches. The plot, dialogue and characters must, of course, follow proper dramaturgical form and relationships, and the exposition and preparation must be clear, sufficient and not obvious.

THE TELEVISION PLAY

Television's Special Characteristics

The television audience and some problems of censorship were analyzed in Chapter 1. Arbitrary censorship has hampered television's potentially high level of dramatic production, and the television playwright must perforce adapt himself to these restrictions.

The special characteristics of the television audience require a special approach on the part of the writer for this medium. The playwright may combine the subjective relationship of the viewer to the television screen with the electronic potentials of the medium to create a purposeful direction of the audience's attention. The television playwright may direct his audience toward the impact of the critical events in the character's life and toward the subjective manifestations of the character's existence. The ability to focus the viewer's sight, attention and even feeling so specifically permits the writer to orient the consciousness of the audience closely to the inner character of the person on the screen. In choosing his subject and developing his play, the television writer should consider the above points. Paddy Chayefsky was very successful with his "slice-of-life" plays on television. The time and space limitations of television discussed in the following pages, in addition to the censorship of controversial ideas, combine with the direction of the audience's attention to suggest that the intimate, searching play may be a logical candidate for television success.

The direct relationship of the television performer to his audience suggests a further kind of orientation: a presentational approach which is possible at the same time as the illusionistic, and which permits an exciting combination of intellectual and emotional stimulation for the audience.

It has been pointed out, in Chapter 2, how the writer must develop the script in terms of TV's technical potentials and incorporate these potentials within the action of the play. Perhaps the most important contribution of the mechanical and electronic devices of television is to enable the writer to direct the audience toward the intimate, toward an examination of the inner character in a manner not possible on the stage or in radio. The ability of television to capture significant details through the camera implies a greater concentration on the visual than on the verbal elements (the latter, of course, dominate the stage and radio play). Indeed, television's most effective means for capturing the intimacy of its presentation is the close-up, which permits physical action to substitute for what sometimes would have to be done through dialogue or sound on the stage or in radio.

Inasmuch as the "live" play of early television is now taped or filmed, the writer has even greater opportunity for an expansion of action over the stage play, and can include a greater number of transitions than otherwise might be possible. Television is not bound by the conventions of the theatre. Through cutting, dissolves, fades and other electronic devices, there are no restrictions of time and place. Television does not need a curtain or blackout convention, but can signify a change of time or place with an effect lasting as short as a few seconds. Other techniques, such as the split screen, the wipe and the superimposition, also permit excellent fluidity. Even in situations where a play is a one-shot live presentation — as in some of the smaller commercial and ETV stations — the incorporation of film, tape and electronic effects permit fluid, flexible drama.

In live-type TV several mechanical and electronic approaches may be used to enable the actor to change costume or to alter make-up, situations which would require an intermission in the theatre. The control room may cut to other characters on another set, the camera may concentrate on an action which does not show a particular character while giving the impression that he is involved in the action, or a tape or film clip may be inserted. These techniques provide the television play with a tighter unity of action than has the stage play.

Time and space are two more special characteristics of the television medium which the writer must understand and apply in the creation of his play. One of the most important problems of all for the television playwright is that of time. The hour drama is really only about 51 minutes long, the half-hour drama 24 minutes in length. Even the hour-and-one-half dramatic program permits only about 75 minutes for the play. The television play must be extremely tight; it can have no irrelevancies. It should have as few characters as possible, and one main, simplified plot line, containing only material relating to the conflict of the major character or characters.

These limitations often result in characters who are stereotyped figures with little richness of human personality. The writer sometimes may concentrate on plot at the expense of character, or stress character without including any valid action. Neither approach makes for good playwriting.

Leading former television playwrights Paddy Chayefsky and Reginald Rose have stated that the primary limitation in television is time. Chayefsky has written that the playing time of the one-hour program permits only one subplot, never two. He adds that it is impossible to have a multiple story — stories of several people around one focal incident — something easily attempted on the stage.[4] Reginald Rose has stated that time limitations permit only brief fragments of people if the plot is an involved one, or brief sketches of plot if the characters are well developed. In describing the writing of his television play, "Thunder on Sycamore Street," Rose indicated that he originally planned to cover three families in different houses on the street in terms of their reactions to one focal incident. Time limitations made possible only 13 minutes per family. He therefore was forced to change the play to revolve around the action rather than around the people who created the action.[5]

Space limitations are of two major kinds in television. First is the physical size of the room within the studio in live-type TV drama. Second is the decreasing smallness of the objects in a picture picked up by an increasing camera distance, and viewed over the narrow and constricting viewing area of the relatively small television screen.

The limitation of space suggests two major considerations for the writer: the number of characters on a screen at any one time, and the number and scope of sets in a play. In order to avoid a situation where the small television screen is choked with a mass of humanity, the writer must be sure that only a few characters are on camera at the same time. Stage convention permits ten people to represent a crowd. Ten people on television likely would appear too small individually and too jumbled as a group.

The lack of physical space in the studio implies further difficulties. Generally, except in the newer Hollywood television centers, small studios doing live or live-type taped shows have to eliminate or greatly restrict exteriors. The writer also should avoid, on live-type TV, nature effects pertaining to exteriors, such as fires and floods.

The limited number of sets and the limited size of a given set imply the need for short scenes. The actors cannot move around enough to warrant long scenes because long scenes require movement to break the monotony. Although smaller sets may be necessary, the fluidity possible through television's electronic devices permits frequent change from set to set and quick and easy re-use of sets.

The space limitations and the time limitations combine to indicate an approach for the television play: an intimate probing of a short span of the subjective life of the character. This approach is reflected in the following analysis of the special dramaturgical concepts for the television play.

Dramaturgical Concepts for Television

Unity. The most important changes in the unities as applied to television relate to time and place. Television can transcend boundaries of time and place that even the most fluid stage presentation cannot match. In the theatre, a scene cannot be changed every other minute; television can present many scenes in relatively few minutes or even seconds. In the theatre, the movements of time and place often are aural as well as visual; television transitions are more visual because of the utilization of mechanical and electronic techniques. The use of film or tape in television permits a wider scope of time and place that can be achieved in even the most flexible theatre, at least in selective realism terms, or can be achieved with a television drama that depends solely on live-type continuous action in its production. Television has been able to achieve what August Strindberg hoped for in the theatre: a situation where "anything may happen: everything is possible and probable." Strindberg looked for dramatic presentation where "time and space do not exist," where "imagination spins and weaves new patterns: a mixture of memories, experience, unfettered fancies, absurdities and improvisations."[6] Television does not preclude the realistic, and though it has more restrictions than Strindberg wished, it does have the same potentials. In television one not only can change setting and change time as on the stage, but also can change time without changing setting and change setting without changing time — and do so much more quickly and easily. The unities of time and place are completely loose and fluid in television.

The unity of action or impression is as vital to the television play as to any other form of drama, and the television writer must be certain that this most important unity is present.

Plot. The dramaturgical rules relating to plot apply to the television play as to the stage play. The problem of time, however, necessitates a much tighter plot line in the television play, and a condensation of the movement from sequence to sequence. The television script must be oriented around a single action and should exclude sub-plots. It should concentrate on a single, simplified plot.

The art of drama is selective. In brief minutes we must present what life may have played out in days or years or centuries. Life is unemphatic, while drama must be emphatic. The short time for the television play requires the plot to be the essence of reality, to contain only the heightened extremities of life. The television writer should aim for the short, terse scene.

Although the emphasis on plot seems to make this the motivating factor in the television play, the exploration of television's intimacy and subjectivity leads to the inner character and, to a degree, enables the writer to utilize character as a plot-motivating element.

The problem of space also has a direct effect on plot construction. As noted earlier, actors cannot move around enough to warrant long scenes which often require movement to break the monotony, and the television writer must make the scenes short.

In condensing the play structure to conform to the time and space requirements, the writer would do well to consider several of the approaches presented by George Pierce Baker in his *Dramatic Technique*. First, the dramatist may "bring together at one place what really happened at the same time, but to other people in another place." Second, episodes happening to a person in the same setting, but at different times may be brought together. Third, events that have "happened to two people in the same place, but at different times may . . . be made to happen to one person." Finally, "what happened to another person at another time, and at another place may at times be arranged so that it will happen to any desired figure." Baker concluded: "The essential point in all this compacting is: when cumbered with more scenes than you wish to use, determine first which scenes contain indispensable action, and must be kept as settings; then consider which of the other scenes may by ingenuity be combined with them."[2]

The dramaturgical rules relating to conflict also are modified in the television play. Because of the shorter running time, the conflict must come much sooner than in the stage play. The television play may open immediately with the conflict, with the exposition cut virtually to nothing. The point of attack in the television play should come quickly, and should bring with it the first important moment of pressure. The television play cannot show that pressure slowly develop, as can the stage play; therefore, the writer should include the basic expository elements, if possible, in this moment of conflict. The writer should tell who the people are, show where they are, place the time of the story, and reveal what actions or events have caused the conflict.

The kind of conflict in the television play differs from that in the stage play. On the stage almost any conflict may be successful. Because of the intimacy and subjectivity of television, the conflict between individuals usually is more effective than are those between man and nature, or between groups, or between any large bodies or forces.

The use of complications in the television play follows their use in the stage play. Although television's time limitation permits fewer complications, the writer must include a sufficient number to validate and build the actions of the major characters. Each complication should move the characters and the action closer to the climax. The final complication should be the crisis, and should reach a valid and inescapable climax which is the result of the conflict reaching its peak.

The modern playwright, influenced by the plays of ideas and more recently by the Brechtian epic drama, has put less and less emphasis on the resolution. Television often dispenses with the resolution entirely, unless some doubt remains about the moral principle involved. Indeed, time frequently does not permit the inclusion of a resolution. Sometimes the writer can incorporate the resolution as a part of the climax.

Character. The character in the play is not the person one sees in life. The playwright cannot validate the actions of the character by saying "but that's what he did in real life." Drama is heightened life. The playwright reveals the character by showing the character's actions in moments of crisis. The television writer must be especially careful of this rule. Not only must he concentrate on the action that strikingly reveals the individual character, but he must concentrate also on the few characters whose actions strikingly reveal the purpose of the play. Do not use unneeded people. If a character does not contribute to the main conflict and to the unified plot line, then he does not belong in the play. If the character is essential, then he must be in the script. If there are too many essential characters, then the entire approach to the play must be rethought.

The presentation of depth, of the intimate, inner character, is one of the advantages of television. Mechanical and electronic devices permit physical and psychological closeness and empathy that are not possible in the theatre. The television writer can direct the audience's attention to the details relating to the inner character; the television camera can focus the audience's eye on the elements which most effectively project the character's feelings. Television cannot present the group as a protagonist so effectively as can the theatre. The scope of the camera and the size of the viewing screen do not permit a breadth in which many characters can be dealt with at the same time with equal and effective attention. The television writer must concentrate on the individual as protagonist.

With a minimum of motivating exposition and clarifying background, because of the lack of time, the development of sufficient characterizations for more than one or two persons is sometimes difficult. The writer should select depth-delineating elements with care. Good visual action indicated by the writer, and effective camera work, can often present exposition which, on the stage, would have to be explained verbally.

Although plot is the motivating factor in most television plays today, writers of quality plays — I exclude most of the hack-written private spy-western-adventure-situation comedy fare — are beginning to understand more and more that characters, and the relationships among them, are the basic factors in television drama. There is more and more byplay between character and plot, with character determining incident and vice versa. The concentration on the subjective and the intimate, while applying the basic dramaturgical rules for television, is leading to the emergence of character as the motivating force in the too rarely presented quality television play.

Dialogue. The rules of dialogue for the television play are the same as for the stage play. The dialogue must forward the situation; it must be consistent with the characters, the situation and with itself; it must be dramatic, and heightened in comparison with the dialogue of real life.

Television requires one significant modification in the use of dialogue to forward the situation and to provide exposition. In television, the visual element can often substitute for the aural. If the writer can show the situation or present the expository information through action instead of through dialogue, he should do so. The use of the camera, with the long shot as well as the close-up, has made it possible for the writer to eliminate time-consuming dialogue in which the character describes things or places. The television writer is able to concentrate not only on action but on "reaction," keeping the dialogue at a minimum and the picture the primary object of attention. Anything that can be shown on television through a close-up should not be described, as it would have to be on the stage. The television writer must be careful, however, not to go too far in substituting visual action for dialogue. Pantomime and the close-up should be used cautiously and only when they are the most effective ways of presenting the material.

The condensing and heightening of real-life dialogue in the drama is of great importance in television. Television dialogue should avoid repetition; it should condense the ideas presented; it should be character-delineating; it should be written so that the purpose of every exchange of speeches is clear to the audience and so that the sequence carries the plot line forward; it should contain the necessary exposition and background for the characters even when presenting the continuing action of the play.

Exposition.   The short time alloted to the television play results in a minimum of exposition. The writer will find it difficult to present sufficient background material necessary to characterization, and to present exposition subtly or as a natural part of the action because of insufficient time for a slow unfolding of the situation. Because the conflict should be presented almost as soon as the television drama begins, the exposition must be highly condensed and presented with all possible speed. The problem here is that, although film and theatre audiences generally have some foreknowledge of the drama they are about to watch, the television audience often has no preparation for what it is going to see. This implies that exposition may be even more important in the television play than in the film or stage play. The television medium itself provides the writer with some means for solving the problem, including super-impositions and voice-over narration. Mechanical and electronic devices permit the cutting of much exposition that might be necessary on the stage. Fluid and mobile camera work, as well as the close-up, can pick out things that would have to be explained by the characters in the stage play.

Preparation.   The rules for preparation apply equally to the television play as to the stage play. The writer must prepare the audience in a subtle and gradual manner for the subsequent actions of the characters and the events of the play. Nothing must come as a surprise. The audience should be able to look back, after something has taken place, and know that the action was inevitable because of the personality of the character who performed the action or because all of the circumstances leading to the event made it unavoidable.

The electronic and mechanical elements of television enable the writer to achieve valid preparation effectively and subtly in a minimum of time.

Setting.   There have been, and are now, many physical kinds of dramatic settings: the Greek open stage, the Italian spectacle and painted backdrop, the cluttered stage of the naturalistic play, the use of light and shadow in expressionistic staging, and the Appia-influenced plasticity of modern production. But the physical areas of the television set are different from those of the stage. Television drama today essentially conforms to the modern play of selective realism in content and purpose, and realistic settings usually are required. Both the limitations and the potentials of television have combined to modify the realistic setting, however. First, the live-type TV setting must be smaller than the writer might wish it to be. Second, there can be few exteriors in live-type TV drama and no large nature effects. On the other hand, the fluidity of television makes up for these restrictions by permitting, within reason, a greater number of changes of setting and a considerable broadening of setting through the uses of film and tape. Television can "open up" the setting, and the playwright can have frequent changes of time and place.

The writer must be certain that all of his scenes, backgrounds and set descriptions are integrated carefully with the forward action of the drama, and that they serve as valid and delineating locales, environment and atmosphere for the characters and for the play.

> ● *1) Examine the action summary and functional analysis beginning on page 297 and analyze the play excerpt beginning on page 299. Note both the form of the television script and the application of the principles of television playwriting. 2) Analyze one or more television scripts of acknowledged merit written by a leading author or authors, including Reginald Rose, Paddy Chayefsky and Rod Serling. (In addition to a number of hard-cover publications, paperback collections of television plays are available. Two such editions worth examining are Paddy Chayesfky's* Television Plays, *Simon and Schuster, and* Best TV Plays: 1957, *edited by Florence Britton, Ballantine Books.) Study the writer's creation of character, plot, dialogue, exposition, preparation, unity and setting. Relate his use of these elements to the principles outlined thus far in this chapter. What is the relationship between technique and creative inspiration in the script or scripts analyzed?*

The Soap Opera

The daytime adult dramatic serial, or soap opera, has been described by Gilbert Seldes as "the great invention of radio, its single, notable contribution to the art of fiction."[7]

Although the soap opera on radio is now no longer with us, its place has been taken to a great degree by the soap opera on television. This form of drama is directed at the woman at home who takes time out of a busy schedule to watch. The drama must be something with which she can identify, and at the same time something in which she can find a vicarious kind of excitement. The setting should be familiar: the household, the doctor's office, the school, the small town, the large city, all presented in general terms so that any listener anywhere can have some clear interpretation of their own of the background, and none presented in such specific terms that any listener might not have some notion of the environment.

The characters must be familiar, not necessarily in occupation, but in the kinds of persons they are and in the problems they encounter. Every listener should be able to identify with the main character, whether that character is a housewife, accountant, librarian, policeman, or architect, explorer or even playwright. The writer achieves this by developing the characters, no matter what environment they are in, on the simplest and most obvious level, with simple, direct motivations. For example, the housewife will have to protect her handsome husband from the woman next door, the mistress of the plantation hers from the widow on the next plantation, or the wife of the actor hers from the leading lady in the show.

Though similarly motivated, the characters should be distinct types. There should be no possibility of confusion of characters. One way to avoid such confusion is to limit the number of characters. The dramatic serial should have the hero and/or heroine; the other man and/or other woman; the young man and/or young woman (or teenagers or children); the villain and/or villainess; the interested and well-meaning relatives or friends, including the kindly old judge, the maiden aunt, and their counterparts. The major characters must always be sympathetic. The "good" people must always vanquish the "bad" people. Even age is a factor: the hero is usually middle-aged, the heroine not quite.

Perhaps the most important thing the writer must keep in mind in the creation of characters and situation is that the characters must be provided with the opportunity to get into an infinite variety of troubles. They must face problems that the listener conceivably could have. The problems must be melodramatic, basically real and valid, but slightly exaggerated beyond the probable real-life involvement of most of the listeners. This gives the listener the opportunity to commiserate with people who are worse off than she; the soap opera viewer usually considers herself to have a similarly infinite amount of troubles. At the very least, the listener should be able to find a mutual kind of commiseration with the characters so she can feel that she is not the only one with these kinds of troubles and that somewhere she has "friends" and "compatriots" who come and visit with her for a while each day. In a sense, the soap opera serves many people as a kind of makeshift therapy, a counterpart of Aristotle's purgation.

The characters all must be very emotional, and this emotion must be conveyed to the listener. They must face obstacles of the most difficult sort. Particularly if the protagonists are young people, they must face seemingly insurmountable odds.

At the same time, the characters must have some experiences that are different in some degree from those of the audience. They must meet situations and find themselves in environments that are, to the listener, exciting or exotic or both. The characters' experiences should serve, in some part, as means of escape for the listener who, through empathy, transports herself to wherever the characters are and to whatever they are doing. The characters should do some things that the housewife would like to do, but can't. With the exception of a sensation-seeking show like "Peyton Place," the soap opera protagonist and theme are always ultimately "moral" and, in the very broadest sense, non-controversial and "against sin."

The plot, unlike those of the straight drama, should contain a number of sub-plots, all bearing on the major conflict. They should complicate matters almost beyond endurance for the protagonist. The only limitation is that the complications should stop short of confusion for the viewer.

Inasmuch as the housewife may not be able to give full attention to each episode, day in and day out, because of the distractions of and duties to her home, the plot line cannot always be brisk and sharp, and it cannot continuously contain elements that demand the full attention of the viewer. In addition, the viewer may miss a number of episodes and should be able to go back to the story and not have missed anything of appreciable importance. The plot should move at a snail's pace — as slowly as possible. The soap opera never reaches a climax. The conflict is clear and ever-present and unfolds imperceptibly. It develops with a very minor event at a time. An unexpected knock at the door can be built up into a minor complication lasting for weeks or even months. In each episode only a minute segment of action takes place, and there is little change. The time of the drama sometimes moves as slow as the time of day. Rather than being a heightened and condensed interpretation of life, the soap opera is a slow, drawn-out, detailed report of life, stressing the sentimental, human elements. Over a period of days or even weeks the action in the drama may cover only an hour's time. The viewer wants to believe that the characters are real, and that the events are happening as she hears them. The events, then, should happen as they do in the lives of the audience: slowly, unemphatically, even undramatically, but to the individual they should be of critical and extreme importance, no matter how minor the event. This implies that the dialogue must be like that of real life: slow, melodramatic and non-dramatic, and barely moving the action along.

The writer should start each episode at a peak — the crisis of what seems to be a complication. In each episode, the particular complication should be solved or should take another turn and the drama should level off. Before the program is ended, a new element of complication — and remember, these complications may be the most insignificant happenings — should be introduced. A critical point should be reached just as the episode ends. Like the serial of the silent film days, it should be a "cliff-hanger," making it necessary for the audience to tune in the next episode to learn what will happen.

The writer may make good use of simultaneous action. Instead of continuous action, which would move the story along too fast to permit the slow development of sub-plots, the writer should switch frequently during the drama to different scenes involving different characters — all bearing on the main conflict, of course — and all of these actions occurring at the same time.

The lack of time for much rehearsal or preparation for a five-time-per-week drama implies several restrictions on the writer. He should keep settings and special effects to a minimum. He should keep the characterizations well within the patterns already established for the roles. He should make no change in the form of the plot or dialogue.

Beginning with the second episode, the writer needs a "lead-in." A lead-in is a summary of the basic situation and of the previous episode. The script also needs a "lead out." This is the aforementioned cliff hanger, where the narrator sets up suspense by asking what will happen to the characters in the precarious situation in which they are left until the next episode. The most intense cliff hanger should be that at the end of the Friday episode, for the weekend break needs that much more suspense to keep the audience interested.

> ● *Examine the following excerpts — the beginning and the ending — of a Monday episode of "The Brighter Day." Note how the writer has incorporated the lead-in material as part of the exposition of the play itself. Note, too, how the end of the script moves in a rising conflict toward a peak, but ends in time to keep the viewer in suspense until the next episode. What other elements pertaining to the writing of the soap opera can you find in these excerpts?*

THE BRIGHTER DAY

(FADE IN:)

(THE DENNIS LIVING ROOM - MORNING)

(THE TIME IS A DAY AFTER THE PREVIOUS SCRIPT, #3370.)

(AT THE OPENING, RICHARD COMES DOWN THE STAIRWAY, CARRYING HIS ATTACHE CASE. AT THE SAME TIME, EMILY COMES ON FROM THE GARDEN CARRYING AN ARMFUL OF CUT FLOWERS OF VARIOUS SORTS.)

        EMILY

Richard ... where are you rushing so early in the morning?

        RICHARD

My office at the University. There's a student coming in for an early counseling session.

        EMILY

A pity your own brother won't give your opinions the same respect as do complete strangers . . .

        RICHARD

(WITH A WRY SMILE)
Isn't that to be expected . . . A man — they say — is no hero to his own family.

(EMILY GOES TO HIM, SMILING FONDLY)

EMILY

Oh you're a hero to us — believe me.
(SHE KISSES HIM)
With just that one exception.

RICHARD

Walter's entitled to go his own way —

EMILY

His own way? Walter's been ten times around the
world . . . and a hundred times on his way to fame
and fortune . . . And where has it all led him?

RICHARD

Emily —

EMILY

Right back to living on his brother and sister . . .

RICHARD

Just because he is staying here a few days as our guest . . .

EMILY

An uninvited guest — remember! And probably a permanent one.

RICHARD

(SMILES)
If that's what's worrying you, relax. You know that nothing
can keep Walter nailed down in any one place for long.

(EMILY CASTS A BALEFUL GLANCE UP THE STAIRWAY.)

EMILY

I don't suppose he shows the faintest signs of getting up from bed.

RICHARD

Sooner or later, when he gets hungry enough to want his breakfast —

EMILY

Oh yes . . . that was my theory too. An hour ago I marched upstairs and
into the guest room with a breakfast tray. Do you think that got Walter
up from bed? Not on your life? Ten minutes later he shouted for me
to bring him a second pot of coffee . . . and more toast.

(RICHARD LAUGHS)

RICHARD

Walter the Magnificent . . . You'll admit at least that Walter has the
grand style . . .

EMILY

Oh yes . . . the grand style . . . and what else?

(RICHARD GLANCES AT HIS WATCH AND STARTS
TOWARD THE FRONT DOOR.)

RICHARD

Excuse me . . . I'm going to be late.

EMILY

I know I seem like an everlasting scold when it comes to Walter . . .

RICHARD

Let's just say that you're a little too concerned about him.

EMILY

Has he given you the slightest indication of whether he has any
kind of job in mind . . . or business . . . or any way of making his living?

RICHARD

(EVASIVELY)
Well, from what I gather, he's just wound up one business connection . . .

EMILY

Went bankrupt again . . . or was fired?

RICHARD

(AVOIDING AN ANSWER)
. . . and hopes very soon to start something new . . . right here in this area . . .

EMILY

That's what he told you?

RICHARD

Generally speaking . . .

EMILY

(WITH A SIGH)
Yes . . . generally speaking . . . which is the way Walter has always gone
through life — generally speaking. And if there were money to be made
from castles in Spain, he'd be one of the richest men alive.

* * *

RICHARD

(SHAKING HIS HEAD)
Walter, you're refusing to face reality.

WALTER

Anybody can see —

RICHARD

The reality is that with your business record, nobody
is going to be in a hurry to recommend you for any new business deal.

276

WALTER

(SHAKING HIS HEAD)
Wrong. I'm 'way ahead of you on that.

RICHARD

As a simple matter of trust and confidence —

WALTER

The fact that I'm your brother . . . and that Yvonne recommended
me so highly to this fellow Jouvet —

RICHARD

He'll accept you on just that basis . . . ?

WALTER

He said it's all the reference he needs . . .

(RICHARD STARES AT HIM IN STUNNED SILENCE)

WALTER (CONT'D)

And now it's all set . . .

RICHARD

You deliberately let Yvonne get involved in all this . . . ?

WALTER

I'm on my way. This time I can't miss.

RICHARD

I can't tell you how shocked I am . . . I'm sure that if Yvonne
had any idea of your bankruptcy troubles —

WALTER

Why ruin what may be my last chance?

(WITH THIS, THERE IS A KNOCK AT THE DOOR)

Because the fact is, Richard —

RICHARD

(CALLING TOWARD THE DOOR)
Yes . . . ?

YVONNE

(THROUGH DOOR)
It's me, Richard . . .

RICHARD

Just a moment, please, Yvonne . . .

YVONNE

(THROUGH DOOR)
You're expecting me for lunch, I thought . . .

WALTER

(HASTILY)
Yes . . . I was just about to tell you about that . . . My idea . . .

RICHARD

What . . . ?

WALTER

. . . that we celebrate the deal . . . my new start . . . by all
going out to lunch together . . .

(AGAIN THERE IS A KNOCK)

YVONNE

(THROUGH DOOR)
Richard?

(WALTER CLUTCHES RICHARD TENSELY BY THE ARM)

WALTER

Richard, you're not going to spoil everything . . . You're not
going to rob me of my last chance . . .

(MUSIC UP)

(FADE)

(COMMERCIAL)

Written by David Davidson; Proctor & Gamble Productions, Inc.; From Program Broadcast
on the CBS Television Network.

Perhaps the best way to learn how to write the soap opera is to spend
several weeks listening to and watching the programs on the air. In summary:
Don't be artistic. The protagonists should be simple, sympathetic characters with whom the audience can easily identify. The main characters should
be faced with obvious, but almost insurmountable trouble. The good people
should be good people, the bad people should be bad people. The dialogue,
characterization and situation are directed at the epitomy of the mass audience. All must be sentimental. All must be obvious. All must be simple.
Don't be intellectual. The audience wants emotion, not ideas. Platitudes
usually comprise the whole of soap opera thinking. If you do want to say
anything, if you do believe you can use the soap opera to raise the cultural
level of the listening audience (and the soap opera may very well be one of
the most powerful forces within the mass media for the potential accomplishment of something of value), present your ideas subtly. Disguise them. Make
them come from the mouths of characters who are very sympathetic, who are
the kinds of characters who usually give good advice. Make your philosophy
homey and friendly, and then cross your fingers and hope for the best.

The Television Play on Film and Tape

The basic techniques for writing a good play are applicable to whatever
production form the television drama takes. As the 1960's progressed, more and

more TV plays were filmed, until most television drama was produced "Hollywood-style." Some plays put on tape were produced "New York-style" — essentially live productions, with continuous action, in sequence, for transmission at a later time. Other plays put on tape combined both techniques: essentially live action, but taped out of sequence and later edited.

The writing approaches for each of these styles are affected by common considerations. The play is being produced for viewing on the small screen, with the same time restrictions, for the same audience and under the same limitations of subject matter. Only the technical elements, the use of mechanical and electronic devices, differ. The plot structure and creation of characters and dialogue are similar. The writer is still limited by the amount of material he can put on the screen at any one time. In live-type tape, edited-tape, and film presentation the visual elements are more important than the aural. In each the close-up remains the most important shot.

The filmed approach does offer some advantages to the director, although it takes much of the creative responsibility away from the writer. Live-type television is continuous, and once the production is under way the script cannot be changed deliberately. Filmed and taped television permits editing, and even after the script is shot, the director can virtually rewrite the entire play in the editing room.

The filmed play permits a looser unity of time and place than does the live-type. The filmed play has a break at each cut or other transition. That is, each sequence may last two seconds or two minutes. Between sequences the director can change sets, costumes, makeup, reset lights and cameras, and even reorient the actors. The action itself may seem to be jerky. The actual sequences are shorter than in live-type TV because they are shot separately. However, a number of sequences may be edited into one smooth-flowing scene. It is more difficult to achieve a clear and concrete unity of impression in the filmed play than in the continuous-action or semi-continuous-action taped play.

The filmed play and, to a degree, the edited-taped play permit outdoor sequences, on-location scenes, chase sequences not possible in the studio, scenic exteriors and so forth. The filmed and taped play permit an expansion of the setting and the integration of many more and a greater variety of sets than does the live-type play. With more settings and background, and the showing of a sequence for only a few seconds, if desirable, the writer of the filmed or taped play can bring in exposition and background easier than can the writer of the live play. Several fragments of incidents and backgrounds can establish exposition and, sometimes, preparation much better than can one long, continuous scene when the entire play is only a half-hour or an hour long.

The filming or taping of a play for television also permits the writer to include sequences which might be extremely difficult for the actor and director if done live. The use of movie techniques, the retaking of shots until the sequence is perfect, and the editing of the material after it is shot avoid the possibility of a scene not being technically perfect.

At the same time, the filmed play suffers from its advantages. The lack of live, continuous performance often results in mechanical and contrived writing. Rarely has television produced a good filmed play that has created the stimulation of the good live play or continuous-action taped play.

The filmed play requires a slightly different form in writing, as well as different techniques, than does the live or taped play. Instead of writing scenes, the writer writes shots. Each shot is set in terms of a picture rather than in terms of character action, although the latter should be the motivating factor. The writer states the place, such as INTERIOR or EXTERIOR, and the shot, such as FULL SHOT or CLOSE-UP. He also describes the setting, states the characters' physical relationships to the set and to each other, and then presents the dialogue for that shot. The dialogue may be only one speech long. For example, the description may read:

> 1   INT. JOE'S LIVING ROOM--JOE AND
> MABEL are seated on the couch,
> quarreling. FULL SHOT Joe and
> Mabel.
>
> JOE
> This is the end, Mabel, do
> you hear? This is the end.
>
> 2   CLOSE-UP--MABEL
>
> MABEL
> I hear, Joe. I hear.

The individual shots are numbered in consecutive order so the director easily may pick out any sequence he desires for initial shooting (the filmed play is not shot in chronological order), retakes or editing.

● *Examine the following excerpts from a script of the "Have Gun, Will Travel" program. Although "Have Gun, Will Travel" is now seen only in reruns, it is a classic of its type, and is an excellent example of quality writing for the filmed television series. 1) Note the numbering of shots and the specific descriptions of camera angles, distances, transitions, and visual setting and action. 2) Look for evidences of frequent cutting and short sequences, usual in film scripts, especially through shots 4-7 and 39-43A. The usual Western would have a great number of exterior sequences, with the cutting from outdoor shot to outdoor shot as frequent as the cutting in this script between interior shots. 3) There are not so many transitions and changes of place and time in this script as one might find in the more mundane Western. Nevertheless, note the ease of transitions where called for, specifically in shots 17-18, 25-26, 29-30, and 55-56. 4) Pay special attention to shots 14 and 38. The continuity here and in several other comparatively long sequences is similar to that found in the live-type TV play. The writing in this series frequently reflects other characteristics of the good live play, particularly the character-oriented and motivated development of the story and action. 5) Compare your analyses of items 1 through 4 with the probable treatment of these elements if the same basic script were to be rewritten for live-type production. 6) Note that this script is written in what is called the "Hollywood" format — the format for the film script. The script beginning on page 299 is written in the television two-column form.*

FADE IN:

1.   EXT. SAN FRANCISCO - ESTABLISHING STOCK - NIGHT   1.

                                                   DISSOLVE TO:

2.   INT. FULL SHOT - CARLTON LOBBY - NIGHT   2.

The usual lobby crowd. Paladin appears as from outside, his hat in his hand, a newspaper under his arm. HEY BOY, carrying a tray appears at right from the dining room and they cross toward the stairs.

3.   MED. SHOT - THE STAIRS   3.

As they meet. Hey Boy does a take that almost slips the tray from his grasp. Paladin takes in his dismay.

> PALADIN
> Hey Boy.

> HEY BOY
> He ordered black-eyed peas, brussel
> sprouts, hominy grits and chili!

Paladin peeks under the silver covers and is appalled.

> PALADIN
> He must have a copper stomach . . .

> HEY BOY
> You know soon enough; he is in your room.

> PALADIN
> He? Who?

> HEY BOY
> Little man say you expect him . . .

Paladin gives a start and peeks under the silver covers again as though the secret guest's identity were to be discovered under them.

> HEY BOY (CONT'D)
> . . . he had your card . . .

Paladin turns in horror and sprints up the stairs.
Hey Boy begins to follow and we . . .

                                               DISSOLVE TO:

4.   OMITTED.   4.

5.   INT. PALADIN'S BEDROOM   5.

Featuring his ornate bed. MONK, in Sybaritic if rancid splendor, sprawls in the middle of Paladin's satin bed spread. He is surrounded by food and nibbles daintily from a kumquat and a whole apple pie. CAMERA MOVES IN to show a plate of oysters precariously askew at his elbow. He is as happily oblivious as ever and is clad as when he was last seen. Putting aside his other food, he plucks up an oyster and pokes and studies it at length. He doesn't quite trust the thing but finally plops it into his mouth. He stiffens, his eyes widen, he half rises and looks as if he might become sick.

6.   MED. SHOT - THE ROOM DOOR - MONK POV   6.

As it opens and Paladin steps inside, followed by Hey Boy. He gives an anguished, outraged, indignant roar and stops short.

MED. CLOSE SHOT - MONK

He starts to his feet with his most engaging smile.

                         MONK
               Lotsa durned fools woulda swallered
               that. Don't guess I like oysters.
                    (brightly)
               Hidey, Mister Palydine! Set down!
               Care for a kumquat?

                         * * *

10.   EXT. BORDELLIS - NIGHT   10.

Paladin and Monk approach it down the sidewalk. It has an ornate gold door
but no other particular sign it is more than another of the houses in this
street, which is as close to old time Barbary Coast as we can get.

                         MONK
               Be careful now . . .

The door opens, and a bouncer, POWER, looks down. He is not glad to see
Monk.

                         MONK
               He split the inside of my mouth yesterday.

Power looks away from him to Paladin, deliberately ignoring him.

                         POWER
               Come in sir . . . Don't mind him.

                         PALADIN
               He is with me.

                         POWER
               He ain't welcome . . .

                         MONK
               I 'bout decided to fire you . . .

                         PALADIN
               Monk.

Monk falls silent.

                         PALADIN (CONT'D)
                    (to Power)
               We're here to see Augusta.

                         POWER
               So? She don't want to see you.

                         PALADIN
               Suppose you let her decide?

Power now turns his full attention on Paladin. He is menace incarnate.

                         POWER
               And who are you?

Paladin delivers the card.

11.   INSERT - THE CARD   11.

Music sting.

282

12. BACK TO SHOT   12.

As Power flips it into the street.

                            POWER
           And you go after it.

Paladin grapples with him, and swings him around into the street with superior
science and strength. He grabs Monk and shooshes him inside. He follows quickly.
Power stumbles in the muddy street trying to catch his balance.

13. INT. BORDELLIS - NIGHT   13.

As Paladin and Monk enter and look around. It is ornate, gorgeous, full of
elegant looking men and women. Some dance, some gamble. A string
quartet plays. This is San Francisco high life, not frontier style.

                            MONK
           Heeeee.....YAH!

The music, the dancing, the gambling, the talk all stop as though Monk had hit
the switch. In the silence everyone turns to see:

14. TWO SHOT - PALADIN AND MONK   14.

Paladin looks acutely pained. Monk looks around with purest pleasure,
speaking loud enough to reach the farthest corners of the room.

                            MONK
           I seen bout a hundred women in my life,
           and that one is the purtiest I ever seen.

He refers to Augusta, a tall, elegantly dressed woman of Monk's age, and
under the dress and the makeup and the affected San Francisco manners,
basically as earthy and tough as he. She is walking through the frozen
tableau of the dancers towards them. She stops, making a small signal
that brings BOUNCERS out of the woodwork.

                            AUGUSTA
                       (to Paladin)
           Mister, you ought to be ashamed of the company you keep.
                       (to Monk)
           Out.

                            PALADIN
           Madam, I think you should talk to him. Under
           his rough hewn exterior beats a heart of sweet
           corn. And he owns a half share in your
           establishment.

Power appears in the door behind them. Dirty, ready for revenge.

                            AUGUSTA

           Who says — his Uncle Mort?
           Listen, when I say play, the orchestra plays.

The orchestra catches this and begins to play as though making up for lost time.

                         AUGUSTA (CONT'D)
           When I say, sing and dance and enjoy yourselves,
           my friends enjoy.

The customers quickly resume, dancing, playing, drinking.

                         AUGUSTA (CONT'D)
           That's the way it was when Mort was alive, and it's
           the way it is now he's dead. Throw 'em out.

This to Power.

                              283

                              MONK
                Ma'am, it ain't right nobody as purty as you should
                see what I'm gonna do to him.

He is grabbed from behind and the sides and thrown to Power who throws
him out the door. They turn now to Paladin, a little more warily.

                              AUGUSTA
                No use him hirin' a lawyer or
                whatever you are. He don't fit in here . . .

Monk fires himself like a small projectile through the door and all hell
breaks loose between him and the bouncers for another ten seconds before
he disappears bodily out the door again.

                              AUGUSTA
                . . . and these men will just kill him if he keeps on trying.

Monk darts back in for a last try, this time carrying his pepperbox at the
ready. He catches the bouncers off guard this time, and it is Paladin who
has to step in and disarm him. The pepperbox erupts weakly, spewing
sparks and smoke. In the shambles around the door, of broken tables and
torn plush drapery, Paladin regards Monk sadly.

                              PALADIN
                Perhaps you're right. He doesn't fit in here.

He releases Monk who instantly goes for Power and is thrown out for the
last time. Paladin bows to Augusta who bows back.

                              AUGUSTA
                You're welcome anytime. By yourself.

Paladin nods, glares at Power and exits. The life in the establishment
picks up again.

15.   EXT. BORDELLIS - NIGHT   15.

The street. Monk is picking himself up out of the mud puddles as Paladin
descends the steps.

                              MONK
                Now, if that ain't the most stupid, onreasonable,
                no-good, purtiest woman you ever saw . . .

Monk disgustedly grabs a handful of mud and flings it down in disgust.

16.   CLOSE - PALADIN   16.

As he regards Monk and resignedly begins helping him up. He is making
up his mind. With the hook in his cane he draws Monk up into a TWO SHOT.

                              PALADIN
                Come on. You smell like a cross between cooked
                cabbage and a wet Airedale!

Paladin drags a squealing Monk out of the mudhole and off down the street
by the ear, holding him at arm's length.

                                              DISSOLVE TO:

17.   INT. FULL SHOT - PALADIN BATHROOM - NIGHT   17.

An old fashioned bathtub has been hauled in and filled with warm water.
A grim, scowling Monk regards it. Steam arises and Hey Boy and Paladin
try industriously to disrobe a loudly recalcitrant Monk who is as shy as
a Junior High School girl at her first gym. It is a fight every inch of the
way but they get Monk's coat off only after Paladin is ready to flatten him.
They finally get his coat off to reveal his union suit. The right shoulder
and sleeve are intact but the other top half has been torn off — except for
the sleeve on the left arm which he wears. It is tied to the rest of the
garment with a string tied across the collarbone. As a gesture towards
going along, Monk haughtily unties the bow of the string holding up the left
sleeve. It drops.

                              PALADIN
                  Get in that tub.

                              MONK
                  I will not!

Paladin moves in on him.

                                                    LAP DISSOLVE TO:

18.   MED. CLOSE SHOT - MONK IN TUB   18.

But not too happy. He begins to like the idea. . . .

                              * * *

25.   CLOSER ON MONK - ANGLE HOLDING PALADIN   25.

Paladin watches not without sympathy, Monk's rather forlorn face. The
men work, the barber cutting and the tailor measuring and cutting, etc.

                                                    LAP DISSOLVE TO:

26.   INT. MED. SHOT - PALADIN'S ROOM   26.

The attendants stand by, each beaming at his own contribution to the New
Monk who subjects himself to critical admiration in front of the mirror.
He seems to have grown several inches taller and takes several views.

                              MONK
                  I ain't a bad lookin' feller —
                  I get duded up.

Paladin goes to join him, squinting at his handiwork. Behold! It is very
good. Paladin signals and the retinue quietly exits.

                              PALADIN
                  How is that?

                              MONK
                  It's better than a poke in the eye with a sharp stob.
                       (worriedly pushes hair)
                  Let's take a little more off the top.

27.   MED. SHOT - THE MIRROR   27.

Monk and Paladin reflected in it.

Monk proudly fluffs the frilled shirt front and scrutinizes the fancy cuffs.
He is seriously delighted like a child, with his first long pants. He checks
his new grandeur against Paladin's. He is worried about the sleeves, and
crosses to Paladin, where he critically compares his sleeves with his
model's.

                              285

MONK
Could we shorten these sleeves
'bout a hen's tooth? I always like
to show a leetle more cuff.

PALADIN
You never even had a shirt before!

Paladin goes o.s. and comes back to hand Monk hat, gloves and stock.

PALADIN
Come on, it's late.

Paladin reaches for his watch in his vest pocket but it is gone and he frisks
himself looking for it. He regards Monk's image in the mirror and sighs
deeply. He spots it.

28.   CLOSE SHOT - MONK'S VEST   28.

Paladin's watch fob is slung between the pockets. Paladin's hand comes
on to snatch it out.

29.   TWO SHOT - PALADIN AND MONK   29.

Paladin glares accusingly and swings the watch a moment before restoring
it to his own pocket. Disappointed Monk.

MONK
It's purty.

PALADIN
Monk. How do you feel?

MONK
Like downtown, only not so crowded.

PALADIN
You think you can make an entrance to Bordellis
without causing a scandal?

MONK
Bordellis!

He whips out the pepperbox, and Paladin disarms almost by automatic reflex.

PALADIN
Leave that thing here. We're doing this my way.

DISSOLVE TO:

30.   EXT. FULL SHOT - THE STREET - NIGHT   30.

As Paladin and Monk make their way along it.

31.   MED. SHOT - MONK AND PALADIN   31.

As they APPROACH CAMERA. A HORSE IS HEARD approaching from o.s. and
as it passes there is a splash and Monk and Paladin both are forced to jump
out of the way to avoid being drenched. Monk's veneer of good manners abruptly
vanishes.

MONK
You clobber footed, hominy headed horn toad!

PALADIN
Monk!

286

MONK
(after rider)
I'll stomp your eyeballs!

Paladin grabs him. Monk sobers.

PALADIN
You say you're a good mimic —
then start imitating me.

Monk opens his mouth to speak.

PALADIN (CONT'D)
Imitate me keeping my mouth shut.

Monk clamps his mouth shut with determination as they proceed as before.
Paladin points ahead and nods, indicating the site is Bordelli's.

32.   EXT. STREET - FRONT OF BORDELLI'S - NIGHT - DOLLY SHOT   32.

Monk and Paladin move down the sidewalk towards the door which opens,
and two ladies emerge on a gust of giggles and come down the steps,
turning up the street towards Monk and Paladin. As they pass, Paladin
with the automatic instinct of a gentleman, tips his hat. Monk glances
up at him, watches the gesture, and tips his hat, although by this time
the girls are past and out of sight. They turn up the steps and Paladin
raps on the door.

33.   CLOSE - DOOR   33.

It opens and Power glares at Paladin, and then to Monk. He stares at him
suspiciously and then back into Paladin's blandly smiling face.

PALADIN
I liked it here so well I decided to come back.

Power looks Monk up and down, and decides it's impossible. He swings
the door open and nods them in.

34.   INT. BORDELLI'S - NIGHT   34.

It is as before. Music, dance, low murmur of voices. At the door a girl
takes Paladin's hat and stick and reaches for Monk's. He is absorbed in
the spectacle and wrestles momentarily when she grabs for his possessions.
He is about to let her have it when Paladin's look intercepts his and he
subsides. She looks at him a little oddly and departs.

35.   CLOSE - PALADIN AND MONK   35.

MONK
Kinda got out of the habit of trusting this place.

Paladin reminds of silence and Monk straightens up. Power is behind still
watching. They cross now, following one of the bouncers (who double as
waiters) to a table.

36.   NEW ANGLE - THE TABLE   36.

It adjoins the dance floor. They are seated. Monk is making new and
wonderful discoveries in everything. He keeps checking his behavior
against Paladin's and trying to simulate his savoir-faire. It comes out
a parody of stuffy self-consciousness.

PALADIN
(to the waiter)
A bottle of Dom Perignon.

287

Monk leans close to whisper.

>   MONK
>   Kin I get supper? I had dinner at breakfast.

>   PALADIN
>   And some white whiskey for my friend.

The waiter starts to go.

>   PALADIN (CONT'D)
>   And will you ask the owner if she will join us?

The waiter nods and departs.

>   PALADIN (CONT'D)
>   Let me have the paper. Now — as soon as I've
>   convinced Augusta you're housebroken I'm
>   leaving — and you're on your own.

But Monk isn't listening. He sees Augusta.

>   MONK
>   Oh, Lordy, looky at her!
>   (a trifle wistfully)
>   Am I doin' all right?

>   PALADIN
>   You're talking. Here she comes . . .

As they prepare themselves for the test.

37.   TWO SHOT - POWER AND WAITER   37.

The waiter is on his way to the kitchen. Power catches him by the arm.

>   POWER
>   You take the door.

He takes the waiter's tray and towel. The waiter shrugs. Power advances
determinedly toward the table.

38.   THE TABLE   38.

As Augusta stands over them. She grins at Paladin.

>   AUGUSTA
>   Mr. Paladin.

>   PALADIN
>   Madam. Will you join us?

She looks at Monk, smiles and begins to sit down.

>   AUGUSTA
>   What'd you order?

>   PALADIN
>   Dom Perignon. And a white whiskey.

Half way down into her seat she looks aside at Monk and puts together
white whiskey with the vaguely familiar profile. She freezes. Power
arrives on the scene watching. Monk grins at her hopefully, then his
grin fades and he squirms uncomfortably.

                              MONK
            Ye better set, Ma'am, or you'll stick that way.

Augusta stands back up.

                             AUGUSTA
                            (to Paladin)
             I don't believe it.

                             PALADIN
             It is true; a miracle of modern science and
             American plumbing. Please sit.

She sits and gasps to Power.

                             AUGUSTA
             You better bring me a white whiskey.

Power waits, staring at Monk. Paladin casts him a glance.

                             PALADIN
             We're waiting.

Power goes, but we feel his sullen rebellion growing.

                              MONK
             Well, what's his trouble?

                             PALADIN
             Monk . . .
                        (cautions for silence)
             . . . still it's a good question.

                             AUGUSTA
             Woman alone, every musclebound clown with
             ambition thinks he can swindle or bully or just
             plain cheat her. I been aiming to fire him, and
             I just might get around to it. Now you.

She means Monk. He snaps to alertness like a twelve year old for the
teacher.

                             AUGUSTA
             What's your game?

                             PALADIN
             It's not a game. Your partner left him his interest.

                             AUGUSTA
             What makes you think so?

Paladin lays out the paper on the table. She glances at it, reads it and
looks at Monk. She rather craftily reaches for the paper, but Paladin
draws it back, out of reach.

                        AUGUSTA (CONT'D)
             That don't mean a thing.

                             PALADIN
             Is it Mort's handwriting?

                             AUGUSTA
             What if it is? You think I'm takin' in some scruffy
             little crook looks like he just finished a wrestling
             match in a cowlot?

                               289

PALADIN
He could learn to behave himself.

AUGUSTA
Mister, I clawed my way into this place, and I made
it into somethin' I'm proud of, that'll keep me in my
old age so nobody can put me down. Mort was like an
extra mortgage on the place, and about as good for
business as a bagful of rattlesnakes. What do I want
takin' care of him?

Power has arrived back and stands ready for the impending ejection.
Monk has been staring at her throughout this. His voice comes very
small and subdued now.

MONK
I can sing, fer the folks.

AUGUSTA
Sing!

She turns to Paladin, and we do not see Monk slip away from the table.
Power looms over them.

AUGUSTA (CONT'D)
I'll tell you somethin' Mister. That paper don't mean
a thing, and Power here is gonna see to it it don't.

Monk's song comes from o.s. like a bell. They stop and turn, astonished.

39.   FULL SHOT - MONK   39.

His foot on a chair, a guitar borrowed from the orchestra in his arms, he
sings, obviously to Augusta. We play the song, with Augusta growing more
and more interested, the patrons listening with pleasure, Power watching
Augusta with growing anger. Toward the end of the song Paladin quietly
rises. He takes a last look at:

40.   CLOSE - AUGUSTA   40.

Transported.

41.   BACK TO PALADIN   41.

He drops money on the table, and Monk's paper on top of it. He nods
to Monk.

42.   CLOSE - MONK   42.

Singing, winking broadly at Paladin. A man in control of his fate.

43.   BACK TO THE TABLE   43.

Paladin quietly leaves. DOLLY IN TO POWER . . . He leans over and
picks up the paper and examines it with interest. The last lines of the
song play out. SPLATTER OF APPLAUSE UP.

43A.   TWO SHOT - MONK & AUGUSTA   43A.

As Monk crosses into it, blushingly taking bows. Augusta greets him and
they turn.

AUGUSTA
(grudgingly)
You're all right.

Power tears up the paper.

MONK
Hey thar, what're you doin' with that paper . . .

He reaches toward Power, who belts him, and Monk swings the guitar
full in Power's face. Augusta screams, the bouncers charge out, the
patrons scream, and furniture splinters. It is the same old disastrous
scene all over again, and Monk is ejected by Power . . .

* * *

55. CLOSE SHOT - PALADIN   55.

CAMERA MOVES with Paladin as he goes to a secret compartment in his
bureau and removes his trail gun which he straps on with easy familiarity.
He checks the chamber of his gun to satisfaction and holsters it.

PALADIN
Monk, the most you can do is stay out of the way.
Everyone on this earth is equipped to handle certain,
specific problems. This is in my domain.

Paladin fumbles for his watch but it is gone. He is concerned for an instant
only. He fixes Monk with a flat glance, extends his hand and snaps his fingers.
Monk absently hands over his watch. Paladin pockets it.

DISSOLVE TO:

56. EXT. STREET IN FRONT OF BORDELLI'S - NIGHT   56.

The street is deserted as Paladin takes his stand and calls out.

PALADIN
It's time, Power! I'm here!

He looks around for a trap but a muffled call comes from o.s. in the house.

POWER
I'm coming out, Paladin!

Paladin settles his trail holster and faces the door of the place. Power comes
out, followed by the two others. All are armed. Power takes his place facing
Paladin with his assistant heavies slightly off to one side in back of him.

57. CLOSE SHOT - PALADIN   57.

He is plainly worried at the bad odds.

PALADIN
Power, I'm looking at you! Not that gang!

POWER (O.S.)
This is a duel. We can both have seconds.

PALADIN
You have a third and a fourth!

POWER
And you have three or four seconds to raise your
army!

291

58. FULL SHOT - THE STREET   58.

From the shadows at one side, Monk comes broiling into the street to take
his place behind and aside Paladin.

                              MONK
                        (yells)
                    He's got one!

Paladin turns to regard him in shock and surprise.

59. TWO SHOT - MONK AND PALADIN   59.

Monk has redeemed his pepperbox. Paladin is not pleased to see him.

                              PALADIN
                    Monk! Get out of here!

Paladin affords him only a cursory glance, not wanting to take his eyes off
the competition. Nor does Monk. Both are ready for an immediate draw.

                              MONK
                    I got a right to kill the ones you miss!

Paladin can't palaver further. He would prefer not to have Monk as an ally
but the opposition is even less appetizing.

60. FULL SHOT - THE AREA   60.

                              POWER
                    Lotta talk here. Paladin.

                              PALADIN
                    Any time you want to die, pull your gun.

Power draws and Paladin beats him. Power falls dead, and Paladin begins
to turn to face the others.

61. FULL SHOT - ANOTHER ANGLE   61.

A bullet from a heavy sings past Paladin's head and he hits the deck.
Monk's pepperbox is out and he charges forward with a roar. He pulls
the triggers and there is something of a conflagration. The minor
explosion hurls him backward to rest in his usual mud puddle.

62. MED. SHOT - THE TWO HEAVIES   62.

They fall in unison, crumpling into each other like melting snowmen.

63. MED. SHOT - PALADIN   63.

It takes a moment for him to realize it is all over and CAMERA PANS
him to Monk who sits in the puddle wringing his numbed hand and sucking
his burned fingers.

                              PALADIN
                    Are you all right?

                              MONK
                        (nods)
                    Man! That gun smarts! They all dead?

                              PALADIN
                    Yes. All ten of those barrels went off at the same
                    time. You laid down a barrage that . . .

MONK
(disappointed)
All went off at the same time? Shucks, I thought
I got 'em all with one shot.

They both turn as they hear an o.s. cry from Augusta.

AUGUSTA
Monk!

She comes on frame, all concern for Monk.

Augusta leans over Monk protectively.

PALADIN
Monk.

MONK
What?

PALADIN
The gun. You can't be trusted with it.

AUGUSTA
Honey, you don't need it.

Monk looks at her, aghast and delighted. He hands the pepperbox to Paladin.

PALADIN
Augusta, you have what every woman should have:
a man she can train almost from scratch.

MONK
And that's one step after itch!

64.   CLOSE - PALADIN   64.

Monk's cornball humor revolts him, but he can't help a smile at them.

PALADIN
Good night, young lovers.

He bows and exits.

65.   SHOT WIDENS TO A FULLSHOT OF THE DESERTED STREET   65.

The two lovers kneel in their mud puddle, as Paladin walks up the street
whistling the air of Monk's gay song.

FADE OUT

THE END

Script written by Jay Simms for the CBS Television Network program HAVE GUN,
WILL TRAVEL.

The Adaptation

Adapting a short story, novel or play to television is in some respects more difficult than creating an original. The greatest problem is in getting away from the original work. When adapting a short story or novel, the writer is in danger of attempting to follow the original's action sequence and even the dialogue, which are usually undramatic, repetitious and introspective when compared with the heightened and condensed structure and dialogue of a play. The author of a prose work can describe people, explain their feelings and clarify the situations, motivations and even the action through examples or illustrations. The playwright cannot do this. He can *explain nothing;* he must *show everything*. The adapter of the short story or novel must therefore get away from the craft of the original and create anew, using as a base the essence of the theme, background, characters and plot of the original.

It is advisable for the adapter to read the original work enough times to become thoroughly familiar with it, and then lay it aside. There should be no need to take it up again. From his thorough knowledge of the material, the adapter should be able to create the radio or television script. From the short story or novel the adapter takes only the elements of character, plot, theme and background, and maybe a hint of the dialogue style, although non-dramatic dialogue frequently sounds ludicrous when read aloud.

Adapting the stage play is somewhat easier. The adapter has the basic elements of content and construction already at hand. The primary problem is one of condensation. The application of the special characteristics of time, space, audience, subject matter and mechanical and electronic devices, and the rules of dramaturgy for the television play as modified from the dramaturgical rules of the stage play, should result in an effective adaptation.

The adaptation of the stage play has contributed heavily to the dramatic fare on radio and television. The adapter may approach his task from two major viewpoints. On one hand, he may consider the original inviolate and attempt to keep it as intact as possible, cutting and condensing only where necessary to comply with a time limit, and changing the original work only in the most dire emergency. At the opposite pole, the adapter may consider the play a peg on which to hang his own creative ability. He may select the barest essence of the original and write what may be virtually an entire new or different play. The approach of most adapters seems to be somewhere between the two extremes. Many times in the 1960's the adapter of the stage play has attempted to get the essence of the play in scenario form and then, selecting parts of the original that could be used intact, he has rounded out the script with his own original work.

In adapting any form of literature the adapter should retain the original author's intent and the essence of his story. He should retain the basic character motivations and delineations. He should attempt to capture the style, feeling and mood of the original. Over and above all this, however, he should add, subtract, change and modify so that the original work is translated most effectively in terms of the techniques of the television or radio medium. The adapter frequently has to delete some sequences, add scenes, combine two or more sequences into one, transpose scenes, delete and add characters, combine several characters into one, change characterizations, and introduce a narrator.

The writer must choose the approach to adaptation in terms of his own abilities. Some writers are better at working with characters and plots already created. Others are better at working from a basic theme or outline and creating their own characters and plot lines. Writer-adapter Irving Elman has analyzed some of the pitfalls as well as the advantages in the two approaches to adaptation. Mr. Elman has written:

> ". . . The tendency with the first type is for the writer's creative urge, with no outlet through original creation of his own, to use the material he is adapting merely as a point of take-off, from which he attempts to soar to heights of his own. If he happens to be a genius like Shakespeare those heights can be very high indeed. But if he is not a genius, or even as talented as the man whose work he is adapting, instead of soaring to heights, the adaptation may sink to depths below the level of the material he "adapted."
>
> "The second writer, with sufficient outlet for his creativity through his own writing, is less tempted (except by his ego!) to show up the writer whose work he is adapting, proving by his "improvements" on the other man's material how much better a writer he is. But if he genuinely likes and respects the material he is adapting, he will restrain himself to the proper business of an adaptor: translating a work from one medium to another with as much fidelity to the original as possible, making only those changes called for by the requirements of the second medium, trying in the process not to impair or violate the artistry of the original."

The Scenario

The scenario — the detailed outline — should indicate to the writer who has been conscientious in his planning and who knows the rules of dramaturgy whether or not he has a good play. Careful construction and analysis of the scenario can eliminate the bad points in the play and strengthen the good ones. The scenario is also valuable because it is not only a way-station toward the completion of the whole, but a check point which can save exhausting work and valuable time on the actual writing of the play.

The scenario is the same for the television and the radio play. At first, the writer should set down the purpose of the play, its theme, background, characters, basic plot line and type of dialogue. The writer should have before him the case histories of all of his characters. Next, the writer should prepare a plot summary of each projected sequence in chronological order. The character motivations in each scene should be noted. The writer should mark off the elements of exposition and preparation. As the writer develops the plot sequences he should insert important lines of dialogue that emerge from his thinking. The result of the scenario, even in its simplest form, will be at the very least a clarification of all of the structural elements of the play.

In the radio play scenario the writer should note important sound effects and music, as well as changes of place and time. The same is true for the television play scenario, with the additional notation of pertinent mechanical and electronic requirements, plus the listing of the necessary sets.

The serious playwright is urged to go a step further in his outlining, or scenario-making. To make certain that the scenario does truly indicate the strengths and weaknesses of the play, and does give the author an opportunity to correct faults, the writer might use the following approach. Use two columns for the scenario. On the left side put the elements that go into a detailed outline, that is, the action summary, as indicated above. On the right side note the specific functions of each line or action. This right side may be called the technical plot or functional analysis. For example, if a particular piece of business in the plot summary serves as preparation, this would be stated in the analysis on the right. A good scenario should clearly show at which point the conflict is introduced, whether there is sufficient exposition accompanying it, where the complications occur, whether they lead inexorably to a climax, and so forth.

The following *condensed* action summary and functional analysis of Act I of a television play, "With Wings As Eagles," will provide the reader with the basic form for the scenario. The scenario can be much more detailed, with more precise analyses of character elements and dialogue as well as play structure, and can be much longer than space allows here. Following the scenario here, the reader may study the first act of this play, noting how the playwright filled out the various elements indicated in the scenario.

● *Analyze the first act of the script in terms of the principles of dramaturgy for the television play.*

Action Summary	Functional Analysis

(1)

The scene is a Jewish ghetto in an unnamed Near East country. The camera opens on a muddy village street and pans one wood and mud-baked hut to another. A Narrator sets the time and place, describing the poverty of the inhabitants, and how their history shows that though they live in hunger, sickness and oppression, they will find the promised land.[1] The Narrator mentions that few have ever seen an automobile and few would believe that such a thing as an airplane exists.[2] He stresses that in all their ignorance and poverty the people have hope of going to the promised land.[3]

Exposition: the place, time, situation, the background and needs of the people. (Is this exposition too obvious, coming through a narrator in addition to the visual?)

(2)

Preparation: for their eventual departure for Israel and for the climax involving the airplane flight.

(3)

Preparation for the conflict: the stress on the hope of going to a promised land subtly suggests the conflict: will they or will they not be able to go?

(4)

Reb Simcha goes from house to house, calling the people to a meeting. He does so stealthily, undercover.[4]

Exposition: shows the kind of existence of the people: fear, oppression.

(5)

At one house, that of Simon and his son, Aaron, Reb Simcha encounters opposition to the meeting. At Aaron's insistence Simon finally agrees to go. We see that Simon's house is well-furnished, unlike the others.[5]

Preparation: for Simon's opposition, and for Aaron's opposition to his father.

(5)

Exposition: shows another aspect of the village life; someone in comparatively good circumstances.

(6)

We follow Simcha to his own house. The house is fixed up as a small synogogue. He prays: "Please, God. This time, make men's words truth."[6]

Conflict: Without a clear statement yet, we learn something may be in opposition with something else. This is preparation for the revelation of the conflict.

(6)

Exposition: Reb Simcha's environment and profession.

(7)

His daughter, Leah, enters. Reb Simcha complains about his tired feet.[7]

Preparation: The tired feet play a humorous part throughout and are particularly important for comic pathos at the end of the play.

(8)

Leah says she saw some of the people, and that Aaron saw the rest, and that all are coming.[8]

Preparation and complication: We are prepared for Aaron's break with his father through the revelation that he is working on Reb Simcha's side. We are prepared for the relationship between Leah and Aaron in that they are working together. This preparation ties in with the later complications: Aaron vs. his father; Aaron and Leah's love.

(9)

Leah sees her father is worried and gets him to tell what it is. He says he hopes the words he heard from the government representative are true. His people are supposed to leave for the promised land the next morning; but from an open field and without belongings.[9]

Conflict: It is made clear here. The people are supposed to go to the promised land. The doubts set up the conflict: the people against the government powers. Will they or will they not reach the promised land?

297

This worries him. He does not know how they will go, from an open field. "How do we go?" he asks. "We fly, maybe, like a bird?"(10)

He doubts that his people will believe him and be ready, and if they are not ready they will not be able to leave again. He doubts, himself, for such promises have been broken for centuries.(11)

Aaron comes for Leah. Leah and Reb Simcha talk about her intended marriage to Aaron. Leah is worried because his father, Simon, is friendly with the authorities and makes money as the official merchant in the ghetto and may not want to leave. He may prevent Aaron from leaving. Reb Simcha tells Leah that when they go to the promised land, she and Aaron will go hand in hand.(12)

The next scene, in the Police-Military office in the town. Dr. Ezam, the diplomat, arranges with the Lieutenant in charge for transportation and clearance. The Lieutenant does not want the people to go because they are helpful to the town. "They stay in their place," he says. They work for the town's businessmen at low wages.(13)

Dr. Ezam insists that they be permitted to leave, citing a United Nations ruling. The Lieutenant says he will agree to that, but if they are not ready and at the open field on time, he will not let them leave. He says a lot of people in the town would not like them to go. He intimates that they may not leave, anyway. They verbally fence with the political, moral and practical considerations.(14)

The next sequence is in Simon and Aaron's house, where Simon and Aaron argue. Aaron is disturbed because his father cooperates with the authorities. Simon explains that he must do it to live well and to keep his promise to Aaron's dead mother that he would provide for him. Simon doesn't want to go to the meeting, fearing trouble from the authorities. Simon also wants his son not to see Leah again. They argue bitterly, and Simon decides to go to the meeting to stop Reb Simcha's foolish plans.(15)

(10)
Preparation: Again, the reference to flying, preparing the audience for the climax.

(11)
Preparation for complication: the dissension among the people themselves, which might prevent them from achieving their goal, is foreshadowed here.

(6-11)
In the revelation of Leah's and Reb Simcha's actions, we get their characterizations.

(12)
Preparation for complication: Will Simon stop Aaron and Leah: will this result in a delay or complete betrayal of all of the people?

(12)
Exposition: Simon's background and profession is revealed more clearly.

(12)
Reb Simcha's need to assure Leah prepares the audience for trouble in this respect.

(13)
Exposition: We see the attitude of the officials toward these people and the people's place in the community.

(13)
Preparation: We are prepared for the attempt of the town to keep them from going; the motivation: cheap labor.

(14)
Preparation for complication: It is clear that the Lieutenant will try to stop the departure.

(13-14)
The discussion and action reveal character.

(15)
Complication: The conflict is complicated by Simon's avowal to stop the proposed exodus, to fight Reb Simcha. It is further complicated by the avowed intention to step between Leah and Aaron. The rising action, moving toward an inevitable clash, is apparent.

(15)
Exposition: We have further understanding about Simon and Aaron's background and motivations.

(15)
Preparation: Simon's reasons for what
he does are understandable, if not
acceptable, and we see he is not a one-
dimensional tyrant, thus preparing the
audience for his actions at the end of
the play.

(15)
The sequence is character-delineating.

(16)
Complication: Another block in the way
of the people's exodus, thus heightening
the conflict.

The next sequence is in the Lieutenant's
office. The Lieutenant makes plans with
one of the town's merchants, Rasin, to
stop the departure. They decide to detain
one of the villagers. "They're a thick
people. If one were detained they
wouldn't leave without him." Because of
Dr. Ezam, they look for legal grounds
for detention, such as one of the villagers
"leaving" the ghetto without permission.(16)

(16)
Preparation: We learn what the
probable trick will be for detention and
for stopping the departure.

WITH WINGS AS EAGLES

ACT I

Open FS Map of Middle East

NARRATOR (VOICE OVER)

This is a map of the Middle East: Egypt,
Syria, Iraq, Jordan, Israel. Of Arabs and
Jews. Of cities and deserts, of camels
and motor cars, of hopes and fears, but
mostly of people. This is the city of
Mabbam. In what country? It doesn't
matter. Like in many other of these towns
outside of Israel there are small Jewish
populations. Hebrew might be a better
term, for these people are the direct
descendents of Isaiah and Abraham, those
who were led by Moses through the wilder-
ness to the promised land, who fell by the
waysides. The waysides grew into
sections and streets . . .

Pan across map, picking no special spot,
dolly in, dissolve to a miniature of a
small city, several new white buildings
and off, at one side, a dingy, dirty-
looking section, with mud huts and shacks.

Dolly in closer to the miniature of the
town, showing the street of the mud huts
and shacks.

. . . like that one. Aviv Street, it's called.
Aviv means hope. That is about all they
have, these Hebrews—hope. There is no
special industry, no principal occupation—
unless one can call hunger, fear, sickness
and poverty occupations.

Pan down street, show dirt streets, wood
and mud-baked huts.

It is not easy for the Hebrew these days.
The new state of Israel has been steadily
growing and the other countries hold no
love for these people whose kinsmen they
have fought and continue to fight. The
Hebrews are beaten, jailed and starved.
Everything the centuries have visited upon
their brethren has not stopped because they
are suddenly thrust into the middle of the
20th century. And that is an odd thing, too,
for although the calendar of the western
world reads in the 1960's, the environment

299

of these people is that of centuries before. No newspapers, no movies, no automobiles. Few have ever even seen an automobile. And as for airplanes, why none in this out-village of Mabbam would believe you if you told them that such a thing exists. But whatever else may be lacking, they have a rich heritage of spiritual inspiration. They have a Rabbi. They have hope—the hope of the promised land. Poverty . . . hope . . . . . . fear . . .

Dissolve to live set. CU of a fist knocking on a door. The door opens revealing a small, cluttered room. Several small children cower in the back. Hannah, a woman of about 40, but looking tired and worn and much older, in tattered clothing, is at the door.

VOICE (OF KNOCKER, REB SIMCHA)

(Reb Simcha is not yet on camera.) Half-an-hour after sundown. Tonight. At my house. (THE DOOR CLOSES).

CU feet moving along the dirt street. CU fist knocking again. Door opens. A man, Schloem, the street-washer, old and wizened, stands in back of the door. Esther, his wife, stands in back of him. They are both in their late sixties.

VOICE (REB SIMCHA; OFF-CAMERA)

Half-an-hour after sundown. At my house. Tonight. (SCHLOEM CLOSES THE DOOR FURTIVELY.)

CU feet moving again. This time they reach a small concrete patch in the street. The fist knocks on a door, ignoring the knocker there. The door is opened by a good looking young man of about 25. This is Aaron.

VOICE (REB SIMCHA; OFF-CAMERA)

Your father? You haven't told him?

AARON

No. A moment, please.

(AARON RETURNS A MOMENT LATER WITH A LARGE, PORTLY MAN OF ABOUT FIFTY. THIS IS SIMON, HIS FATHER, THE MERCHANT OF THE GHETTO. THE INSIDE OF THE HOUSE CAN BE SEEN. THERE IS SOME FURNI-TURE, INCLUDING A BED WITH A BED-SPREAD, TWO COMFORTABLE CHAIRS, A TABLE WITH A CANDELABRA. IT IS POOR, BUT WEALTHY IN COMPARISON WITH THE HOMES OF HANNAH, THE WIDOW, AND SCHLOEM, THE STREET-WASHER. SIMON IS DRESSED IN A SUIT, NOT IN RAGS LIKE THE OTHERS.)

                    SIMON

What? What do you want?

          VOICE (REB SIMCHA; OFF-CAMERA)

Tonight. At my house. At a half . . .

                    SIMON (INTERRUPTING)

Again? More trouble-making?

                    VOICE

It is important.

                    SIMON

Always it is important. And always it causes
trouble. I've no time. I have to see about
some goods.

                    AARON

We should go, father.

                    VOICE

(INSISTENT.) It is most important.

                    SIMON

Well . . . all right.

                    VOICE

Half-an-hour after sundown.

                    SIMON

(ANGRILY) All right! (HE SLAMS THE
DOOR.)

CU feet again, walking down the street.
They stop in front of a door. This time the
fist doesn't knock, but the hand opens the
door, instead. The feet go in, past two
humble cots, an old table and two rickety
chairs, to a corner of the room where a
shelf is seen, with several old and tattered
books, two brass candlesticks. In the
wall there is a recession, the "Ark," in
which is seen a rolled up scroll. This is
the "Torah." CU of the Torah as a face
bends toward it and kisses it. Dolly out
and see, finally, the person of the feet and
the voice. It is Rabbi Simcha, a man of
about 50, dressed in a black gown, wearing
a "yarmulka," the black skullcap. He is
bearded, a gentle face, worn, but with
eyes bright with hope.

REB SIMCHA

Please, God. This time, make men's words
truth. (HE BEGINS TO PACE BACK AND
FORTH ACROSS THE SMALL ROOM. THE
FRONT DOOR SLOWLY OPENS. A
PRETTY YOUNG GIRL, ABOUT 23, A
SOFT FACE AND LARGE EYES, HER HAIR
LONG BEHIND HER BACK, COMES IN.
SHE IS UNHEARD BY THE RABBI. SHE
WATCHES HIM A MOMENT. THIS IS HIS
DAUGHTER, LEAH.)

LEAH

Father, your feet will wear off before the
floor will.

REB SIMCHA

(COMING OUT OF DEEP THOUGHT) Oh,
Leah! (HE LAUGHS, LOOKS AT HIS
FEET.) Oh, of course. The head some-
times pays not enough attention to the feet.
(SITS DOWN ON ONE OF THE COTS,
RUBS HIS FEET.) They hurt. These feet
will be the death of me yet. (AFTER A
MOMENT) Did you tell them, Leah? About
tonight?

LEAH

Those I was supposed to. Aaron saw the
rest.

REB SIMCHA

They're coming?

LEAH

Yes.

REB SIMCHA

Good. (HOLDS HIS HEAD IN HIS HANDS,
AGAIN IN WORRIED THOUGHT.)

LEAH

(SITS DOWN NEXT TO HIM.) You can tell
me, father.

REB SIMCHA

(SMILING) Tell? There is nothing to tell.

LEAH

Mother used to say—may she rest in
peace—"When your father says he has
nothing to tell, it is a sure sign he is
bursting to talk."

REB SIMCHA

(FONDLES HER FACE, WISTFULLY) You
are like your mother. (AFTER A MOMENT)
I am worried.

LEAH

About the meeting?

REB SIMCHA

About the meeting, about the authorities,
about our people, about whether what my
ears heard today was really true or just
another one of their stories.

LEAH

But you said it was a government official,
a diplomat in a dark suit and bright shoes
who told you.

REB SIMCHA

And since when is it that diplomats don't
lie?

LEAH

Tell me again. Exactly what he said.

REB SIMCHA

He said "Be at the field in the north of the
city with all of your people and without
belongings at nine o'clock tomorrow
morning. If you are there, you will go to
the 'promised land.' If you are not, you
will not go." That's all he said. Not one
word more.

LEAH

This time I don't think it's a lie. Not this
time.

REB SIMCHA

Last time, you said not last time. Next
time, you'll say not next time. But how do
we go, if we go? We fly, maybe, like a
bird? And with no belongings. They want
to loot the few pitiful things left in the
ghetto, perhaps?

LEAH

Perhaps, father. Perhaps not.

REB SIMCHA

But will the people believe me **this** time?
Will they take the chance and come to the
field? If we're not there, we won't go, he
said.

LEAH

Aaron says they'll come. I say so.

REB SIMCHA

So many days I have been promising the
people. Soon you will go to the promised
land, I tell them. Days? Years! Centuries!
Every day it is the same. Naaman, the
carpenter, comes to me and asks, 'Reb
Simcha, when is it? Today? Tomorrow?'
I smile and say, 'not today, maybe
tomorrow.' Schloem, the street-washer,
says 'tell me when it is, Reb. Today?'
And his eyes shine for a moment and I
answer 'maybe tomorrow' and he is sad
again. For how long now this has gone on.
Why should they believe me now, just because a diplomat has told me 'tomorrow'?
I begin to doubt. Is there a tomorrow?

LEAH

Don't doubt yourself. You can't take them
on a magic carpet. You can only give them
faith and lead them.

REB SIMCHA

Faith! Words from a book. I should find
a magic carpet for them. (GETS UP,
GOES TO THE DOOR, LOOKS OUT.) A
ghetto: mud, dirt, barefoot people. (TURNS
BACK) What if they ask me how do we go?
What do I tell them? On the wings of an
eagle, like Isaiah prophesied? Or do we
walk for forty years, like Moses? We have
walked and wandered enough, they will tell
me. How many years!

LEAH

But remember, the authorities did bring
us here from the desert to get ready for
the promised land.

REB SIMCHA

For cheap labor. To use our shoemakers
and carpenters. What is it now? Two—
three years.

LEAH

And that is why we must keep hoping and
trying. Fifty-four are left, father. Of all
those from the desert, only fifty-four
left in the ghetto.

REB SIMCHA

There you are. So, I ask you, how can we
believe them now?

LEAH

We must. And so must our people.

REB SIMCHA

They will think like Simon.

LEAH

Aaron will try to make him understand.

REB SIMCHA

There are so many doubts, Leah. Do we
walk? Do we ride a camel? They will not
give us camels. What other way is there?
One of the machines with wheels that spit
poison? I have seen one in the city. How
many can there be in the whole world? A
dozen? Twenty? None for us, at any rate.
Besides, the people are afraid of them.

LEAH

When the people are together and have
faith, then they will find a way. (PATS
HIM ON THE SHOULDER) We will find
a way, father.

REB SIMCHA

(SLOWLY LOOKS UP, SMILES) My
daughter is wiser than her father. I can
read from the Holy Book, so they say I am
wise. (SHAKES HIS HEAD) Wisdom comes
from here (POINTING TO HIS HEAD).
(GETTING UP) I feel better.

(LEAH GOES TO THE DOOR, LOOKS OUT,
COMES BACK)

REB SIMCHA

Is there someone?

LEAH

I hoped.

REB SIMCHA

Aaron?

(LEAH NODS HER HEAD)

REB SIMCHA

A good boy. An honest boy.

LEAH

You don't mind my seeing him?

REB SIMCHA

Should I mind?

LEAH

Some of the people say a girl should not
see a young man until they know they are
to be married.

REB SIMCHA

So? There is something wrong in seeing
a young man? Your mother used to see a
young man. (POINTING WITH PRIDE TO
HIMSELF) Me! (AFTER A MOMENT)
But Aaron's father, that's another matter.

LEAH

Will he try to stop the people from going
tomorrow?

REB SIMCHA

I don't know.

LEAH

Simon has worldly goods here. He's
friendly with the authorities. They let him
do all the selling in the ghetto. He won't
want to take the chance.

REB SIMCHA

My child, about Simon I don't know. But
when we go to the promised land, you and
Aaron will go hand in hand. Aaron will
go . . .

SLOW DISSOLVE TO POLICE-MILITARY
OFFICE OF MABBAM. The Lieutenant,
dressed in a military uniform, about 35,
hard-looking, authoritative, is seated at
his desk, going over some papers.
Standing in front of the desk is the
diplomat, Dr. Ezam, about 50, dressed
well, immaculately. He is distinguished-
looking, with a gentle, yet determined
manner.

DR. EZAM

They'll go, Lieutenant. They'll all go.

LIEUTENANT

It's your idea, Dr. Ezam, not mine. A lot
of people in this town don't like the idea of
you diplomats coming from the government
and changing the way we do things here.

DR. EZAM

Perhaps. But this is an official agreement
made with Israel through the United Nations. And the Americans are providing
the transportation.

LIEUT.

There are people in this town who do all
right by these Jews. They stay in their
place. They work for us when we want
them. It saves us money, and they don't
need so much to live on. You know the way
they live.

DR. EZAM

I have heard that there have been many
deaths in the ghetto here.

LIEUT.

(STARTING TO SAY SOMETHING, THEN
IGNORING THE LAST REMARK) All right.
You gave me the orders. (NODS TO THE
OFFICIAL PAPERS) I'll grant them free
passage to the field at the north of town at
nine in the morning. But I don't approve
of this whole idea.

DR. EZAM

Approving is not your job.

LIEUT.

I will do my job, Dr. Ezam. But if they're
not ready, then they don't go. They stay in
the ghetto. The orders say tomorrow at
nine and nothing else.

DR. EZAM

It's been a long time they've been searching for the promised land. They'll be
ready.

LIEUT.

You almost seem to feel sorry for them,
Doctor.

DR. EZAM

Sorry? No. A little envious, perhaps.

LIEUT.

Envious? Of Jews?

DR. EZAM

Why are you so bitter against Jews,
Lieutenant?

LIEUT.

Why? Well, because . . . well . . .
because . . . they're Jews!

DR. EZAM

It must be a good feeling for them,
Lieutenant, to be living the fulfillment of a
prophecy. Think for a moment. For five
thousand years there has been prophecy,
expectation and hope. The greatest thing,
you feel, that history has to offer mankind.
Then, suddenly, in your lifetime, in your
generation, in your year, your minute, it
happens, and you are part of it.

                    LIEUT.

You don't have to preach to me.

                    DR. EZAM

(QUIETLY) I didn't intend to. You are an
officer. Your job is duty. I am a diplomat.
My job is understanding.

                    LIEUT.

If I had my way, we military would be the
diplomats, too. Diplomats! Talk, talk,
talk! Sometimes I wonder whether you
ever accomplish anything.

                    DR. EZAM

So do I. But, then, when I look back, I
know. Civilization lives by talk. It dies by
force.

                    LIEUT.

Well, I suppose we both have a job to do.

                    DR. EZAM

(HALF TO HIMSELF) And I wonder where
the balance lies . . .

                    LIEUT.

(SIGNING AND STAMPING SOME PAPERS)
Hmmm?

                    DR. EZAM

Nothing.

                    LIEUT.

Here are your papers. Clearance for them.
I tell you again, Dr. Ezam. They're
scheduled for nine in the morning. If
they're not ready they don't go. That's
my duty. A lot of people in this town would
like to keep them here.

                    DR. EZAM

That's the second time you've said that,
Lieutenant. Why?

                    LIEUT.

No matter.

                    DR. EZAM

(AUTHORITATIVELY) Why?

                    LIEUT.

(SMILING, CONFIDENT) Some of those
Jews know when to be good Jews. There
are some . . . who like it here.

                       308

                                              DR. EZAM

                              I've told their Rabbi. He'll have them ready.

                                              LIEUT.

                              The Rabbi's a troublemaker. They know
                              it. They're poor people, with no education,
                              your Jews. A wrong word here, a wrong
                              word there . . . well, we'll see.

                                              DR. EZAM

                              I think they'll be ready. It's their only
                              chance.

                                              LIEUT.

                              (STILL SMILING) We'll see . . . you don't
                              know those Jews! You don't know that
                              ghetto!

DISSOLVE TO SIMON'S HOUSE. SIMON
AND AARON ARE ARGUING.

                                              AARON

                              You don't know this ghetto, father. You
                              sell them goods, you take their money.
                              But you don't know them.

                                              SIMON

                              I know them well enough to know they're
                              not so stupid as to keep following that
                              Reb Simcha. Another meeting. For
                              what? To pray? To tell stories? To cry
                              about how bad things are? To make more
                              promises about a promised land?!

                                              AARON

                              It gives them hope. It gives me hope.

                                              SIMON

                              A false hope. He promises, so they
                              depend on him. I have the goods. It's me
                              they should depend on.

                                              AARON

                              (PLACATING) They need your goods.

                                              SIMON

                              They need his promises more, it seems.
                              (MUSING) If it weren't for him, I could
                              control them all, work closer with the
                              authorities and really be wealthy.

                                              AARON

                              Wealth, goods, money. I am ashamed for
                              my father. He seems to have no concern
                              for people, only wealth.

AARON

That's my business. With the Rabbi. With
his daughter.

SIMON

And I, your father? It's not my business?
Understand me, my son; I know what is
happening.

AARON

What do you know?

SIMON

You and that girl, Leah. You think you are
in love with her.

AARON

Have I told you that?

SIMON

You don't have to tell me. I am your father.

AARON

Talk! If you have anything to say about
her, say it to my face.

SIMON

She is like her father. Headstrong.
Foolish. She has caused you trouble
already. (AARON STARTS TO SPEAK,
BUT SIMON SILENCES HIM) You ask me
to speak, so I tell you! By seeing her you
will only learn more trouble. I ask you to
stop seeing her.

AARON

(WITH SARCASM) For me? Your son?
You do all this? Don't make me laugh!

SIMON

Yes. For you. You are young and you act
like you are both young and stupid. Keep
away from her.

AARON

And what if I told you I were really in love?

SIMON

Then I would tell you that it is not love.
In this world one loves only his own, and
himself.

AARON

Then you don't know what love is. You
couldn't know what love is.

SIMON

I have concern for you, Aaron, my son.

AARON

Not for my feelings. Not for my thoughts.
If you did you would help our people, not
live off them.

SIMON

For you, Aaron. I do it for you. (AFTER
A MOMENT, QUICKLY, BUT STRONGLY)
I promised myself that what happened to
your mother will not happen to you. When
there is hunger, you will eat. When
authorities want tribute, you will have
enough to buy your life. (SADLY AND
SOFTLY) They took your mother because
I was too poor to pay tribute. Thin and
weak and hungry, they took her as a
work-slave because I did not have enough
money. I fought them. And two months
later they let me come out from jail to
get her body and bury her. (SHOUTING)
Because I did not have enough money for
tribute! No more! No more! Not in my
lifetime! Not to my child!

AARON

If our people stand together, they could
not hurt us.

SIMON

Did our people stand with me? Did our
people stop the authorities from taking
your mother? You can't fight the
authorities, my son. You can only buy
them or cooperate with them. (AFTER A
MOMENT) I'd do well to stay away from
this meeting.

AARON

This one is important. You have to go.

SIMON

Important? Have to go? You know more
about it than you let on.

AARON

I know that it's important.

SIMON

You have a hand in it, too. Again. When
the authorities threw you into jail for a
fortnight, it wasn't enough. So much money
it cost me to get you out. Now you have to
get mixed up with that troublemaker Rabbi
and his daughter again.

310

SIMON

(SLOWLY) With more than my life, I loved
your mother.

AARON

I'm sorry.

SIMON

Then understand what I say.

AARON

I understand. But you do not. This ghetto,
the whole terrible life of the Jew makes
you hard and bitter. Father . . . let me
tell you this . . . soon, maybe very soon,
we will be in the promised land. There,
there will be no authorities. There we
will live like human beings. There a man
and woman can love without fear.

SIMON

Foolishness. Idle dreams. Trouble-
making. Is this what the meeting is
tonight? Some more stories about the
promised land?

AARON

This time it's true. We will leave for
there tomorrow morning.

SIMON

Tomorrow morning! Fah! More promises
from that Rabbi. Well, not tonight. I'll
go to that meeting and I'll put an end to
this foolishness. Whatever promises he
has, I'll open the eyes of the people . . .

DISSOLVE TO THE POLICE-MILITARY
OFFICE.

The Lieutenant is talking with a large,
portly man, a leading citizen of the town.
He is dressed well and looks much like
Simon, except big-joweled, prosperous
and well-dressed from the proceeds of
his clothing establishment. His name is
Abd-Rasin.

RASIN

(EXCITED) This is true, eh? They're
going, eh? Who's idea? Your idea? Not
your idea . . .

LIEUT.

You take me for a fool . . . ?

RASIN

(INTERRUPTING) I take you for a fool!

311

LIEUT.

Now, look here, Abd-Rasin . . .

RASIN

(INTERRUPTING) You look here! I have a
clothing establishment, eh? It costs a
great deal for workers nowadays. They
read too much. They want more money.
But now I have these Jews working, eh?
Good workmen. I'll say that much for
them. And they cost me practically
nothing. My neighbor, Hezaf, the pottery-
maker. Fourteen Jews in his factory.
Good potters. The blacksmith. With the
Jews to work he's opened another shop.
If the Jews go, it doubles our costs, it
reduces our business, eh?

LIEUT.

What do you want me to do? It's an order.
From the government.

RASIN

We have done well by you, Lieutenant, eh?

(THE LIEUTENANT NODS)

If this ghetto is allowed to leave . . .
well . . . the citizens of this town won't
have it.

LIEUT.

You think I want it!

RASIN

Then we must do something. (AFTER A
MOMENT) Listen to me. I have one of
their carpenters, a fellow called Naaman,
working for me today. I'm building an
addition, you know. Now, they're a thick
people. If one of them were detained . . .
this Naaman, for instance . . . they
wouldn't leave without him, eh? And if
they don't leave tomorrow morning,
then . . .

LIEUT.
This Dr. Ezam. I'd have to find legal
grounds.

RASIN

Then find them.

LIEUT.

Now, if one of them left the ghetto, without
permission, or committed some similar
breach of the law . . . (SMILES AND BE-
GINS TO NOD HIS HEAD TO RASIN, AS

FADE OUT, END OF ACT I

The Manuscript

Following the first scenario, and subsequent scenarios which should improve with each attempt, the writer will arrive at the point where he feels the scenario is as complete as he can make it. His next job is to write the play. This is where the pleasure of accomplishment comes in. If the writer has done a good job with the scenario, the play will virtually write itself. The good scenario is flexible and permits much change, expansion or condensation, as the characters come to life and the play fills itself out. If the writer finds that some radical changes are needed from the scenario, he may justly conclude that his preparation was not so good as it should have been, and he should go back to the scenario and start again. Otherwise he will find that though he may complete the first draft of the play, he will need many more extra drafts before he has achieved an acceptable final product, requiring much more time and work than he would have needed with the proper scenario preparation.

The final manuscript should have all the dialogue and stage directions complete. In addition, the author may indicate sound, music, camera and electronic effects which are vital to the action. Ordinarily, producers and directors frown upon the writer offering directions that they believe belong exclusively in their domain. However, when the visual effect in television or the sound effect in radio is part of the action, when it serves the script in place of or as importantly as dialogue, then the writer must indicate what it is. In addition, the writer should always indicate a change of time or place, stating whether the effect is a dissolve, fade, wipe, musical bridge or other device.

The form for the television manuscript varies, but the most frequently used approach utilizes a divided page — the right-hand column containing all of the audio, that is, the dialogue plus the characters' movements, and the left-hand column containing the video, that is, the mechanical and electronic effects. The left-hand column also may contain special sound effects and music. The uses for the right- and left-hand columns may be reversed. In some instances all of the material, audio and video, is placed in one column, leaving the other column free for the director's notes. The name of the character should be typed in capital letters in the center of the column, above the dialogue of the character. Script editors prefer that the dialogue be double-spaced, with double-spacing between speeches.

The radio manuscript form uses the full page, with the character's name in capital letters at the left-hand margin or, sometimes, in the middle of the page, depending on the wishes of the individual script editor. There should be double spaces between lines of dialogue and between speeches. All sound and music directions should be indicated in capital letters.

There is yet another manuscript representing a further step in the writing — or rewriting — of the play. This is the production script, the final version of the play. This script contains the director's notations for all technical effects and for revisions in content, style and form.

Whether the production script will have any relationship to the writer's original manuscript is problematical. The script may contain changes in which the author not only may not have had a hand, but of which he may not even have been informed. The author of the radio or television play usually has no say in casting or in production; the producers, directors, advertising agencies and networks can virtually do whatever they wish to his play. CBS has stated its commitment "to obtain the talents of those writers . . . whose outstanding abilities and dedication permit no compromise with anything less than their best efforts at all times"; CBS commits itself at the same time to a "continuing participation of the Network's programming officials at every stage of the creative process from the initial script to the final broadcast."[8] It often happens, as Paddy Chayefsky has written, that a work is "butchered" in the production process. This is in addition to the changes made in the script before it even reaches the rehearsal stage. The writer can only hope that his script is not altered too greatly as it runs the gamut of script editor screening, agency approval, production planning, rehearsals and performance. All the writer can do is offer a script of the highest artistic merit of which he is capable. He may at least take some comfort in the feeling that no matter what anyone else has done he, at least, has done his best. If worst comes to worst he can always request that his name be taken off the credits, a request and occurrence not unheard of in network television.

A Final Word

Thus far television has not lived up to its potential. Radio almost did, but became too prosperous and sacrificed its achievements for a common denominator. Television drama, as well as most other forms of television production, seems to have fulfilled the dire prediction made by Gilbert Seldes as far back as 1931. Television, Mr. Seldes wrote, will be as bad as or worse than the most mediocre aspects of radio. "Each new form of entertainment drains off the cheap and accidental elements of its predecessors." The commercialization of television is a great fault, he warned, for although it is a magic miracle, it will be used as "a miracle made for money."[9]

This need not be so, of course. Television and radio both have the potentials to be most effective art forms. They can contribute a great deal to entertainment and culture. Whether they will or not depends not alone on a handful of writers or producers or directors or critics. It does not even depend alone on the advertisers. The FCC of Newton Minow and of E. William Henry has had, through "friendly persuasion," some effect on the quality of broadcasting, but the legal power of the government commission is limited. A concerted effort by responsible members of the audience, by the public at large — through letters, phone calls and other communications on the part of each individual viewer and listener — can most effectively influence a change in the programming practices of the mass-oriented and product-controlled media.

With little likelihood that either the public or the broadcasters will radically change the television or radio media in the immediate future, we can operate only in the framework that we now know. Although in 1967 one-sixth of all TV stations on the air were non-commercial educational, they still did not have the economic support necessary to provide a large number of positions for writers. The writer economically dependent on the commercial mass media for his existence can take comfort in the fact that despite all the restrictions put upon him by the many areas of sponsorship, network control and production, he is still the prime mover, the one element upon which all the other elements stand or fall. With a script of high quality, with writing of ethical and artistic merit, the writer may at least take pride in knowing he has made an effort to fulfill some of the mass media's infinite potentials.

NOTES TO CHAPTER 9

[1] Brander Matthews, *The Development of the Drama* (New York: Charles Scribner's Sons, 1903), p. 19.

[2] George Pierce Baker, *Dramatic Technique* (New York: Houghton Mifflin Company, 1919), p. 241. Second reference, pp. 126-128.

[3] Terrence Rattigan, "The Characters Make the Play," *Theatre Arts* XXXI (April, 1947), 45.

[4] Paddy Chayefsky, *Television Plays* (New York: Simon and Schuster, 1955), pp. 130-131.

[5] Reginald Rose, *Six Television Plays* (New York: Simon and Schuster, 1956), pp. 107-108, 150.

[6] August Strindberg, "A Dream Play," *Collected Plays*, Thomas H. Dickinson, editor (New York: Houghton Mifflin Company, 1935), II, 64. Strindberg makes these comments in his Author's Note to the play.

[7] Gilbert Seldes, *The Great Audience* (New York: The Viking Press, 1950), p. 113.

[8] Columbia Broadcasting System, *Annual Report to Stockholders* (New York: Columbia Broadcasting System, 1963), p. 12.

[9] Gilbert Seldes, "A Note On Television," *New Republic*, LXIX (December 2, 1931), 71.

INDEX